18⁵⁰

Ping Chang

HARVARD ECONOMIC STUDIES

Volume CXX

The studies in this series are published by the Department of Economics of Harvard University. The Department does not assume responsibility for the views expressed.

AIR TRANSPORT
AND ITS REGULATORS

‹‹‹‹‹‹‹‹‹‹‹‹‹‹‹ AN INDUSTRY STUDY

Richard E. Caves

HARVARD UNIVERSITY PRESS

CAMBRIDGE · MASSACHUSETTS

‹‹‹‹‹‹‹‹‹‹‹‹‹‹

ACKNOWLEDGMENTS

Discussions with many people and in many places have helped to form the contents of this book. The following are the claimants to my greatest debts: Professor John R. Meyer and Robert Gordon, Harvard University; Professor H. Douglas Price, Columbia University; Professor Joe S. Bain, University of California; Mark Massel, Brookings Institution; Warner Hord, William Weinfeld, and Paul Y. Seligson, Civil Aeronautics Board. Richard Ernst served as my research assistant in the early phases, David E. Johnson at the close. The Institute of Business and Economic Research of the University of California furnished a number of essential services, and the Brookings Institution supplied a valued working base in Washington, D.C. This study would not have been possible without the generosity of the Ford Foundation, whose Faculty Research Fellowship allowed a year's leave and an extended stay in Washington. None of these men or organizations bears any responsibility for the results.

This study undertakes the difficult task of making timeless generalizations about a fast-changing subject. The reader should be warned that I have been able to keep the book up to date only on material becoming available before the middle months of 1961. Anything since then has had to be included on a hit-or-miss basis.

R. E. C.

Berkeley, California
February 1962

CONTENTS

TABLES

FIGURES

AIR TRANSPORT
AND ITS REGULATORS

Introduction

The "industry study," like the can opener, has proved to be a useful if unlovely tool for getting at many desirable things. It provides one of the major methods open to the economist for testing the predictions of the theory of markets. Does an oligopolistic industry, producing a homogeneous product and enjoying only moderately high barriers to the entry of new firms, tend toward a rigid selling price? One way of seeking an answer to this question is to turn to some industry in which such conditions and their consequences can be examined in the context of the industry's other major structural traits. How much can be proved from the microscopic examination of one industry? In a formal sense, nothing about the general economy. Nonetheless, reading the more competent industry studies consecutively gives one a cumulative impression of certain stable relations between the physical or structural characteristics of industries and the patterns of conduct, and thereby of economic performance, exhibited by their member firms. The reader gains in the ability to predict the market-structure patterns that will cause any given conduct pattern to arise. And since an industry's performance is essentially its market-conduct pattern evaluated through the application of norms of economic welfare, links can be established between market structure and market performance. These links can supply numerous ideas about making changes in structure to improve performance.[1]

The present volume seeks to add to the inventory of industry studies and shares the objectives implicitly common to its predecessors. It seeks to analyze the market structure, conduct, and performance of the United States domestic passenger airlines, and to point out the degree of consistency and the apparent causal relations among these elements. However, there is an influence in the airline industry which has not been previously subjected

[1] For general background, see Joe S. Bain, *Industrial Organization* (New York, 1959) and Everett E. Hagen, *Handbook of Industry Studies* (Glencoe, 1958).

to a major investigation. That is the detailed regulation of the industry's day-to-day business decisions by the Civil Aeronautics Board under the authority of the Civil Aeronautics Act of 1938 (now the Federal Aviation Act of 1958). The business decisions of the airlines are constrained both by the Civil Aeronautics Board's regulations and requirements and by the environmental situation created by the industry's market structure.

When the Board's influence touches almost every important managerial decision, do the economic elements of market structure still play a vital role? An affirmative answer to this question is a result, not an assumption, of this study. In such matters as the determination of effective barriers to the entry of new firms, decisions of the regulators completely override the underlying economic factors. But in many ways the converse is also true — aspects of the regulatory pattern are determined almost entirely by the economic elements of market structure.

There are very great potential advantages in relating the airlines' market conduct and performance both to the regulatory pattern and to the economic elements of market structure. From market structure alone we can get some idea of what conduct and performance the industry would exhibit in the absence of public regulation. By comparing these theoretical patterns with the actual conduct and performance of America's airlines, we can discover how much difference the presence of regulation makes. Does it lead to lower profits than otherwise? In its absence, would there be more or less product competition among airlines, and more or less price competition? Answers to these questions would in turn provide definite evidence for evaluating the often-heard suggestion that competition be given a greater role in governing the industry, a suggestion generally supported by reference to a market structure favorable to competitive adjustments. For instance, the Air Transport Association, the domestic certified carriers' trade association, declared recently:

The trunkline carriers are competitive. Each of them must generate maximum traffic — including the most it can pull away from other airlines — to prosper. Under these circumstances, differing as they do from the "natural monopoly" utilities — airline managements could well be accorded a substantial measure of discretion in pricing their services. Any mistake — either overpricing or underpricing — would speedily fall on the management that made the mistake. Accordingly, fares would tend to adjust for the airlines — to levels consistent with over-all economy, and to do so promptly if such adjustment (upward or downward) could be made without protracted formal board proceedings.[2]

The industry study is designed to establish or test just such propositions as these.

How good an industry's economic performance appears to be depends, of course, on what standards are used to evaluate performance. An economist's usual standard is an ideal norm drawn from general economic theory. The virtue of this ideal is that, if all industries matched up to it, the static economic well-being of the society would be at a maximum.[3] Now there is nothing divine about this standard. For a vast number of good and bad reasons, social policy follows many goals in addition to maximization of economic welfare in the private sector of the economy. Public regulation of air transport has sought many goals, some compatible with outright economic maximization, some not. The standard of performance used in this study will therefore be a two-headed one. I shall weigh the performance of the airlines, and by implication that of the Civil Aeronautics Board, both in terms of the general economic criteria for welfare and the special goals stated in aviation legislation or followed consistently by the Board. The analysis attempts to give some idea of ways in which policies might be changed to improve the industry's performance by either set of standards.

This investigation is frankly after bigger game than a scholarly evaluation of the air-transport industry. Direct regulation by public bodies affects major segments of the American economy — urban gas, electric, water, and transportation utilities, the telephone industry, broadcasting, all forms of public transportation, and natural-gas transmission. Partial direct regulation touches many other industries, such as insurance, banking, and petroleum extraction. Many federal, state, and local regulatory agencies are involved. This sort of direct regulation of industry seems to be spreading. For instance, Canada and Great Britain have been shifting their policies on civil aviation away from monopoly by

---

[2] Air Transport Association, Brief, General Passenger Fare Investigation, Docket No. 8008.

[3] Technically, this means a Paretoan optimum under static conditions; the resulting income distribution might not be the most desirable one.

public enterprise toward a pattern similar to that in the United States. Debates have raged among economists and the general public alike about the usefulness of direct public control of business. Yet no techniques have emerged to guide an impartial investigator, and vague, untested platonic generalities have ruled the field. No set of theoretical tools or verified factual propositions guides the scholar who tries to decide what would be the net impact on economic welfare of imposing direct control on an industry, compared to permitting the free play of market forces or applying some other scheme of social control. One possible source of assistance is the set of concepts and tested propositions that make up the body of knowledge in the field of industrial organization. This field contributes the technique of the industry study, based on those concepts of market structure, conduct, and performance already mentioned and defined more fully in the material that follows. The field also contributes some factual material on the relations discovered in the unregulated segment of the United States economy which may be usable in predicting or evaluating the behavior of its regulated segment. No old hand in industrial organization would claim it to be well enough developed to provide sure solutions for the problem of studying and evaluating economic regulation. Still, it seems amply promising for an experiment. It is hoped that the success or failure of this investigation of air transport will give some guidance to fruitful research in other regulated industries or regulatory agencies.

The framework of the industry study dictates the four-part organization of this volume. The major economic elements of the industry's market structure are outlined in the first part. Initially these are studied without reference to regulatory policy. Barriers to the entry of new trunk airlines are considered independently of the fact that the Civil Aeronautics Board has blocked the way to all entrants since the passage of the Civil Aeronautics Act in 1938. After analyzing the relevant traits of market structure, I try to suggest, by reference to the existing literature on industrial organization, what sort of market-conduct patterns and market performance an industry with such structural features might exhibit if the intervening factor of regulation were not present.

The second part of the study contains a necessarily sketchy

treatment of the policies of the Civil Aeronautics Board, as molded by the underlying statutory requirements, by the practical problems of administration, and by the various political pressures on the agency. Here I lean on the large amount of legal scholarship already available on the Board's decisions, though it still proves necessary to rework the primary material. Most research by political scientists on this and other regulatory agencies has followed one of two lines: legalistic analysis of formal decisions to ascertain the underlying standard of judgment, if any; and outright political appraisal of the influences and pressures on the agency and its response to them. Both approaches are useful and necessary; they are complements, rather than substitutes. Some of the Board's policies devolve from clear-cut lines of legal precedent. Many types of issues, however, either are subject to vague and flexible standards or are normally handled by informal procedures. In these substantive areas the Board is free to lean with the wind, and my argument is that in the past political processes have acted in certain systematic ways to affect the regulation of the airlines.

The third part of the study turns to the problems of describing the airlines' patterns of market conduct, the way the carriers' policies on the product they offer and the price they charge are evolved and adjusted within the industry. Finally, the fourth part turns to the problem of assessing market performance. Here I take up the general economic criteria of efficiency — the rate of profit earned by the industry, the appropriateness of the size of firms and their achievement of minimum costs (technical efficiency), the reasonableness of expenditures on advertising and product differentiation, and the amount of progressiveness and innovation. I also consider the extent of the Board's success in achieving some chosen goals which lie outside this list and then offer some suggestions about how policies might be changed to improve performance in terms of either set of standards.

In an industry that has risen as rapidly as air-passenger transport, it is difficult to decide what historic time span to cover in gathering information. One wants policy conclusions that are correct for the present and near-future situation of the industry, a situation that has changed greatly even since the end of World War II. Analytical conclusions, however, are valuable for the past as well as the present. Furthermore, a look at the existing literature on air transport will quickly warn the investigator that there are grave dangers in becoming preoccupied with whatever seem to be the major problems of the industry at the moment. This volume concentrates on the industry and its evolution since World War II, and it has very little to say about the airlines prior to the passage of the Civil Aeronautics Act in 1938. World War II constituted an enormous break in the industry's development. It worked a complete change in the nature of the short-run problems facing the industry and postponed the time when the novice Civil Aeronautics Board would come to establish normal relations with the carriers. Also, it changed the market for air-passenger transport by accustoming many more Americans to flying and by subsidizing the development of aircraft much larger, more efficient, and more comfortable than those previously in use. Thus in the postwar period the airlines and their regulators were essentially starting out from a new set of initial conditions. It is from this departure that the study begins its intensive coverage.

Every industry study faces a major problem of sources of information, and almost no good one has been written without the aid of evidence unearthed in judicial proceedings under the antitrust laws. Fortunately, the problem is less severe for the air-transport industry because of the public information generated in the airlines' dealings with the Civil Aeronautics Board and the Board's dealings with Congress. In addition to the decisions and orders of the Board, and the statistics it collects, very heavy reliance has been placed on exhibits filed in several important dockets. Another major source has been the numerous trade magazines and journals serving the industry. Of course these exhibits and trade publications seldom breathe the cool air of detached scholarship. A great deal of reading between lines has been necessary, and it has not been possible to explain the whole process of judgment in each particular footnote.

This volume could have been three times as long as it is, or one third as long, or anywhere in between. Limits on time and available resources prevented a more extensive job; considerations of marginal productivity ruled out a shorter one. The strategy of research has been to pursue every facet to the point where an approximately right answer seemed evident. More thorough research on a number of matters would have yielded more precise results and perhaps rather different ones. In particular, more elaborate statistical procedures would be worth applying to several problems. In any case, doubters are invited to try their hand.

PART I

MARKET STRUCTURE

1 Seller Concentration

It is always a troublesome problem of judgment to know what elements need to be included under the heading of "market structure." There is a methodological problem created by the hypothesis that market structure determines market conduct and performance. It takes the form of a temptation to stretch the rather flexible notion of market structure to cover everything that seems *ex post* to affect market conduct. One way of avoiding this problem is to deal with only those market-structure elements that appear significant on a cross-sectional basis, somewhat independently of the industry in which they are observed. However, this limiting procedure is also unsatisfactory. Existing empirical evidence would hardly sustain through a wide range of American industries the significance of more than three or four market-structure traits: seller concentration, buyer concentration, height of barriers to entry, and extent of product differentiation. Yet individual industry studies have uncovered many more traits that seem important, at least in particular cases. An example would be heavy excise taxes, which seem to restrict price competition in such industries as cigarettes and distilled liquor. Rapidly growing demand seems to encourage competitive rivalry for shares of the market in the rayon industry. In still other cases, the longevity of capital goods or high fixed costs (the old "overhead costs" problem) seems to encourage price rigidity and various conduct devices aiming at market stabilization.

In the domestic airline industry it is clear that several important market-structure traits exist besides the obvious ones of the number and size distribution of sellers, considered in this chapter, and the height of barriers to entry, discussed in Chapter 4. It is necessary to refer also to certain features of the demand facing the air-transport industry, including its growth rate, price and income elasticity, and product differentiability (Chapter 2), and to present finally some evidence on the relation between the airlines and their input suppliers (Chapter 5).

NUMBER AND SIZE DISTRIBUTION OF FIRMS

The Civil Aeronautics Board tightly controls the number and loosely controls the size distribution of firms in the airline industry. The firms in the industry are administratively divided into three separate groups. The twelve trunkline carriers[1] which comprise most of the domestic industry have all existed at least since 1938; at that time they received certificates of convenience and necessity pursuant to section 401(a) of the Civil Aeronautics Act, the "grandfather provision," rendering automatic the certification of all carriers which had previously been in continuous operation. These trunkline carriers are the only airlines with operating rights between most major pairs of American cities, and they claim primary attention in this study.

The second group of firms is the so-called local-service carriers, now numbering thirteen, created around the end of World War II by the Civil Aeronautics Board as an experiment in developing further the network of domestic air transport to serve smaller cities lacking trunkline service. Originally granted temporary certificates subject to renewal, the surviving local carriers received permanent certificates by congressional mandate in 1955. In 1958 these local-service carriers produced only 3.4 percent as many passenger-miles of transportation as the trunkline carriers; in some ways they constitute a fringe of the trunk industry. Along with the local-service carriers could be classed the territorial carriers, seventeen of which operate within Hawaii or Alaska or between Alaska and the United States. However, in 1958 these carriers produced only one eighth as many passenger-miles of transportation as the local-service carriers. Hence they will be largely ignored in the following discussion.

The third group of carriers significant in United States domestic air transport is the supplemental carriers, the "nonskeds," which have proved a continuing policy problem for the Civil Aeronautics Board in the postwar period. After a long series of proceedings before the Board, described briefly in Chapter 8, some of these carriers were given special certificates to carry on charter and

---

[1] Since the major work on this study was completed, a merger between United Air Lines and Capital Airlines reduced the number to eleven. The Civil Aeronautics Board is now considering the promotion of other mergers among the trunks.

irregular or nonscheduled service. In 1957 and 1958 there were forty-nine of these carriers legally existing, of which thirty-six appear to have been operating. However, the special certification procedure was recently overturned by the courts, and the supplemental carriers' legal status is again in doubt. A final segment of the air-transport industry requiring mention is the intrastate carriers which have operated in a few states such as California, Texas, and Tennessee, where the principal cities are some distance apart. Apparently the only large operator among them currently is Pacific Southwest Airlines, which, according to trade publications, is a well-equipped carrier holding 25 to 30 percent of the traffic between San Francisco, Los Angeles, and San Diego.[2]

Both the trunkline and local-service segments of the industry have lost firms through normal processes of attrition. Since the Civil Aeronautics Board has never permitted any new firms to enter either segment, the absolute number has shrunk. Originally, nineteen carriers were active in certified domestic service. One, essentially a shuttle operation, has suspended business. By the end of 1960, six others, all of them small and economically weak as compared with the leading firms in the industry, had disappeared by merger or by absorption into existing carriers. Before World War II, Mayflower Airlines was combined with Boston and Maine Airways, Inc., the resulting firm subsequently becoming Northeast Airlines; and Marquette Airlines was sold to Transcontinental & Western Air (later Trans World Airlines). Several other trunklines resulted from important mergers before the passage of the Civil Aeronautics Act. Since World War II, four trunks have disappeared through merger: Inland Airlines with Western Air Lines (completed in 1952); Mid-Continent Airlines with Braniff Airways (1952); Chicago and Southern Airlines with Delta Air Lines (1953); and Colonial Airlines with Eastern Air Lines (1956).[3] Still other mergers have been threatened from time to time. In 1936 the Interstate Commerce

[2] *Airlift*, XXIII (Aug. 1959), 62. See also Richard Van Osten, "Hustling PSA Bucks Big Lines With Low Fares and Makes It Pay Off," *Airlift*, XXIII (Dec. 1959), 33–34.

[3] *Monopoly Problems in Regulated Industries — Airlines*, hearings, U.S. House of Representatives, Committee on the Judiciary, Antitrust Subcommittee, 84th Cong., 2nd sess. (Washington, 1957), I, 491 (hereafter cited, *Monopoly Problems in Regulated Industries — Airlines*).

Commission, which then held jurisdiction, blocked a merger between United Air Lines and Pennsylvania Airlines & Transport Company, a firm which later became the foundation for Capital Airlines.[4] The Civil Aeronautics Board has disallowed several mergers in formal proceedings, although it has not been continuously hostile to them There are hardly any pairs of trunk carriers that have not joined in merger considerations at one time or another.

The mortality rate among the local-service carriers has also been rather high. Of twenty originally given temporary certificates, only thirteen survived to receive permanent certification in 1955, with the routes of a fourteenth being operated by a trunkline carrier. A total of eighteen appear to have provided service at some time or other. Four began operations in 1946. Three more started in 1947, three in 1948, seven in 1949, and the final one in 1950. The disappearing carriers have gone out primarily through business failures and Board action; the geographic isolation of the local-service systems has militated against mergers.[5] Among nonscheduled airlines the mortality rate has been very high. This is a reflection of lack of capital and business experience on the part of many operators. It is true that the direct cause of the disappearance of many of them was an inability to live within the narrow scope of legal operations defined by the Board;[6] but, apart from this, there is clear evidence that only the larger supplemental carriers and those with better managerial talent had the ability to survive the shake-out process.[7]

In the certified segments of the industry, it would seem wise to expect occasional mergers as normal. No two airlines have

[4] Frank J. Taylor, *High Horizons — The United Airlines Story* (rev. ed., New York, 1958), p. 104.

[5] *The Airlines Industry*, report pursuant to H. Res. 107, U.S. House of Representatives, Committee on the Judiciary, Antitrust Subcommittee (Subcommittee No. 5), 85th Cong., 1st sess. (Washington, 1957), p. 23. See also J. P. Adams, "Future Airline Service Depends on State Support," *Journal of Air Law and Commerce*, XX (Autumn 1953), 403–415.

[6] The nonscheduled carriers' woes are told at length in *Future of Irregular Airlines in the United States Air Transportation Industry*, hearings before a subcommittee, U.S. Senate, Select Committee on Small Business, 83rd Cong., 1st sess. (Washington, 1953).

[7] See, for example, Fred Hunter, "Pattern for the Future: Fewer, Stronger Nonskeds?", *American Aviation*, XVIII (March 28, 1955), 82–83.

exactly identical route structure; the vicissitudes of economic
fortune are likely to strike them unequally, providing an inducement to mergers. In the industry's periods of relatively hard
times, mergers have been contemplated of much greater scope
than any which have actually occurred. Furthermore, an airline
management is frequently faced with grave problems affecting
the firm's revenue prospects, which call for discrete decisions to
be made on the basis of sadly incomplete information. An error
in judgment can easily threaten the carrier's prospects for survival. In deciding on the purchase of aircraft, a choice of equipment that proves economically inefficient or unpopular can
readily cause trouble and in one case was partly responsible
for the absorption of a local-service carrier by a trunkline.[8]

There has always been considerable disparity in size among the
domestic trunklines. The industry has always had a clearly recognizable Big Four — American, Eastern, TWA, and United. It has
been the practice since World War II to distinguish in the remaining carriers a Middle Six and a fringe of smaller carriers.
This last group, depleted by mergers, now includes only Northeast and Continental; furthermore, changes in route structure
allowed them by the Civil Aeronautics Board since 1955 have
rendered them not significantly different in size from the Middle
Six. It is now more common in airline circles to hear all of the
smaller eight referred to as "regional carriers."

In developing data on the size distribution of firms in an industry, it is customary to devote prayerful attention to the choice
among various measures of business size — sales, employees, or
assets. The problem here does not seem a serious one. It is market
power that is at issue, and the factor most commonly said to
cause sales measurements to give a distorted idea of market power
— vertical integration — is absent. For various reasons, the
number of employees and the stock of capital furnish deceptive
measures. There is a question of choosing between a measure of

[8] Pioneer was absorbed by Continental Air Lines in 1955 after the Board had
refused to grant it extra subsidy to finance losses from the replacement of its
old DC-3s with Martin aircraft; the latter offered lower unit costs but were
too large relative to traffic over Pioneer's routes. See Eric Bramley, "CAL's
Goal: Subsidy-Free Operation by 1957," *American Aviation*, XVIII (May 9,
1955), 66.

sales (passenger-miles) and a measure of output (seat-miles). A
service industry cannot produce for stock, and of course the two
measures can diverge substantially if load factors (the portion of
seat-miles actually sold) vary among air carriers. Though the
divergences between available seat-miles and revenue passenger-
miles, and the determinants of load factors, will be discussed later,
the long-run relative market strength of carriers is clearly better
reflected by the measure of passenger-miles.

Returning to the trunkline carriers, and using the customary
measure of the portion of trunkline passenger-miles produced by
the largest four sellers, we find that there was a decrease in concentration from before World War II to the postwar period and
no substantial change thereafter until roughly 1956, when the decline of the share of the Big Four continued. Table 1 shows

Table 1.   Market-share percentages of revenue passenger-miles held by U.S.
air carriers and carrier groups, 1939–1959[a]

Carrier group	1939[b]	1946[b]	1955	1957	1959
Big Four carriers	81.9	66.0	69.3	68.4	64.9
American	29.3	22.0	20.6	19.5	18.7
Eastern	14.9	13.5	16.7	17.0	14.8
TWA	15.1	12.5	13.9	14.2	15.3
United	22.6	18.0	18.1	17.7	16.1
Other trunklines	18.1	34.0	23.6	26.4	29.0
Local-service carriers	0	0	2.5	2.9	3.4
Noncertified carriers	0	0	4.0	1.6	2.2
Other certified carriers[c]	0	0	0.6	0.7	0.5

[a] Percentages may not total 100 percent because of rounding errors.
[b] Figures for 1939 and 1946 cover the trunklines only; however, only tiny
amounts of service were produced by other groups and so these figures are nearly
comparable with those for later years.
[c] Includes helicopter and Alaskan and Hawaiian territorial operations.
Source: U.S. House of Representatives, Committee on the Judiciary, Antitrust
Subcommittee, *The Airlines Industry*, report . . . pursuant to H. Res. 107, 85th
Cong., 1st sess. (Washington, 1957), table 3; Civil Aeronautics Board, *Monthly
Report of Air Carrier Traffic Statistics* (various issues).

market-share percentages in five selected years for the Big Four,
the other trunk carriers, and, from 1955 on, the local-service
carriers, other certified carriers (helicopter and Hawaiian and

Alaskan territorial), and the irregular or supplemental carriers.[9] The fall in the Big Four market share since before World War II may be attributable mostly to a decline in the shares of American and United, the largest firms and two of the three historic occupants of the transcontinental market. It is not possible here to explain completely this pattern of concentration and its changes, but it is probably reasonable to associate the fall during World War II with the fact that the transcontinental market was the first to develop — the airplane's advantage over other forms of transport is primarily conspicuous in long-haul markets. The recent changes reflect a conscious Civil Aeronautics Board policy of granting new routes almost entirely to the smaller carriers. One writer has estimated that, if the trend resulting from this policy of the last few years continues, the share of the largest four carriers will be down to 50 percent by 1968.[10]

The sharp decline in the share of the supplemental carriers is directly the result of Board policy and litigation ending the life of one of the largest firms. It could be argued, though, that economic forces in the 1950s would have produced this result in any case.[11] Within the irregular-carrier sector, the same forces curtailing the number of firms have left a large share of the business in the hands of a few firms. In 1952 it was estimated that the top three or four supplemental carriers held 60 percent of that sector's business. This same figure holds for the largest four in 1958.[12]

CONCENTRATION IN CITY-PAIR MARKETS

In a transportation industry, of course, the significance of national aggregate market shares is bound to be limited, although

---

[9] Service between continental United States and Alaska and Hawaii is excluded because available data do not allow it to be unscrambled from the other international service of Pan American and Northwest. No reliable data on passenger-miles sold for the supplemental carriers are available except for recent years.
[10] William V. Henzey, "Challenge to Big 4 . . . ," *American Aviation*, XXI (Nov. 4, 1957), 29.
[11] See Dero A. Saunders, "The Airlines' Flight from Reality," *Fortune*, LIII (Feb. 1956), 220.
[12] *Future of Irregular Carriers*, p. 189; Civil Aeronautics Board, *Monthly Report of Air Carrier Traffic Statistics*, March 1959. Throughout the source notes, the Civil Aeronautics Board will hereafter be abbreviated CAB.

not negligible. Certain forms of product rivalry in the industry are clearly not confined to city-pairs alone, and price adjustment in the industry is almost never thus restricted; but in day-to-day competition for customers the relevant market is that comprised of persons actually or potentially desiring to travel between a particular pair of cities. The Chicagoan weighing vacations in Florida and Hawaii may find airline trips to these places good substitutes for one another.[13] But such situations are not common, and in any case the business traveler is not likely to feel that much substitutability in destinations exists for him, except perhaps in such long-run planning that the location of business activity is significantly affected. In the days before long-distance nonstop flights became common, service along a roundabout route by a single carrier or by connecting carrier was a significant competitive force. Thus, at one time United Air Lines' New York–San Francisco monopoly was limited by the possibility of travel via Los Angeles.[14] However, as nonstop flights grew more important and common, the influence of circuitous routings as a competitive factor has dropped sharply.

The many aspects of seller concentration in individual city-pairs require selectivity for investigation. Four questions will receive principal attention. First, to what extent does competition exist in individual city-pair transport markets? Second, to what extent has competition increased? Third, how stable are market shares in city-pair markets? Fourth, do individual airlines tend to face different rivals in each of the markets which they serve competitively, or do they tend to encounter the same competitors in a number of markets?

One fundamental and obvious trait of the patterns of competition in city-pair markets simplifies the expositional task considerably. It is the fact that the number of airlines competing in a city-pair market tends strongly to increase with the size of the market in terms of total revenue passenger-miles. As we shall see

[13] "The Florida market . . . has been cut into somewhat, according to Eastern, by the increased accessibility of more distant resort areas with jet travel. The airline cites the Chicago market as an example, with some potential Florida business diverting to Hawaii." Glenn Garrison, "Florida Market Stirs Stiff Competition," *Aviation Week*, LXXII (Jan. 18, 1960), 36.

[14] Frederick W. Gill and Gilbert L. Bates, *Airline Competition* (Boston, 1949), pp. 213–214.

subsequently, this fact is partly a reflection of the industry's cost characteristics, partly a function of Civil Aeronautics Board policy.[15] The relation of number of airlines to market size in passenger-miles is clear, but passenger-miles as a size measure raises a subsidiary question. This measure is a product of the number of passengers and the number of miles between cities. Do both terms of the product have something to do with the relation? There is no way of giving a very formal answer to this question, either by statistical analysis of market data or by interpretation of Board decisions on admission of new carriers to particular city-pair markets. Inspection of the data conveys a strong impression that the number of carriers serving a city-pair tends to be a positive function of both the number of passengers moving between two cities and the distance between the points. The former relation is a strong one; the latter exists but is definitely weaker.[16] The net result is that between two city-pairs generating equivalent passenger-miles of transportation, the pair the shorter distance apart will tend to have more carriers, since the distance relation is weaker than the relation to the number of passengers.

The data available to answer the questions raised above about seller concentration in individual city-pair markets are of a very special sort. Until 1960, the airlines took two surveys each year of the origin and destination of all ticketed passengers. Each survey covered all passengers moving by air in a period of two weeks — the first two weeks of March and the last two weeks of September. The resulting data were complete enumerations for the periods; but because they covered only four weeks out of fifty-two in the year, they have to be used with care to avoid certain wrong impressions. There is no particular reason for

[15] The Board controls not only the number of scheduled carriers participating in a given market but also, to some extent, the distribution of market shares among them. The latter is effected by restrictions on service, such as requirements of intermediate stops, which make the service of one carrier necessarily less desirable than that of another.

[16] The reason why the number of carriers should be related to distance traveled between points will become apparent below. The relation has to do largely with the fact that airlines' historic pricing policies and competition with other forms of transportation have rendered long-haul air carriage more profitable than short-haul runs. This has caused the Board in turn to tend to certify more carriers into long-haul markets where several could compete and still earn normal profits.

thinking that market shares normally show any seasonal variation (this is not an issue here), but the relative importance of such seasonal markets as the Florida and Arizona resort cities becomes much greater in the winter. When dealing with only the larger city-pairs in terms of traffic generation, one must note, in conjunction with the March survey especially, that many city-pairs appear among the leaders which would not so appear on a calendar-year basis.

We shall examine the largest one hundred city-pairs in terms of number of passenger-miles generated. Tables 2 and 3 show

Table 2. Distribution of 100 leading city-pairs by market shares held by the largest one, two, and three carriers, March 1–14, 1958

Number of sellers	Percentage of market held								Total number of city-pairs
	100	90–99	80–89	70–79	60–69	50–59	40–49	30–39	
Largest 1	14	9	4	11	24	27	9	2	100
Largest 2	48	32	12	7	1	0	0	0	100
Largest 3	85	13	2	0	0	0	0	0	100

Source: CAB, Office of Carrier Accounts and Statistics, *Competition Among Domestic Air Carriers, September 17–30, 1957* (Washington, D.C.: Air Transport Association of America, 1958), vol. 4; *idem*, March 1–14, 1958, vols. 4, 5.

Table 3. Distribution of 100 leading city-pairs by number of carriers certified, March 1–14, 1958

	Number of carriers								
	1	2	3	4	5	6	7	8	9
Number of city-pairs	11	26	30	14	7	3	5	2	2

Source: CAB, *Competition Among Domestic Air Carriers, March 1–14, 1958* (Washington, D.C.: Air Transport Association of America, 1959), vol. 4.

selected aspects of seller concentration in these markets for the two-week survey period of March 1958, the most recent figures available at this writing. One major abnormality had to be removed from the data for this period — a strike, which affected

Western Air Lines' share in all markets it served. These markets were treated as if the shares were the same as those in the sampling period immediately preceding — September 17–30, 1957. Table 2 gives the distribution of city-pairs by market shares held by the largest one, two, and three carriers. The average level of concentration is obviously quite high, though the distribution of the shares held by the largest single carrier is not *J*-shaped but rather bimodal. As we shall see later, Board certification policies in the 1950s have been such that they tend strongly to place the dominant carrier in any particular market somewhere in the 50 to 70 percent range of the distribution. Table 3 shows a different sort of distribution — the one hundred leading city-pairs classified by the number of carriers certified to serve them. In comparing Tables 2 and 3 it is important to keep in mind that a carrier's being certified to serve a particular market does not mean that it will claim a significant share of the market or indeed any share at all; for it may have postponed the initiation of service in a market long after authorization. This is even more likely because certifications are occasionally granted which were sought by a carrier solely for the defensive purpose of keeping out a rival. Another important possibility is that a carrier may be certified to serve a particular market but subject to such restrictions that it finds it unprofitable to provide more than token service.

Allied to the question of the level of seller concentration in particular city-pair passenger markets is the issue of the ways in which this concentration has been changing over time. Several students of Civil Aeronautics Board policies have published tabulations reflecting this evolving pattern. F. W. Gill and G. L. Bates have calculated the percentage of each domestic trunkline's route-miles over which it faces competition, defined as another certified carrier holding at least a 10 percent market share. Table 4 gives their calculations for 1940, 1947, and 1954 (the most recent year covered in their study).[17] Table 5 shows a similar measure for more recent years — the portions of various carriers' revenue passenger-miles sold in competitive markets. The portions of

[17] Gill and Bates, *Airline Competition,* chap. 1; Gilbert L. Bates, "Current Changes in Trunkline Competition," *Journal of Air Law and Commerce,* XXII (Autumn 1955), 379–405.

Table 4. Percentage of trunkline route-miles subject to competition, selected years[a]

Carrier	1940	1947	1954
American	41.3	75.9	81.0
Eastern	22.4	65.2	56.5
(Colonial)	0	0	100.0
TWA	76.2	82.0	83.9
United	58.1	86.7	89.0
Delta	0	68.0	45.0
(Chicago & Southern)	38.6	34.3	—
Capital	0	61.8	68.7
Northwest	34.1	41.6	59.4
National	23.2	100.0	100.0
Braniff	31.3	58.6	45.9
(Mid-Continent)	0	0	—
Western	16.2	68.6	69.4
(Inland)	0	38.9	—
Continental	0	12.9	9.4
Northeast	0	47.1	11.7

[a] The carriers whose names appear in parentheses have disappeared by merger with the carrier listed immediately above each.

Source: Gilbert L. Bates, "Current Changes in Trunkline Competition," *Journal of Air Law and Commerce*, XXII (Autumn 1955), 384.

Table 5. Percentage of carrier passenger-miles sold in competitive markets, trunkline and local-service carriers, selected years

Trunk airline			Local-service airline		
	1954	1957		1955	1957
American	51.0	72.5	Allegheny	25.9	32.6
Braniff	29.5	44.6	Bonanza	6.7	10.3
Capital	42.5	74.0	Central	21.6	18.7
Continental	13.6	32.5	Frontier	13.1	16.5
Delta	25.6	39.3	Lake Central	15.3	13.9
Eastern[a]	36.4	59.5	Mohawk	15.8	25.5
National	62.4	90.4	North Central	24.0	26.1
Northeast	6.0	53.2	Ozark	29.8	30.3
Northwest	39.5	57.4	Pacific	8.2	41.7
TWA	52.8	73.3	Piedmont	20.6	24.1
United	55.9	75.0	Southern	26.9	23.3
Western	49.5	53.5	Trans Texas	18.6	19.7
			West Coast	18.4	18.0

[a] Includes Colonial Airlines, with which Eastern merged in 1956.

Source: United Research, Inc., *Federal Regulation of the Domestic Air Transport Industry* (Cambridge, Mass., 1959), table B-19.

traffic gained in monopoly markets shrank considerably from 1940 to 1947 but stayed fairly stable from 1947 to 1954. The changes that produced these increases in competitive mileage also saw the typical airline derive its business from more and more city-pair markets. The average trunkline drew half its revenue from only six markets in 1940, ten in 1947, and fifteen in 1954. Since 1954, major grants of competitive route awards by the Civil Aeronautics Board have raised the portion of traffic drawn from competitive markets for all the trunks, as Table 5 shows. The greatest proportional increases were for several regional carriers which won entry into major markets — Braniff, Capital, Continental, Delta, and Northeast. The local-service carriers, though still primarily monopolists, are entering more and more into competitive service.

Having noted the patterns of seller concentration in the industry at large and in individual markets, we can consider some of the relations between them. Are some airlines larger than others because they operate in more markets, because they operate in larger markets, or because they hold larger shares of the competitive markets in which they operate? Each of these possible explanations contributes part of the answer. The latter two factors are particularly important, as is shown in some recent work by the geographer E. J. Taaffe.[18] Table 6 shows Taaffe's calculation of the share held by each of the largest four trunklines and by seven of the smaller carriers in total passenger-miles and in passenger-miles of travel between the one hundred city-pairs generating the most traffic. The tabulations are for 1940, 1949, 1954, and 1956.[19] They show that the dominant trunklines have always had a significantly greater share of the largest traffic-generating city-pairs, but that this margin has been shrinking over the years. Only Eastern Air Lines, dominating the Florida resort traffic, retains a substantially greater share in the traffic of the one hundred largest pairs; only Braniff and Delta have sig-

---

[18] E. J. Taaffe, "A Map Analysis of United States Airline Competition. Part I — The Development of Competition," *Journal of Air Law and Commerce,* XXV (Spring 1958), 121–147. See also the second part of the same article, *Journal of Air Law and Commerce,* XXV (Autumn 1958), 402–427, and his "Air Transport and United States Urban Distribution," *Geographical Review,* XL (April 1956), 219–238.

[19] More precisely, the data cover the September survey period for 1940 and both the March and September surveys for the postwar period.

Table 6. Market shares of trunkline carriers in total domestic passenger-miles and in passenger-miles generated in largest city-pair markets, selected years (percentages)

Carrier	1940			1949			1954			1956		
	Hundred largest	Total	Difference[a]	Hundred largest	Total	Difference	Hundred largest	Total	Difference	Hundred largest	Total	Difference
American	36.4	30.0	6.4	24.9	23.3	1.6	22.2	20.8	1.4	21.8	22.1	-0.3
United	26.2	21.4	4.8	23.0	19.6	3.4	22.0	19.3	2.7	20.9	19.5	1.4
TWA	20.9	14.9	6.0	18.2	14.4	3.8	16.5	16.1	0.4	15.2	15.1	0.2
Eastern	12.9	15.2	-2.3	17.1	15.4	1.7	21.3	17.5	3.8	21.6	17.5	4.1
Big Four	95.3	81.4	13.9	83.2	72.7	10.5	81.9	73.7	8.3	79.7	74.2	5.4
Capital	1.1	3.6	-2.5	3.6	5.4	-1.8	2.2	4.6	-2.4	4.5	4.7	-0.2
National	0	0.5	-0.5	3.0	2.6	0.4	6.9	4.3	2.7	7.2	4.4	2.9
Northwest	2.4	4.9	-2.5	5.5	6.5	-1.0	3.3	4.6	-1.3	3.0	4.0	-1.0
Delta	0.5	2.8	-2.3	1.5	4.9	-3.4	2.4	4.8	-2.5	2.6	5.2	-2.6
Western	0.2	1.5	-1.3	1.9	1.6	0.3	2.8	2.5	0.3	2.2	2.1	0.1
Braniff	0.4	4.1	-3.6	1.1	4.6	-3.5	0.5	3.2	-2.8	0.8	3.3	-2.5
Northeast	0	0.4	-0.4	0.2	1.0	-0.8	0.1	0.6	-0.5	0.1	0.6	-0.5
Regional carriers	4.7	17.7	-13.1	16.8	26.5	-9.8	18.1	24.6	-6.6	20.3	24.2	-3.9

[a] Row differences and column totals may not reconcile because of rounding errors.
Source: E. J. Taaffe, "A Map Analysis of United States Airline Competition," Journal of Air Law and Commerce, XXV (Autumn 1958), 128, 132, 136, 142.

nificantly smaller shares.[20] If we took not the one hundred largest city-pairs, but the twenty-five or fifty largest, then the largest four carriers would probably again show greater shares of the top markets because of their transcontinental routes. The point remains, however, that the dominant carriers owe their present position to a greater number of routes, and dominance in larger markets is less significant than it was.

Are the shares the trunklines hold in city-pair markets highly stable, or are they relatively flexible subject to successful marketing strategies? This question is obviously an historical approach to the problem of product differentiation and demand characteristics (discussed below) and to the measurement of cross-elasticities of demand between carriers (impossible historically because of absence of competitive price adjustments in individual markets). Unfortunately, no particularly satisfying evidence can be constructed. Obviously we should examine only those markets where the number of competing carriers has remained constant. The ability of new carriers to seize a share of a city-pair market is of interest, but it is a different question from that of market-share stability. Since the mid-1950s and early 1940s saw numerous increases in the number of carriers certified to serve particular markets, relatively few markets could be studied back to World War II. Hence it was decided, for what it may be worth, to tabulate changes of market shares in selected city-pairs among one hundred largest in terms of passenger-miles, using the period from March 1955 to March 1958. Excluded from the tabulation, which appears in Table 7, are those markets which were monopolized throughout the period and those in which a significant addition to the number of carriers certified took place. By "significant" addition is meant one extra carrier's gaining as much as a 5 percent market share. Under these rules, fifty-eight of the top one hundred markets could be included. Table 7 shows the distribution of changes by the number of percentage-point variations; it excludes shares not over 10 percent in either 1955 or 1958 and subdivides the remaining changes according to

[20] Route awards not reflected in the 1956 surveys are probably now washing out these disparities. See Taaffe, "A Map Analysis of United States Airline Competition," pp. 139–143.

Table 7.   Changes in airline shares of major city-pair markets, March 1955–
March 1958, by size of share

Number of percentage-point changes	Shares in 10–50% range	Shares exceeding 50%	All shares over 10%
+41 to 50	1	3	4
+31 to 40	2	2	4
+21 to 30	3	2	5
+16 to 20	6	0	6
+11 to 15	6	9	15
+6 to 10	7	4	11
+1 to 5	9	5	14
0	4	4	8
−1 to −5	8	9	17
−6 to −10	6	3	9
−11 to −15	7	8	15
−16 to −20	0	3	3
−21 to −30	3	8	11
−31 to −40	1	5	6
Total changes	63	65	128

Source: Calculated from CAB, *Competition Among Domestic Air Carriers*, March 1–14, 1955, and March 1–14, 1958 (Washington: Research Department, Air Transport Association of America, 1959); see text.

whether or not they involved a market share greater than 50 percent at either the beginning or the end of the period.

Of the 128 share changes tabulated, 89, or 69.5 percent, were greater than five percentage points, and 69, or 53.9 percent, were greater than ten percentage points. By any comparison to other industrial markets or submarkets in the American economy, these shares would have to be judged rather flexible. Even though shares of the trunkline carriers in the national passenger market have been much more stable, their positions in particular markets do not strike one as being tightly entrenched. The large increases of market shares, those greater than twenty percentage points, in most cases obviously resulted from conspicuous competitive moves. By far the most important of these was the introduction in the 1955–1958 period by Capital Airlines of the British-made Vickers Viscount turboprop aircraft. The Viscount's great popularity and the failure of Capital's competitors to secure comparable equipment until the end of 1958 (when an American turboprop plane became available) raised Capital's market share enormously. The company moved from 1 percent to 22 percent of the Chicago–New York market, from 3 percent to 47 percent of Detroit–New York, 18 percent to 63 percent of Chicago–Washington, and from 24 percent to 58 percent of Chicago–Pittsburgh.[21] Other strategies which had conspicuous effects on market shares included introduction by the large transcontinental carriers of less austere forms of coach-class travel, involving service of meals at nominal cost in the fastest available aircraft.

The final question raised above concerning the trunk airlines' shares of city-pair markets dealt with the extent to which individual carriers face the same rivals in a number of different markets. Before turning to the facts, it may be well to indicate on *a priori* grounds why this question might be important. Consider two schematic models, each involving four city-pair markets of identical size, with two carriers competing in each. The airline industry consists of four carriers, *A, B, C,* and *D,* each operating between two city-pairs. Markets are shared as shown in Table 8. In Model I, *A* faces *B* in each of its markets; any

Table 8. Hypothetical alternative patterns of airline competition in a series of city-pair markets

	City-pair			
Model	1	2	3	4
I	A, B	A, B	C, D	C, D
II	A, B	B, C	C, D	A, D

of *A*'s competitive strategies will threaten all of *B*'s operations and hence will be likely to provoke retaliation. In Model II, however, *A*'s strategies may affect both *B* and *D*, though not the whole operation of either. A move by *A* to capture a larger share of markets 1 and 4 might cause *B* and *D* not to retaliate effectively, but rather to seek to recoup their losses at *C*'s expense in markets 2 and 3. The chances of mutual dependence being fully recognized and impeding competitive strategies would seem to be less in Model II.

[21] These changes are noted in Taaffe, pp. 137–138.

By inspection of the route patterns of the United States trunk-lines, something can be said about which pattern prevails. The three large transcontinental carriers, American, TWA, and United, are clearly in the situation of Model I. Each competes with at least one of the others in numerous long-haul east-west city-pairs. Western, and to a lesser extent Northwest and Continental, constitute a "fringe" to these three large carriers. Eastern and its rivals, by contrast, are more in the situation of Model II. Eastern's principal routes in the eastern half of the country fan out to the north from the Florida resort cities and also connect a number of large middle-Atlantic and northeastern points. In those of the one hundred largest city-pairs which it serves, it faces as principal rivals seven other airlines. American Airlines has a larger total number of rivals, but the distribution of their importance is much more skewed. Among the remaining regional trunks, Capital, Delta, and Braniff, like Eastern, face a variety of market rivals. Capital operates a dense network of routes running both east-west and north-south in the northeastern portion of the country. Delta's more widespread operations are more or less north-south in the east and central portions of the United States; it competes extensively with Eastern but with numerous others as well. Braniff's situation is similar to Delta's. On the other hand, National, Northeast, and Northwest face more limited sets of rivals. National and Northeast compete largely with each other and with Eastern up and down the east coast. Northwest faces primarily United and Capital along its routes between New York and the Pacific northwest.

These relations can be studied with something resembling Louis Guttman's scaling methodology: essentially, a simple procedure for ranking the members of an interrelated population to test for chainlike or recursive relations. Table 9 shows the number of city-pair markets among the hundred largest in which each of the trunk carriers faced each of the other trunks. To be a significant rival a carrier was required to have a market share of more than 2 percent. The distribution of each carrier's rivals appears as the L-shaped row and column of numbers headed by its name. The carriers have been arranged in Table 9 roughly to minimize the number of cases of competition far off the diagonal of the table. Our ability to make such an arrangement reflects the extent to which carriers in the industry (or subsets of carriers) face only limited numbers of rivals. Table 9 generally confirms the findings of the preceding paragraph. The distribu-

Table 9. Number of cases of market rivalry between all pairs of trunklines, 100 largest city-pairs, 1958[a]

Carrier	WA	NW	UA	TW	AA	CA	CO	BN	DL	EA	NA	NE
Western		7	2									
Northwest		6	1	4								
United			28	21	10	4			1			1
TWA				24	6	5	1		2			
American					7	1	5	3	5		1	2
Capital									2	3		
Continental								2				
Braniff									4	2		
Delta										7		
Eastern											8	8
National												6
Northeast												

a The column headings are common abbreviations of carrier names and are in the same order as the row headings.
Source: Calculated from CAB, *Competition Among Domestic Air Carriers, March 1–14, 1958* and *September 17–30, 1958* (Washington: Research Department, Air Transport Association of America, 1959, 1960); the March survey was used except for carriers affected by strikes, in which case the September survey was used.

tions for American, TWA, United, Western, and Northwest have strong central tendencies (toward the diagonal). So do National and Northeast, but the distributions for Eastern and its rivals are significantly more scattered.

CONCLUSION

The domestic airline industry is one of moderately high and stable seller concentration in the aggregate national market. Concentration in the typical city-pair market is very high but has been falling in recent years. Furthermore, shares in city-pair markets seem rather variable over time. The high concentration in most city-pair markets strongly implies effective recognition by the carriers of their mutual interdependence, as does the pattern of the identity of rivals from market to market that appears for the east-west Big Three and their smaller competitors. But rivalries among the remaining trunklines are more scattered and perhaps more conducive to active competition.

2 Demand Aspects of Market Structure

In this chapter there are grouped several features of market structure which, according to *a priori* theory and the experience of other industry studies, might play a role in determining the market conduct and performance of the airlines. The first of the following sections deals with aggregative evidence on the price elasticity and income elasticity of demand for air-passenger transport and, collaterally, the way in which these traits are perceived by airline managements. Then we turn to evidence from consumer surveys on the same matters and on substitutability between classes of air service and between air and rail travel. The final section deals with the conceptually difficult matter of product differentiation as a market-structure trait.

ELASTICITY OF DEMAND

In industries of relatively high concentration, the size of both price and income elasticities of demand can be an important market-structure trait. Where market rivals are few and interdependence is recognized, managements must resolve two conflicting objectives. One possible route to increased profits for the firm is cooperative action to raise joint industry profits closer to the theoretical monopolistic maximum. Another is unilateral action to increase its share of the market, even at the expense of joint profits to the industry. Which sort of policies will the typical firm choose, those leading toward joint maximization or those leading toward a greater market share? Theoretical discussions have touched on many of the factors determining this choice, but one which has certainly not been overemphasized is the magnitude of price and income elasticities. The reasoning is simple. If the industry faces an aggregate demand with relatively high price elasticity, cooperative action to achieve a given price increase probably has a small effect on joint profits. Likewise, any strategies aimed at increasing a firm's market share will do relatively little damage to joint profit levels if the whole industry price level should be dragged down as a result.

The reasoning with respect to income elasticities is less direct and, indeed, pertains not to income elasticity alone but to any condition which affects the growth rate of aggregate sales of the industry. Writers interested in the organizational aspects of business behavior have often suggested that profit objectives are best described not by the pursuit of maximum profits but rather by the pursuit of a satisfactory and rising level of profits. If this be the case, then an oligopoly facing a rapidly growing demand is likely to be satisfied with a submonopoly price and with profits that are increasing through the impact of a steadily widening market. The pressure on managements to formulate policies aimed at *either* an increased share of the market or greater joint industry profits is reduced. Entrepreneurial attention will be drawn more to the internal problems of organization and control that face a rapidly growing firm. Conversely, firms in an oligopolistic industry facing a low income elasticity of aggregate demand (or a low growth rate of sales for any reason) will tend to be under more pressure to choose some sort of policy likely to give an upward trend to the firm's profit record. These *a priori* arguments concerning the effects of price and income elasticities deal with possibilities rather than necessities. Nonetheless, various industry studies seem to set forth behavioral patterns consistent with these notions.

For air transport it is hard to unscramble from available data on demand the income elasticity, pure price elasticity, and substitution elasticity with respect to surface transport. The money price of airline trips has changed relatively few times, and on the occasions when it has changed the short-period behavior of the demand for air transport has usually been subject to other strong influences at the same time. The price of air travel relative to that of surface travel by common carrier (and probably relative to surface travel by private automobile) has been falling rather steadily for many years, and we have considerable experience with substitution between the two modes of transportation. However, any statistical measures that might be based on this experience would be rather hard to interpret. At the same time that the relative prices of air and surface transportation have been changing, more and more travelers have overcome their fear of flying and come to use air transport. That is, people who were once not sensitive to the relative prices of air and surface carriers in choosing means of transportation have gradually become susceptible to choice on the basis of a price comparison. The significance of this is that any calculation of a cross-elasticity of substitution between air and surface transportation would be overstated because of the constant presence of this element of "learning" among the airlines' customers. The elasticity would not be reversible for rises in the price of air as against surface transport; it would overstate the loss of traffic to the airlines.

With these precautions in mind, let us turn to what evidence is available on the various demand elasticities for air transport. Consider two attempts to calculate something resembling a "pure" demand elasticity for air transport with all other factors held constant. One was contained in an exhibit presented by American Airlines in a recent lengthy Civil Aeronautics Board proceeding called the *General Passenger Fare Investigation*.[1] This presentation, using rather crude data, sought to isolate the influence of average price on traffic volume by relating the annual percentage change in aggregate passenger-miles to the annual percentage change in the average fare yield per passenger-mile (gross passenger revenue divided by passenger-miles).[2] Taking the years 1949–1956, the constant term of the regression equation (annual growth in the absence of a price change) turned out to be 16 percent, the implied price elasticity to be −0.2. No correlation coefficient was given, but it clearly would have been very low. The American Airlines document conceded that these calculations were of the roughest sort. However, it also discussed most of the other plausible methods of attempting to measure the elasticity of demand for air transport and put forth convincing arguments for why they would not work.

Another estimate of demand elasticity appears in a recent study

[1] Docket No. 8008. This complex proceeding was begun in May 1956, by Board Order Serial No. E-10279, and sought to deal with the appropriateness of the prevailing general level of air-passenger rates and also with the appropriate method for determining the correct rates, an issue which the Board miraculously had never previously treated. Problems of the fare structure were excluded from the case. Because of procedural delays, this case was not heard before a Board examiner until May 1957. Interrupted by pleas from the carriers for emergency interim fare increases, the examiner's report was not issued until May 1959. This case is discussed below, pp. 146–153.

[2] American Airlines, Inc., Exhibit No. AA-12, Testimony of Robert E. Kimble, General Passenger Fare Investigation, Docket No. 8008, pp. 9–10; see also Transcript of Hearings before Examiner, pp. 6745–6754.

coming from the Civil Aeronautics Board's Office of Carrier Accounts and Statistics. This was an attempt to use multivariate analysis to explain the changes in airline passengers and passenger-miles, 1939–1957, by the movement of four independent variables: average airline yield per passenger-mile, average railroad yield per passenger-mile, disposable personal income per person, and a time trend. The monetary variables were deflated by the consumer price index, and the equations were fitted to logarithms of the percentage changes of the variables. The statistical procedure is acceptable, except for being somewhat light on degrees of freedom, and the perverse results can be taken as establishing the hopelessness of efforts along this line. The equations for both passengers and passenger-miles yielded delectably high price elasticities (-2.57 for passengers, -2.46 for passenger-miles). Furthermore, the sign of the substitution term relating to the price of rail transport was appropriate in both equations. However, in both cases, the time trend was *negative* and significant, and the income elasticity was implausibly low (less than 0.50) and not significant. Because of high intercorrelation of the independent variables, obviously the influence of both time and income growth has turned up in the price-elasticity term, and none of the coefficients can be accepted.[3]

It is possible that an elaborate cross-sectional study of fares and travel in particular city-pair markets might yield acceptable evidence on the elasticity of demand for air travel, but it is beyond the resources of this study. The best guess an economist could make from the available qualitative and quantitative evidence on demand elasticity might run as follows: for small changes in the fares for all classes of service between given city-pairs, there are probably few instances in which a demand response indicating more than unit elasticity would be observed within a year, with everything else held constant. This appears to be the view of most economists who have studied the industry.[4] It is also the view that seems to prevail among manage-

[3] These difficulties are fully recognized in the study. See CAB, Office of Carrier Accounts and Statistics, Research and Statistics Division, *Forecast of Airline Passenger Traffic in the United States: 1959–1965* ("Air Transport Economics in the Jet Age"), Dec. 1959, pp. 24–26.

[4] For example, Paul W. Cherington, *Airline Price Policy* (Boston, 1958), p. 437 and *passim*. Cherington is not even optimistic about the elasticity of demand for particular classes of service, holding the price of other classes constant.

ments, at least in their representations to the Civil Aeronautics Board. For instance, in calling for a 12 percent fare increase in *General Passenger Fare Investigation,* a Capital Airlines spokesman declared: "In today's inflationary atmosphere and with the declining value of the dollar, an increase of this amount will deter very few people from traveling. This is particularly true among the business people who constitute the primary segment of Capital's traffic. The business traveler is accustomed to increasing costs in his own business and accepts increasing transportation costs as an inevitable portion of his own costs." [5] Similar statements could be drawn from innumerable airline sources.[6] This is also the prevailing airline view of historic experience with changes in the general level of air fares.[7] Sometimes carrier assertions about effective demand elasticity turn on relatively subtle interpretations of general-equilibrium cost-price relations.[8] Sometimes they reflect an unsubtle faith that any travel discouraged by higher prices will be offset by the pull of a high income elasticity of demand. The only airline dissenters to the low-elasticity view are the short-haul carriers who feel themselves to be in close competition with surface transportation. In the 1940s the smaller trunklines were in this position; now it is the local-service carriers which frequently behave as if they faced a highly elastic demand.[9]

There is, in short, no clear evidence about the value of the aggregate demand elasticity for air transport at the present time. There is equal uncertainty about whether it is rising or falling. A strong force is working in each direction. On the one hand, as we shall see below, the steady deterioration of rail service seems

[5] Brief of Capital Airlines, Inc., General Passenger Fare Investigation, Oct. 29, 1958, pp. 51–52.

[6] See, for example, American Airlines, Inc., Exhibit No. AA-11, Testimony of Walter H. Johnson, Jr., *passim;* and Transcript of Hearings before Examiner, General Passenger Fare Investigation, pp. 6438–6439.

[7] Testimony of United Air Lines President, W. A. Patterson, in *Air-Line Industry Investigation,* hearings pursuant to S. Res. 50, U.S. Senate, Committee on Interstate and Foreign Commerce, 81st Cong., 1st sess. (Washington, 1949), II, 656.

[8] Transcript of Hearings before Examiner, General Passenger Fare Investigation, p. 6443.

[9] See, *Guaranteed Loans for Purchase of Aircraft and Equipment,* hearings on S. 2229, U.S. Senate, Committee on Interstate and Foreign Commerce, Subcommittee on Aviation, 85th Cong., 1st sess. (Washington, 1957), p. 120.

to be cutting down the substitutability between rail and air (at least over the range of fares actually observed) and thus cutting down the effective demand elasticity for air transport. On the other hand, the portion of airline travel purchased by presumably price-conscious individuals has been rising. Personal consumption expenditures were about 39 percent of total expenditures on air travel at the beginning of the 1950s, when coach service was first introduced; at the close of the 1950s they were hovering around 43 percent.[10] The balance of these forces is certainly hard to strike.

Turning from evidence on price elasticity to evidence on the income elasticity and growth trend of passenger travel, we recall the failure of the Civil Aeronautics Board's effort to separate these factors. Even a simpler attempt at separating the effect on air-transport demand of income growth from the time trend (shift of consumer preferences toward air transport) would probably be impossible. Nonetheless, any income elasticity derived by simple regression from time-series data will be biased upward or at the very least will give incorrect results when applied to anticipate the result of income reductions. For what it is worth, a Department of Commerce calculation of this sort gives an income-elasticity measure of +2.7 for air transport, based on the relation of personal disposable income to personal expenditures on air travel. Calculated in the same way, the income elasticity for intercity bus travel is 0.0 and for rail travel −0.6.[11] But, as it was argued above, the important thing for predicting business conduct in the air-transport industry is not so much income elasticity as the over-all growth rate of demand. This has been enormous — around 15 percent annually since the end of World War II. Aside from some violent oscillation in the reconversion period, the quarterly figures for revenue passenger-miles sold by the certified carriers show steady growth with a steady seasonal pattern[12] and no marked sensitivity to business fluctuations.

[10] Calculated from Department of Commerce, *Survey of Current Business* (various issues); *Statistical Abstract of the United States* (various issues); and Federal Aviation Agency, *Statistical Handbook of Aviation* (Washington, 1960), p. 84.

[11] Louis J. Paradiso and Clement Winston, "Consumer Expenditure-Income Patterns," *Survey of Current Business,* XXXV (Sept. 1955), 29.

[12] The seasonal ranking of the quarters of the year from highest demand to lowest would be third, second, fourth, first. This pattern holds for the whole

There has been endless discussion in the industry over whether the recent years portend a permanent fall in the growth rate of demand.

SURVEY EVIDENCE ON DEMAND

To supplement this unsatisfactory evidence on the traits of general elasticity demand for air transport, there is a good deal of survey material on air-transport demand. Some of this is worth noting for the additional light it sheds on the conclusions reached above and also for its implications for another feature of the demand for air transport — the substitutability between the two classes of service. This last matter, the relation of the demand for coach and for first-class air travel at the going fare structure, has often been under study by both the Board and the carriers. A survey of United Air Lines passengers made during the first week of August 1956 sought the reasons for the journeys undertaken by coach and by first-class passengers.[13] It presented results both for passengers on all United flights and for those taking

Table 10. Reasons for travel stated by first-class and coach passengers on United Air Lines, August 1–7, 1956 (percentages)

Class	Pleasure	Business	Other
All passengers			
First class	29	43	28
Coach	58	10	32
Passengers traveling more than 1000 miles			
First class	34	38	28
Coach	65	6	29

Source: United Air Lines, Inc., Exhibit No. U-116, General Passenger Fare Investigation.

trips longer than a thousand miles. The data are summarized in Table 10. Superficially at least, they tend to bear out the air-

trunk industry and also for most of the east-west carriers individually. However, carriers operating mostly in winter-vacation traffic have almost the reverse seasonal pattern. This condition is a strong inducement for either route patterns involving both winter-vacation and other routes or the use of seasonal leasing of equipment. Neither adjustment has, however, actually been very extensive.

[13] United Air Lines, Inc., Exhibit No. U-116, General Passenger Fare Investigation.

lines' contention that the great bulk of first-class air travel is by businessmen, who can be assumed to be indifferent, within wide limits, to the level of air fares. Especially on journeys greater than a thousand miles, the portion of business travelers using coach flights seems scarcely larger than the number that would use them for convenience of scheduling even if first-class comforts were preferred. However, there is one qualification of unknown significance which must be placed on this conclusion. Among the 28 to 32 percent of travelers journeying for reasons other than pleasure or business, an important fraction, 11 or 12 percent of all passengers, were traveling for reasons of combined business and pleasure. If these are lumped in with the coach passengers traveling purely for business reasons, then the percentage of coach travelers moving to some extent for business purposes rises to the more appreciable fraction of one fifth. This figure is more or less in line with one drawn from surveys by the Port of New York Authority and cited by counsel for the Civil Aeronautics Board in *General Passenger Fare Investigation*. Of business travelers enplaning at New York City in 1956, the Authority found that 15.7 percent used coach accommodations, the figure varying seasonally between 19.5 percent during the winter and 12.7 percent in a summer survey. The chief attraction of coach travel was asserted to be lower fares, not scheduling convenience.[14] The rather wobbly conclusion to be drawn from these surveys is that a fairly small but significant portion of business travelers display sensitivity to the price of air travel by using less luxurious tourist or coach facilities.[15] This sensitivity

---

[14] CAB, Brief of Bureau Counsel, General Passenger Fare Investigation, p. 309.

[15] Of course, even if all business travelers used first-class flights by dictate of the social mores, this would still not prove that the demand for first-class business air travel is completely price-inelastic. Travel is normally substitutable for other business inputs; the business faced with a rising cost of travel can reallocate its inputs to increase the size of its fixed-base sales and supervisory force, use more mail advertising and less direct solicitation, employ telephone and telegraph for internal communication rather than travel, and so forth. This substitutability is well discussed in American Airlines, Inc., Exhibit No. AA-11, General Passenger Fare Investigation. But from it is drawn the fallacious conclusion that because the existing use of business travel (versus other business inputs) can be presumed to maximize business profits, any smaller amount would decrease profits, and hence a rise in the price of air travel would not decrease its use.

is sometimes many years in appearing. During 1960 the transcontinental carriers sought successfully to raise their coach fares as numerous businesses and the federal government began to urge their employees to use coach service. The differential between coach and first-class fares had been about the same for ten years before this adjustment occurred, although the differential in the quality of service had fallen significantly.

There is a good deal of survey information on the relation between personal income and demand for travel. Strong backing is given the notion that the income elasticity of demand for air travel is high, both because at present high-income groups are more frequent air travelers and because they are more likely to choose air over surface means. Material from four surveys will be cited — those by the University of Michigan Survey Research Center (1955 and 1956), the United States Department of Commerce (1957), and the Port of New York Authority (December 1955 to March 1956 and June-September 1956).[16] Information from the Michigan survey indicates how clearly the number of trips by air for both business and nonbusiness reasons varies with the level of family income. Table 11 shows that not only were individuals in high-income groups more likely to take a trip in any given year, but also that they were likely to have taken substantially more trips. The latter part of the generalization shows up even more in the figures for business travel. It would be desirable to have information on the amount spent for air travel by persons in various income categories, but unfortunately the only survey that seems to contain this information lumps air travel into a generic category "plane, ship, etc." However, results of this survey are presented in Table 12 because of other highly interesting information contained therein. The amount spent on travel is shown broken down not only by family-income category but also by region of the United States and by the type of city in which the traveler resides. The classification according to these last two variables produces some striking results. Persons in any given income bracket high enough to do substantial traveling spend much more on "plane, ship, etc." if

[16] Citations here will be to the useful summary of the results of these surveys contained in CAB, Bureau Counsel Exhibit No. BCR-188 (Sup.), General Passenger Fare Investigation.

Table 11.   Frequency of air travel for business and nonbusiness purposes, by
family-income level, 1956 (percentages)

| | Family-income level | | | |
Travel category	Under $3,000	$3,000– $5,999	$6,000– $9,999	Over $10,000
Took nonbusiness trip	1.4	2.7	7.3	20.5
Number of trips: 1	1.0	2.0	5.2	13.0
2	0.2	0.5	1.2	5.2
3	0.1	0.2	0.5	1.3
4–9	0.1	0.0	0.3	1.0
10 or more	0.0	0.0	0.1	0.0
No nonbusiness trip or not ascertained	98.6	97.3	92.7	79.5
Took business trip	0.2	1.2	6.1	18.6
Number of trips: 1	0.1	0.5	3.2	5.9
2	0.1	0.3	1.2	1.3
3	0.0	0.1	0.3	1.3
4–9	0.0	0.2	0.9	5.5
10 or more	0.0	0.1	0.5	4.6
No business trip or not ascertained	99.8	98.8	93.9	81.4

Source: CAB, Bureau of Air Operations, Bureau Counsel Exhibit No. BCR-188 (Sup.), General Passenger Fare Investigation, table 8, p. 14.

they live in northern or western rather than in southern cities; they spend much more if they live in large cities or suburbs than if they live in small cities. As one would expect, the surveys show a strong positive relation between family-income level and the choice of first-class service. The Port of New York Authority survey of passengers enplaning at New York indicated an average income of first-class nonbusiness passengers of $9,125, whereas the average coach passenger had a family income of $7,244. Of the first-class passengers, 18.6 percent had incomes in excess of $20,000 and 35.8 percent in excess of $10,000; only 10.2 percent of coach passengers had incomes over $20,000 and 27.8 percent had incomes over $10,000.[17] Evidently there is a

[17] *Ibid.*, p. 24. In assessing the precision of these figures for the income distribution of air travelers, it is well to note that almost 20 percent of both first-class and coach passengers failed to indicate family income.

DEMAND ASPECTS 41

Table 12. Average family expenditures on travel by "plane, ship, etc.," 1956 (dollars)

Income range	Northern cities			Southern cities			Western cities		
	Large	Suburban	Small	Large	Suburban	Small	Large	Suburban	Small
0–1,000	0.52	0.00	0.00	0.72	0.00	0.00	0.00	18.81	0.00
1,000–1,999	3.91	0.21	0.00	0.87	0.00	0.00	0.78	1.84	0.01
2,000–2,999	1.58	1.49	0.50	1.15	1.33	0.00	2.90	1.99	2.74
3,000–3,999	2.53	0.66	2.63	1.40	6.41	0.45	6.03	0.60	2.53
4,000–4,999	1.78	7.36	9.12	3.58	2.72	0.00	9.06	5.56	2.99
5,000–5,999	8.60	0.91	0.00	2.42	5.67	0.00	8.29	0.80	4.11
6,000–7,499	7.11	0.62	0.00	3.34	9.76	6.58	21.26	1.67	14.64
7,500–9,999	23.01	15.96	0.00	2.04	10.71	5.60	22.96	29.20	30.33
10,000 and up	88.84	43.04	22.77	18.02	16.54	0.00	35.31	33.88	13.98

Source: Bureau of Labor Statistics survey collected for University of Pennsylvania, Wharton School of Finance and Commerce, and appearing in their *Study of Consumer Expenditure, Income and Savings* (Philadelphia, 1957), XVI, table 2, part 2, p. 52.

substantial income elasticity for more luxurious service in non-business air travel.

Another important sort of information on the relation of income to demand for air transportation that emerges from these consumer surveys lies in the family incomes of travelers choosing the various modes of public transportation. As one would expect, air travel is the mode chosen by those with relatively high incomes. In 1956 the median family income of air travelers was $8,300, that of rail travelers $5,500, intercity-bus travelers $3,900, and private-automobile travelers $5,400. The median income for travelers by any mode of transportation was $5,500, higher than the median family income for all United States families of $4,783.[18] When weighted by the number of trips taken annually by each traveler, the income differences among passengers using the various types of transport become even more marked.[19] This fact implies that persons with very high incomes are more likely to be repeat travelers on airlines than on other modes of transport. Another check on these generalizations appears in Table 13, which shows for each mode of travel the number of trips

[18] *Ibid.*, table 1.
[19] *Ibid.*, table 3, p. 5.

Table 13.   Number of trips per 100 adults for nonbusiness purposes, by
             income group and mode of transportation, 1956

Income class	Mode of transportation			
	Air	Rail	Bus	Private auto
Under $1,000	1.7	6.0	8.5	37.8
1,000– 1,999	1.4	9.3	14.9	60.7
2,000– 2,999	2.4	13.6	7.9	91.3
3,000– 3,999	3.0	9.7	8.1	130.8
4,000– 4,999	3.4	12.0	5.8	126.4
5,000– 5,999	5.8	13.8	8.9	192.6
6,000– 7,499	11.6	10.4	4.8	194.3
7,500– 9,999	11.6	13.8	9.8	271.1
10,000–14,999	21.2	13.9	8.1	295.7
15,000–19,999	54.7	17.2	5.6	276.5
20,000 and up	76.2	38.4	13.1	201.1

Source: CAB, Bureau of Air Operations, Bureau Counsel Exhibit No. BCR-188 (Sup.), General Passenger Fare Investigation, table 11, p. 18.

made for nonbusiness purposes per one hundred adults in each income category. The use of air travel and private automobiles strongly increases with income, while bus travel looks slightly like an inferior good and rail travel shows no discernible pattern. It is interesting and perhaps significant that one can argue from the figures that private-automobile travel becomes an inferior good for families with incomes over $15,000, while the use of air travel continues to increase sharply.

Not only do high-income families tend strongly to use air transportation; the survey data also show that more of them have at least sampled air travel at some time. The 1955 Michigan survey showed that of the population at large, 77 percent had never taken an air trip, while only 31 percent had had no rail trip, 53 percent no bus trip, and 11 percent no automobile trip. Air travel was unknown to 88 percent of those with incomes under $4,000, while only 41 percent of those with incomes over $10,000 had never been aloft.[20]

One final facet of the relation of family income to the choice of air travel remains to be explored—namely, its connection with the distance the passenger travels. Information from the Port of

[20] *Ibid.,* p. 8.

New York Authority survey shows a good inverse relation between the average income of nonbusiness travelers and the distance traveled. The average family income of passengers traveling by air on journeys under 250 miles was $9,200, but only $6,800 for persons traveling more than 1500 miles.[21] Table 14 goes fur-

Table 14. Portion of travelers using air transport on most recent trip, by miles traveled and family income (percentages)

	Family income				
Miles traveled	Under $3,000	$3,000–$5,999	$6,000–$9,999	$10,000 and up	All classes
100–499	1.4	14.4	25.0	60.9	16.7
500–999	10.7	31.2	52.6	—a	25.4
1,000 or more	41.7	48.0	75.0	85.7	62.3

a "Too few cases to be percentagized."
Source: CAB, Bureau of Air Operations, Bureau Counsel Exhibit No. BCR-188 (Sup.), General Passenger Fare Investigation, table 16, p. 26; data originally from University of Michigan Survey Research Center.

ther by showing the portion of travelers selecting travel by air for their most recent journey, classified both according to distance and according to family income. The results are quite dramatic. For example, only 1.4 percent of travelers with incomes under $3,000 had selected air travel for journeys between 100 and 500 miles, whereas persons with incomes over $10,000 chose to travel such distances by air 60.9 percent of the time. Once more, there is cross-sectional evidence of an extremely strong relation between the preference for air travel as a superior means of transportation and the level of family income.

If the data of Table 14 give an accurate impression, then for any given length of journey air travel is the preferred means of transportation in the sense that the higher is a person's income the greater is the chance that he will journey by air. This fact leads directly to the role of price as a determinant of this choice and to evidence on the substitutability between air and surface

[21] *Ibid.*, p. 25. For some slightly different ideas about the significance of air travel by different income groups, see J. B. Lansing, J.-C. Liu, and D. B. Suits, "An Analysis of Interurban Air Travel," *Quarterly Journal of Economics,* LXXV (Feb. 1961), 89.

travel over various distances. The barest facts of market shares held by air and surface carriers testify to the large numbers of travelers who have switched from surface to air transportation and can be presumed to have considered the merits of both. Since World War II the absolute volume of travel on intercity buses has fallen moderately, while intercity train travel has dropped precipitously. Table 15 shows these figures and also the per-

Table 15. Airlines' share of intercity travel market, selected years

Year	Volume (billions passenger-miles)				Airlines' percentage of common-carrier total	Airlines' percentage of grand total
	Class I railroads	Bus	Domestic airlines	Auto[a]		
1939	18.6	11.2	0.7	80.6	2.3	0.6
1940	19.8	11.6	1.1	87.2	3.4	0.9
1946	58.8	25.6	6.0	99.4	6.6	3.2
1947	40.0	23.4	6.1	106.5	8.8	3.5
1948	35.3	23.0	6.0	108.8	9.3	3.5
1949	29.4	21.5	6.8	112.0	11.8	4.0
1950	26.7	21.3	8.0	120.5	14.3	4.5
1951	29.7	22.3	10.6	136.6	16.9	5.3
1952	29.3	21.1	12.5	147.6	19.9	5.9
1953	27.0	19.6	14.7	158.1	24.0	6.7
1954	24.6	16.9	16.7	163.8	28.7	7.5
1955	23.7	17.2	19.7	175.0	32.5	8.4
1956	23.4	17.0	22.3	190.0	35.6	8.8

[a] Trips over 50 miles.
Source: P. W. Cherington, *Airline Price Policy* (Boston, 1958), pp. 28–29; data originally from Port of New York Authority, Civil Aeronautics Authority, Bureau of Public Roads, Interstate Commerce Commission.

centage relation of the volume of air travel to all intercity common-carrier travel and to long-distance travel by both public and private conveyance. The main problem to be faced in compiling such statistics is that of getting a reasonable estimate of travel by private automobile; the estimates by Cherington used in Table 15 are probably as good as any. This drastic shift of traffic toward air carriers from other common carriers has been accompanied by a fall in the average price of air travel relative to rail and bus transport. Table 16 shows average fare levels for a few representative years.

Table 16. Passenger revenue per passenger-mile, major domestic common carriers, selected years (cents per mile)

Year	Air	Rail	Bus
1938	5.12	2.07	1.62
1940	5.05	1.90	1.46
1945	4.93	1.92	1.64
1949	5.75	2.64	1.85
1953	5.44	2.78	2.06
1957	5.29	2.95	2.29

Source: CAB, Office of Carrier Accounts and Statistics, Research and Statistics Division, *Forecast of Airline Passenger Traffic in the United States: 1959–1965*, tables 15, 16.

These figures are useful background for discussing the substitutability between air and surface carriers, but they tell nothing about it directly. Ideally we would like experimental data showing the response of relative shares to a small change in relative prices, occurring without the clutter of exogenous events; naturally, nothing of the sort exists. Instead we must revert to descriptive material on particular cities or city-pair markets and to information on the extent to which the airlines' fare structure is pegged to rail rates. The trip distances over which airlines are in effective competition with other means of public transportation received some consideration in the hearings and exhibits of the *General Passenger Fare* case. As the Bureau counsel's brief pointed out, there was general agreement that the competition is most significant over the range of 150 or 200 miles to 1000 miles. This range of distances covers a very substantial portion of the airlines' business; in 1957, 49 percent of air-passenger journeys were between 150 and 999 miles in length, and only 11 percent of air travelers took journeys greater than 999 miles, for which the airlines on the whole do not face effective competition.[22] An analysis of passenger traffic to and from Chicago showed how rail service was a formidable competitor with the airlines on certain types of hauls. Overnight rail service tended to furnish relatively strong competition with first-class air travel; rail runs offering evening service were a threat because rail coach fares then

[22] Brief of Bureau Counsel, General Passenger Fare Investigation, pp. 300–302. See also Gill and Bates, *Airline Competition*, p. 438.

became the relevant price for comparison.[23] Similarly, Gill and Bates indicate in their study of airline competition the importance which rail competition has had in such short-haul markets as Boston–New York. They hold that the high quality of airline service given this market in the days prior to 1944, when it was a single-carrier monopoly, can be explained in part by effective rail competition.[24] Finally, S. B. Richmond's intensive study of air traffic to and from Denver and Dallas seems to identify a break in the competitiveness of air service at 170 to 200 miles.[25]

Without any direct evidence on the size of the elasticity of substitution between air and surface transportation for various distances, it is necessary to look at the results of this competition in the relation between air and surface fare structures. If air and rail are strongly competitive at certain distances, one would expect fares for comparable classes of air and rail service at those distances to be either close together absolutely or at least closer together than air and rail fares over hauls where the two media are less competitive. Table 17 classifies the ratios of air to rail fares, taking first class and coach separately, for hauls over and under roughly 1200 miles. The 1200-mile division between long and short hauls was selected to maximize the difference between the distributions. Looking at the half of Table 17 dealing with coach fares, the expected pattern does appear. Of forty short-haul ratios, fourteen lie between 0.99 and 1.10, while seventeen of the twenty-six long-haul ratios lie between 1.21 and 1.40 and only one is under 1.10. In the pattern of first-class fare ratios, how-

[23] Edward J. Taaffe, *The Air Passenger Hinterland of Chicago,* Department of Geography, Research Paper No. 24 (Chicago, 1952), pp. 73–83.

[24] Gill and Bates, p. 377.

[25] Samuel B. Richmond, "Interspatial Relationships Affecting Air Travel," *Land Economics,* XXXIII (Feb. 1957), 65–73, especially pp. 72, 73. Users of this article should be cautioned against accepting another of Richmond's conclusions that beyond distances of 200 miles or so "air travel comes into its own" so that "as distances increase beyond this point of discontinuity there seems to be no systematic change in the degree to which traffic is produced." In testing the familiar gravity or P_1P_2/D hypothesis about interspatial movement, in the formula Richmond substitutes the number of hotel registrations from the other city for the size of its population. Since hotel registrations are surely inversely related to distance between cities, the distance variable sneaks into the relation twice, causing *one* of its appearances to seem to have no significance and permitting the invalid conclusion quoted above to be drawn.

Table 17. Distribution of ratios of air to rail fares, selected major city-pairs, by distance of journey

Ratios of first-class air to rail pullman fare			Ratios of air-coach to rail-coach fare		
Range	Short haul[a]	Long haul	Range	Short haul[a]	Long haul
1.21+	2	1	1.71+	2	0
1.16–1.20	3	0	1.61–1.70	1	1
1.11–1.15	4	1	1.51–1.60	6	1
1.06–1.10	2	8	1.41–1.50	5	1
1.02–1.05	6	7	1.31–1.40	4	9
0.99–1.01	2	3	1.21–1.30	3	8
0.96–0.98	1	6	1.11–1.20	5	5
0.91–0.95	4	0	1.01–1.10	13	1
0.86–0.90	3	0	0 –1.00	1	0
0.81–0.85	8	0			
0 –0.80	5	0			

[a] Under 1200 air miles.
Source: Calculated from Trans World Airlines, Exhibits No. TWA-11 and TWA-12, General Passenger Fare Investigation.

ever, a different pattern appears, with the short-haul fares having a bimodal distribution and only ten of forty lying between 0.99 and 1.10. Furthermore, the first-class fares show more of a tendency to cluster around parity with rail fares for long hauls. What these data probably indicate, if we take them as a representative sample, is that high cross-elasticities of demand exist between air and rail coach fares at distances under a thousand miles or so, but that first-class air and rail travel are not viewed by most travelers as very good substitutes; thus cross-elasticities are somewhat lower than for coach fares at any given distance.

Assembling the information on substitutability between air and surface travel, it is apparent that in some city-pair markets for hauls up to one thousand miles substitutability is quite high. This conclusion qualifies the findings stated above on the aggregate price elasticity of demand for air transportation. But, as a final note, one should be cautious about extrapolating the significance of surface-carrier rivalry into the future. In 1958 the airlines sought the elimination of certain discounts once installed to match similar ones of the railroads, on the grounds that the declining frequency of rail service had drastically cut the extent of competition between them.[26]

PRODUCT DIFFERENTIABILITY

A good deal of evidence contained in the general literature of industrial organization leads one to rank the differentiability[27] of an industry's product as potentially one of the most important traits of market structure. The obvious reason for this is that substantial differentiability of the product manufactured by a moderately concentrated industry is almost sure to influence the character of competition and, for better or worse, lead to substantial product competition and rather little price competition. Product differentiability goes much further than this in its influence because it tends to interact over time with the elements of market structure and work changes in them of significant and often undesirable kinds. One of these is the important role which product differentiability plays in determining the height of barriers to the entry of new firms. Bain's study of barriers to new competition tended strongly to establish for a sample of twenty industries the primary role of product differentiation in controlling entry.[28] Since an industry in which the barriers to new firms remain high over a substantial period of time usually comes to show moderately high seller concentration, there is also an indirect link between product differentiability and the number of firms in the industry. A good example of these interrelations is the United States automobile industry, which underwent a series

[26] See State of California, Public Utilities Commission, Decision No. 57990, February 10, 1959, p. 4.

[27] I use the awkward term "differentiability" instead of the familiar "product differentiation" in order to make it clear that it is a physiological structural condition that is under scrutiny. Product differentiation can be and is thought of both as an inherent trait of certain kinds of goods and as a set of policies employed by firms in certain types of industries. The trouble with mixing the two areas is that firms in highly concentrated industries sometimes undertake elaborate product-differentiation strategies in part *because* their common product is not readily differentiable. They may do this because interdependence is not fully recognized or because their market-share objectives are not compatible, so that the alternative is an undesirable amount of price competition. Thus, whether the presence or absence of "product differentiability" in a given industrial setting implies the presence or absence of "production differentiation" depends on the other market-structure traits prevailing.

[28] Joe S. Bain, *Barriers to New Competition* (Cambridge, Mass., 1956), p. 142.

of changes in its market structure in the decade following World War I. To oversimplify the story considerably, the discovery by a key firm of methods of establishing product differentiation and product obsolescence rapidly and effectively raised the barriers to entry and constricted the entry of new firms. With economies of scale acting at the same time to induce consolidations among the existing firms, the industry was set on the road toward its present highly concentrated pattern.[29]

Weighing the differentiability of an industry's product is not in principle an easy matter. We must decide on *a priori* grounds whether its properties are such that its producers can readily make consumers think that separate brands have unique and distinguishing characteristics. The producer of a successfully differentiated product creates a body of customers who consider his brand somewhat superior to others. He can elevate his price above the prevailing market level without losing all his business. The cross-elasticity of demand for his product brand with respect to the price of other brands becomes less than infinite. What of the case where the "product" can be and is produced in various varieties or qualities and where noninfinite cross-elasticities prevail among the qualities produced by different sellers? Here the presence of product differentiability still has clear-cut meaning. If any one producer imitates the physical quality or variety of another producer's output, will purchasers always choose the cheaper variety? The signs of product differentiability, then, are product traits which make it likely that a producer can create the illusion in the buyer's mind that his brand possesses certain virtues that cannot be duplicated and that are worth a slightly higher price.

It should be stressed that product differentiability should be detected from traits of the product rather than from actions of the producer. Heavy advertising expenditures are the mark of attempts at product differentiation, not necessarily the proof of its success. We should be concerned with whether the typical customer has the ability and the incentive to assess the quality of a particular product brand. Does he buy it sufficiently often to be well informed of the varieties available? Is it purchased

[29] See H. G. Vatter, "Closure of Entry into the Automobile Industry," *Oxford Economic Papers,* n.s. IV (Oct. 1952), 213–234.

strictly for the buyer's use or for motives of social esteem? Is its price a sufficiently large outlay that the buyer gives some attention to the choice of brand rather than purchasing casually? Are the physical qualities of the product immediately apparent to the buyer, or do they reveal themselves only over a long period of use or through unmeasurable contributions to the buyer's gastric ease or social magnetism? Evidence based on observed market conditions should be used only as it contributes direct answers to these questions.

By such tests, air transportation should not be a readily differentiable product. At least for the traveler paying his own way, the expenditure is usually relatively large enough to call for prudent shopping. The physical dimensions of the prospective journey are generally readily measurable by the purchaser. The time that the trip will require can be learned from published schedules if flights are normally completed in scheduled times. Airlines use standardized aircraft, and it seems most unlikely that travelers could be convinced that a particular type of aircraft could be flown better by one airline than another. Other relevant dimensions of the product for the air traveler are the comfort and convenience of arrangements within the plane and of ground passenger-handling facilities. Again, it is fairly simple for the passenger to inform himself of the seating density of various airlines' craft (the principal dimension being the number of seats in a row across the plane) and of the quantity and quality of food, liquor, and other free merchandise dispensed along the way. A large portion of air passengers frequently travel by this means, enhancing their ability to evaluate the product of various airlines.[30] Even those who lack the experience of regular air travel can easily get the relevant information through travel agents, who write airline tickets at no extra charge to the traveler and who are responsible for about a fourth of the revenues of the domestic trunklines.[31] There would seem to be only one dimension of the quality of the air journey which the prospective traveler cannot evaluate reasonably well himself — its safety, or

---

[30] According to a trade publication, in 1954 there were 35 million passenger journeys on the domestic carriers, but most were repeated travelers and only 8 million different persons were carried. See *American Aviation*, XIX (Oct. 10, 1955), 26, and also *American Aviation Daily*, January 17, 1959, p. 32.

[31] See *Aviation Week*, LXIX (Nov. 24, 1958), 41.

the chances of getting there intact. This concern might be the basis for the view, often expressed in several congressional hearings, that the certified carriers have what is essentially a product-differentiation advantage over the nonscheduled or irregular carriers.[32] However, safety seems to be a rather slender basis for building a differentiated product, especially when it is well known by the traveling public that the federal government establishes and enforces rigorous safety standards on the carriers. And in fact it is not so used.

This information points rather strongly to the conclusion that if two airlines producing service of comparable quality operate between a pair of cities, one of them can do nothing to cause a significant number of passengers to take its flights if the price is above that of the other carrier. In studying the airlines, however, it is not wise to leave the consideration of product differentiability at this point. As we shall see later, competitive product improvement is a very important aspect of the market-conduct patterns of airlines.[33] Air travelers seem to be particularly responsive to certain product-improvement strategies. Insofar as these strategies cannot be matched immediately by an airline's competitors, they can constitute in the short run an effective product differentiation even though they do not fit the formal definition of this phenomenon used above. The consumer appeal of three sorts of product improvement seems especially worth considering: reducing scheduled time of flights, increasing the frequency with which flights are available, and employing faster, larger, and more comfortable aircraft.

It is clearly an article of faith among airline executives that reducing the elapsed time of journeys is a mode of product improvement highly valued by the traveling public. At least this is regularly said in their public statements explaining the purchase of new and speedier aircraft. Undoubtedly this public preference for speed exists; witness the almost complete dominance of the airlines over railroads on relatively long passsenger hauls. It is doubtful, however, whether small changes in flight

---

[32] See *Future of Irregular Airlines in the United States Air Transportation Industry*, hearings before a subcommittee, U.S. Senate, Select Committee on Small Business, 83rd Cong., 1st sess. (Washington, 1953), p. 213 and *passim*.
[33] See Chapter 14.

times are viewed as significant or, indeed, even perceived by travelers. A trade magazine reported that one airline had checked incoming calls for reservations for several days and found the public almost totally disinterested in elapsed time of flights. There were frequent questions about the various departure times available, but little concern over arrival times.[34] Airline spokesmen in recent years have at times voiced doubts over the payoff to extra speed in the air, especially in view of the fixed cost in terms of time of the ground journeys to and from airports.

Though the appeal to passengers of a little more speed per se is slight, it becomes enormous when the extra speed is one feature of a newer and more comfortable sort of aircraft. An ideal setting in which to observe this phenomenon is in the current conversion of the local-service carriers from DC-3 aircraft to new turbine-powered craft; in this case there is little or no competitive diversion of traffic from other air carriers to obscure the "pure" effect of a higher-quality product on the aggregate demand for service. In replacing the twenty-year-old DC-3 with a fast, pressurized, turboprop plane, West Coast Airlines found traffic on a number of noncompetitive routes increased by a weighted average of 48.8 percent from September to October 1958, a time of year when business normally shows a seasonal decline.[35] If new equipment has such power to generate business among people who would otherwise not have traveled by air at all, it is easy to imagine its power as a competitive weapon. To put it mildly, this truth is not lost on airline executives, and, as we shall see below, it is a crucial determinant of market-conduct patterns. One example is the impact of the introduction by Capital Airlines of the Vickers Viscount, the first turboprop aircraft to go into commercial service in the United States. Capital's market share immediately more than doubled in most of the markets where the new aircraft was introduced. More recently, introduction of American-made turbojets has had the same sort of effects both on market shares and total traffic. Load factors of more than 90 percent persisted for what one writer called "more than the customary period of inaugural enthusiasm," in contrast to normal

[34] *American Aviation,* XXII (June 16, 1958), 47.
[35] William S. Reed, "F-27s Boost West Coast Revenue Miles," *Aviation Week,* LXX (March 2, 1959), 28.

load factors on comparable routes in the range of 55 to 65 percent.[36] A Trans World executive has testified that TWA reached its persuasion of the potency of the appeal of new equipment from studying the British Comet jet operations in 1951 and 1952. They decided that "the preference was invariably for the turbine aircraft regardless of any other faults that it had; a tremendous attraction due to its speed." [37]

Further evidence of the drawing power of more comfortable equipment stems from the numerous cases in which passengers have shown a willingness to pay for such blessings. One example of this was American Airlines' experience with installing a deluxe version of transcontinental coach service using DC-7 aircraft. This cost $99 as compared to $80 for a more spartan service available on certain days of the week. Yet, in the price-conscious market for coach travel, it outsold the inferior service on the days the latter was offered by three to one.[38]

Another type of product improvement which seems to have a strong appeal to passengers is an increase in the frequency of departures on a given route. Again, the experience of local-service carriers is useful for seeing the pure impact of more frequent scheduling on the demand for air transportation. North Central Airlines found that increasing flights serving Oshkosh, Wisconsin, from eight to fifteen a day raised the average number of passengers from three to five and two tenths, and that correspondingly increasing the number of flights serving Duluth, Minnesota, from eight to twenty-four a day raised the average number of passengers from six to seven and three tenths.[39] This instance has its

[36] William V. Henzey, "Phenomenal Jet Loads Forecast Boom," *Airlift*, XXII (May 1959), 39–40.

[37] Transcript of Hearings before Examiner, General Passenger Fare Investigation, p. 6510.

[38] American Airlines, Inc., Exhibit No. AA-11, General Passenger Fare Investigation, p. 11.

[39] Robert H. Cook, "North Central Mass-Schedules Traffic," *Aviation Week*, LXX (Feb. 16, 1959), 38. There are two difficulties with using this bit of evidence for illustrating the traffic-generating power of more frequent sheduling. First, on a local-service carrier most passenger journeys are quite short, so that there is substantial competition with surface carriers; hence more frequent scheduling diverts traffic from other forms of transportation, for one thing. Second, the particular source cited here failed to state the time period over which the load-factor increases occurred; thus it is possible that an income effect or seasonal change may have played a part.

counterparts in the experience of the competitive trunkline carriers. Indeed, it often appears that a carrier suffering a reduction in its market share and absolute traffic volume in some city-pairs is uncertain about what strategy to follow to minimize the impact on its profit. Curtailing the number of flights per day it can offer its customers may reduce its average load factor rather than increasing it, and thus reduce its total revenues by more than its total costs.[40] Apparently air travelers have strong proclivities to contact the airline which is known to offer frequent flights. This fact is an article of faith among carrier managements.

To conclude this section on the product differentiability of air transportation, we find almost no characteristics in the product to lead us to expect that it would prove readily differentiable. We would expect airlines, therefore, to charge identical prices for equivalent classes of service and to orient their advertising primarily toward specific information on prices, schedules, and equipment. Traffic does respond strongly, however, to certain types of product improvements which in theory can be made by any carrier. This fact has great significance for explaining market-conduct patterns and the efforts made by airlines to avert situations in which competitors steal a march with product-improvement strategies. It also has important consequences where competing carriers are constrained from fully matching these improvements.

[40] See Chapter 14.

3 Cost Aspects of Market Structure

This chapter is an attempt to develop evidence on market-structure elements relating to the characteristics of cost and productive plant in the air-passenger transport industry. Many different features require attention. The first and most generally significant is the determinants of the average cost levels of different firms. The search for these determinants is one of the elements which give some airlines advantages in cost levels over others, thereby affecting the nature of competition. Included here is the question of economies of scale, important not only for assessing the position of small air carriers but also for measuring barriers to entry into the industry, discussed in Chapter 4.

Many other potentially important features of market structure are reflections of firms' cost patterns. The relation of fixed to variable costs is important for knowing how much pressure reduced demand or rising costs will place on profit margins. The relative costs of producing ton-miles with various types of aircraft must be considered, to see whether they are such as to grant cost advantages to airlines whose route structures are suitable for the most efficient types of aircraft. Another important structural aspect of the industry's capital goods is the ease with which aircraft can be transferred from firm to firm and the closely related matter of the degree of perfection in the used-aircraft market and price trends in that market. A final topic related to the cost structure of the industry, discussed in Chapter 5, is the general nature of markets in which airline managements purchase their inputs — particularly new aircraft, skilled labor, petroleum, and airport services — and the way conditions in these markets affect competition among the airlines themselves.

DETERMINANTS OF COST LEVELS

Considerable information on airline costs appears in reports required of the airlines by the Civil Aeronautics Board. Furthermore, the uniform accounting practices imposed by the agency help somewhat in rendering different airlines' costs comparable, although serious differences still exist even for broad categories of costs.[1] The domestic trunklines, for example, are known to differ significantly in the conservatism of their depreciation policies and in the classification of certain cost components. Simple and straightforward techniques have been used numerous times by writers seeking to explore the airlines' cost determinants; more sophisticated techniques have not been used as much, perhaps because there are convincing reasons why the existing data have traits which make them difficult to employ.

The question that has motivated the most work on airline cost structures has been that of the relation of average costs to scale of operation and the presence or absence of economies of scale. The most direct method of searching for economies of scale is to inspect the average cost levels of the domestic carriers in various size classes; this has been done at various times by John B. Crane[2] and by Harold D. Koontz.[3] Crane, working with data for fiscal 1940 and 1941, found that the second-largest four carriers in the trunkline industry had average operating costs per seat-mile slightly lower than the largest four carriers, while the smallest seven had appreciably higher costs. The same pattern appeared in operating costs per airplane-mile flown, when adjustments were made for the differences in the types of aircraft operated by different carriers. Crane concluded that diseconomies of small scale affected only very small carriers, since the medium-sized four had average assets of less than one fifth of those of the largest four and yet performed at least as well.[4] Koontz's more thorough examination of 1949 data yielded about the same conclusions. He found the relation between cost and size inconclusive except for the smallest four to six carriers. As in the pre-World War II period, costs per available ton-mile[5] showed no

---

[1] Cherington, *Airline Price Policy*, pp. 44–45.

[2] John B. Crane, "The Economics of Air Transportation," *Harvard Business Review*, XXII (Summer 1944), 495–509.

[3] Harold D. Koontz, "Economic and Managerial Factors Underlying Subsidy Needs of Domestic Trunk Line Air Carriers," *Journal of Air Law and Commerce*, XVIII (Spring 1951), 127–156; and his "Domestic Air Line Self-Sufficiency: A Problem of Route Structure," *American Economic Review*, XLII (March 1952), 103–125.

[4] Crane, pp. 502–505.

[5] This measure, representing salable ton-miles of air transportation produced, is conceptually the best measure of output to use in studying cost patterns. Not

differences among the larger carriers that were systematically related to size, though the differences among the larger carriers were considerable. The average operating expenses of the ninth-largest carrier, the lowest in the industry, were only 79 percent of those of the third-largest carrier, the highest among the larger carriers.

Koontz also examined expenses in particular categories to isolate those cost elements which account for the limited economies of scale that do exist. These appear in ground-operation expenses and in general and administrative expenses. The data seem to show economies of scale in flying-operation expenses, but Koontz rightly pointed out that this reflects not differences in airline size but differences in route structures. Larger carriers typically fly longer hops, and ton-miles can be produced more cheaply, *ceteris paribus,* on long hauls.[6] Even in aircraft maintenance, a process subject to mass-production and assembly-line techniques, no distinctive pattern of cost differences related to scale appeared. Koontz argued, furthermore, on the basis of direct experience in the industry, that the apparently random relation of costs to scale was not the result of accounting differences but rather that carriers, large and small, reporting low maintenance costs came by them honestly through good management and efficient facilities.[7]

Thus, the studies made to date of comparative airline costs seem to indicate that diseconomies of small scale afflict, if at all, only the smallest of the domestic trunklines. Average costs are definitely a negative function of the scale of operations and increase sharply in the neighborhood of the size (a decade ago, at least) of the small trunkline carriers, Northeast and Continental. The local-service carriers are particularly affected by diseconomies of small scale.

To illustrate these disadvantages of very small carriers and to

---

infrequently one sees airline costs calculated per *revenue* ton-mile (or seat-mile), the amount of ton-miles actually sold. This procedure mixes together an airline's ability to produce ton-miles with its ability to sell those it produces. Such a practice may be desirable in particular cases, but the issue should be decided in each instance on explicit grounds.

[6] Koontz, "Domestic Air Line Self-Sufficiency," pp. 108–113; "Economic and Managerial Factors Underlying Subsidy Needs of Domestic Trunk Line Air Carriers," pp. 138–140. See also Cherington, pp. 46–47.

[7] Koontz, "Economic and Managerial Factors Underlying Subsidy," pp. 136–138.

check these conclusions against the most recent data available, those for 1958,[8] let us consider the distributions of carrier costs per available ton-mile shown in Fig. 1 and Table 18. Fig. 1 plots

Table 18.   Indexes of costs of other carrier groups relative to Big Four carriers'
by cost category, 1958

Cost category	Big Four lines[a]	Medium-sized lines[b]	Small lines[c]	Local-service carriers
Flying operations	100.0	96.3	100.9	186.3
Maintenance	100.0	94.3	83.9	182.2
Passenger service	100.0	94.0	89.4	125.2
Aircraft and traffic servicing	100.0	101.2	110.9	305.2
Promotion and sales	100.0	101.9	118.1	125.6
General and administrative	100.0	89.8	131.9	290.5
Depreciation and amortization	100.0	101.8	102.5	79.2
Total operating expenses	100.0	97.4	101.6	187.9

[a] American, Eastern, TWA, United.

[b] Braniff, Capital, Delta, National, Northwest. Western, normally a member of this group, was excluded because it did not operate for almost four months due to a strike.

[c] Continental, Northeast.

Source: Calculated from CAB, Office of Carrier Accounts and Statistics, *Quarterly Report of Air Carrier Financial Statistics*, December 1958; CAB, *Monthly Report of Air Carrier Traffic Statistics*, December 1958.

average carrier operating expenses per available ton-mile against the quantity of ton-miles produced. There is a good deal of variation from carrier to carrier; the highest-cost carrier's average costs for 1958 were about one fifth higher than the lowest-cost carrier. There was, however, no significant relation between size and average costs among the trunklines, although the local-service carriers suffer very substantial diseconomies of small scale. Their costs are represented by the cluster of points in the upper left corner of the figure. This apparent flatness of the cost curve over the range of outputs represented by the trunkline carriers is a relatively new occurrence. Indeed, the 1958 figures probably give

[8] Unfortunately, 1958 was not the ideal year. Four of the trunklines, American, Eastern, TWA, and Capital, were affected by short strikes. Western Airlines was shut down for more than three months, rendering its cost figures unusable in this study. Also, air traffic was relatively heavily affected by the 1957–58 recession, so that the industry's excess capacity was abnormally great.

a false impression of how little relation of cost to size there is, for two of the Big Four had abnormally high costs that year. Nonetheless, the finding of Crane and Koontz, that many of the smaller carriers suffer no significant cost disadvantage, now seems to extend downward to almost the smallest of the trunklines. If the minimum scale of operations at which lowest average costs can be achieved has been increasing at all, it has not been increasing as fast as the size of the smallest trunklines.[9] The average-cost curve in Fig. 1 embodies the conclusions suggested

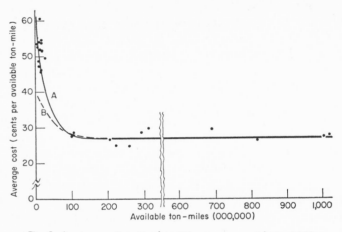

Fig. 1. Average unit costs, domestic passenger airlines, 1958

above. Although it could be drawn in other ways,[10] it seems to agree well with all available evidence. It suggests that the minimum scale of operations needed for carriers like the domestic trunklines to achieve minimum average costs lies between 100 million and 200 million ton-miles annually. Line segment A includes the local-service carriers; the dashed-line segment B

[9] Cherington gives average costs per available ton-mile for large, medium, and small carriers from 1946 to 1956 (p. 43). They also give the impression of a steady shrinking of the relative disadvantage of small carriers.

[10] For instance, one might fit a slightly U-shaped curve with a minimum point at about 500 million ton-miles, rising slightly to the right for very large firms and rising also to the left but less sharply than the one actually drawn.

assumes that they do not have the same cost function as the trunks.

Table 18 elaborates on the data presented in Fig. 1 by showing the behavior of individual cost categories of the carriers in 1958 and by grouping the airlines into four classes, large, medium, and small trunklines, and local-service carriers. The costs of the Big Four in each category are used as an index base. Looking only at the trunklines for the moment, only three cost categories seem to reveal significant cost disadvantages for the smaller carriers — aircraft and traffic servicing, promotion and sales expenses, and general and administrative expenses. Each of these reflects certain types of costs that are likely not to increase proportionally with output. General and administrative expenses, of course, cover the central administrative and managerial function. Aircraft and traffic servicing involves expenditures for airport-station facilities, reservations systems, and the like; given the number of cities a carrier is to serve, these tend not to be fully variable with the number of ton-miles produced. Finally, promotion and sales efforts by any given carrier, to be effective, probably must more or less match in quantity and quality those of other carriers; this may in part explain the appearance of economies of scale in promotion and sales expenses. The smaller carriers largely offset their disadvantage in these three cost categories by their advantages in maintenance and passenger service. Maintenance costs in most years would probably not show this pattern so conspicuously. Passenger-service expenditures are lower for the smaller carriers in part because of shorter average passenger journeys and because they tend to provide less elaborate service to the average passenger. Turning now to the local-service carriers, we notice that their greatest disadvantage lies in aircraft and traffic servicing and in general and administrative expenses, categories whose fixed-cost nature was noted above.[11] Their low depreciation and amortization costs result from the fact that in 1958 they operated old DC-3 aircraft almost exclusively. Other-

[11] Similarly, low expenses in these categories explain the successful operation of some of the nonscheduled carriers. A 1948 comparison of Standard Airlines with Colonial, Continental, and Mid-Continent (three small certified trunks) showed that Standard's low operating costs, 3.84 cents per passenger-mile compared to 9.06, 7.66, and 7.18 cents for the scheduled carriers, stemmed from the fact that all ground and indirect expenses were only 32.5 percent of Standard's costs but about 57 percent of the costs of the three trunks. See

wise, their smallest disadvantage is in passenger service and promotion and sales expenditures, expense classes which include many types of discretionary promotional expenditures which they are able to forgo.

Because it is somewhat surprising that no economies of scale seem to appear in the technical side of airline operations, we shall check the information from Table 18 by examining the airlines' flying-operation costs and maintenance costs on individual types of aircraft. This is done in Table 19, whose entries consist of average costs per flight-hour for each of several major kinds of aircraft. Table 19 more or less reinforces the impression of Table 18 and of Koontz's earlier results. The Big Four have a slight advantage in flying-operation costs for most types of aircraft, but for four aircraft out of seven they have a perceptible disadvantage in maintenance costs. No significant economies of scale are in evidence.

Paul Cherington, Stephen Wheatcroft, and other writers with considerable knowledge of the air-transport industry have pointed out that carrier experience and testimony in Civil Aeronautics Board proceedings indicate a number of other factors influencing the airlines' cost levels besides the scale of operations. Cherington's list of cost determinants includes route turnover (number of daily plane-miles per route-mile), average length of the passenger's journey, average length of airplane hop, amount of traffic per terminal operated, and volume of coach operations.[12] Other factors that are commonly suggested include average size and speed of airplanes used, number of types of airplanes operated, number of hours per day during which planes are used, size of metropolitan populations served, climatic conditions in the region where the carrier operates, and the extent to which the carrier faces direct competition from other carriers.[13] The list could be

William B. Saunders, "Comparative Expenses and Unit Costs of Irregular and Scheduled Air Lines," in *Air-line Industry Investigation,* hearings pursuant to S. Res. 50, U.S. Senate, Committee on Interstate and Foreign Commerce, 81st Cong., 1st sess. (Washington, 1949), I, 266–270.

[12] Cherington, p. 49.

[13] Sources which list and analyze these cost determinants in some detail include Stephen Wheatcroft, *The Economics of European Air Transport* (Manchester, Eng., 1956), chap. 3; and Jesse W. Proctor and Julius S. Duncan, "A Regression Analysis of Airline Costs," *Journal of Air Law and Commerce,* XXI (Summer 1954), 282–292.

Table 19. Flying-operation costs and maintenance costs by size of carrier
and by type of aircraft, 1952–1957 (dollars per flight-hour)[a]

Type of aircraft	Carrier group		
	Big Four[b]	Medium-sized[c]	Small[d]
	Flying-operation costs		
DC-6	134 (2)	136 (3)	
DC-6B	144 (2)	150 (3)	
CV-240	78 (1)	84 (1)	91 (1)
CV-340	92 (1)	83 (3)	86 (1)
DC-7, DC-7B	180 (2)	187 (2)	
L-49	137 (1)	140 (2)	
L-749	146 (2)	142 (1)	
	Maintenance costs		
DC-6	57 (2)	61 (3)	
DC-6B	56 (2)	45 (3)	
CV-240	47 (1)	40 (1)	51 (1)
CV-340	38 (1)	33 (3)	35 (1)
DC-7, DC-7B	92 (2)	88 (2)	
L-49	66 (1)	82 (2)	
L-749	60 (2)	63 (1)	

[a] Dollar amounts are simple averages of six-year (or less) average figures for separate carriers. The figures in parentheses give the number of carriers included in each average.
[b] American, Eastern, TWA, United.
[c] Braniff, Capital, Delta, National, Northwest, Western.
[d] Continental, Northeast.
Source: Calculated from CAB, Bureau Counsel Exhibit No. BC-986 (rev.), General Passenger Fare Investigation, table 4.

extended much further if we recognized temporary factors such as the costs of phasing a new type of aircraft into a carrier's fleet, initial operation on a newly authorized route, and the like. Good *a priori* arguments can be made for the significance of all of the factors listed above. Several pertain to the extent the carrier can spread certain costs which are partially overhead in nature. The existence of fixed costs per station, for example, implies that the carrier enplaning more passengers per station will have lower average costs. Similarly, there are costs of passenger ticketing that are independent of the length of the passenger's journey, and so the longer the average passenger's journey the lower should be the airline's average cost of transporting him. If depreciation charges are a function of calendar time only, as is usually the case, then the airline using its planes more hours of the day will tend to have lower costs. There are other items in the list that are not fully variable, although they are not exactly overhead costs. For example, numerous components of flying costs, such as pilots' salaries, are proportional to elapsed time rather than to distance flown. Hence, lower average costs should go with higher average speed of planes and with longer hops, on which higher average speeds can be attained. Still another type of *a priori* argument applies to certain factors affecting costs which essentially represent variations in the airline's product. A higher proportion of coach services, associated with lower service costs per passenger, should mean lower average costs. Also, a large amount of product competition, a manipulation of cost levels as a sales inducement, should generate higher average costs.

Turning from theoretical arguments to factual reporting, the situation immediately becomes more complex. One would like to identify the result of varying each of these cost determinants while the others are held constant. With the large quantities of data available on airline costs, multiple regression techniques are obviously tempting. Various difficulties, however, turn out to make this procedure of limited use. Changing relative input prices block the analysis of time series, and no satisfactory adjustments or deflations can be found. If one proceeds to take a cross-section of the domestic industry in a particular year, it turns out that trunklines and local-service carriers cannot reasonably be lumped together, and so the sample is very small. This limitation is critical because the number of independent variables determining airline costs is clearly very large. One published regression analysis by Proctor and Duncan illustrates some of these difficulties. They attempt to relate total operating expenses per revenue ton-mile to seven independent variables. Though *a priori* considerations and independent evidence tell us that all of these variables should be significant, only three of them prove to be so at the 5 percent level of confidence. Worse yet, serious multicollinearity appears, and costs per ton-mile in their results appear to increase with average length of flight though all other evidence suggests the opposite. The reason, as the authors note, is the high correlations among average length of flight, airplane capacity, and average speed of planes.[14] Multicollinearity would probably frustrate any analysis designed along these lines. Many of the cost-determining variables discussed above are strongly intercorrelated in their effect on domestic air carriers. A large airline typically has a large amount of traffic per station, a large average length of hop, and a high volume of coach operations. It tends to operate large aircraft and to utilize them a relatively large number of hours per day.

In the face of these difficulties, one must use the simpler but less comprehensive techniques of simple regression and scatter diagrams, as have Wheatcroft and Cherington. Cherington's simple correlation coefficients show average costs to be significantly influenced by the airline's proportion of coach traffic and its average length of passenger journey, but not by its scale of operations (total revenue ton-miles).[15] In the same way, Wheatcroft's scatter diagrams show a weak inverse relation between average cost and a composite variable reflecting the size and speed of aircraft operated.[16] Finally, it should be mentioned that one definite conclusion does emerge from the Proctor-Duncan analysis — that average costs fall significantly as the average number of hours that aircraft are utilized increases.[17]

Thus there is fairly good qualitative evidence on what results would appear if a multiple correlation of airline costs were possible. Another trait which could be inferred from such an imaginary multiple correlation is that it would have a significant amount of unexplained variance. This is simply because carrier managements vary substantially in their efficiency, a fact attested by many long-term observers of the industry.[18] Furthermore, there are numerous instances which show that the average cost level of a particular carrier can change sharply relative to the industry in a short period of time. Thus a conscious five-year effort by the management of Northwest Airlines was said to underlie a decline of its

[14] Proctor and Duncan, pp. 282–292.
[15] Cherington, p. 52.
[16] Wheatcroft, pp. 83–84; see also Cherington, p. 47.
[17] Proctor and Duncan, p. 291.
[18] See, for example, Koontz, "Domestic Air Line Self-Sufficiency," pp. 114–115; Koontz, "Economic and Managerial Factors Underlying Subsidy," pp. 143–144.

costs from 33.5 cents per available ton-mile in 1953 to 24.6 cents in November 1958. One of the local-service carriers succeeded over four months in shaving the cost of its DC-3 operations from $1.25 to $0.96 per plane-mile at a time when the local-service industry's average was $1.10.[19] These features of cost-level flexibility and differences in managerial efficiency from carrier to carrier should be recalled both as background to the discussion of barriers to entry (Chapter 4) and the consideration of conduct patterns in Part III.

AIRCRAFT TYPES AND THEIR OPERATING COSTS

An extremely important feature of the structural environment of the domestic airlines is the relative cost of operating various types of aircraft over various route systems. Is an airline with short average hops between stations at a cost disadvantage compared to one with long hops?[20] Have the aircraft more recently introduced into service in the postwar years been lower-cost conveyances than their predecessors? Are the fastest aircraft also the cheapest to operate, or must an airline choose between thrift and speed? Are the most comfortable aircraft, from the passenger's viewpoint, the cheapest to operate, or must an airline choose between thrift and comfort? Do aircraft types differ in their flexibility so that an airline must, in order to gain speed or comfort, take an aircraft that is ill suited to some of its routes? These questions are of great importance as a background to discussing those market-conduct patterns dealing with the choice of carrier equipment. They also underlie a major test of market performance: whether or not the industry's investment decisions can be said to offer the public the optimal sort of choice of equipment.

In view of the importance of comparative operating costs, it is unfortunately very difficult to know what sense to make of the large amounts of available data. These come in several different forms. First, there are engineering figures commonly quoted for

[19] Robert H. Cook, "Northwest Cuts Overhead, Boosts Profits," *Aviation Week*, LXX (Feb. 9, 1959), 40; Eric Bramley, "The Amazing Four-Month Comeback of a Local Service Line," *American Aviation*, XVIII (Aug. 30, 1954), 39–40.

[20] A major emphasis of Stephen Wheatcroft's study of the managerial problems of European air transport is the lack of a large aircraft designed to operate efficiently in the short-haul European market.

new aircraft, based on designed performance characteristics and certain assumptions about conditions of operation. All manufacturers issue such engineering cost estimates on the basis of a formula first developed by the Air Transport Association in 1944 and revised periodically. Sometimes these estimates appear as average figures per plane-mile or per seat-mile, sometimes as functional relations between operating costs and the length of hop. Equipment manufacturers also make engineering estimates of the cost of new aircraft over the routes of potential customers; sometimes these are printed for the public. A second type of available cost information is that based on actual airline experience. Such figures normally appear as an average per plane-mile or per seat-mile, unrelated to the route pattern on which the aircraft was used. Civil Aeronautics Board accounting requirements introduce some standardization into the ways in which carriers report the costs of operating various types of equipment, but of course these cost figures reflect not only the physical properties of the aircraft in question but also innumerable features of the individual carrier's operations — average length of hop and haul, weather conditions, average load factor, average portion of the day during which the aircraft was in service, and so forth. A final class of cost information consists of special studies that have built up cost information on some *ad hoc* basis from a combination of engineering and experiential data.

No one of these three types of cost data logically suffices for the purposes of this study. The engineering estimates are more often than not all that is available to an airline when it makes a decision about the purchase of equipment; for studying such decisions, a review of the engineering estimates would seem appropriate. Social performance, however, is a matter of actual and not anticipated costs; actual statistical figures would be needed to assess performance. If the two sorts of information yielded reasonably similar results, the problem would disappear. Unfortunately, the engineering figures and those based on experience often diverge greatly. Prices used in the Air Transport Association's formula tend to get out of date, and approximate constants are used for factors which are subject to managerial discretion and which in any case vary from carrier to carrier. Thus the formula shows costs per seat-mile (in first-class seating density) for the Vickers Viscount (V-745) and Douglas DC-7 aircraft, respectively, as 2.34 and 1.77 cents. Yet in 1958 Capital Airlines reported an actual figure of 1.84 cents for the Viscount and two major operators 1.94 cents for the DC-7.[21] The two sets of figures seem to differ squarely and sharply on which is the lower-cost aircraft.[22] Moreover, this is apparently not at all a special case; it is often suggested that the formula systematically overstates the cost of operating turboprop aircraft.[23] The usefulness of engineering estimates is limited not only because they fail to agree with experience, but also because they do not necessarily reflect the cost information carriers actually use in making their equipment commitments. In addition to securing special cost analyses for their own routes, carriers normally make modifications of their own in the Air Transport Association formula.[24] Actual operating costs reported by the carriers have almost as many limitations. There is the problem of the extremely high break-in costs which carriers normally experience in phasing a new type of aircraft into their fleets. There is the problem, when comparing costs per seat-mile, of the substantial differences in the number of seats different carriers place in the same aircraft. With straight engineering cost figures and straight statistical cost figures both called into question, the best alternative might seem a judicious combination of the two in some synthetic estimate. But only one thorough study of this sort seems to exist,[25] and, though some use will be made of it shortly, it omits certain cost components that it would be desirable to have included.

With no single satisfactory type of information at hand, it seems best to use all three types for what they may be worth. First, consider Table 20, which shows the results of the Sobotka study, the one generally available attempt to develop a consistent

[21] As a caution, different airlines might not have reported the same ranking of the costs of these aircraft.

[22] "Costrender" (pseud.), "ATA Formula Misleading on Costs," *Airlift*, XXIII (June 1959), 33–34.

[23] See CAB, Bureau Counsel Exhibit BC-987, General Passenger Fare Investigation, Docket 8008 (Written Testimony of Thomas G. Harris on ATA Aircraft Cost Formula).

[24] Transcript of Hearings before Examiner, General Passenger Fare Investigation, pp. 6389–6392.

[25] Stephen P. Sobotka and others, *Prices of Used Commercial Aircraft, 1959–1965: A Research Report* (Evanston, 1959).

Table 20. Operating costs of major types of commercial aircraft, by stage length (dollars per thousand passenger-miles)

Aircraft	Stage length (miles) 0–200	200–400	400–600	600–800	800–1000	1000–1500	1500–2000	2000–2500	2500 and over[a]
Douglas DC-3	42.41	31.62	30.13						
Convair CV-240	34.30	24.06	22.58						
Martin M-202	38.06	27.56	26.09						
Martin M-404	34.72	25.16	23.79						
Convair CV-340	33.45	22.38	20.74						
Convair CV-440	33.80	22.55	20.89						
Vickers V-700	36.47	24.22	22.38	20.03	19.64				
Douglas DC-4	40.89	26.88	24.79	22.14	21.68	21.22			
Lockheed L-049	53.65	31.45	27.90	24.42	23.63	22.84	22.29		
Douglas DC-6	54.85	30.81	26.91	23.43	22.56	21.73	21.11		
Douglas DC-6B	45.00	26.93	24.09	21.18	20.56	19.95	19.47		
Lockheed L-749	53.76	30.49	26.71	23.31	22.47	21.68	21.07	20.46	
Lockheed L-1049	53.01	30.62	27.02	23.61	22.81	22.03	21.45	20.83	21.08
Douglas DC-7	62.24	34.01	29.40	25.43	24.42	23.41	22.66	21.17	21.63
Douglas DC-7B	62.61	34.27	29.53	25.56	24.52	23.50	22.78	21.29	21.72
Lockheed L-1049G	51.40	32.84	28.89	25.19	24.32	23.47	22.85	21.85	22.08
Lockheed L-1049H	57.24	32.74	28.80	25.12	24.25	23.41	22.78	21.76	22.00
Douglas DC-7C	65.03	35.09	30.18	26.05	24.28	23.95	23.18	21.67	22.12
Boeing B-377	57.43	34.75	31.18	27.52	26.72	25.94	25.38	24.68	24.96
Lockheed L-1649	67.66	36.47	31.36	27.06	25.91	24.86	24.04	22.49	22.92

[a] 3000 miles is used as midpoint in calculating figures for this class.

Source: Stephen P. Sobotka and others, *Prices of Used Commercial Aircraft* (Evanston: The Transportation Center, Northwestern University, 1959), table 14. p. 45.

cost comparison of all major aircraft in United States domestic service just prior to the re-equipment boom beginning in 1959.[26] The calculations rest on salaries for operating personnel based on current contracts, maintenance costs based on the Air Transport Association formula, and fuel-consumption figures, employee-welfare expenditures, public-liability and property-damage insurance, and landing fees based on actual 1957 costs. Excluded are passenger-service costs (they would normally be independent of the type of aircraft) and depreciation and insurance (for reasons peculiar to the objectives of the Sobotka study). Because the figures in Table 20 exclude depreciation charges, they represent

[26] *Ibid.*, p. 45.

something akin to average variable operating costs rather than average total unit operating costs. Also, they allow for the fact that short-haul operations normally show a lower load factor, so that they are useful for showing the way the costs of operating various types of equipment vary with the length of hop. They also show the relative costs of different types of equipment where it is clear what the effect would be of adding the omitted cost components. For example, the DC-7 is more costly to operate at stages under 2000 miles than the DC-6; since its original cost is also higher per seat and since its depreciation period is the same, its total cost would also be greater than the DC-6 on short and medium flight stages.[27]

One thing that appears in these figures is the way operating costs fall sharply as the length of hop increases. Plotted against stage length, all aircraft models have U-shaped curves. The fixed costs of take-off and climb to cruising altitude explain the decreasing portion. Many costs of aircraft operation are proportional to the number of hours flown. The block time of flying a given distance, in turn, is often estimated from the formula of distance divided by cruising speed plus a fixed time for climb-out and descent.[28] The eventually increasing portion (not shown in the table) is due to the fact that, given the basic aircraft design, it is necessary at some flight stage to start sacrificing payload in order to carry sufficient fuel. At very short stages, under 400 or 500 miles, the larger, newer, and faster four-engined aircraft are at a very considerable disadvantage. Furthermore, at medium stages of 1000 to 2000 miles, the table gives a strong impression that the lowest-cost aircraft are not the latest piston-engined designs (the DC-7 series and L-1049s) but rather the models

[27] For those unfamiliar with aircraft types, the DC-3 was the standard two-engine transport in use domestically before World War II. The Convair 240, 340, and 440 and the Martin 202 and 404 were successive versions of postwar two-engine aircraft. The Vickers Viscount is a four-engine turboprop craft introduced in the 1950s. The DC-4, -6, -6B, -7, and -7B and the Lockheed L-049, -749, -1049, -1049G, and -1049H are two series of four-engine transports developing from World War II aircraft; they have been the mainstays of the postwar medium- and long-haul domestic routes. The DC-7C, Boeing B-377, and L-1649 are the most recent and fastest piston-engine aircraft, all designed for very long flight stages.

[28] See, for example, George Gardner, "Some Aspects of Future Air Transport Possibilities," *Canadian Aeronautical Journal,* V (Oct. 1959), 326.

MARKET STRUCTURE

which came into service just before them (the DC-6s and L-749). By and large, each successive piston aircraft has offered greater cruising speed than its predecessors, though the increases in the last decade were minor. Increases in passenger comfort were very significant in the first aircraft emerging after World War II, but such gains have been relatively insignificant since then up to the emergence of the quiet and vibration-free turbine-powered aircraft. Thus the impression received from Table 20 is that aircraft development up through the DC-6s and contemporary Lockheed aircraft combined reductions of cost with increases of speed and passenger comfort. More recent aircraft, however, have bought greater speed and nonstop operating range at the cost of somewhat higher operating costs.

Once we move from the Sobotka tabulations, there are no comprehensive comparisons of large numbers of aircraft types on the basis of engineering costs; there are only numerous scraps of information released by various carriers and manufacturers. Of substantial interest, naturally, are the cost comparisons made by the carriers between the most fully developed piston-engined transports and the turbine equipment currently going into use. All evidence points to the conclusion that the carriers were not at all sure that the large turbojet craft would be cheaper to operate than the most modern piston-engined airplanes.[29] An anonymous Braniff Airways executive was quoted to this effect in 1956,[30] and later the same airline anticipated costs per seat-mile for the Boeing 707 on domestic routes which would be 19 percent greater than for the DC-6 and about 30 percent greater than for the DC-7C.[31] United Air Lines, however, claimed in material submitted in connection with the general fare investigation that it

[29] One highly qualified authority, the chairman of British European Airways, declared: "The economic characteristics of an aeroplane are considerably more difficult to forecast than its performance. This has been so even with piston-engined transports, whose operating costs one would expect to estimate with fair precision as an extrapolation of previous experience. The turbine transport with its new type of prime mover, raises entirely new problems in cost estimation . . . it must be recognized that, to a large extent, air transport is at present an industry in the dark." See Lord Douglas of Kirtleside, "The Economics of Speed . . . ," *Journal of the Institute of Transport*, XXVII (May 1957), 118–119.

[30] Dero A. Saunders, "The Airlines' Flight from Reality," *Fortune*, LIII (Feb. 1956), 222.

[31] *American Aviation*, XXII (Sept. 8, 1958), 53.

expected costs for the DC-8 and the intermediate-range Boeing 720 on 1500 mile flight stages to be substantially less per seat-mile than for the DC-7 and slightly lower than for the DC-6.[32] Similarly, United's transcontinental competitor, TWA, anticipated in 1957 that both of the two turbojet aircraft it had on order would cost less per seat-mile to operate than its mainstay, Lockheed L-1049G. The figure given for the L-1049G was 2.40 cents per seat-mile; for the Convair 880 jet, 1.92 cents; for the Boeing 707, 1.68 cents.[33] This would be a 30 percent advantage for the Boeing, a 20 percent advantage for the Convair.

To get something more reliable than these unexplained published comparisons, an attempt has been made to assemble manufacturers' performance estimates for the generation of turbine-powered aircraft now coming into use in the United States. Included were four turbojet aircraft, two turboprops, and one turboprop conversion of an existing piston-engine aircraft. Many uncertainties surround such a calculation. First, there are innumerable problems in obtaining separate manufacturers' specifications on a comparable basis. Second, there are some basic doubts about what seating configurations to assume — a crucial matter in calculating costs per seat-mile. For instance, the fuselages of several turbojet aircraft are wide enough to place five standard first-class seats abreast across the cabin, but most of the airlines have used only four. In a fully first-class plane this would make a 20 percent difference for the resulting seat-mile costs. The practice chosen here has been to make all calculations on a first-class basis, assuming the seating patterns now in most common use. The tentative results of this experiment appear in Table 21 and Fig. 2. At most stage lengths the cost difference between the lowest and next-lowest aircraft was very slight. Hence it seems undesirable to identify the aircraft responsible for the low-cost points. Both Table 21 and Fig. 2 show the "envelope curve," giving the lowest direct costs attainable if the most efficient aircraft were used for every stage length. In Fig. 2 another envelope

[32] Transcript of Hearings before Examiner, General Passenger Fare Investigation, pp. 6671–6672. It should be noted that United assumed that the jets would be used as many hours a day as the piston-engine planes, an optimistic assumption by most standards.

[33] Bernard Brown, "TWA Report: Jets Will Not Tolerate Inefficiency," American Aviation, XXI (Nov. 4, 1957), 47.

curve shows the costs at various stage lengths for the most appropriate aircraft in use before 1958. This curve is derived from the data in the Sobotka study (Table 20) by converting them from a passenger-mile to a seat-mile basis and adding estimates of depreciation and insurance costs computed on the same basis as for the turbine aircraft. Note that this curve rises for stages longer than 2000 miles because the faster transcontinental aircraft that have been developed in the 1950s have higher costs than the DC-6B, which cannot make the United States transcontinental hop nonstop without significant sacrifice of payload. Unfortunately, no cost figure for piston-engine aircraft operating at stages under 200 miles was thought reliable enough to include.

Table 21.   Relation of direct operating costs to length of flight, pre-1958 and turbine aircraft (cents per available seat-mile)[a]

Length of hop (miles)	Pre-1958 piston and turbine aircraft	Turboprop and turbojet aircraft now in service
100	—	3.04
200	2.43	2.26
400	1.83	1.63
500	1.75	1.57
600	—	1.54
700	1.68	1.50
900	1.65	1.49
1250	1.64	1.47
1750	1.63	1.47
2250	1.70	1.47

[a] Figures for piston and pre-1958 turbine aircraft are in 1957 prices; figures for currently new turbojet aircraft are primarily in 1958 prices.
Source: see text.

Fig. 2 shows that the switch to jet aircraft involves a cut in direct operating costs per seat-mile for the airlines. It involves, however, only minor changes in the shape of the cost curve with respect to distance — no diseconomies for long hops and perhaps a slightly greater relative cost disadvantage on very short ones, though this latter is quite uncertain. The size of the real productivity gain at any stage length is worth noting. Indeed, if the

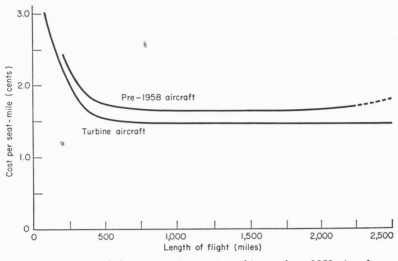

Fig. 2. Estimated direct operating costs, turbine and pre-1958 aircraft

manufacturers' estimates for the new turbine aircraft are not too optimistic, the operating costs of the most efficient piston aircraft *not* including depreciation lie above the fully allocated operating costs of turbine aircraft. In a wholly competitive situation a DC-6B operator could not cover his variable costs in competition with the most efficient jet aircraft, even if travelers made their choice on the basis of price alone.

CHANGING OPERATIONS AND CHANGING COSTS

It was argued above that straightforward multiple regression techniques cannot isolate the determinants of the airlines' average costs. However, flying operations and maintenance costs have already turned out to be explainable independently on the basis of airplane type and stage length. Can the same be done with the remaining categories of indirect costs? Experimental fitting of the major classes of indirect cost[34] shows that the variation of each of them from airline to airline can be fairly well explained

[34] The data used, drawn from the CAB's *Quarterly Report of Air Carrier Financial Statistics,* September 1959, cover the twelve months ending September 30, 1959.

by one or two independent variables.[35] The following regression equations summarize the results; standard errors are presented beneath each regression coefficient, and the coefficient of determination appears at the right of each equation.

Passenger-service costs bear a close relation to total revenue passenger-miles for each carrier. The equation implies an extra passenger-service cost of 0.43 cents for each additional revenue passenger-mile:

$$y_1 = \$280,000 + 0.00429x_1 \quad (0.9781).$$
$$(0.00020)$$

Reservation and sales costs are slightly more complicated. On *a priori* grounds one would expect them to relate closely to the number of passengers enplaning, but revenue passenger-miles turns out to be a better explanatory variable. Revenue passenger-miles are the product of the number of passengers and the average length of the passenger's journey, but it is not desirable to lump these two independent variables into one if reservation and sales costs are unequally sensitive to changes in them. This turns out to be the case. Relating reservation and sales costs (y_2) to passengers enplaning (x_2) and average passenger journey (x_3), we get:

$$y_2 = -\$8,870,000 + 3.2284x_2 + 15,117x_3 \quad (0.9738).$$
$$(0.2151) \quad (15,040)$$

The elasticity of reservation and sales costs in relation to changes in the number of passengers enplaned [36] is 1.04, not significantly different from the unit value one would expect on *a priori* grounds. The elasticity of these costs with respect to average journey is 0.71. Two points obviously need explaining about the equation — the large negative intercept and the sensitivity of reservation and sales costs to length of journey. A single economic explanation is sufficient (though not necessary) for both. A longer journey is

---

[35] Although the airlines often seem to estimate the behavior of their indirect costs in an even simpler way than is done here, a few documents stemming from the carriers have been of help in suggesting determinants for these cost components. See Capital Airlines, Inc., Exhibit No. CAP-12, "Profit and Loss of a V-745 First Class Roundtrip in the New York–Chicago Market," Short-haul Coach Service Case, Docket No. 9973; see also Delta Air Lines, Inc., Exhibit No. DL 3, in the same case.

[36] Calculated at the mean using the relation $b\overline{X}/\overline{Y}$, as an approximation to $(dy/dx)/(y/x)$.

more likely than a short one is to involve changes of planes and hence more complex reservation procedures, so some sensitivity of reservation costs to distance of journey would be expected. Besides this, however, the long-haul airlines have historically been much more profitable than the short-haul carriers and have tended to offer a better reservation service in terms of such things as having each reservation employee handle fewer telephone calls. This gives a high value to the coefficient of x_3 in the equation above, though it would probably be much smaller over other ranges of observations of the length of passenger journeys. This would explain the substantial negative intercept. There are some independent estimates that can be compared to the coefficient of x_2 above. In 1952 Eastern Air Lines put its own reservation cost per passenger at $1.54 and that for the industry at $2.02. Five years later a TWA executive mentioned the same two-dollar figure.[37] This evidence makes the $3.22 figure look high (assuming that the independent estimates cover the same types of costs); possibly the explanation is similar to that for the size of the coefficient of x_3.

Aircraft- and traffic-servicing costs would be expected to vary with the number of flights and the size of the aircraft involved. An acceptable fit results from using the product of these two variables — total number of seats available on flights operated — as the sole independent variable. The relation is:

$$y_3 = \$1,940,000 + 1.6663x_4 \quad (0.5849).$$
$$(0.4439)$$

Advertising and promotion costs predictably seem to relate closely to carrier revenue from passenger services. The relation is:

$$y_4 = \$740,000 + 0.02305x_5 \quad (0.7833),$$
$$(0.00002)$$

implying that 2.3 cents are spent to buy the marginal dollar of revenue at the mean revenue level.

General and administrative costs represent the general "central office" function in air transport. They do not seem to relate closely

[37] *Aviation Week,* LVI (April 14, 1952), 86; *Guaranteed Loans for Purchase of Aircraft and Equipment,* hearings on S.2229, U.S. Senate, Committee on Interstate and Foreign Commerce, Subcommittee on Aviation, 85th Cong., 1st sess. (Washington, 1957), p. 75.

to any single independent variable. The best fit is with total cash expenditures less general and administrative costs, but the relation is not linear. A good linear fit exists for the smallest eight trunklines, given by the equation

$$y_5 = \$1,152,000 + 0.02141x_6 \quad (0.9866).$$
$$(0.000001)$$

The observations for the Big Four, however, lie well above this line, indicating possible diseconomies in administration and coordination of their far-flung operations. Visually fitting a trend line to the relation of general and administrative costs for these four carriers would give a regression coefficient of about 0.052, compared to 0.02141 for the smaller airlines.

These relations, along with the information above on the direct costs of flying operations and maintenance, can be shuffled to show some of the ways in which the cost environment can influence market conduct in the air-transport industry. First, consider the crucial matter of the way in which average total unit costs (per revenue passenger-mile) vary with the length of the average passenger's journey. This is an extension of the information of Fig. 2, which answers a related question for direct costs per seat-mile. Table 22 develops the relation for average total

Table 22. Average costs per revenue passenger-mile at various stage lengths
(cents in 1958 prices)

Stage length (miles)	Passenger service	Reservations and sales	Aircraft and traffic servicing	General and administrative	Advertising and promotion	Total indirect	Direct	Total
100	0.43	1.31	2.50	0.47	0.34	5.05	3.34	8.39
200	0.43	0.85	1.25	0.26	0.24	3.03	2.46	5.49
300	0.43	0.70	0.83	0.19	0.20	2.15	2.24	4.39
500	0.43	0.58	0.50	0.14	0.18	1.83	2.07	3.90
700	0.43	0.55	0.36	0.12	0.17	1.63	2.00	3.63
900	0.43	0.48	0.28	0.10	0.16	1.45	1.96	3.41
1250	0.43	0.46	0.21	0.09	0.15	1.33	1.99	3.32
1750	0.43	0.45	0.13	0.08	0.14	1.23	1.95	3.18
2250	0.43	0.43	0.12	0.07	0.13	1.18	2.05	3.23

Source: see text.

costs on the basis of certain supplementary assumptions. First, load factors (average percentage of available seats sold) have been assumed for each stage length on the basis of historical experience. Second, since some fare structure had to be assumed to determine advertising and promotion expenditures, the one chosen was roughly that prevailing in 1958 and 1959, the years to which the cost data pertain. Third, to transform some of the equations for indirect-cost components it was necessary to assume that the airline in question was of average size among the eight smaller trunklines. Different results would emerge for the Big Four, not to mention the local-service carriers. Table 22 shows the industry cost pattern as it existed just before the introduction of the most recent turbojet and turboprop aircraft; very tentatively it also covers the average cost pattern for the new turbine aircraft on the assumption that the indirect-cost formulas require no changes. As with the direct-cost curve shown above, the average-total-cost curve flattens out somewhere between 500 and 1000 miles. Since the average length of passenger journey for the various trunklines ranges between 400 and 800 miles, roughly, and since the average airplane hop between stops is less than that, the higher unit cost of short-haul operations is obviously of great significance. As we shall see later, until 1952 there was no significant tapering off in the fare structure with respect to distance, and only in the very recent past has it come to be enough roughly to equalize the profitability of service on all but quite short hauls.

There is another dimension of possible tapering off in airline costs and revenues, and that is with respect to the volume of travel over a route. A relatively thin route is likely to involve low load factors for the carrier. A very thin one necessarily will, if there is not enough traffic to fill a minimal one or two flights a day.[38] It is harder to construct a curve showing cost variation with respect to density than it was to concoct the figures in Table 22. A simple but useful approach is to compare the load factors achieved in routes of varying passenger densities. A 1953 study by D. W. Bluestone yielded a visually fitted curve relating segment load factors to traffic densities from which the following observations can be read:

[38] Or, alternatively, if "reasonable" load factors can be achieved only by using aircraft of smaller capacity and higher seat-mile costs.

Passengers daily	Percent load factor
100	55.9
500	63.5
1000	66.9
1500	69.6
2000	72.3
2500	75.0

The last two observations are from the extrapolated portion of the curve.[39] As Bluestone points out, the load-factor estimates for the relatively larger flows of traffic are not of much use, for such routes are typically competitive. Their load factors then reflect the pattern of competition in flight scheduling as well as the presence or absence of any cost problems associated with indivisibilities in flight equipment. Bluestone's approach is hardly the whole answer to the question of a cost taper with increasing traffic density. It is an aggregation over routes of varying distances. It sheds no light on the way indirect costs might vary with route densities. It would be possible to construct curves similar to those in Fig. 2 for variations in the density of traffic over a given distance. However, when light densities and higher costs are involved, it matters a great deal what assumptions we make about the general route pattern in which our imaginary city-pair segment is embedded. Is it a dead-end segment, so that one station has to be maintained solely to serve traffic over this segment? Is it a connection between two of the airline's existing stations, so that the only indirect costs are those associated with the extra passengers? Is it between two points strung out between larger terminal cities, so that through flights can be stopped rather than maintaining more expensive turnabout service for this particular segment? Experimental calculations show that the assumptions made about these matters are too significant to allow the presentation of any simple information about the relation between average costs and traffic densities.

[39] David W. Bluestone, "The Problem of Competition among Domestic Trunk Airlines," *Journal of Air Law and Commerce*, XX (Autumn 1953), 384–387. For similar evidence based on European experience, see Wheatcroft, pp. 52–53.

FIXED AND VARIABLE COSTS

Another aspect of an industry's cost structure that can affect its market conduct substantially is the degree to which costs are fixed or largely fixed with respect to short-run changes in output. The "overhead cost" problem is as familiar in general economic theory as it is in the industrial-organization literature. If typical firms in two industries have identically shaped marginal-cost functions, then a given reduction in demand or a shift to the left of the demand function will tend to cut more into the profits of the industry with the greater fixed costs. If the industry is uncartelized and of atomistic structure, relatively heavy fixed costs are likely to mean substantial losses to many firms and "cutthroat competition."[40] If it is relatively highly concentrated industry, then a greater overhead-cost problem in times of depressed demand sometimes seems to generate greater caution in the industry about expanding capacity in prosperous times and to induce a more acute consciousness of mutual interdependence and greater heed to maintaining effective tacit collusion.[41]

If business costs fell neatly into the "fixed" and "variable" categories of economic theory, measuring this aspect of industry structure would be simple. In fact they do not, and the task is correspondingly difficult. Some capital goods may be readily detachable from the firm by open-market sale, so that the cost of their services to the firm is effectively variable even if it is normally financed through the issue of long-term securities; this is an important feature of the airlines and is discussed below. On the other hand, a firm may be quite unwilling to adjust expenditures for strictly variable inputs for fear that its long-run position may be harmed. One example is a reluctance to discharge skilled employees and administrators for fear that suitable replacements will ultimately be needed and be unavailable.

---

[40] Comparing conditions in the United States bituminous-coal industry with those in the less capital-intensive cotton-textile industry during the 1930s gives an idea of what differences in conduct and performance can result. See Lloyd Reynolds, "Cutthroat Competition," *American Economic Review*, XXX (Dec. 1940), 736–747; Waldo E. Fisher and Charles M. James, *Minimum Price Fixing in the Bituminous Coal Industry* (Princeton, 1955), chap. 1.

[41] Steel and some of the nonferrous smelting and refining industries have fairly heavy fixed costs and often seem to show conduct patterns of this sort.

Another example is a reluctance to cut back promotional expenditures for advertising and customer service lest long-run sales-promotion efforts suffer. It is because of these considerations that a discussion of the issue of fixed and variable costs must cover more than the simple measurement of capital turnover and debt ratios.

Viewed as a structural trait, fixed costs do not constitute a heavy burden on the airlines. This is commonly recognized by students of the industry in the form of a contrast drawn between the airlines and other publicly regulated industries. For instance, Bluestone notes that "the heavy fixed capital charges which pressed many unregulated utilities toward cut-throat competition are minor here." [42] Not only is capital a more minor factor of production, but also some of the most expensive fixed capital needed in commercial aviation is publicly provided in the form of airports and airways. Finally, airplanes, making up the bulk of the industry's capital goods, can readily be sold or leased among firms or even outside of the country. Aircraft are by and large of standard design, and any conversion costs from one airline's specifications to that of another are usually very small when compared to the construction cost of the aircraft. Needless to say, aircraft are readily transferred from one city-pair market to another, and it is hard to see why aircraft in a particular city-pair market should ever suffer subnormal imputed earnings for long periods of time without being put to other uses, unless managerial considerations relating to a larger route system or public subsidy were at work. [43] Despite all these considerations, a great deal of thinking within the industry and a certain amount of its conduct proceeds as if costs are almost entirely fixed in the short run. Break-even load factors are regularly calculated by the Civil Aeronautics Board on the assumption that costs are completely fixed. It is common to hear concern voiced over the airlines' relatively high ratio of debt to equity capital as a danger to "the staying power of the airlines in the face of economic

[42] David W. Bluestone, "The Problem of Competition Among Domestic Trunk Airlines: Part II," *Journal of Air Law and Commerce*, XXI (Winter 1954), 58.
[43] See Stanley Berge, "Subsidies and Competition as Factors in Air Transport Policy," *Journal of Air Law and Commerce*, XVIII (Winter 1951), 1–11.

fluctuations." [44] And, as a matter of fact, the airlines' net income is more sensitive to the business cycle than the cyclical sensitivity of the industry's volume of passengers would lead one to expect.[45] Apparently some unraveling is required here.

The calculations of capital-output relations in the air-transportation literature usually appear as rates of capital turnover, the reciprocal of a capital-output ratio. In 1956 the Air Transport Association prepared a calculation of annual capital-turnover rates for the trunkline carriers 1938–1953 and compared them with other public-utility industries. The average figure for the airlines was 144.4 percent, lower than Class I motor buses (175.5 percent) but much higher than Class I Railroads (34.9 percent) and electric utilities (25.9 percent). There appeared to have been a rough upward trend in the figure for the airlines (that is, a downward trend in the capital-output ratio); the figure for moderately prosperous 1939 was 155.3 percent, that for highly prosperous 1953 was 175.3 percent. The upward trend for the other industries in the comparison was much more marked.[46] Rather clearly, the airlines are close to the highway bus industry rather than to the highly capital-intensive public utilities.

Another indication of the extent to which airline costs are variable in the short run is to consider the result of an airline's output level that changes drastically due to a strike. This has been done, using figures for Western Air Lines, by the Civil Aeronautics Board staff in an exhibit prepared for the general fare investigation. It goes without saying that a strike is not the same thing as a market-determined change in the level of output. Management policy toward many discretionary cost items would not be the same in the two cases. Still, the comparison has a certain amount of interest in suggesting which cost categories defy reduction under such conditions. The comparison takes the form of percentage changes of various categories of the airline's costs from February 1955, a period of normal operations, to

[44] Testimony of CAB chairman, J. J. O'Connell, in *Air-line Industry Investigation*, p. 116.
    [45] *Monopoly Problems in Regulated Industries — Airlines*, U.S. House of Representatives, III, 2010, table 19.
    [46] *Ibid.*, III, 2050.

February 1956, when nearly all operations were shut down by a lengthy strike. Between the two months seat-miles sold fell by 99.7 percent. Changes in the standard cost categories were: flying operations, −94.1 percent; direct maintenance-flight equipment, −68.8 percent; depreciation-flight equipment, −20.1 percent; total aircraft operating expenses, −76.4 percent; ground operations, −75.7 percent; ground and indirect maintenance, −30.3 percent; passenger service, −95.2 percent; traffic and sales, −48.5 percent; advertising and publicity, −71.8 percent; general and administrative expenses, −16.6 percent; depreciation-ground equipment, +5.5 percent; total ground and indirect expenses, −55.2 percent; total operating expenses, −66.1 percent.[47] In short, even with the prospect of only a temporary stoppage of operations, two thirds of the airline's total expenses were avoidable. This would seem to confirm the previous impression that the overhead-cost problem for the airlines is relatively slight.

This is not the point at which to raise the question of whether the behavior of airline costs and profits actually fits this pattern of few fixed-cost elements. We can, however, note why an oligopolistic service industry such as air transport *could* give the appearance of operating under a burden of heavy fixed costs. First, a service industry does not produce for inventory; there is no positive check in the form of rising inventories that exert pressure on managements to key production to sales. Second, the levels of most activities carried on by an airline are not rigidly related to one another. Total passenger-miles sold can vary significantly without causing proportional changes in plane-miles flown, aircraft operated, reservation and sales personnel employed, or many other factors. Third, in airlines and the other service industries it is hopeless to try to make a distinction between production costs and promotion expenditures. Faced with a seasonal or cyclical fall of demand, an airline may well maintain its output level as an investment in protecting its future market share. Thus there is a great difference between the *structural* variability of costs in the industry and the minimum *actual* variability we might observe as a reflection of market conduct under imperfect competition.

[47] CAB, Exhibit No. BC-708, "Contractibility of Airline Expenses," General Passenger Fare Investigation, p. 1.

CONCLUSION

Viewed broadly, the domestic trunklines make up an industry with relatively constant costs, minor economies of scale in the national market, and no major fixed-cost burden. However, as we turn to the details of their cost patterns, the appearance of many different determinants of cost levels and of the heavily discretionary nature of costs provides several qualifications. There are many ways in which an airline might come to find itself at an advantage or disadvantage as compared to its close rivals. Hence, even if we observe approximately the same cost level for all carriers at a given time, this affords no guarantee for the relative profitability of their operations. It is also no guarantee that the impact of any exogenous change will be similar for all airlines.

4 Barriers to Entry

Although the Civil Aeronautics Board has never admitted a new carrier to full-fledged trunkline status and probably never will, the height of the economic barriers to entry still seems to be a significant element of market structure. The importance of the purely economic problems of entry for new carriers is two-fold. First, the entry situation has been a major factor conditioning the Civil Aeronautics Board's pattern of regulatory policies — policies not only on entry but also in such matters as pricing and route structure. Second, the height of barriers to entry has major indirect effects on the airline industry's conduct and performance that are independent of the Board's antientry policy.

The concept of barriers to entry employed here is substantially that developed by Joe S. Bain in his *Barriers to New Competition*.[1] He identifies three major sources of disadvantage to new firms. The existence of economies of scale forces an entrant firm to produce at a small scale and suffer higher costs than existing firms, or it must start at a size sufficient to achieve minimum long-run average costs and fight for the market share which such production would constitute. The existence of significant product differentiation compels the new firm to employ some market strategy that implies at least temporarily lower profits than established firms earn; it can strive through advertising or product improvement (spurious or significant) to create a separate identity and consumer preference for its product, or it can take a relatively lower price for its product than do sellers who have succeeded in establishing differentiated products. The third source of barriers to new firms is called absolute-cost disadvantages. These have the common effect of placing the average cost level for new firms significantly above that for existing firms at any given level of output. An example of an absolute-cost disadvantage would be control by existing firms of all known high-grade deposits of an ore basic to production in an industry. The notion of an absolute-cost disadvantage also covers the higher

[1] Joe S. Bain, *Barriers to New Competition* (Cambridge, Mass., 1956).

cost of capital which lending institutions may extract from the new firm.

For various reasons the measurement of the barriers to entry into air transport cannot be given as a simple relation of percentage cost disadvantage or the like. For one thing, one must specify the time at which the ease of entry is being assessed. It has changed significantly over the past two decades and will no doubt continue to change. For another, it matters what sort of route structure and operation is contemplated by the entrant. The number and density of routes, distribution of route stage lengths, and other traits of the route structure all affect the cost structure of the potential entrant and its cost disadvantage relative to existing firms. To deal with the problem of disadvantages to the entrant firm that change over time, I shall simply indicate what these changes have been, as well as how the present situation can be described. The diverse traits of possible entrants to the industry demand a more complex solution. First I shall consider the barriers to entry by airlines with route structures, product mixes, and cost characteristics similar to the existing trunklines. Then I shall compare the ease of entry for a conventional trunkline carrier with that for alternative firms such as a specialized coach carrier, a carrier operating among very few cities, and a carrier operating in markets of similar traffic density and distance. This approach first covers the information about barriers to entry contained in our knowledge of the existing industry, then checks the results by experimental calculations for imaginary cases.

OBSTACLES TO NEW TRUNK CARRIERS

As we saw in Chapter 3, examination of the average costs of the scheduled domestic carriers suggests that, below a certain size, firms suffer significant diseconomies of small scale. On the basis of 1958 data, the output level at which firms seem to achieve minimum optimal scale appears to lie around 100 to 200 million available ton-miles annually (see Fig. 1 above). Comparing this result with the cost structure of the industry in earlier years indicates that the minimum optimal scale has probably been increasing significantly. A decade earlier it was probably a little less than 50 million ton-miles.

The minimum optimal scale of 100 to 200 million ton-miles a year represents only about 2 to 4 percent of the available ton-miles produced in 1958 by the domestic trunk industry. In terms of the national market, then, the minimum optimal scale is of relatively insignificant size. However, no existing trunk serves all city-pairs that make up the national market and an entrant certainly would not do so. Hence we should also compare the figure for minimum optimal scale with the size of particular city-pair markets. No data are available on the ton-miles produced annually in individual city-pair markets, but some reasonable estimates can be inferred from the Civil Aeronautics Board's two annual surveys of passenger origins and destinations. Table 23 shows these figures (and the assumptions necessary to derive them) for twenty of the largest city-pair markets in the year ending June 30, 1958.[2] Only two exceed in size the upper boundary indicated for the minimum optimal scale, and only five are larger than the lower boundary. However, if an entrant carrier served only one city-pair market, it would certainly need a smaller scale of operations to achieve all economies of scale. Of the two smallest trunklines, Northeast served forty-six stations in 1959 and Continental served fifty-two. Consequently, if the relation which minimum optimal scale bears to the size of the *national* market for air-passenger transportation understates the problem created by economies of scale, then its relation to single city-pair markets surely overstates it. Just what might be the minimum efficient scale for operations in one or a few markets will be discussed below.

How substantial would be the disadvantages of operating at less than the minimum optimal scale? Segment *A* of the curve in Fig. 1 (Chapter 3) implies that this disadvantage would be very great. A carrier producing at one half to one fourth of the minimum efficient scale would have average costs roughly 50 to 75 percent higher than those of the medium-sized or large trunks. But this estimate can bear no substantial weight because the slope of the curve is determined entirely by the difference in

---

[2] Since the September 1958 survey was not available when this information was prepared, those for September 1957 and March 1958 were used. If these can be taken as a basis for estimating traffic over any twelve-month period, it is the year July 1957 through June 1958.

Table 23. Estimated available ton-miles of air service produced in 20 leading city-pair markets, year ending June 30, 1958 (thousands of ton-miles)[a]

City-pair	Annual available ton-miles
Miami–New York	244,000
Los Angeles–New York	220,000
New York–San Francisco	138,000
Chicago–New York	134,000
Chicago–Los Angeles	123,000
Chicago–Miami	97,000
Chicago–San Francisco	82,500
Los Angeles–San Francisco	73,000
Los Angeles–Washington	56,000
San Francisco–Washington	45,000
Dallas–Los Angeles	43,500
Detroit–New York	42,000
Chicago–Seattle	40,000
New York–Seattle	37,500
New York–Washington	36,000
Detroit–Miami	36,000
Boston–New York	35,500
Los Angeles–Seattle	33,500
Dallas–New York	32,500
Chicago–Washington	32,000

[a] To compute these figures, it was necessary to assume that (1) the March and September traffic surveys, covering two weeks each, cover exactly 1/13 (4 weeks of 52) of the year's traffic in each market; (2) a ton-mile was equivalent to 10.53 passenger-miles in all markets, the national average for the year; (3) the volume of nonpassenger ton-miles was proportionally the same in all markets; (4) the over-all revenue load factor was the same in all markets and equal to the trunks' national average.

Source: Calculated from Air Transport Association, *Competition Among Domestic Air Carriers, September 17–30, 1957* (Washington, D.C., 1958); *idem, March 1–14, 1958* (Washington, D.C., 1959), V, part 2.

costs between the trunklines and the local-service carriers. These two groups are unquestionably different types of firms. All of the trunks have at least a few high-density routes on which large aircraft can profitably be used. The local-service carriers by nature operate on thin routes and under severe restrictions on through scheduling or on overflying their weaker stations. Hence the figure given above for the cost disadvantage of inefficiently small trunklines should be viewed as a maximum one rather than as a best guess. Going back a decade to a time when only about half of the trunks had achieved minimum optimal scale, one can get a more meaningful estimate of the disadvantages of small scale. Three carriers operating at 40 to 60 percent of minimum efficient scale — Western, Chicago and Southern, and Mid-Continent — had costs roughly 16 percent higher than the average of the carriers producing beyond the minimum efficient scale. Four very small carriers operating at between 12 and 35 percent of minimum optimal scale were, on the average, at a 35 percent cost disadvantage. These estimates are the basis for segment *B* of Fig. 1. Whether these figures are still appropriate today is not known because all of the trunks are now at or above minimum efficient scale; but they probably are much closer to the truth than any figures drawn from the local-service carriers' experience.

A second possible source of barriers to new competition in an industry, product differentiation, was held in Chapter 2 to have little significance as a general feature of market structure in the airlines. This was not because the "product" produced by different airlines is necessarily homogeneous, but rather because the dimensions of the product which control consumers' choices are features which any airline can adopt. Air travelers, or at least most of them, are in a good position to evaluate the products of competing carriers and decide strictly on the basis of tangible merits. Only one exception to this general pattern was indicated — the feature of safety, which the traveler can evaluate only on a crude statistical basis. This would hardly seem to be important among established carriers except in rather unusual conditions; when considered as a possible source of barriers to new competition, however, it becomes rather more significant. The new airline, particularly if it seeks business on the basis of low price and relatively spartan service, might well face a disadvantage due to consumer suspicion of its safety, whether objective information warranted this or not. Possibly this is a partial explanation of the substantial price differentials between fares of scheduled intrastate carriers and trunks which offer nearly identical service. Thus Pacific Southwest Airlines in 1959 quoted a one-way San Francisco–Los Angeles fare of $11.81, compared to $15.05 for coach service on an interstate carrier, although its equipment is as modern as that of its certified competitors. Similarly, Lone Star Airlines, a new intrastate carrier proposing high-frequency service between Dallas and Houston, quoted a fare of $10.80, compared to $14.50 for the certified carriers' coach service.[3] These instances would seem to suggest a substantial disadvantage for the new carrier. However, it is doubtful that they should be taken at face value. First, given the pricing rigidities that are standard in the airlines, there is no reason for thinking that the differentials quoted represent any sort of equilibrium. Indeed, there is ample evidence that the scheduled carriers affected by intrastate competition would like to see the differential reduced.[4] Second, the certified carriers certainly have a product-differentiation advantage of some significance in the very fact that they receive authorization to operate from a federal agency; this is not open to the intrastate carriers. The question before us is whether an existing certified carrier would have a product differentiation over a new one or alternatively, with no certification, whether a carrier with a well-known history of regular operation would have such an advantage. In this setting the product-differentiation advantage of an existing carrier would probably be small or transient or both.

What of the existence of absolute-cost barriers to entry, elements which place the costs of the new carrier above those of existing carriers at any given scale of operations? Only one of these seems to be important in the case of the airlines, but that one may be very important indeed. This is the presence of capital requirements that are large in comparison to the capital-rationing practices enforced by lending institutions. In order to achieve minimum optimal scale, a new trunkline carrier would have to attain a size at least equal to that of Northeast Airlines and Continental Air Lines. During 1958 the average capital (equity plus long-term debt) of these carriers was $19,038,000 and $36,256,000, respectively.[5] The size of the investment in a trunkline of minimum efficient size has increased sharply over the postwar pe-

[3] Richard Van Osten, "Hustling PSA Bucks Big Lines With Low Fares and Makes It Pay Off," *Airlift*, XXIII (Dec. 1959), 33–34; also *Airlift*, XXIII (Dec. 1959), 16.

[4] United Air Lines has claimed to make no profit on its routes competing with Pacific Southwest, whereas Pacific Southwest has often shown substantial profits. See California, Public Utilities Commission, Decisions No. 56849 (June 17, 1958) and No. 57990 (February 10, 1959).

[5] CAB, Office of Carrier Accounts and Statistics, *Quarterly Report of Air Carrier Financial Statistics*, Dec. 1958, p. 38.

riod. A decade ago it was about $6.5 million, and at the end of World War II probably no more than $2 million. These figures are guesses based on the invested capital of actual carriers whose size probably placed them at the threshold of minimum efficient scale at those times. But they underestimate the capital requirements for a new carrier of similar size and equipment by the amount of loss suffered in getting operations under way. Moreover, the initial investment required of a new carrier to achieve minimum optimal scale will probably go on increasing as the industry converts fully to turbine-powered aircraft. This is not so much because of the high initial cost of jet planes; their high productivity and prospective long life appear to offset this, and one cost study sets their depreciation costs at a significantly smaller fraction of total direct costs than for the Lockheed L-1049G, one of the last major piston-engine planes.[6] Rather, the problem is the heavy auxiliary investment in maintenance facilities, employee training, and the like, that is associated with the use of turbine-powered equipment. American Airlines figures place the investment in ground facilities and support equipment at 44 percent of the investment in the jets themselves, and crew-training costs have been reported as running quite high.[7] The data are not yet available to support a clear-cut statement that modern aircraft have raised the ratio of other carrier investment to flight-equipment investment, but appearances strongly suggest that this is true and that the capital costs of starting a carrier of any given size are rising as a result.

There is another way to get at present-day minimum capital requirements in the industry besides reading them directly from the costs of particular carriers. They can be estimated from information giving the minimum efficient scale for particular aspects of an airline's activities. In testimony before a Civil Aeronautics Board examiner in *General Passenger Fare Investigation,* the president of Northwest Airlines, Donald Nyrop, gave apparently well-founded figures on the minimum numbers of several types of modern aircraft needed for efficient maintenance and

[6] Bernard Brown, "TWA Report: Jets Will Not Tolerate Inefficiency," *American Aviation,* XXI (Nov. 4, 1957), 47; see also Chapter 3 above.

[7] George Hart, "Ground Support: Carriers' New Cost Headache," *American Aviation,* XXI (April 21, 1958), 42; Per A. Norlin, "The Jets Outpace Industry's Economics," *Airlift,* XXII (May 1959), 43–44.

operation.[8] Many other statements by the managements of American and foreign carriers and the recent agreement of the two Canadian DC-8 operators to pool the maintenance of their six aircraft support Nyrop's estimates of the "minimum efficient fleet." By inspecting the consolidated balance sheet for the trunkline industry in 1957 and 1958, one can develop a crude estimate of the ratio of total capital required to undepreciated flight-equipment investment. This seems to lie in the range between 1.4 to 1 and 1.65 to 1. Applying these ratios to the cost (including spare parts) of Northwest's estimate of a minimum efficient fleet, we get the following estimates of total capital requirements: an airline using five or six long-range turbojet aircraft, $46 to $67 million; an airline using seven to ten medium-range jets, $41 to $69 million; and an airline using "about ten" large turboprop airplanes, $40 to $48 million. In the light of the preceding paragraph, if there is any bias to the historic ratios of total investment to flight-equipment investment, it is downward.

Has this amount of required capital now grown so large that it could be secured by a new carrier only at a relatively high cost? Or, to phrase the question more realistically, would the lending institutions' capital-rationing practices deny a new firm such large quantities of capital? That market, with its emphasis on past profitability rather than on future net productivity, tends to handle the airlines rather roughly in any case (see Chapter 5). And the recent difficulties and uncertainties faced by most of the trunklines in financing purchases of turbine equipment suggest that capital requirements for a new airline are probably substantial enough to make financing a major problem. The fact that the federal government felt it necessary to assist the financing of the local-service carriers by means of a guaranteed-loan program suggests the same conclusion, as do the tales of financing woe and

[8] Q.: "Do you consider that there is a minimum of any particular type of aircraft which can be successfully used by a carrier?" A. (Nyrop): "Yes, sir . . . With regard to the large jet airplane, the DC-8 or 707-320, we think it is either five or six units . . . With regard to a turboprop airplane, we believe that a minimum fleet initially would be in the neighborhood of ten. With regard to the medium sized jet, that could be any place from seven to ten . . . The spare parts provisioning problem, together with the training problem, will be very substantial with regard to these new types of airplanes. If you buy too few number of units I think your unit costs will be higher." Transcript of Hearings before Examiner, General Passenger Fare Investigation, pp. 6394–6396.

turmoil surrounding even the more successful of the large irregular carriers started after World War II.[9]

Having surveyed the major sources of barriers to entry to the trunkline industry, we can attempt a summary statement of how substantial an economic discouragement they provide to new firms. Probably the most meaningful way to do this is to compare the entry situation in the airlines with that in the industries covered by Bain's *Barriers to New Competition*. The three categories employed there are "very high barriers" (including such industries as automobiles, cigarettes, typewriters, farm tractors), "substantial barriers" (copper, petroleum refining, soap, steel), and "moderate to low barriers" (cement, flour, meatpacking).[10] The industries with the highest barriers to entry are, broadly speaking, those with substantial product differentiation or, less often, with major absolute-cost barriers. Certainly in the early years after World War II the airlines would have ranked among the industries with the lowest barriers. The actual pattern and frequency of entry to the industry just before the passage of the Civil Aeronautics Act in 1938 certainly bears out this impression.[11] However, by the end of the 1950s, the barriers had probably crept up to the bottom boundary of the "substantial" class. The shift is primarily due to the changing capital requirements and the resulting effect on the relation between the markets for new and used aircraft; to a lesser extent, increasing minimum optimal scale plays a role.

There is also some circumstantial evidence of rising barriers to entry in the general decrease of concern among the certified trunk carriers over the threat of competition from the large irregular or supplemental carriers, which gained authorization to carry out charter operations plus limited and nonscheduled coach service. (Recent court decisions have thrown even this limited authority into uncertainty.) This relaxation comes partly from the awareness that the economic role allotted by the Board to the supplemental carriers, that of charter or tramp operations, has limited

---

[9] For a journalistic account of one such carrier's problems, see Richard Thruelsen, *Transocean: The Story of an Unusual Airline* (New York, 1953). The initial equity investment in this carrier was $190,000.

[10] Bain, p. 170.

[11] See J. H. Frederick, *Commercial Air Transportation* (4th ed., Homewood, 1955), p. 174.

possibilities both as a base for an airline operation and as a profitable venture in and of itself.[12] But, more important, the trunklines are said to recognize that the current re-equipment cycle, bringing to the trunks aircraft with enormous appeal to passengers, averts much of the economic threat which entry posed to their revenue positions shortly after World War II. Then secondhand aircraft which were competitive with those of the trunk carriers could be purchased with very little capital. Though secondhand equipment is again relatively inexpensive, it is viewed by passengers as substantially inferior to the best that is available. Thus, the supplemental carrier seeking to compete with the trunklines must use economically obsolete equipment and face the resulting product-differentiation disadvantage, or it must attempt to purchase the most modern equipment and tangle with the serious problems of capital rationing that would arise.[13] Of course, this situation is conditioned by the circuitous way in which the Civil Aeronautics Board has handled the "nonsked problem" over the past fifteen years, but its relation to the purely economic aspect of barriers to entry is clear enough.

OBSTACLES TO ENTRY INTO LIMITED MARKETS

In the preceding section I have tried to evaluate the barriers to entry into air transport by a new firm that generally resembles the existing trunks in route structure and types of service provided. This is a useful way to approach the question of the condition of entry, for it allows of rather revealing comparisons between the airline industry and the unregulated industries on which we have information. But it is not a full treatment of this aspect of market structure, since a new carrier might offer a greatly varied quality of product and route structure. The present-day trunkline is only one type of airline that might conceivably exist in the industry.

My concern here is not with indicating what sort of entrant

[12] See, for example, Frederick, p. 219; Eric Bramley, "Outlook for Supplementals — Prosperity Despite Jets," *Airlift,* XXIII (March, 1960), 34–36; R. H. Cook, "Nonskeds Take New Look at Certification," *Aviation Week,* LXVIII (April 14, 1958), 41.

[13] Dero A. Saunders, "The Airlines' Flight from Reality," *Fortune,* Feb. 1956, p. 220. Saunders attributes this view of the changing entry situation to W. A. Patterson, president of United Air Lines.

would be most likely to appear under present economic conditions in the industry. Why most would-be entrants to the industry have been long-haul carriers offering a coach service is an interesting analytical question, but it is not one that necessarily has much to do with barriers to entry. Barriers put the potential entrant at a cost or price disadvantage relative to existing firms. Whether an entrant in fact will attempt to surmount whatever barriers exist, be they trivial or massive, depends on present profits in the industry and the prospective reaction of existing firms to a new rival. The appearance of operators wishing to supply long-haul coach service could mean only that the industry's price structure has yielded an abnormally high return to productive facilities put to this use. Or it may mean, instead or in addition, that the entrant providing this sort of service is at less of a disadvantage relative to existing firms than one which attempts to provide any other pattern of air service. The market-structure element is the disadvantage in cost or price facing the particular entrant; the potential profits for the entrant that overcomes it stem from a concatenation of structural and behavioral features.

How might a potential air carrier choose a different structure or operation from those of the existing trunklines so as to reduce the disadvantages it faces? How nearly could it come to eliminating them entirely? These questions lead to the type of information called for by the considerations discussed in the preceding paragraph. The planner of a new airline, striving to avoid the problems raised by economies of scale and by the absolute size of the capital requirements facing him,[14] might try several tactics. Most obviously, he might serve fewer stations or operate in fewer city-pair markets than existing carriers of comparable size. He might select a route network with similar stage lengths throughout, so that a single type of aircraft could be used efficiently on all of his operations. He might offer only one type of service (all coach, for example). He might lease flight equipment rather than purchase it in order to reduce capital requirements. He might contract out operations that involve some scale economies, such as engine overhauls. To make a long and inconclusive story short, the only one of these tactics that would substantially cut the entry barriers

---

[14] Avoiding the product-differentiation disadvantage would seem to be impossible if it rests solely on the greater experience of existing carriers.

is serving a smaller number of stations. Leasing of equipment appears not to be a very promising way of avoiding capital-cost barriers to entry. One authority holds that leasing arrangements are "usually a more expensive way of financing equipment than if it were done directly by the airline with its own credit." [15] The gains from offering a single class of service are small in view of the present-day flexibility of jet aircraft. The advantages of a homogeneous route structure (similar stage lengths and densities) boil down largely to those of using a minimum number of different types of aircraft, discussed above in connection with the size of a "minimum efficient fleet."

The advantages of serving a limited number of stations, however, are more substantial. Lower administrative or indirect costs certainly result, as can be seen from comparisons of the more efficient postwar "nonskeds" with certified carriers of similar size.[16] The gain essentially lies in the smaller minimum efficient scale of operations for an airline serving a limited number of city-pair markets. Capital requirements would drop to about $15 million for a carrier entering a single major city-pair market.[17] Though most individual city-pair markets are small relative to the scale of a carrier with a route structure like the existing trunks', as was shown above in connection with Table 23, minimum efficient scale for a carrier serving a single market would be reasonably small compared to the size of the larger markets. It would be extremely desirable to have an accurate estimate of the number of airlines (whether they are single-market carriers or conventional trunklines does not matter much) which can serve a city-pair market of any given size without incurring significantly rising average costs. The Civil Aeronautics Board has worried about this problem for twenty years without reaching any solution, and it seems necessary to agree with the excellent United Research study that the only workable approach seems to be

[15] Selig Altschul, "Trunklines Face Crucial Financing Problems," *American Aviation*, XXI (Sept. 9, 1957), 44.

[16] The "North American" group of irregular carriers had general and administrative costs that were 32.5 percent of total costs, while the same figure for three small trunks averaged 57 percent. See *Air-line Industry Investigation*, hearings pursuant to S. Res. 50, U.S. Senate, Committee on Interstate and Foreign Commerce, 81st Cong., 1st sess. (Washington, 1949), I, 266–270.

[17] United Research, Inc., *Federal Regulation of the Domestic Air Transport Industry* (Cambridge, Mass., 1959), p. 118.

the behavioral one of looking at the number of carriers actually operating in various sizes of city-pair markets.

There are two kinds of evidence of this — the number of carriers operating in intrastate city-pair markets where entry is unrestricted and the number of certified carriers *not* operating in multiple-carrier markets in which the Civil Aeronautics Board has given them authority to serve. The only large intrastate city-pair of significance is San Francisco–Los Angeles. This market has grown very fast and ranks near the top in total number of passengers; the number of certified carriers authorized for nonstop service is now three, with one serving on a restricted basis.[18] Intrastate carriers have been active in this market throughout the postwar period, but no more than one has ever operated with substantial success at any one time. Thus four carriers would seem to be about the maximum number that can operate in this market efficiently at any one time. For other large city-pair markets United Research has tabulated the carriers that, though authorized to give nonstop service, were not providing it to any extent as of October 1959. In the top twenty-five city-pair markets in terms of passenger-miles, the study found six authorized carriers that were offering no nonstop service. In other cases only token service was provided. United Research's conclusions, which seem to follow properly from the data, are that considerations of minimum efficient scale prevent more than four or five carriers from offering nonstop service in short or medium-haul markets and more than two or three in the long-haul transcontinental markets.[19] The scale factors affecting the number of airlines serving individual city-pair markets rest partly on technical matters and partly on sales considerations. Probably somewhat larger numbers of carriers than those just indicated could produce a given total number of seat-miles in a market without incurring significantly higher costs, but efficient marketing of these seat-miles raises the minimum scale for the simple reason that would-be travelers are likely to contact the airline known to have numerous flights and thereby probably able to provide a desirable departure time. Considering smaller city-pair markets, one probably need not go far beyond the largest one hundred to reach the

[18] TWA can serve this market only on flights continuing beyond one terminal.
[19] United Research, pp. 29–30 and table B-12.

point where no more than two carriers can efficiently operate. Many of the smaller city-pair markets would yield normal profits to a single carrier. As we shall see in Part Four, perhaps half of the five-hundred-odd cities in the United States receiving air service would get none at all without public subsidy to the local-service carriers and "internal subsidy" by the trunks whereby the profits on the larger routes support loss operations to and between smaller points.

Considering the vigorous growth of the air-transport industry, one would expect the number of carriers that could efficiently serve a given city-pair market to rise over time. Unhappily, technological factors have more than offset this market growth. The Civil Aeronautics Board calculates on a cross-sectional basis an estimate of the number of ton-miles an airline must generate per airport in order to break even. Ignoring competitive factors, this measure can be identified with the size of a city's traffic flow that will allow a single carrier merely to break even. Between 1953 and 1959 this figure rose by about 80 percent, while average traffic per city served by airlines rose by about 50 percent.[20] This trend, which will probably continue at a growing rate, is related to the increasing size and speed of jet aircraft.

This evidence confirms what was said earlier about barriers to the entry of new carriers of the trunkline type. Barriers to these firms are moderately high to substantial and are clearly rising. Barriers to entry of *any* sort of airline, not restricting the new firm to the traits of existing trunks, are at least moderate because of the effective economies of scale in the combined production-marketing operation on a single city-pair route. Viewed from the standpoint of the single market, the barriers are rising very rapidly.

[20] CAB, Office of Carrier Accounts and Statistics, *Quarterly Report of Air Carrier Financial Statistics* (various issues); United Research, pp. 117–118, chart B-1, table B-33.

5 Input Markets for Air Transport

A feature of the cost environment that can have some bearing on an industry's conduct and performance is the nature of the markets in which inputs are purchased. If the markets for an industry's supplies are workably competitive, subject to full information, and free from geographic segmentation or similar rigidities and obstructions, we can think of conditions in the supplying markets as having neutral effects on the industry's performance. Production of inputs would yield just normal profits. Particular firms would have no advantages over others through superior bargaining power with suppliers. Indeed, these two traits of input "neutrality" could appear even where the buying industry has some monopsonistic power. This would simply mean that firms recognize the influence of the volume of their own purchases on the market-wide price of an input and therefore demand somewhat fewer units than the number that would equate the cost of the marginal unit to its marginal value product.[1]

Where these conditions of neutrality are missing from some input markets, the conduct and performance of the industry buying them can be affected in various ways. For instance, where labor is purchased either in a perfect market or under industry-wide collective bargaining, a single wage must be paid to a given class of labor by all firms. However, where each firm bargains with its own employees, an element of ability to pay is likely to creep into the wage bargain. Firms with inherent marketing or real production-cost advantages, ordinarily permitting them to earn higher profits than competing firms, may be forced to share these profits with their employees.[2] Another situation in which input markets can affect market conduct and performance in the buying industry is that of imperfect competition among input sellers. If the buying industry behaves competitively in purchasing

---

[1] Formally, perfect monopsony requires input purchases curtailed to the point at which the change in total industry cost occasioned by the last unit of a particular input purchased equals that input's marginal-value product.

[2] For statistical evidence, see Sumner H. Slichter, "Notes on the Structure of Wages," *Review of Economics and Statistics,* XXX (Feb. 1950), 80–91.

its inputs, then the most likely case is the simple one in which the price paid for inputs includes an element of monopoly profit. Where the buying industry is oligopsonistic, all sorts of cases can result. An empirical instance is the metal-container industry, a highly concentrated sector that purchases its most important input, tin plate, from the rather highly concentrated steel industry. In the past the price of tin plate has been set over the whole market through bilateral negotiations between American Can Co., the dominant tin-can producer, and Carnegie Illinois Steel Co., a subsidiary of United States Steel and the dominant producer of tin plate.[3] Another possible outcome where both buyers and sellers are concentrated is bilateral bargaining which yields lower input prices to the large buyers than to the small ones. Though there are legal restrictions on such an outcome in the United States, many historical examples are widely known, such as the rate concessions once extracted by the large oil companies from the railroads. Still another possible outcome when buying and selling industries are both concentrated is more or less traditional connections between particular buyers and particular sellers which introduce imperfections that prevent the regular establishment of a single market price.

Having seen the potential importance of the condition of an industry's input markets, let us turn to a survey of the markets in which the United States domestic airlines purchase their major inputs, especially new and used aircraft, airport services, petroleum products, skilled labor, and finance.

NEW AIRCRAFT

The market for new aircraft is a highly unusual one, showing major changes over the last three decades. It will receive further attention below when we consider the equipment-investment policies of the trunklines as a form of product competition.[4] In the 1930s, before the passage of the Civil Aeronautics Act, there were legal ties and commercial agreements between the major United States aircraft manufacturers and some of the major airlines. A large vertical holding company, broken apart in the

---

[3] James W. McKie, *Tin Cans and Tin Plate, A Study of Competition in Two Related Markets* (Cambridge, Mass., 1959), chap. 4.
[4] See Chapter 13.

mid-1930s,[5] had included United Air Lines Transport Corp. and Boeing Airplane Co. as well as United Aircraft Corp. North American Aviation, a holding company controlled in turn by General Motors, had contained Douglas, a major aircraft manufacturer, and also the predecessor firms of three major airlines — Eastern, TWA, and Western. The last of the airlines to be detached from this complex network, Eastern, was cut loose in 1938.[6] After the disappearance of these corporate interconnections, the illegality of which was reaffirmed in the Civil Aeronautics Act of 1938,[7] major communities of interest existed between airlines and aircraft manufacturers through collaborative efforts toward the development of new aircraft. A number of airlines were at times parties to an agreement with Douglas Aircraft to develop the DC-4, a four-engine transport. TWA (then Transcontinental & Western Air, Inc.) had backed the aircraft manufacturer Lockheed in developing the Constellation series.[8] There is evidence that these arrangements embodied significant actual or potential market impediments. The TWA-Lockheed agreement on developing the Constellation contained a provision that the resulting aircraft not be sold to other transcontinental carriers.[9] Before United Air Lines was freed from its corporate ties to Boeing, it had suffered severely from its lack of freedom in equipment purchases and the inferiority of Boeing equipment to newly developed Douglas airplanes.[10] Interlocking relations of this type could clearly operate to the disadvantage of a particular carrier or, alternatively, to the advantage of a carrier which thereby gained exclusive use of a superior aircraft. Finally, a cooperative agree-

[5] This was a result of provisions of the Air Mail Act of 1934, preventing persons holding air-mail contracts from having any interests in companies engaged in other phases of aeronautics.

[6] Elsbeth E. Freudenthal, *The Aviation Business, From Kitty Hawk to Wall Street* (New York, 1940), pp. 200–212.

[7] Sec. 408(a) makes unlawful mutual control without Board approval of an air carrier and any firm "engaged in any phase of aeronautics otherwise than as an air carrier." Under Sec. 408(b), such arrangements can be approved by the Board when found consistent with the public interest, provided that they do not result in a monopoly or monopolies or jeopardize another air carrier not party to the agreement (49 U.S.C.A. 1378).

[8] Frank J. Taylor, *High Horizons — The United Air Lines Story* (rev. ed., New York, 1958), pp. 113–115, 150.

[9] *Ibid.*, p. 150.

[10] *Ibid.*, p. 110.

ment such as the one with Douglas to develop the DC-4, which covered standardizing design and allocating new planes among member airlines, was a substantial factor in the market situation. Its overt objectives were to insure volume production of a single-aircraft, and thereby a lower price to the airline, and to protect against monopolistic exploitation by the manufacturer. But, as one commentator pointed out, "there is inherent in such an arrangement the possibility of discrimination, at least for the first year or so of production, against carriers which might not be allowed to join the agreement first off." [11]

The years during and since World War II have brought substantial changes and development in the market for new commercial aircraft. One of these changes was enormous expenditures on research and development of military aircraft. The aircraft manufacturers have grown to be corporate giants and have ceased to lean on airline commitments and assistance to finance the development of transports for commercial use. Thus Douglas Aircraft disclosed in 1958 that it had spent more than $200 million on payrolls, engineering, facilities, tooling and material for the DC-8 jet airliner before the first plane had flown,[12] and on the sole basis of numerous but revocable orders by the airlines. No aircraft manufacturer, except possibly Douglas, has made significant profits from development and production of commercial aircraft in the past,[13] and none seems likely to profit significantly from the current introduction of turbine-powered equipment.[14] Still, the aircraft industry has continually offered new types of planes either in the advanced planning stage or as prototype models. Relations of individual airlines to particular manufacturers have grown less firm. Three new manufacturers, Convair, Fairchild, and Martin, have appeared in the commercial market, joining the three prewar giants, Douglas, Lockheed, and

[11] Kent T. Healy, "Workable Competition in Air Transportation," *American Economic Review*, XXXV (May 1945), 230–232.

[12] *American Aviation*, XXI (April 21, 1958), 51.

[13] John McDonald, "Jet Airliners: Year of Decision," *Fortune*, XLVII (April 1953), 127.

[14] Write-offs of more than $500 million have already been taken by the industry on turbine development expenses. Accurate profit figures on commercial aircraft production are impossible to come by because the great bulk of the airframe industry's sales have been to the military. See Charles J. V. Murphy, "The Plane Makers under Stress," *Fortune*, LXI (June 1960), 134–137.

Boeing, which still dominate the industry. Other firms have been on the verge of entering and have helped create effective competition in airframe design; a partial list would include Republic, Beech, Northrop, and Frye.

Finally, a development of the 1950s that is playing a major part in creating workable competition in the new aircraft market is the rise of European producers of highly competitive aircraft along with an increased willingness of domestic airlines to consider the use of planes not of United States manufacture. The British especially have sought a leading position in the world civil-aircraft market. Thus, in 1953, a count of aircraft producers with serious plans for introducing turbine-powered aircraft (turboprop or turbojet) unearthed ten companies — four American (Douglas, Lockheed, Boeing, Convair), five British (de Havilland, Bristol, Vickers Armstrong, A. V. Roe, Handley Page), and one Dutch (Fokker).[15] Seven years later, all of these were still in the race, one more British, one French, and one Canadian firm had joined them, and still other firms were considering entering active competition. Equally important as the rise of foreign producers has been the evolution of a willingness on the part of United States airlines to purchase foreign aircraft. Though de Havilland's Comet jet had been seriously considered, it was not until Capital Airlines introduced the British-made Viscount turboprop in 1955, with enormous commercial success,[16] that it became clear that new aircraft were being sold in an effective competitive world market. In 1957 a trade publication pointed out that, by the end of 1956, United States trunklines had placed orders with seven different foreign and domestic manufacturers.[17]

Of course, a rising number of sellers plus an elastic supply of entrants does not remove all the important peculiarities from the aircraft market. For instance, there is the question of product differentiation. At one time Douglas seemed to hold a slight product-differentiation advantage over other aircraft manufacturers because of the high reputation of its product and the personal familiarity of its personnel with airline executives

[15] John McDonald, "Jet Airliners II," *Fortune*, XLVII (May 1953), 127.

[16] See McDonald, "Jet Airliners: Year of Decision," pp. 244–248; and pp. 52–53 above.

[17] Joseph S. Murphy, "Jet Sales Competition Shapes Buyers' Market," *American Aviation*, XX (April 22, 1957), 62.

responsible for equipment purchases.[18] But there is little prospect that Douglas or any other aircraft manufacturer will glean significant profit rates on aircraft sales. The most recent reports of all United States manufacturers of turbine aircraft indicate very high break-even sales levels to recover the development costs;[19] and in any case Douglas currently seems to be facing displacement by Boeing as the leading firm.

A very important problem not eliminated by the increasing number of competing aircraft manufacturers is that of optimal variety in types of aircraft offered on the market. In the decade when piston-engine aircraft reached their peak of development, ending in the early 1950s, the duopolistic rivalry between Douglas and Lockheed led them to concentrate on development of an aircraft that would capture the largest single market — that of airlines flying United States transcontinental or trans-Atlantic routes. Relatively forgotten were the airlines in need of large planes efficient on relatively short hops, as well as the airlines needing low-cost equipment to serve low-density routes.[20] This situation has improved with the appearance of more diverse designs, but the general problem has not changed. Airlines and aircraft manufacturers are both relatively few in number; airlines seek to minimize the number of different airplanes in their fleets for efficient maintenance purposes. These facts guarantee a standing pressure for aircraft manufacturers (operating under considerable uncertainty) to bias their research and development efforts toward the largest single market, whatever the structure and conduct of the airline industry may cause that to be. As already indicated, over the years the resulting bias has normally been toward long-haul, luxury aircraft.[21]

As one would expect from the all-or-nothing character of

---

[18] See, for example, Anthony Vandyk, "Jet Race Quickens: UAL Orders 30 DC-8's," *American Aviation,* XIX (Nov. 7, 1955), 24.

[19] Selig Altschul, "Will Jet Builders Make Money?" *Airlift,* XXIII (June 1959), 37, 40.

[20] Stephen Wheatcroft argues the former shortcoming at convincing length in his *The Economics of European Air Transport.* See also, P. G. Masefield, "Anyone Want the 'Economy' Transport?" *Airlift,* XXIII (July 1959), 29.

[21] For carrier complaints of this, see *Permanent Certificates for Local Service Air Carriers,* hearings on S. 651, U.S. Senate, Committee on Interstate and Foreign Commerce, Subcommittee, 84th Cong., 1st sess. (Washington, 1955), p. 34.

equipment orders, agreements or close working arrangements between a manufacturer and one or more airlines are still the rule, and these have many side effects. Technical collaboration takes place between the manufacturer and one or two airlines for years before a new plane is produced. The cooperating airlines are then normally the first to order the plane and take delivery.[22] One consequence of this developmental collaboration grew from the agreement of Eastern and TWA in securing the Martin 4-0-4 aircraft in the early 1950s. Apparently the consolidated order for sixty-five aircraft from these two giants constituted such a substantial all-or-nothing offer that Martin (in wresting the order away from Convair) set too low a price and was finally forced into financial reorganization.[23] More important for workable competition in air transport itself is the possibility that through such agreements large carriers may obtain hidden price concessions, early delivery dates, or other terms giving them an advantage over smaller point-to-point rivals. Although neutral observers believe that large carriers (when placing large equipment orders) typically get price concessions, this is difficult to prove from public information because each carrier specifies its own equipment on a plane, and thus no two airlines buy exactly the same "product." Sometimes financing and trade-in deals are involved. It is clear that, in the case of piston-engine planes produced since World War II, the reported sales prices of a given aircraft have normally shown distinct increases over time.[24] This could be due to the forces generally raising the price level, but *de facto* the larger carriers normally get most of the early deliveries and pay a lower price, whether through superior bargaining power or simply through being first in line. Finally, the all-or-nothing

[22] For a good description of this pattern, see *Aviation Week*, XLIX (Dec. 13, 1948), 29–33.

[23] See *Aviation Week*, LII (Feb. 13, 1950), 15; Alexander McSurely, "Eastern and TWA Order 65 Martin 4-0-4s," *Aviation Week*, LII (March 13, 1950), 11–12, and his "Management Key to Martin Money," *Aviation Week*, LVI (Jan. 14, 1952), 18.

[24] See the figures given in *Reinvestment of Capital Gains on Sale of Airlines Flight Equipment*, hearings on S. 3449, U.S. Senate, Committee on Interstate and Foreign Commerce, 84th Cong., 2nd sess. (Washington, 1956), p. 14. A tabulation for five piston-engine transports bought by several airlines each showed that delivery prices during the second year after introduction ran 5 to 10 percent over those in the first year, and deliveries in the third year 25 to 33 percent above those of the first.

character of large equipment orders and of agreements between carriers and manufacturers opens the possibility of exclusionary terms requiring the manufacturer of a new and popular aircraft not to give early deliveries to smaller competitors. As we shall see in Chapter 13, there are at least a few well-documented cases of such exclusion.

There is one final important implication of the relatively high seller concentration in the aircraft-manufacturing industry. That is the possibility that the industry indulges in "planned obsolescence," a form of tacit product collusion often associated with certain industries producing consumer durable goods. It is highly plausible that this would be so. No reader of airline trade journals can fail to be aware that until the very recent past nearly all airlines have been managed by pilots who have an endless fascination for new aircraft. Internal funds generated by depreciation allowances have always been a major means of paying for new planes. The carriers, with the acquiescence of the Civil Aeronautics Board, have taken short depreciation periods on aircraft relative to their prospective technological lifespan. Thus a given type of plane is seldom anywhere near worn out by the time its owner has generated enough depreciation allowances to afford a replacement. The question is: have the aircraft manufacturers, facing this situation, spaced their innovations in time to maximize their profit by a higher rate of equipment turnover? Consider the following statement by an executive of one of the smaller aircraft producers:

There is a sensitive interrelation between product improvement vs. the introduction of a new design from a timing standpoint. The improvements or new design must not be offered too soon to affect the sales of the present product, but not too late either to lose a part of the market or to have a low spot in factory employment. Also, the stretch design or new design must not come too soon to require the investment of new capital before a reasonable return on the investment from sales of the present product is realized. In addition, the timing of the introduction of a new design must be keyed to the airlines' ability to absorb a new transport as related to amortizing their previous and present equipment. Also, it must be considered whether the state-of-the-art of the design and major components such as the power plants will be sufficient to interest the airline in making a new purchase.[25]

[25] W. H. Arata, Jr., "Aircraft Growth, Local Transport Category," *Aero/ Space Engineering*, XVIII (Nov. 1959), 46.

This statement does not seem to misrepresent the general thinking of aircraft manufacturers. It calls forcible attention to the connection between the appropriate rate of technical progress in transport construction and the airlines' gross margin over current costs (not simply their reported profit rates).

USED AIRCRAFT, AIRPORT SERVICES, PETROLEUM

Another important input market is that for used aircraft, although the domestic trunklines participate in it almost entirely as sellers. Used aircraft are feasible substitutes for new ones, due to the exceptionally rigorous standards for maintenance. At least in recent years the market for used aircraft seems to have been relatively perfect and world-wide. Buyers and sellers appear to be well informed both of market conditions and the physical condition of particular pieces of equipment. For years, aviation trade publications have periodically quoted the going prices for the major types of commercial transports. Several developments of recent years should improve the market further. Brokerage firms have arisen to handle transactions either on a commission basis or by taking full title to equipment.[26] In January 1959, a "curb market" for used aircraft opened in New York and London, charging a 1 to 3 percent commission on sales and publishing regular weekly price quotations.[27] Still another recent development is the acceptance of trade-ins by some aircraft manufacturers of late-model piston-engine planes on orders for new turbine-powered equipment.[28] These used aircraft are either disposed of through brokerage channels or converted to air-freight configurations; the deals can be viewed either as price concessions to the airlines in question or as inventory speculations by the relatively liquid manufacturers to help the airlines avoid losses from distress sales of used equipment to meet payments on new orders.

An interesting confirmation of the impression that the market for used aircraft is an effectively competitive one comes from a

[26] The firm of Frederic B. Ayer and Associates is "probably the largest used aircraft dealer in the world." See Bernard D. Brown, "The Great Used Transport Mystery," *Airlift*, XXIII (July 1959), 26–27; also *Aviation Week*, LXIX (Nov. 10, 1958), 43, and LXIX (Dec. 8, 1958), 29.
[27] *American Aviation*, XXII (Dec. 15, 1958), 21.
[28] *American Aviation*, XXII (Sept. 22, 1958), 54.

recent study by the Transportation Center of Northwestern University.[29] This project sought short-run predictions of the market prices of used aircraft from a linear-programming model which assumed these aircraft to be assigned to world air routes in such a way as to minimize total costs of producing air transportation. Prices were then calculated from discounted net earnings, with scrap value used as a minimum. The study was greeted by an anguished outcry from the air-transport industry, for it estimated prices generally lower than had been anticipated; the impression coming from scattered information in recent months, however, is that the predictions have come quite close to the mark, both for the general level and for particular aircraft types.

Another trait of potential significance for airline market conduct has been the variations in the ratio of the prices of used to new aircraft. Through the first decade after World War II, the prices of nearly all types of used transport aircraft were close to and sometimes above their current new price. To the extent that the trunklines actually sold aircraft in this market, they received substantial capital gains in the excess of the used market price over residual book values, and *ex post* profits were substantially redistributed forward in time. More important for market conduct, an airline under these conditions faced much less market risk from placing too large an order for new aircraft than from too small an order. Furthermore, airlines able to get particularly good prices on new aircraft (through early deliveries or otherwise) could count on substantial internally generated funds from depreciation throw-off plus capital gains to finance the purchase of any newer aircraft types. By contrast, the airline which had paid a high price for its planes, lacked the liquidity to time its aircraft sale-purchase transactions properly, or had made a bad equipment choice (yielding no capital gains on ultimate sale) had trouble generating funds for subsequent equipment purchases. During the "jet revolution," the price of used piston-engine aircraft has generally plunged to residual book value. It is not clear yet whether or not the secondhand market for jet aircraft, once it comes into being, will have the traits of the 1945–1956 market for piston-engine aircraft.

[29] Stephen P. Sobotka and others, *Prices of Used Commercial Aircraft, 1959–1965: A Research Report* (Evanston, Ill., 1959).

Another significant input requirement of commercial air transport is airport services — covering landing area, terminal, and hangar facilities. Airports are normally run by agencies of local governments and thus are highly diverse in their pricing practices. Available information seems, however, to indicate that certain uniformities occur. Airport managers view their function as one of serving the airlines and promoting air travel to and from their city; thus they tend to price services provided to the airlines at cost (somehow measured) or as near to cost as possible, but to extract what the traffic will bear from other airport tenants — restaurants, souvenir shops, and the like. Landing fees are normally a function of the number of flights a carrier offers and the weight of the planes. Sometimes "value of service" elements creep into these charges by means of a relation to the number of revenue-passengers.[30] On the other hand, there is often a quantity discount in the form of a declining taper as the carrier's number of flights increases. It is doubtful whether this taper reflects any trait of airport costs.[31] Recently there have been complaints from the airlines of sharp increases in landing fees and efforts of airport managers to "make a profit" rather than to "break even." [32] One would guess that a "profit" in this context means earnings in excess of current costs and that, except at a few large and important airports, the airlines pay little for the airport capital at their disposal. Indeed, it is shown in Chapter 17 that airports in the aggregate earn a negative rate of return, though large airports tend to make significantly smaller losses. But uniformities are few and arbitrariness and diversity the main rules in airport pricing; one authority has held that the terms are "arbitrary and unrelated to cost and profit." [33]

[30] John H. Frederick, *Commercial Air Transportation* (4th ed., Homewood, 1955), pp. 55–56.

[31] Richard W. Lindholm, *Public Finance in Air Transportation, A Study of Taxation and Public Expenditures in Relation to a Developing Industry,* (Columbus, 1948), pp. 34–39. Lindholm's table 36 shows the form of landing-fee contracts of Pennsylvania-Central Airlines with thirteen airports.

[32] See, for example, "Should Airports Reap a Profit?" *Airlift,* XXIII (July 1959), 25.

[33] Healy, p. 232. See also, State of New York, Department of Commerce, *Survey of Landing Fees at Airports in the United States, September 1952* (Albany, 1953).

A number of less important airline inputs seem to be available to all airlines at reasonably identical price schedules and, however priced, do not seem to involve much price discrimination within the industry.[34] This is true of such things as petroleum products, although testimony before a 1949 Senate investigation asserted that the noncertified airlines were forced to purchase these at prices 25 percent over what the scheduled airlines paid.[35] The scheduled airlines all pay the same fees to travel agents, since these fees are set collusively through the Air Traffic Conference of the Air Transport Association; the current rate on domestic tickets is 5 percent of the price of the ticket.[36] Noncertified carriers of various sorts, such as intrastate airlines, frequently pay a higher percentage,[37] but this difference probably represents not a cost disadvantage but rather a marketing opportunity created by the trunklines' monopsonistic policy. The market for aviation insurance apparently is effectively cartelized by two large pools — United States Aviation Insurance Group (sixty-two firms) and Associated Aviation Underwriters (forty firms).[38] Aviation-hull and casualty-insurance rates moved downward in the mid-1940s, following investigations of the insurance industry by the Civil Aeronautics Board and the Air Transport Association and a threat by the latter to organize its own insurance group. They have risen sharply since 1958, when a price-cutting firm was eliminated from the industry.

INPUTS OF LABOR AND CAPITAL

The price of labor services to the airlines seems to tend toward a wage scale that is the same to all buyers. The airlines face

[34] Frederick, p. 187.

[35] *Air-line Industry Investigation,* hearings pursuant to S. Res. 50, U.S. Senate, Committee on Interstate and Foreign Commerce, 81st Cong., 1st sess. (Washington, 1949), I, 273. The charge was backed by evidence from an independent consultant's report, but other testimony held that the price difference was due to purchasing by the nonskeds in small quantities on shaky credit.

[36] *Aviation Week,* LXIX (Nov. 24, 1958), 41.

[37] California's Pacific Southwest Airlines pays 8 percent. See *Airlift,* XXIII (Dec. 1959), 34.

[38] *The Insurance Industry: Aviation, Ocean Marine, and State Regulation,* report pursuant to S. Res. 238, U.S. Senate, Committee on the Judiciary, Subcommittee on Antitrust and Monopoly, Report No. 1834, 86th Cong., 2nd sess. (Washington, 1960), pp. 12–59.

relatively strong unions that press for standardized rates of pay except where regional differences in living costs are substantial.[39] In the past the local-service carriers have paid less for some classes of labor than the trunks, but these differentials are being reduced and may have disappeared by now.[40] Much information is available on the bargaining practices of the most important union the airlines face, the Air Line Pilots Association.[41] The pilots are in a strong position because of many factors making the short-run demand elasticity for their services very low. Both rivalry in oligopolistic markets and the rigidities of technology and federal safety regulations are responsible for this low elasticity, even though the Civil Aeronautics Board has never made this complete by covering strike losses for subsidized carriers. As a result, the pilots have been very successful in pressing for high wage levels. Initially they were aided by a federal minimum wage when Congress wrote into law through the Air Mail Act of 1934, as amended, a 1933 National Labor Board decision (Decision 83). This wage settlement gave the pilots access to productivity gains coming in the form of faster aircraft; in the 1947–48 round of bargaining, productivity gains coming through increased size and weight of aircraft were also drawn into the agreement. In the 1951–52 period, the Pilots Association successfully sought modification of the speed component of the pay arrangement so that the cost per mile of a pilot's services increases with the number of miles he flies in a month. Their aim was to protect the number of jobs for pilots in the face of rapid increases in the speed of aircraft.

In general, the pilots' strategy has been to resist industry-wide bargaining vehemently and instead use "whipsawing" and single-carrier bargaining to establish general precedents for contract settlement. The very success of this technique is testimony to the nature and intensity of oligopolistic rivalry in the major segments of the trunkline industry. Individual airlines strongly

[39] Healy, p. 229; Frederick, p. 187.

[40] *Permanent Certificates for Local Service Air Carriers*, pp. 211–212, 220.

[41] See Mark L. Kahn, "Wage Determination for Airline Pilots," *Industrial and Labor Relations Review*, VI (April 1953), 317–336. For a good general discussion of the airlines' labor-relations situation, see Mark L. Kahn, "Regulatory Agencies and Industrial Relations: The Airlines Case," *American Economic Review*, XLII (May 1952), 686–698.

wish to avoid shutdowns when their rivals in major markets are still flying because of the widespread belief of carrier managements that market shares are a function of travelers' habits and of the volume of service offered by the various competitors. Recently the carriers have tried to reduce their vulnerability to whipsawing tactics by an unusual mutual-aid strike pact which seeks to restore to struck carriers the extra profits earned by their rivals from diverted traffic during shutdowns.[42] Perhaps the pilots, like the aircraft manufacturers, use their bargaining power to extract some of the airlines' potential monopoly profits. Certainly this is true of the productivity advantages of carriers that own relatively superior aircraft, and probably it is true of the industry as a whole. Otherwise, the influence on the industry's conduct and performance of conditions in its labor market probably lies in the barriers unions create to agreements among airlines. A major administrative problem in every airline merger case is agreeing on an integrated seniority list, and Civil Aeronautics Board decisions on mergers often expend more effort on labor-protection provisions of the agreement than on the results for public welfare. Another alleged restriction on intercarrier agreements lies in the Pilots Association's hostility to equipment interchanges among the carriers.[43] The seasonal traffic peaks of the trunklines differ greatly, and the pilots' opposition to interchanges may explain why these have always been much less common in the past than the casual observer of the industry would expect.

Turning to the market in which the airlines secure loanable funds, the problem is not finding information but knowing whom to believe. The airlines' financing woes are often aired in public and before the Civil Aeronautics Board. Apparently no problems of oligopoly or oligopsony exist, since both the carriers and their creditors participate in a market for funds that serves many industries other than airlines. However, there are certain patterns in the conduct of the lending agencies that substantially influence the conduct of the airlines and also the policy environment in which the Board operates. Since these conduct patterns, which deal with the method of appraising loan prospects, are external to the airlines, it is appropriate to consider them as a structural

---

[42] See Chapter 8.
[43] *Aviation Week*, LII (March 20, 1950), 49.

feature of the environment in which the carriers operate. The impression one gets from studying reports from investment houses on airline securities, statements from the investment banking community, and complaints by the airlines themselves is that prospective lenders base their appraisal of the loan's safety not on the prospective contribution of the capital injection to the airline's net revenue so much as on the past and present net profits of the carrier. The evidence behind this assertion is necessarily impressionistic. During 1957–58, when airline earnings were temporarily depressed by a general economic recession, the industry kept the Civil Aeronautics Board under continuous fire for the Board's refusal to grant all the industry's requests for fare increases. The result, the airlines asserted, would be to make it impossible to finance their enormous orders of turbine-powered equipment. In the hearings and briefs compiled in the *General Passenger Fare Investigation,* this theme is echoed again and again.[44] The same view was stressed to a lesser extent in the early 1950s. Part of the outcry, of course, was tactical; the Board feels strong promotional responsibilities for the airlines' general development and thus has a strong desire to avoid blame for hampering the re-equipment programs by stinginess on allowed profit margins. But in view of the historic difficulties the airlines have had in securing capital, there is more than tactics involved in the charges.[45]

To develop these ideas more fully, I shall argue the following points. First, there is evidence that the airlines are afflicted by capital rationing and shortages of loanable funds. Second, there is an explanation for this in terms of the motives of the lenders of funds. Third, the situation has potentially major consequences for the industry's conduct and performance.

To consider the evidence on capital rationing, there are many cases of the cancellation or changing of equipment orders when

[44] For examples, see William V. Henzey, "Airlines Need 6% Fare Increase, 'Or Else' . . . ," *American Aviation,* XXI (July 15, 1957), 67, and the briefs of all the carriers to the Board in the General Passenger Fare Investigation, Docket No. 8008.

[45] *Airline Equipment Investment Program,* communication from President of United States transmitting report concerning status and economic significance of airline equipment investment program, U.S. House of Representatives, H. Doc. 430, 85th Cong., 2nd sess. (Washington, 1958), pp. 27–28. Hereafter cited, Cherington Report.

finance proved unavailable, such as Northeast Airlines' having to switch an order from British Bristol aircraft to Vickers because the latter company would aid in financing the purchase.[46] The president of Capital Airlines complained publicly that, although purchase of more Viscount aircraft would expand the firm's markets and eliminate losses, he could find no lenders willing to finance the purchase.[47] Earlier, there had been fairly clear evidence of capital rationing's cutting into the investment plans of Capital, Northwest, and TWA.[48] Although the local-service carriers receive a subsidy according to need that sharply cuts the chances of loss or a low rate of return to the investor, they have complained of being unable to establish a credit position.[49] Even where no such definite consequences have ensued, the airlines have had trouble in selling various types of securities[50] and must perform strange shenanigans to finance particular equipment orders. It has been common for the airlines to seek financial assistance from aircraft manufacturers; partly this reflects the financial constraints upon the carriers; partly also it reflects the relatively stronger financial position of the aircraft manufacturers (until recently) due to military contracts and the increased post-war competition among aircraft producers, inducing them to use credit arrangements as a sales attraction.[51] Airlines rent or finance purchase of engines and even propellers through their manufacturers in order to hold down capital requirements.[52] In

[46] *American Aviation,* XXII (June 30, 1958), 57; XXII (July 28, 1958), 54.

[47] *Aviation Week,* LXVI (June 24, 1957), 42.

[48] *Aviation Week,* L (Jan. 24, 1949), 33; LI (Oct. 24, 1949), 50–51; LI (Nov. 21, 1949), 50–51; LVII (Nov. 10, 1952), 90.

[49] *Guaranteed Loans for Purchase of Aircraft and Equipment,* hearings on S. 2229, U.S. Senate, Committee on Interstate and Foreign Commerce, Subcommittee on Aviation, 85th Cong., 1st sess. (Washington, 1957), p. 47; *Permanent Certificates for Local Service Air Carriers,* p. 41.

[50] See the material submitted by the Air Transport Association in *Monopoly Problems in Regulated Industries — Airlines,* III, 2089–2090.

[51] For instance, the planned purchase of nine Convair 880 jet aircraft by Capital Airlines was to be partly financed by General Dynamics, Convair's parent firm. The loan included financing the balance of Capital's payments due on previously purchased equipment of other manufacturers. See *American Aviation,* XXI (Feb. 10, 1958), 40, and *Aviation Week,* LXXII (Feb. 1, 1960), 30.

[52] American Airlines leases engines from Pratt & Whitney, the manufacturer, for its turbine aircraft. On these arrangements generally, see L. D. Adkins and D. Billyou, "Developments in Commercial Aircraft Equipment Financing," *Business Lawyer,* XIII (Jan. 1958), 199–219.

1959 the Air Transport Association sought congressional action
to let airlines issue valid security interests in propellers alone
and to exempt holders of engine and propeller security interests
from liability. An association representative testified that one
airline hoped to cut capital requirements for its turbine-powered
fleet by $1.5 million through leasing propellers.[53] Yet another
curious financing practice is that of the local-service carriers'
peddling of their debentures to large firms dependent on their
transport services.[54] In sum, capital rationing in the form of high
interest rates or absolute constraints or both can be taken as
established.

Why does the finance market restrain the airlines more harshly
than other firms of comparable size? Does it keep the carriers
from unprofitable overinvestment, or does it apply mechanical
standards that distort the allocation of finance? Lenders such
as banks and insurance companies, in dealing with the airlines,
seem mainly concerned with current profit rates. This is, for
lenders, a rational approach. The ability of a going enterprise
to meet interest and repayments on a debt depends not only on
the net earnings secured through the use of the particular loan,
but also on the net earnings of the enterprise's other assets that
are legally available to meet these payments. An investor in any
security of a rich firm other than equity shares should not care
greatly if the project the firm contemplates financing seems a
poor gamble, as long as the firm's over-all position clearly assures
repayment. Conversely, a lender may reasonably be suspicious of
a firm seeking funds to put to a clearly profitable use if its over-
all revenue position is weak. The investment decision for the
borrower of funds, of course, is entirely different. He seeks to
estimate the amount of loanable funds he can currently put to
uses in which the internal rate of return exceeds the marginal
interest rate he must pay. His desire to borrow to undertake such
projects has no necessary connection with how profitable are other
portions of his business operation. The entrepreneur may overestimate the productivity of investments in his own firm; in this

[53] *Aviation Week,* LXX (April 6, 1959), 48.
[54] *Permanent Certificates for Local Service Air Carriers,* hearings on S. 3579
and H. R. 8898 and Amendments I and J to S. 2647, U.S. Senate, Committee
on Interstate and Foreign Commerce, 83rd Cong., 2nd sess. (Washington, 1954),
p. 30.

case it is desirable that the capital market deny him funds. The market may not want to do so, however, if his total "credit rating" is good enough. Or it may deny funds for a profitable venture to a firm that in the past has just barely survived. Now when all participants in the capital market must make decisions under conditions of uncertainty and incomplete information, further complications of the same type ensue. The entrepreneur is more likely to have to make his investment plans on the basis of educated guesses. Lenders of funds, who presumably are less well equipped than entrepreneurs to appraise the payoff to prospective investments, are likely to place even more reliance upon current profits of the firm and the apparent soundness of its past managerial policies.

If these generalizations about the allocation of funds by large lenders are correct, the market for funds could systematically underrate the investment prospects of certain types of industries. Consider a fast-growing industry with a rate of return that is about normal. Suppose that this same industry tends because of technological progress to go through recurrent re-equipment cycles, periodically investing sums in new cost-reducing or demand-increasing equipment that are very large relative to its previous total capital. Past profit records might reveal nothing of the wisdom of such re-equipment investments, either for individual firms or for the industry as a whole. Risk-avoidance motives and normal modes of evaluating investment safety may cause lenders to underestimate the ability of such an industry to use funds profitably.

At least portions of the domestic airlines industry do not seem to differ drastically from the situation just pictured. The earnings of the trunkline carriers have been approximately normal in the 1950s, as will be argued in Chapter 17. Periodically the industry has sought to make major investments in new aircraft and equipment whose prospective payoff has little to do with past profit records. The current reinvestment in turbines is an excellent example, for, according to one report, it will involve outlays of $2.6 billion by an industry whose total assets in 1958 were only a little over $1.6 billion.[55] It has also been noted that in the current period of turbine acquisition the airlines' annual invest-

[55] Cherington Report, p. 9.

ment expenditures will run to around a quarter of their gross revenues. By comparison, the Ford Motor Company in a period of explosive growth in the early 1950s was investing at an annual rate of 5 percent of its total sales.[56] In the late 1940s the trunklines were in almost the same situation as now, and one former Civil Aeronautics Board member has argued that such "reequipment cycles" are endemic to the industry and can be expected to recur every decade or so.[57]

What are the consequences of this pattern in the airlines' dealings in the finance markets? The carriers tend to retain a large portion of their earnings and to draw heavily on internal funds for current investments. A trade publication's tabulation showed that in the years 1951–1955, relatively profitable ones for the airlines, the domestic trunklines had paid out only 27.7 percent of their net profits in dividends, while all United States corporations had paid out 53.6 percent.[58] An official of the Air Transport Association testified that over the longer period 1946–1955 the rate of dividend payments from net profits had been 32 percent, and that only $91 million had been paid out to stockholders while $1.4 billion had gone to finance new equipment.[59] Not only have most profits been plowed back into internal financing but also most investment has been financed through internal sources. Table 24 shows that a third of the capital requirements were drawn from retained earnings in the years 1946–1956. Airlines have had to use the relatively limited and restricted types of loans and security issues that have been available to them. It is very common for loans of roughly five years' duration to be placed with banks and insurance companies to finance equipment purchases.[60] These loans often carry stringent protec-

[56] Dero A. Saunders, "The Airlines' Flight from Reality," *Fortune,* Feb., 1956, p. 92.

[57] Louis J. Hector, "Problems in Economic Regulation of Civil Aviation in the United States," *Journal of Air Law and Commerce,* XXVI (Winter 1959), 103.

[58] Selig Altschul, "Trunk Airline Dividends Remain Moderate," *American Aviation,* XX (Sept. 10, 1956), 52.

[59] Testimony of Stanley Gewirtz, Executive Assistant to the President, Air Transport Association. See *Monopoly Problems in Regulated Industries — Airlines,* III, 1536.

[60] Saunders, p. 92. It is significant that five years is less than the seven-year depreciation period normally used in the past for aircraft and much less than the service life of the aircraft.

Table 24. Sources of trunkline net-investment funds, January 1, 1946–June 30, 1956 (percentages)

Source	Big Four	Other trunklines
Long-term debt	34.9	36.7
Preferred stock	2.3	3.8
Common stock[a]	29.1	26.3
Earned surplus	33.7	33.2
	100.0	100.0

[a] Including capital surplus.
Source: Foster Associates, *Rate of Return Study* (joint exhibits of Braniff Airways, Capital Airlines, Continental Air Lines, Delta Airlines, and Western Airlines), Joint Exhibit No. 401, General Passenger Fare Investigation.

tive features such as specified equity and working-capital coverage. Often the full amount of a line of credit cannot be drawn out until certain conditions have been met.[61] Almost the only type of marketable security the airlines have regularly used is the convertible debenture, carrying a relatively high interest rate and convertible to common stock at a market price above that prevailing at the time of its issue.[62] This type of instrument combines for the investor a high rate of return with chances for capital gains in an industry where speculative increases in market prices of common shares have often been substantial.

The airlines have always used rapid depreciation to increase internal funds available for re-equipment on short notice and to hedge against the ever-present threat of the economic obsolescence

[61] Selig Altschul, "Money Squeeze Clouds Jet Picture," *American Aviation*, XXI (April 21, 1958), 72; and Transcript of Hearings before Examiner, General Passenger Fare Investigation, p. 6578. The difficulty of securing this type of loan, however, should not be overemphasized, since the airlines have been able to get them at fairly reasonable interest rates. This rapprochement between the airlines and the large banks stems from favorable experience by the banks with such loans in the 1940s and from the airlines' relatively large cash flows before depreciation, taxes, and the like, even when profits are negligible. See William H. Gregory, "Most Trunklines Complete Jet Financing," *Aviation Week*, LXIX (Dec. 15, 1958), 37.

[62] See, for example, *American Aviation*, XX (June 4, 1956), 37; XX (July 2, 1956), 33. Between 1946 and 1956 one fourth of the airlines' capital expansion came through common stock, but four fifths of the common-stock issue represented conversion of senior securities. See Initial Decision, General Passenger Fare Investigation, p. 27.

of recently purchased aircraft. Eastern Air Lines, forced by the Civil Aeronautics Board to switch from four-year to seven-year depreciation of aircraft, is only a moderately extreme case; Eddie Rickenbacker, Eastern's board chairman, declared: "We should be able to depreciate in two years. There's nothing so cancerous as having money tied up in obsolete book value. Destroy the old and buy the new — that's the key to progress." [63] Because of this outlook in the industry, there has been a running battle with the Civil Aeronautics Board, which has fought for depreciation periods keyed to what it considers the economic life of an aircraft type. There has been acrimony generated over the Board's treatment of capital gains. Finally, the carriers voiced substantial complaints in early 1957 over a decision by the Office of Defense Mobilization that terminated the issue of tax-amortization certificates allowing accelerated depreciation of new aircraft.[64]

How does all of this affect the airlines' market conduct and performance? A carrier's ability to raise capital funds depends doubly on past profits — because they are a source of internal funds and because they give comfort to would-be external lenders. Owing to historic differences among route structures, the larger of the domestic trunks have always been the most profitable. The effect is that the capital market gives the larger trunks a much warmer welcome and encourages mergers in order to insure itself a more trustworthy group of customers.[65] The favoring of large carriers was reflected in a recent decision of the Civil Aeronautics Board which conceded a need for a rate of return that was higher for the "regional" trunks than for the Big Four and higher for the local-service carriers than for the regional trunks. This is consistent with the historical order of profitability of the three groups of airlines. The finance market also tends to discriminate on the basis of other features of the airlines that have caused profit differentials. It penalizes managerial inefficiency, but it also penalizes the victim of any current cut-throat rivalry in a city-pair

[63] Eric Bramley, "EAL Set to Battle Stiffer Competition," *American Aviation,* XXII (July 14, 1958), 54.

[64] *American Aviation,* XXI (Dec. 30, 1957), 42–43; Selig Altschul, "Airline Growth: Strong in Traffic, Weak in Earnings," *American Aviation,* XX (April 22, 1957), 60.

[65] *Aviation Week,* LVII (July 14, 1952), 79, reported financial pressure for mergers at a time when several were in the wind for the trunkline industry.

market. The finance market, like the new aircraft market, tends to favor the relative position of the carrier that is large or historically profitable or both. Against this, there was only fragmentary evidence of input markets that penalize large carriers or that tend significantly to appropriate any unimputed surplus of the firm's operations.

Whether the finance market has kept the volume of capital goods owned by the air-transport industry undesirably low cannot be answered directly — the test lies largely in the rate of return these goods have earned, a rate determined by a host of other variables as well. Certainly the large carriers have not suffered any abnormal long-run restriction. Furthermore, at least in the 1950s, the industry seems to have brought on some of its own troubles by not seeking more equity capital at times when both profits and prospects were good. The only solid conclusion, but still an important one, concerns the different treatment given large and small carriers.

PART II

PUBLIC REGULATION

6 The Statutory Basis for Public Regulation

In the years 1918 through 1937, prior to the passage of the Civil Aeronautics Act, there had been, by one count, fifteen major and several minor congressional investigations in the field of aeronautics. Significant legislation was passed in 1925, 1926, 1930, 1934, and 1935. In the years 1934 through 1938, legislation bearing on the economic regulation of air transport was under almost continuous consideration, and some thirty-four separate basic bills were introduced in Congress. The final product combined pieces of several of these. Before we turn to the provisions of the Civil Aeronautics Act itself, it will help to describe briefly the sort of public dissatisfaction with the pre-existing regulatory arrangements and the issues which occupied congressional attention at the time.[1]

The Air Mail Act of 1934, the inadequacies of which are part of the background to the 1938 legislation, was itself a reaction to a crisis. Early in 1934, the Postmaster General had canceled all existing contracts with airlines to carry air mail, on the basis of charges that they had originally been parceled out in 1930 not according to proper competitive bidding but through a collusive spoils session. There followed a period in which these charges were investigated by a special Senate committee headed by Senator Hugo Black, while the Army was assigned to operate the air-mail routes. The investigation was somewhat inconclusive, and the Army's efforts at carrying the mail proved to be costly and plagued by accidents and were soon terminated.[2] In this setting the Air Mail Act of 1934 was developed and passed. It revised the competitive bidding process for air-mail routes and

---

[1] The political history of aviation legislation and the legislative history of the Civil Aeronautics Act have been thoroughly studied before, so reliance here is principally upon secondary sources. Good general references are Charles S. Rhyne, *The Civil Aeronautics Act Annotated* (Washington, D.C., 1939); Claude E. Puffer, *Air Transportation* (Philadelphia, 1941); Lucile S. Keyes, *Federal Control of Entry into Air Transportation* (Cambridge, Mass., 1951), chap. 3; Henry L. Smith, *Airways: The History of Commercial Aviation in the United States* (New York, 1942), chaps. 23, 24.

[2] Puffer, pp. 200–224.

divided responsibility for public control of the air-transport industry among three different governmental agencies. The Post Office awarded contracts for carrying air mail and determined the routes and schedules to be flown. Thus it controlled entry to the industry, since air-passenger travel was then in its infancy and a successful business operation without a subsidized air-mail contract was impossible. Route awards were to be for one year, but they could be extended indefinitely if service was satisfactory during the initial period. It was the duty of the Interstate Commerce Commission to fix fair and reasonable rates of mail pay for each route "as soon as practicable and from time to time." The commission could not set rates higher than a certain statutory maximum; it was charged with reviewing rates annually and revising them downward to eliminate any unreasonable profits. Its authority to raise rates to cover losses was permissive. The Bureau of Air Commerce of the Department of Commerce, responsible for safety and technical regulation since 1926, would supply equipment specifications in advertisements for air mail bids.

It soon became apparent that the 1934 arrangements were untenable for two major reasons. One of these was the distribution of responsibility among three agencies. The second was a loophole in the competitive-bidding mechanism. The jurisdiction of the three agencies overlapped in several areas, such as the control of accounting and auditing procedures. Carriers allegedly could not know what to expect. The competitive-bidding mechanism was unworkable. A carrier winning a route award was stuck with its bid rate of compensation for a year at most; then this rate could be adjusted to a reasonable level by the Interstate Commerce Commission. The opportunities opened up by this situation reached their fullest realization in 1938 when Braniff Airways bid $0.00001907378 per airplane mile for a route from Houston to San Antonio, but was high bidder over Eastern Air Lines' zero cents per mile. Moreover, the bidding provisions could hardly have redrawn the air-route map on a clean slate as the legislation envisioned. One way or other, including through amendments to the act, the existing carriers were able to get back the route structures they had had before the 1934 cancellations.

In the years 1934 through 1938, no agency was a staunch defender of the existing arrangements for economic regulation of air transportation. The Interstate Commerce Commission found the provisions of the 1934 act tangled and difficult to interpret and administer. The Federal Aviation Commission, created by the act to make policy recommendations, came out in 1935 for a wholesale revision that would centralize authority in a single new commission. The form and amount of regulation desired for air transport does not seem to have been a major issue in Congress at this time. The reason that action was delayed until 1938 was the rivalry among the governmental departments (and also the congressional committees) over who should get the enlarged and revised regulatory powers. At first President Roosevelt favored some powers for the Interstate Commerce Commission, and legislation to this effect was considered in 1935. Only after some highly complex maneuvering, including collective efforts by several executive departments to freeze out the Interstate Commerce Commission, was the bill that finally became the Civil Aeronautics Act assembled and passed in 1938.

THE CIVIL AERONAUTICS ACT

The Civil Aeronautics Act of 1938 remains the basic statute governing public control of civil aviation in the United States. The administrative agencies it created have been altered twice and minor substantive amendments have been added, but the essential statutory content of the provisions for economic regulation has not changed since 1938. In 1958 the sections dealing with economic regulation were taken over into the Federal Aviation Act without significant change; to avoid confusion on this score, I shall normally refer to the act under its 1938 title.[3]

Since a 1940 reorganization, economic regulation of the airlines has rested in the hands of a five-man Civil Aeronautics Board. Its members, not more than three of whom can be of one political party, normally serve six-year terms and are removable by the President only for malfeasance in office and the like.[4] A 1950

[3] For the text of the Civil Aeronautics Act of 1938, as amended through 1954, see 49 U.S.C.A. 401ff; the text of the Federal Aviation Act is given at 49 U.S.C.A. 1301ff. Citations will be to the latter statute, though section numbers will be those of the original act since they are still commonly mentioned in airline literature.

[4] Civil Aeronautics Act, Sec. 201, 72 Stat. 741, 49 U.S.C.A. 1321; see also 1940 Reorganization Plan No. IV, section 7, effective June 30, 1940.

reorganization plan sought to centralize the Board's operations by vesting in the chairman certain administrative powers and responsibilities which formerly rested in the Board itself.[5]

Two parts of the act contain provisions dealing with the economic conduct of the airlines. The first of these is Title I, which sets forth a rather unusual general declaration of policy designed to guide the Board in all determinations of public interest or of public convenience and necessity. This section must be quoted in full:

In the exercise and performance of its powers and duties under this Act, the Board shall consider the following, among other things, as being in the public interest, and in accordance with the public convenience and necessity:

(a) The encouragement and development of an air-transportation system properly adapted to the present and future needs of the foreign and domestic commerce of the United States, of the Postal Service, and of the national defense;

(b) The regulation of air transportation in such manner as to recognize and preserve the inherent advantages of, assure the highest degree of safety in, and foster sound economic conditions in, such transportation, and to improve the relations between, and coordinate transportation by, air carriers;

(c) The promotion of adequate, economical, and efficient service by air carriers at reasonable charges, without unjust discriminations, undue preferences or advantages, or unfair or destructive competitive practices;

(d) Competition to the extent necessary to assure the sound development of an air-transportation system properly adapted to the needs of the foreign and domestic commerce of the United States, of the Postal Service, and of the national defense;

(e) The promotion of safety in air commerce; and

(f) The promotion, encouragement, and development of Civil Aeronautics.[6]

The Board, then, is to pursue the activities of both promoting and regulating air transportation. Promotion and regulation in turn are to be carried out in pursuit of multiple objectives — highest degree of safety, sound economic conditions, proper adaptation to the needs of the foreign and domestic commerce of the United

[5] 1950 Reorganization Plan No. 13, effective May 24, 1950.
[6] Sec. 102, 72 Stat. 740, 49 U.S.C.A. 1303.

States, the Postal Service, and the national defense. Competition is to be employed as a means, "to the extent necessary." An economist is prone to notice immediately that policies designed to maximize or optimize the achievement of one of these goals may not achieve the same result for some or all of the others. What if present needs and future needs call for different policies? What if a maximal contribution to the national defense does not square with optimal service of the needs of foreign and domestic commerce? What if "sound economic conditions" require substantial price discrimination? Apparently this statement of policy requires an impossibility of the Board, on the one hand, and leaves it with considerable freedom of action, on the other. Taken literally, it requires an impossibility by suggesting the simultaneous maximization of things that probably cannot be simultaneously maximized. Taken more realistically, it identifies a number of desirable goals and leaves it up to the Board to choose which ones it will pursue.[7]

The detailed features of air-carrier economic regulation appear in Titles IV and X of the Civil Aeronautics Act. Section 401 stipulates that no air carrier shall operate in interstate commerce without a certificate of public convenience and necessity. Such certificates were to be issued to all carriers operating continuously between May 14 and August 22, 1938, though applications to serve any points not covered by air-mail contracts existing on April 1, 1938, required a Board finding of public convenience and necessity and of no adverse effect on other air carriers. This is the so-called grandfather clause. The certificates are to cover particular routes (terminals and intermediate points) and may be restricted as the Board sees fit, with the important exception that they cannot restrict the right of .a carrier to add or change schedules.[8] The Board may amend, modify, or suspend any certificate, or revoke it for intentional failure to comply with regulation; transfers or abandonments of certificates can occur only

[7] For a study of public administration in the face of conflicting goals, see Earl Latham, *The Politics of Railroad Coordination, 1933–1936* (Cambridge, Mass., 1959).

[8] Sec. 401 (a)–(e), 72 Stat. 754, 49 U.S.C.A. 1371. Typical sorts of certificate restrictions which the Board could impose would be the requirement of an intermediate stop between two points or of service to two cities only on flights originating or terminating at some third point.

if the Board finds them to be in the public interest.[9] Besides several procedural requirements, the statute provides a two-part substantive standard for passing on applications for certificates by other than the "grandfather" carriers. Applications are to be granted if the Board finds "that the applicant is fit, willing, and able to perform such transportation properly, and to conform to the provisions of this Act and the rules, regulations, and requirements of the Board hereunder, and that such transportation is required by the public convenience and necessity."[10] New entrants must be both fit and needed; the latter requirement is to be judged by public convenience and necessity as defined in the policy statement of section 2. Once certified, a carrier is under obligation to furnish service "upon reasonable request therefor," to enforce just, reasonable, and nondiscriminatory fares, and to establish connecting service, joint rates, and reasonable divisions thereof with other carriers.[11]

Sections 403, 404, 405, 406, and part of 1002 deal with the crucial matters of levels of air fares and rates and terms for the carriage of air mail. Section 403 requires that carriers establish and adhere to rates in such form as the Board prescribes. Section 404 gives comprehensive authority to the Board to reject, modify, or revise any tariff. It can set exact fares, minimum or maximum limits, or both.[12] The detailed provisions dealing with determining rates come in paragraphs (d) through (h) of section 1002, which is broadly concerned with Board procedures. Either upon complaint or upon its own initiative, the Board may conduct a hearing to decide whether a particular domestic rate, classification, or practice is unjust or unduly preferential. If it so finds, it may

[9] Sec. 401 (g),(h),(i),(k), 72 Stat. 754, 49 U.S.C.A. 1371. The courts have broadly upheld the Board's use of its powers of suspension. It has been sustained in suspending the certificate of an interstate trunk carrier at one point temporarily to see whether a local-service carrier might better meet that point's needs (Western Air Lines, Inc. v. Civil Aeronautics Board, 196 F.2d 933 [1952]); in rescinding a temporary certificate by reconsideration of its prior order (Southwest Airways Co. v. Civil Aeronautics Board, 196 F.2d 937 [1952]); and in temporary suspension of the certificate of a carrier at designated points by virtue of public convenience and necessity (United Air Lines, Inc. v. Civil Aeronautics Board, 198 F.2d 10 [1952]).
[10] Sec. 401 (d), 72 Stat. 754, 49 U.S.C.A. 1371.
[11] Sec. 404 (a), 72 Stat. 760, 49 U.S.C.A. 1374.
[12] Sec. 403 (a)-(c), 72 Stat. 758, 49 U.S.C.A. 1373; Sec. 404 (a)-(b), 72 Stat. 760, 49 U.S.C.A. 1374.

prescribe the lawful fare (or maximum, minimum, or both). Under stated procedures it may suspend any proposed tariff change to determine its lawfulness. The statute lists five factors, among others, which the Board is to consider in determining the lawfulness of rates.[13] The first pertains to the elasticity of demand, the fourth to substitutable services of other common carriers. The remaining three refer to a desired minimum for total revenue — the minimum necessary to secure service of "adequate and efficient" quality.

Section 405 is a lengthy one, of little concern here, setting forth the service standards and conditions for the carriage of air mail. Section 406 governs the determination of pay for the carriage of air mail and, for those carriers receiving more than a "compensatory" rate, has been the instrument controlling the determination of the amount of "need" subsidy they would receive. Here the statute is far more explicit than in its provisions covering fares. Upon its own initiative, that of a carrier, or that of the Postmaster General, the Board can determine fair and reasonable rates of compensation for the carriage of mail; these rates are binding upon the Postmaster General.[14] The postal rates can vary among groups of carriers, among individual carriers, and among classes of service, "considering the conditions peculiar to transportation by aircraft and to the particular air carrier or class of air carriers." In setting mail rates, the Board shall take into account, among other things, the condition that carriers may hold certificates of convenience and necessity only by providing adequate mail service, any prescribed standards for the character and quality of air service to be rendered by air carriers, and finally the need of the carriers for revenue. The "need" component calls for mail compensation

sufficient to insure the performance of such service, and, together with all other revenue of the air carrier, to enable such air carrier under honest, economical, and efficient management, to maintain and continue the development of air transportation to the extent and of the character and quality required for the commerce of the United States, the Postal Service, and the national defense.[15]

[13] Sec. 1002 (e), 72 Stat. 788, 49 U.S.C.A. 1482.
[14] Sec. 406 (a), 72 Stat. 763, 49 U.S.C.A. 1376.
[15] Sec. 406 (b), *ibid.* Broadly speaking, the courts have upheld the Board's freedom of action in determining mail pay. Although the Board could not fix

In 1957, Congress acted to exclude from the "other revenue" entering into the mail-pay determination any net capital gains earmarked by the carrier for investment in new flight equipment.[16] A major administrative change came in the mail-pay provisions in 1953, climaxing several years of movement in its direction. This was a transfer to the Civil Aeronautics Board from the Postmaster General the function of paying each carrier any subsidy in excess of the pay that would compensate it for the cost of carrying mail.[17] This followed the assumption by the Board of the responsibility for indicating how much of each carrier's mail pay was compensation, how much was subsidy.

The striking thing about sections 404, 406, and 1002 is the lack of touch between the provisions governing legal fares and the provisions controlling mail pay. Air-mail compensation fills the gap between the costs incurred by honest, economical, and efficient management and the revenues supplied by just and reasonable rates. In the typical situation of public-utility regulation in the United States, determination of just and reasonable rates is keyed to permitting the regulated firms to earn a fair rate of return on their investment. Because of the mail-pay provisions,

a new mail rate retroactive over a period when an unchallenged final rate was in effect (Transcontinental & Western Air, Inc., v. Civil Aeronautics Board, 336 U.S. 601 [1949], affirming 169 F.2d 893 [1948]), temporary mail rates were held to be not reviewable when the final rate is retroactive over the period of the temporary rates (Seaboard & Western Airlines, Inc. v. Civil Aeronautics Board, 181 F.2d 515 [1949]). It was held not to be the intent of this section to underwrite the profitable operation of a carrier's business (Capital Airlines, Inc. v. Civil Aeronautics Board, 171 F.2d 339 [1948]). An expense adjustment by the Board to take account of a holding-company relation was upheld (Pan American Airways, Inc. v. Civil Aeronautics Board, 171 F.2d 139 [1948]). However, at some points the courts have taken a hand in the details of setting mail rates. A Board attempt to segregate a carrier's earnings from domestic operations from its "need" mail rate on foreign operations was rejected (Delta Air Lines, Inc. v. Summerfield, 347 U.S. 74 [1954], affirming 207 F.2d 207 [1953]). Also it was held that the Board had to include gains from sale of an airline route and profits from airport concessions in "other revenue" to determine mail-pay needs, and that it could not exclude part of the route gain in order to encourage the improvement of the route pattern through voluntary route transfers among carriers (Western Air Lines, Inc. v. Civil Aeronautics Board, 347 U.S. 67 [1954], affirming 207 F.2d 200 [1953]); see also Reopened Western-Inland Mail-Rate Case, Docket No. 2870, 21 CAB 1, pp. 1–3 (1955).

[16] Sec. 406 (d), 72 Stat. 763, 49 U.S.C.A. 1376.

[17] 1953 Reorganization Plan No. 10, effective Oct. 1, 1953.

however, this standard cannot appear in the Civil Aeronautics Act. A just and reasonable level of fares then presumably could be determined in terms of any of the goals mentioned in the policy statement of section 2. Air fares near the zero level would certainly promote the development of air commerce in terms of traffic volume, if they could be reconciled with the act's other goals. And, logically, nothing in section 406 precludes mail pay set to cover a large fraction of the carriers' total costs. At the other extreme, air fares set to maximize industry profits would secure "sound economic conditions" in the industry. Thus in principle the act gives the Board enormous leeway for jointly manipulating air fares and mail pay to achieve its preferred combination of the act's various goals. As we shall see, the interdependence of these two elements of the carriers' gross revenues has been at the root of many major disputes over Civil Aeronautics Board policy, often without its role being fully recognized.

Section 407 gives the Board authority to require any sort of accounts or information from the carriers, including "any contract, agreement, understanding, or arrangement" between carriers or with persons subject to the provisions of the act. The Board can prescribe the form of accounts maintained by the carriers.[18] The provision of section 412 for the filing of intercarrier agreements was one of the numerous antitrust provisions included in the statute. Others, in sections 408, 409, 411, 414, and 415, extend this kind of restriction in various ways. Section 408 requires Board approval of all mergers between air carriers and any firms engaged in aeronautics, whether air carriers or not. It enumerates a number of other possible forms of intercarrier control. The Board may give its approval to any of the merger, lease, or control transactions listed if it finds them in the public interest and the terms reasonable. It may not approve such arrangements if they create a monopoly or jeopardize another carrier not party to the agreement. Surface carriers entering into such agreements are to be put under special scrutiny; their applications may be approved only if they are enabled to "use aircraft to public advantage" and "not restrain competition." The Board can institute investigations to determine whether control arrangements subject

[18] Sec. 407, 72 Stat. 766, 49 U.S.C.A. 1377.

to its jurisdiction exist.[19] Also, section 412 requires filing with the Board all agreements involving pooling of

earnings, losses, traffic, service, or equipment, or relating to the establishment of transportation rates, fares, charges, or classifications, or for preserving and improving safety, economy, and efficiency of operation, or for controlling, regulating, preventing, or otherwise eliminating destructive, oppressive, or wasteful competition, or for regulating stops, schedules, and character of service, or for other cooperative working arrangements.

The Board may disapprove any agreement which it finds contrary to the public interest, even if the agreement has previously been approved.[20]

Section 409 prohibits, in the absence of Board approval, any interlocking directorate or similar relation between air carriers, between an air carrier and a surface common carrier, or between an air carrier and a firm engaged in any other phase of aeronautics.[21] Section 411 of the act gives to the Board power to investigate, on complaint or on its own initiative, and determine whether any carrier or ticket agent has engaged in "unfair or deceptive practices or unfair methods of competition." It can issue cease-and-desist orders.[22] Finally, section 414 provides that any party affected by a Board order under sections 408, 409, or

[19] *Ibid.*, 1378. The courts have sustained the Board's finding that separate companies jointly owned and operated constitute a combination proscribed by this section (North American Airlines, Inc., et al., v. Civil Aeronautics Board, 240 F.2d 867 [1956]), and they have affirmed the Board's power to find a control acquisition not in the public interest on a reasonable construction of the facts, even where a statutory presumption favoring merger was raised (North Central Airlines, Inc. v. Civil Aeronautics Board, 265 F.2d 581 [1959]).

[20] Sec. 412, 72 Stat. 770, 56 Stat. 301, 49 U.S.C.A. 1382. Treble-damage suits can be brought under antitrust laws, the district court retaining jurisdiction until the Board makes a finding on the legality of the agreement (S.S.W., Inc. v. Air Transport Association of America, et al., 191 F.2d 658 [1951], reversing 91 F. Supp. 269 [1950]).

[21] Sec. 409 (a), 72 Stat. 768, 49 U.S.C.A. 1379. A court has held that partners of an investment-banking firm dealing regularly with aeronautics firms cannot serve on the board of different firms within the industry (Lehman, et al., v. Civil Aeronautics Board, et al., 209 F.2d 289 [1953]).

[22] Sec. 411, 72 Stat. 769, 49 U.S.C.A. 1381. Ticket agents were included by a 1952 amendment, 66 Stat. 628. The Supreme Court found that use by a non-certified carrier of a corporate name similar to that of a certified carrier constituted an unfair and deceptive practice (American Airlines, Inc. v. North American Airlines, Inc., et al., 351 U.S. 79 [1956], reversing 228 F.2d 432 [1955]).

412 is exempted from the general antitrust laws of the United States.[23]

Besides its power to require information under section 407, section 415 allows the Board to "inquire into the management of the business of any air carrier" and obtain from it "full and complete reports and other information." One recent circuit-court decision, however, sharply constrained the Board's powers of internal control by denying the right to regulate depreciation except by adjustment or disallowance in rate making.[24]

The final provision of Title IV of the Civil Aeronautics Act is section 416, authorizing the Board to classify carriers, make rules and regulations for each class, and also to exempt from any or all requirements of the title any carrier or class of carriers for whom enforcement would be an undue burden "by reason of the limited extent of, or unusual circumstances affecting, the operations of such air carrier or class of air carriers and is not in the public interest." [25]

STATE REGULATION OF AIR TRANSPORT

Economic regulation of air transport by the states has not taken on much importance and does not seem likely to do so. Most state legislation confines itself to promotional activities or to strictly intrastate matters that incur no conflict with federal regulation, and one survey noted that "the states appear to consider their own regulations more as reiterative of the Federal laws than as supplements to them." [26] Federal regulation has been entirely dominant in the field of air safety since 1926. This supremacy has been supported by the courts, and there have been no efforts by the states to establish competing jurisdiction. Since most commercial air transport is either directly interstate or provided by carriers operating in interstate commerce, very few economic decisions by carriers lie outside the reach of the Civil Aeronautics Board. Of those states having statutes providing for the

[23] Sec. 414, 72 Stat. 770, 49 U.S.C.A. 1384.
[24] Sec. 415, 72 Stat. 770, 49 U.S.C.A. 1385. See also, Alaska Airlines, Inc., et al., v. Civil Aeronautics Board, 257 F.2d 229 (1958).
[25] Sec. 416, 72 Stat. 771, 49 U.S.C.A. 1386.
[26] William J. Davis, "State Regulation of Aeronautics in the Southwest," *Southwestern Law Journal,* VII (Spring 1953), 293–299.

economic regulation of intrastate air transportation, many (for example, Arkansas, Oklahoma, Texas) specifically exclude any controls that would affect the intrastate operations of interstate carriers and thereby confine their jurisdiction to the insignificant activities of intrastate carriers. However, there is a potential conflict of jurisdiction over the intrastate activities of interstate carriers that has been the source of some trouble since World War II, despite the numerous voices raised to argue that state regulation can do no good in this area.[27]

There have been two broad types of movement in state legislation. One stemmed from a 1944 drive by the National Association of Railroad and Utility Commissioners for adoption of a "Uniform State Air Commerce Bill" that would have provided for extensive state certification and regulation, including jurisdiction over the intrastate routes and fares of interstate carriers. This has not been widely adopted, however, and at least three states employing it exclude the activities of interstate carriers and thus avoid the potential conflict with the Civil Aeronautics Act.[28] There seems to be only one state, California, that both asserts economic authority over the intrastate activities of interstate carriers and has intrastate segments of such importance that serious conflicts with federal policy could occur. The other major direction followed by the states' legislation has been that urged by the Eighth General Assembly of the States in 1947 — state activities to promote local air transportation and efforts to find a procedural system to allow for state participation in the determining of air routes by the Board.[29] Many states have followed this lead, and in the round of local-service route cases heard by the Board in the last five years many state aeronautical commissions have filed extensive briefs containing useful recommendations and have sent representatives to plead that their states be adequately noticed in the dispensing of new routes.

Cases of active state-federal conflict have already occurred on

[27] See Oswald Ryan, "Economic Regulation of Air Commerce by the States," *Virginia Law Review*, XXXI (March 1945), 479–513; John H. Frederick, *Commercial Air Transportation*, pp. 146–150; Bernard R. Balch, "Abandonment of Intrastate Segment of Interstate Air Route," *Journal of Air Law and Commerce*, XVII (Winter 1950), 107–112.

[28] H. H. E. Plaine, "The Pattern of State Aviation Legislation," *Insurance Counsel Journal*, XV (Jan. 1948), 63–64.

[29] *Ibid.*, p. 64.

both routes and fares. The Illinois Commerce Commission, which maintains that all carriers serving two or more points within the state are subject to its jurisdiction, in 1954 suspended an Ozark Air Lines tariff approved by the Civil Aeronautics Board and also ordered a hearing on penalizing Ozark for moving its service to Moline, Illinois-Davenport, Iowa, from an Illinois airport to one in Davenport.[30] Also Nevada has recently sought to control the intrastate segments served by Bonanza Airlines.[31] More important for the national situation than these episodes are developments over the last decade in California, even though the conflicts with federal policies have not been substantial to date.[32] The first decision by the state's Public Utilities Commission on air-transport rates, approving the existing coach fares, came in 1950.[33] In the following year the Civil Aeronautics Board urged interstate carriers on the Los Angeles–San Francisco route to raise their coach fares, which were abnormally low owing to the competition of two intrastate carriers. All but one interstate carrier complied, but the Public Utilities Commission, though it approved the increase, ordered rebates by those carriers that had put the increase into effect before its approval was given.[34] The state's jurisdiction was affirmed by the United States Supreme Court on the basis of a lack of a substantial federal question.[35] Since then, fare adjustments authorized by the Civil Aeronautics Board have not gone into effect on California segments until approval has come from the Public Utilities Commission, but approval has been given in each case and the commission has recognized the desirability of a "uniform and systematic fare structure" and shows no signs of trying to combat federal decisions.[36]

---

[30] *Provide Permanent Certificates for Local Service Carriers,* hearings on S. 3759 and H.R. 8898 and Amendments I and J to S. 2647, U.S. Senate, Committee on Interstate and Foreign Commerce, 83rd Cong., 2nd sess. (Washington, 1954), pp. 46–47.

[31] *Airlift,* XXIII (April 1960), 38.

[32] On California regulation generally, see M. M. Taylor, "Economic Regulation of Intrastate Air Carriers in California," *California Law Review,* XLI (Fall 1953), 454–482.

[33] Decision No. 43,932, 49 Cal. PUC 494, p. 496 (1950).

[34] Decision No. 45,624, 50 Cal. PUC 563 (1951).

[35] United Air Lines, Inc. v. Public Utilities Commission of California, 342 U.S. 908 (1952).

[36] Decision No. 57,990, 56 Cal. PUC 779, p. 783 (1959); see also Decision No. 56,849, 56 Cal. PUC 374 (1958), and No. 61,120 (November 23, 1960).

In sum, given the nature of air transportation, the apparent mood of the states, and the comprehensive use of its regulatory powers by the Civil Aeronautics Board, it seems likely that, except for occasional jurisdictional conflicts, all important economic regulatory power will continue to lie with the Civil Aeronautics Board.

MARKET STRUCTURE AND AIRLINE REGULATION

We now have before us the market structure of the air-transport industry and the statutory provisions for the regulation of the airlines, including the Civil Aeronautics Act's policy statement marking out the boundaries of industry performance to be found in the public interest. Before looking at the actual problems that have faced the Board, we shall ask whether *a priori* consideration of the industry's market structure might point to difficulties in keeping performance within these stated boundaries. How, in short, might the consequences of the industry's structure be expected to plague the Civil Aeronautics Board?

The market structure of air transport is not one that would yield abnormally high profits under unregulated operation, judging by conditions in other industries. The barriers to entry, though rising, are not extremely high, and the "product" is not one easily subject to differentiation. Seller concentration has always been rather high in the national market and very high in most city-pair markets. Still, the absence of economies of scale relative to the national market and their only moderate role in city-pair markets probably means that entry or the threat of entry would control profit levels with some effectiveness. The ease of entry of established carriers into new city-pair markets, the near perfection of the secondhand aircraft market, and several lesser traits support this reasoning. Thus, unless entry were interfered with, one would not expect the industry to embarrass its regulators by earning excessive profits. By the same token, prolonged subnormal profits would be very unlikely because of the high seller concentration, the relatively small fixed costs, and the fairly low durability of the chief capital goods and the ease with which aircraft can be switched from city-pair market to city-pair market or even out of the country. Based on these same considerations, one could argue that the unregulated air-transport industry would·

offer its customers a reasonable product variety (classes of service, departure times, and such) and that there would be no significant problems of firms of inefficiently small size.

So far, these traits would seem to conflict with the objectives of the Civil Aeronautics Act in only two respects. The "present and future needs" of commerce, the Postal Service, and the national defense might be (and have been) interpreted as calling for air service to more points than an unregulated industry would provide. Second, the goal of "sound economic conditions" in the industry might be taken as an instruction to maximize commercial revenues at least until subsidy mail pay came to an end; but the act is extremely vague on this matter.

An even more important potential conflict appears, however, when we note the promotional objectives of the act for both air commerce and civil aeronautics generally. An unregulated industry would presumably promote the demand for air travel in that there would be sufficient rivalry to gear travel to various consumer tastes. Also, there is no reason for thinking that the industry's sales-promotion efforts would be inefficiently low. However, there is a major question about the rate of development that the unregulated industry would generate in the technology of aircraft. This rate would presumably be economically efficient. The long technological life of airplanes and the competitive market for used aircraft (and other traits of the industry's cost structure and market rivalry) imply that an unregulated industry would not introduce new aircraft unless their fully allocated operating cost fell below the variable cost of operating existing planes. If this condition were not met, then appeal to the public would have to be such that travelers would pay the higher costs. Now if the Board's mandate to promote air transport and civil aeronautics means anything, it means a faster rate of innovation than this "competitive norm." Such a course might be socially desirable if national defense or national prestige were felt to benefit from it.

The standards of public interest contained in the Civil Aeronautics Act seem to touch on traits of market conduct and market structure as well as of market performance. The Board is to combat "unjust discrimination," "undue preferences," and "unfair or destructive competitive practices." Anyone familiar with trade-

restraint legislation in the United States knows that the economist cannot guess very accurately what such terms will come to
mean in practice. However, because most structural traits in the
industry are compatible with a fair amount of competitive rivalry of one form or another, one might expect some facets of
conduct to rub against these standards. This is so especially since,
in an industry in which a few firms market a relatively homogeneous product, direct price competition often gives way to disguised or selective (discriminatory) price adjustments or to
product and sales-promotion rivalry. Another reason would be
that different groups of customers have different elasticities of
demand, making discrimination relatively feasible.

Finally, there is some question about whether the Civil Aeronautics Act's mandate to maintain sound economic conditions in
the air-transport industry might conflict with the turnover of
firms implied by the market structure of the industry. It has
been stressed that in many ways the firms in the industry (both
as of 1938 and in recent years) face unequal opportunities for
profit and survival. The weaker route networks of the smaller
trunk carriers, and formerly their scale disadvantages as well,
have always placed them at some disadvantage. The capital and
aircraft markets reinforce these effects. Furthermore, the condition of relatively easy entry into the industry (at least in earlier
years) implies the fairly easy and frequent exit of firms. One
might expect, even without knowing the dramatic extent to
which it has actually been so, that sound economic conditions
could be associated with aiding the survival of existing firms and
staving off the invasion of new ones. Yet the Civil Aeronautics
Act does not contain the standard of maximum earnings common
in much public-utility regulation (also long held a minimum
standard by the courts): a "fair return on a fair value" of property dedicated to the public service.

One more possible difficulty in regulating the airline industry
because of its market structure has to do with the ease of turning it from the conduct and performance that would result without regulation. The set of performance characteristics one can
predict for the industry is based on the whole set of conduct
patterns. Suppose a public authority acts to change just one performance dimension under such conditions. Performance is an

evaluation, not an event or a decision, so that this can be done by altering the conduct patterns or the structural features that give rise to them. Thus there is no direct way of changing any performance trait, but there are usually many indirect ways through changing various combinations of structural and conduct features. Each of these indirect courses, however, will change other performance dimensions besides the one initially aimed at; and it will probably change some or many features of the market structure and conduct patterns as well. A commissioner who oversees a somewhat competitive industry thus has a tougher job than the supervisor of a "natural monopoly." There will be many more problems of unanticipated consequences, and it will be much harder to adjust a set of "controls" so that they just reach a given set of "targets." In addition to these predictions of problem areas for Civil Aeronautics Board regulation, the matter of unanticipated consequences should be kept in mind in the analysis of the Board's policies that follows.

7 Regulation of Fares and Fare Structure

The Civil Aeronautics Board has ruled on the fares charged by the airlines, the quality or qualities of services provided, and the profits to be earned in cases presenting a great variety of specific issues. It is hard to organize the cases into a meaningful pattern. For instance, some cases dealing with the creation of new classes or qualities of service are decided primarily with regard to their impact on pricing and price competition; others are decided on the basis of whether undue discrimination will result; still others are decided in light of the probable effect of the change on the carrier's earnings. As a further complication, sometimes the judicial reasoning will deal with one of these sets of considerations when it is clear that the Board's finding was largely motivated by another set. Recognizing these problems, I shall attempt to discuss not types of cases but rather facets of the Board's policies. Thus the following sections will deal with price levels and price competition,[1] the quality of service offered, the use of price discrimination, and managerial incentives and efficiency.

FARE LEVELS AND PRICE COMPETITION

The remarkable thing about the regulation of fare levels by the Board is how little of it there has been. Only recently, two decades after it came into existence, has the Board even pretended to establish any general standard for determining the just and reasonable level of fares in light of the Civil Aeronautics Act. The reason for this rather unusual situation was ambiguity in the statute over the contribution which air fares and public subsidy were to make to airline revenues. The Board has been concerned throughout its history with the control of carrier profit levels but, as long as all carriers received some element of subsidy

[1] My discussion of fare levels and price competition owes a substantial debt to Paul W. Cherington's *Airline Price Policy*, chap. 3, which covers this material thoroughly and with an excellent grasp of the political and organizational considerations involved.

according to their need, profit rates could be controlled by varying the subsidy and leaving the fare levels by and large to the
carriers' discretion. The Board in fact chose this course, bolstering its control of profits through adjustment of mail-pay rates,
with indirect profit control through its decisions on route extensions and classes of service. At times, general economic conditions have changed drastically, altering sharply the level of
fares needed to yield any given rate of return. Only then has the
Board been forced to consider ordering or permitting changes in
the general fare level. By contrast, when satisfactory profit rates
could be achieved through politically tolerable changes in the
amount of subsidy or by other policies not involving fare changes,
the Board invariably chose these methods, leaving the fares
unaltered. It was only after the early 1950s, when most trunkline carriers ceased to receive any subsidy to cover their total
costs, that the Board was pressed to pay more active attention to
fare levels. No longer could the device of subsidy variation be
used. The other methods of controlling profits — competitive
route extensions and the like — were imprecise in both the timing
and magnitude of their effects and in most cases were irreversible
once instituted. Early in the 1950s the Board developed a
rationale for avoiding any frequent review of general price levels,
but it clearly could not justify inaction forever. Let us trace the
decisions and conditions underlying this situation.

Up to World War II there was little concern with the level of
commercial fares. The Board was preoccupied with the initial
round of carrier certifications under the Civil Aeronautics Act's,
"grandfather" provisions and with the difficulties of getting the
carriers' tariffs organized and published in a consolidated and consistent form.[2] The mail-rate cases of this period contain miscellaneous statements on the need for reasonable rates, but no
carriers' fares were specifically disapproved and consequently no
standards for reasonable fares were implied. Western Air Express
was lauded for selective fare reductions that stimulated local
traffic at insignificant marginal cost to the carrier. And in a statement in *Northwest Airlines, Inc. — Mail Rates*, the Board recognized that the promotional objectives of the act left open the
possibility of substantially lower rates and higher mail pay. It

[2] CAB, *Annual Report*, 1941, p. 16.

sought to discourage any strong tendencies in this direction, however, by declaring that reasonable commercial rates imply "a steady progress towards commercial self-support as the total volume of traffic and the number of schedules increase, rather than a steadily mounting dependence on the support of Government with such increase."[3] Here we see an early manifestation of a recurrent theme in the Board's policy toward carrier pricing. Low fares presumably could do most to contribute to the development of air transportation by encouraging people to use it. Commercially compensatory fares, by contrast, presumably would do most to achieve the sound economic conditions also mentioned among the goals of the Civil Aeronautics Act. In choosing between these the Board has always had a tendency to anchor its policy to the existing level of subsidy. Lower fares or other effective price reductions have generally been subsumed to the goals of holding constant or lowering the subsidy and of expanding the availability of air service.

The coming of World War II greatly changed the situation of the carriers. On the one hand, much of their equipment and personnel was transferred to the military establishment. On the other, the demand for air transportation increased enormously. Load factors increased to levels that necessarily implied a large volume of unsatisfied demand. The carriers removed their promotional discounts as of July 1, 1942. The Board by this time had become seriously concerned with the possibility of excess profits. Mail-pay rates were reduced in a series of cases, and after several informal suggestions the Board ordered the eleven largest domestic trunk carriers to show cause why their passenger fares should not be reduced by 10 percent.[4] Ultimately the Big Four carriers plus Braniff and Western complied to the extent of filing reductions of somewhat less than 10 percent. The Board dismissed its investigation of the carriers that had complied, with a notable dissent from Board member Harllee Branch arguing that the general investigation should be continued to establish a standard procedure for handling both questions of fares and of

---

[3] Western Air Express Corporation — Mail Rates, Docket No. 31–406–A–1, 1 CAA 341, pp. 349–350 (1939); Northwest Airlines, Inc. — Mail Rates, Docket No. 129, 1 CAA 275 (1939), p. 283.
[4] Order Serial No. E-2164, Feb. 27, 1943.

mail pay.[5] However, the Board did not press the investigation of the remaining carriers, and the case terminated at the end of 1943.

Nevertheless, numerous additional fare reductions had already resulted from competitive pressures.[6] The wartime pressure for rate reductions in the face of a great excess demand is a problem that frequently haunts price regulation by public bodies. Both the public sense of fairness and the economic theory of competitive equilibrium lead to the conclusion that appropriate prices can be achieved by insuring a normal rate of return. Under special conditions such as those of war and depression, however, the role of price in performing a rationing function diverges from its role in returning a normal yield to factors of production. Price regulation by profit regulation at such times leads to regulated prices that move counter to the general price level, a result that is not necessarily wrong but that certainly cannot be shown to be economically right by any simple argument.

As the war drew to a close, the Big Four carriers met Board orders calling for a substantial mail-pay reduction by proposing a smaller cut in mail pay combined with a further reduction of passenger fares.[7] This compromise proposal had a strong appeal of reasonableness, for it made approximately equal the yield to the carriers from a ton of mail and that from a ton of passengers, so that the proposed mail rate could be branded a "service" or compensatory rate with no element of subsidy. This was adopted over the violent and prophetic objections of some of the smaller carriers, which anticipated the results of the reduced load factors foreseen in the postwar period. Indeed, load factors dropped by nine percentage points from 1945 to 1946, by thirteen more from 1946 to 1947, as the war-swollen travel demand sub-

[5] Order Serial No. E-2302, June 10, 1943; E-2344, July 7, 1943; E-5102, Aug. 21, 1946. Declared Branch: "The development of a proper method of allocation is a major duty of the Board which must be fulfilled before any sound basis of establishing mail, passenger or express rates can be reached. Since it is clear that the Board will never be able to properly discharge this duty if its rate problems are approached in disjointed and piecemeal fashion, a comprehensive formal proceeding for the purpose of simultaneous investigation of all air transportation rates . . . is imperative."

[6] Cherington, p. 83.

[7] Order Serial No. E-3350, E-3351, E-3352, E-3353, Dec. 22, 1944; Order Serial No. E-3950, E-3951, E-3952, E-3953, Aug. 7, 1945.

sided while the carriers' fleets expanded. The years 1947 and 1948 brought significant losses to the industry as a whole, both from unfavorable cost trends and a disastrous series of accidents. The Board was inundated with pleas for higher mail pay; it was under heavy political pressure because of the rising mail-pay bill and the alleged "excessive competition" behind it. Thus it was not only sympathetic with the carriers' proposals for fare increases but took an active hand in soliciting cooperation among the carriers in agreeing what fare changes should be made. The result was a series of three general increases of 10 percent in the level of passenger fares. These were all granted on the basis of significant losses currently reported by the industry. Although the Board was aiming at obtaining indicators of end results, the decisions established no general standard for handling rate-level decisions and stated no precise rate-of-return criterion. Indeed, the decisions seem to have been made by the Board with very little knowledge of the probable effect of the increases either on traffic or on profits.[8] When the third increase was granted, the Board encouraged the carriers to experiment more with promotional fares and incentives for off-peak users, and later allowed a series of tariffs involving promotional price discriminations to go into effect.[9] The Board overruled a recommendation of its staff in order to permit a family-fare plan filed by American Airlines to go into effect. The round-trip discount, abandoned at the beginning of World War II, was reinstated, without elaborate consideration. Finally, and more important, at this time there came the first decision on air-coach fares for the domestic trunk carriers.

The Board's handling of the problem of coach fares in the years 1949–1951 furnishes an excellent example of the way its policies have tended to respond to changing economic conditions in the industry and to changing political pressures. The first

[8] Of the third 10 percent increase, Cherington states that "the Board apparently had little knowledge, and few well-developed ideas, as to the probable effect on traffic" (p. 89).

[9] See *Air-line Industry Investigation,* hearings pursuant to S. Res. 50, U.S. Senate, Committee on Interstate and Foreign Commerce, 81st Cong., 1st sess. (Washington, 1949), I, 98–99.

filing for a domestic coach fare by a certified carrier came from Capital Airlines in October 1948, while the Board still had the third 10 percent increase under consideration and was entirely preoccupied with raising the carriers' net revenues. This tariff was approved, but the Board showed deep concern for avoiding any competitive price cutting through the introduction of coach fares and also put considerable staff effort into studies to determine the extent to which coach flights diverted traffic from first-class service (as opposed to generating new traffic). In September 1949, as the temporary approval given to the early coach tariffs was about to expire, the Board issued an important policy statement aimed at minimizing the diversion of traffic from regular flights and maintaining a substantial difference between the service given on first-class and coach flights. Coach tariffs filed for renewal would have to provide for service only at off-peak hours, presumably at night, and with high-density four-engine equipment. Competitive conditions in the industry kept the Board from sticking to the letter of this policy. Through 1950 it resisted implicit price cutting through the extension or improvement of low-fare coach service, and in some cases it pressed for reductions of coach services which did not contribute to the industry's net revenue. In September 1950, the Board laid down as a condition for further extension of the temporary coach fares that their levels be raised from 4.0 to 4.5 cents per passenger-mile. Its press release at the time placed cardinal importance on maximizing revenues from the lucrative markets where coach services were normally offered in order to maintain adequate rates of return.[10]

The Korean War caused another quick shift in the financial position of the industry, relieving the Board of some of its fears about the industry's welfare. At the same time, it was deciding on the applications of the large nonscheduled coach operators for certification, and was facing heavy criticism from congressional sources for its previous harsh treatment of these carriers and its alleged favoritism of the certified trunks.[11] In July 1951, an important step was taken when a divided Board approved a request for day-

[10] *Aviation Week,* LIII (Oct. 9, 1950), 16.
[11] These political pressures are discussed below in Chapter 12.

time coach services using modern DC-6 equipment between New York and Miami.[12] A statement issued in December urged the extension of high-density coach operations: "It is the Board's considered opinion that coach operations to date have conclusively demonstrated their economic soundness and that the certified domestic carriers should promptly and substantially expand their coach services."[13] The policy statement included a suggestion for off-peak coach service as an alternative to high-density seating, with off-peak fares no higher than four cents a mile. At the end of February 1952, the Board suspended certain carriers' coach tariffs for failing to make this suggested reduction, completing the reversal. Thus in 1951 and early 1952 the Board acted in the pricing of coach service and in other decisions[14] to lower or at least to maintain the fare level and generally to expand low-fare services. The same pattern appeared in prosperous 1953, when with coach fares up for renewal the Board decided to leave highly profitable long-haul coach fares alone but encouraged the carriers to use them to subsidize medium- and short-haul coach service.[15]

Returning to regulations directly affecting the general fare level, the carriers were not satisfied with the financial results for the first quarter of 1952. They sought both a flat increase of fares by one dollar per ticket and elimination of the round-trip discount. By three-to-two votes the Board let the fare increase stand but suspended the request for the discount elimination. And at the same time it issued an order calling for a general investigation of the level and structure of passenger fares.[16]

In conferences between the Board's staff and the carriers, a series of issues was worked out to be covered by this general passenger-fare investigation. It was to determine whether the

[12] National Airlines, Inc., DC-6 Daylight Coach Case, Docket No. 4786 et al., **14 CAB 331** (1951).

[13] Civil Aeronautics Board Policy Statement on Coach Services of Certificated Domestic Air Carriers, Dec. 6, 1951, CCH Av. Law Rep. §23,128.

[14] See also, West Coast Common Fares Case, Docket No. 4586, 15 CAB 90 (1952), in which the Board refused to raise the common fares between Chicago and points east, on the one hand, and the Pacific coast cities farther from Chicago than Los Angeles, on the other.

[15] *Aviation Week,* LVIII (June 8, 1953), 22. This incentive proved insufficient, and the Board was soon involved in a direct dispute with American and Eastern over the level of coach fares in such markets as New York–Washington; see *Aviation Week,* LVIII (June 8, 1953), 20, and LVIII (June 22, 1953), 96.

[16] Order Serial No. E-6305, April 9, 1952.

dollar-per-ticket increase had been reasonable, whether the existing level of fares was reasonable for both tourist and first-class service, and whether the variation of fares with distance traveled was reasonable and not unduly preferential. Before the proceeding reached the stage of a hearing, the airlines came to feel that it was highly desirable to get the investigation dismissed. Earnings for the year 1952 were better than the first quarter had suggested, and it seemed likely that the investigation, if pushed to a conclusion, would not only end in rescinding the previously approved dollar-per-ticket increase but might occasion further rate cuts as well. During the winter of 1952–53, the Board, in one of its periodic phases of being short a member, was deadlocked two to two on dismissing the investigation while the carriers bombarded it with a variety of arguments for dismissal and the staff held that the investigation should be continued. When a fifth member, Harmar D. Denny, was finally added to the Board in April 1953, he sided at first with the two members seeking to continue the general fare investigation, but then he reversed his vote. This reversal later became the center of a stormy 1956 investigation by a subcommittee of the House Judiciary Committee under Representative Emanuel Celler. There it was made clear that Denny was approached by Stuart G. Tipton, president of the airlines' trade association, the Air Transport Association, between the two ballots. Whether it was Tipton's powers of persuasion that turned the trick was not, however, clearly determined in the hearings.[17] The majority opinion dismissing the investigation offered a strange set of makeshift reasons. The investigation would be extremely costly and time-consuming. Carrier earnings had not been unreasonable if averaged out over the whole period of the Board's existence, 1938–1952. The effect of current cost trends, the ending of the Korean War, and the extensions of coach service was uncertain. The industry's earnings are strongly subject to the general business cycle, and so it would not be feasible to vary prices in the short run to maintain a constant rate of return.[18] The majority's one positive contribution to airline rate making was to announce a policy of watchful waiting:

[17] *Monopoly Problems in Regulated Industries — Airlines,* U.S. House of Representatives, II, 950–980, 1187–1230.

[18] General Passenger Fare Investigation, Docket No. 5509, 17 CAB 230, pp. 232–234 (1953).

should earnings fall markedly in the future the carriers will be expected to absorb such losses without resort to fare or mail-rate adjustments unless it can be demonstrated that such earnings are below the level necessary to provide a fair return over a reasonably extended period which includes the good years as well as the bad.[19]

The dissent of Board Member Josh Lee attacked the "good years and bad" solution to the rate problem by pointing out that it was technically inadequate unless an equalization reserve were established to capture the proceeds from the good years, since by standing policy past financial results could be formally reviewed only for those carriers on temporary mail rates. He also attacked the tangled logic of the majority arguments, which dealt with reasons for not reducing rates rather than with reasons for not investigating them.[20] Member J. P. Adams took a similar dissenting position, noting the paradox of the Board's enormous efforts to determine mail pay, contributing 10.1 percent of the carriers' aggregate revenue for 1939–1952, while passenger fares, generating 82.3 percent of aggregate revenue, had been adjusted in the most casual fashion.[21]

A positive suggestion contained in the majority opinion was for continuing the investigation at an informal level by the Board's staff. The two minority members objected that this was inadequate since the Board could take no action on fares without a formal proceeding. The appearance given by testimony at the 1956 Celler investigation is that the staff study proposed as an alternative was indeed a sop. This study was never pursued, and in 1956 the Board's chairman, a new member, Ross Rizley, did not even know that the dismissal order had called for a staff investigation.[22]

In early 1954, with a minor general recession in process, the carriers found themselves in a position similar to that of early 1952. There was a clear short-run reduction in earnings, no growth in the volume of first-class traffic, and only modest expansion in coach service. The opinions of the firms diverged

[19] *Ibid.*, p. 235.
[20] *Ibid.*, pp. 236–238.
[21] *Ibid.*, pp. 243–245.
[22] Lee Moore, "CAB Launches New Airline Fares Study," *Aviation Week*, LVIII (June 15, 1953), 79–80; *Monopoly Problems in Regulated Industries — Airlines*, I, 138–144.

greatly as to whether anything should be done and, if so, whether the appropriate remedy lay in a change in the general fare level or in manipulating the fare structure, the discount structure, or the classes of service offered.[23] The carriers decided to take the novel step of sending the president of the Air Transport Association before the Board to ask permission for the carriers to hold formal meetings to seek agreement on fare policies. This was substantially denied; the Board granted permission for meetings to discuss means of increasing revenue, but excluded from consideration fare levels, the relation of coach to first-class fares, and the round-trip discount.[24] It cited its previously announced policy of permitting such meetings — exempt from the antitrust laws — only where a convincing showing of need could be made, and it noted the advantages of stability in transport fares. It made a formal application of the doctrine employed in the general-investigation dismissal order of considering earning levels only over a period of time, implying that it would not be stampeded by short-term earning conditions (as it had been in the 1952 dollar-per-ticket case). The 1954 situation brought no change in fares, and the industry's profits returned to satisfactory levels in the latter part of 1954 and 1955.

As of 1955, the high profit rates for the 1950s had still induced no Board action dealing with the general level of fares. Profit rates were an important background factor, however, in the Board's effort that year to break a substantial log jam of route cases. Under the new chairman, Ross Rizley, a series of cases was decided in which more carriers were allowed to compete on many major routes; this was especially intended to enlarge the smaller and weaker trunklines vis-à-vis the Big Four. But it did not solve the Board's problems of regulating fares and profits. In March through May 1956, Representative Celler's subcommittee of the House Judiciary Committee hammered away at the Board for its failure to pursue the 1952 general fare investigation. No Board member would actively defend the dismissal order before the subcommittee's questioning, and this surely had much to do with the Board's decision on May 10, 1956, to order a new investigation dealing with the general level, but not the structure, of domestic

---

[23] Cherington, pp. 106–107.
[24] Order Serial No. E-8421, June 9, 1954.

passenger fares.[25] It cited as grounds the trunk industry's rate
of return, which since 1950 had exceeded 10 percent annually,
and the absence of any trend conclusively showing this to be a
temporary condition. Hearings were not instituted immediately,
and in March 1957, again on the basis of slight short-run deterioration of traffic and profits in the last quarter of 1956 and early
1957, seven carriers filed for flat 6 percent increases and Eastern
and Capital asked also for another dollar-per-ticket increase.
These tariffs were suspended, and in the expedited proceeding
that followed the Board decided that emergency conditions did
not warrant the increase sought and that the postponed investigation should again be pressed.

Aside from the evidence of a short-run adverse movement in
earnings, the carriers' case had rested on highly conjectural
arguments that the cost-reducing factors of "greater traffic
volumes, technological improvements, increased productivity, and
operating economies" would operate less strongly in the future;
they also argued that the new aircraft being introduced at the
time (principally the DC-7) were more costly to operate than
their predecessors.[26] These arguments about prospects for changes
in the cost level left the Board unmoved. It rejected the argument based on trends in the carriers' rates of return on two
grounds. First, referring to its "good years and bad" philosophy,
it noted that the 1950–1956 earnings rate for the seven carriers
in the proceeding was 10.87 percent, ranging from 12.86 percent
for Delta to 6.51 percent for Northwest. The average results
adequately exceeded the Board's rule-of-thumb return standard
of 8 percent. Second, the Board cited reasons resting on temporary
factors — development costs on new routes and integration costs
of new equipment — for the temporary low returns of which the
carriers complained.[27] Thus, not only did the carriers find that
the "good years and bad" philosophy could work against them
as well as for them, but also they were faced in the proceeding
with efforts by the Board's staff to secure retroactive accounting

[25] General Passenger Fare Investigation, Docket No. 8008, 23 CAB 803 (1956);
William V. Henzey, "CAB May Be Forced to Conduct Fare Probe," *American
Aviation,* XIX (April 9, 1956), 65–66.

[26] Suspended Passenger Fare Increase Case, Docket No. 8613, decided Sept. 25,
1957, CCH Av. Law Rep. §22,077.01.

[27] CCH Av. Law Rep. §22,077.02.

changes in the residual value of depreciated aircraft. This would have transferred significant amounts of carrier earnings from capital gains to operating profits and made the operating rates of return look higher than ever.[28]

The Board's decision was hardly announced before the 1957–58 recession was upon the industry. Its effects, much sharper than those of earlier postwar recessions and no doubt augmented by the normal impact on profits of the new competitive route awards since 1954, brought industry profits well below normal levels for the first time in the decade. The carriers filed varying fare increases, mostly in excess of 10 percent. The Board suspended these tariffs on January 25, 1958, and announced in a press release that it would grant a temporary fare increase of 4 percent, plus one dollar per ticket, making a theoretical total increase of 6.6 percent.[29] This the carriers promptly took. The Board's decision focused strongly on the temporary problems of the industry; the deficient earnings justifying the increase were those of September–November 1957 and the prospective returns for 1958. The "good years and bad" philosophy went under cover. Later in 1958 the carriers filed for a number of revenue-increasing changes in promotional rates and discounts. The round-trip discount was to be eliminated along with free stopover and related privileges, and the family-fare discount was to drop from one half to one third. The Board let this go into effect without a formal opinion.[30]

Finally in 1960, five years after it began, the Board reached a decision in its general fare investigation. Preliminary details came in a press release of April 29, 1960, indicating the rate of return to be allowed, time periods to be used in calculating depreciation, and a few other matters.[31] With trunkline earnings for the previous three years significantly under the announced standard, the carriers immediately entered filings for diverse increases in the general fare level. The Board suspended these and announced that it would grant an increase of 2.5 percent plus one dollar per ticket, an increase that it held would yield over an extended

[28] Cherington, p. 112.
[29] Trans World Airlines, Inc. — (Interim Fare Increases), Docket No. 9288, decided Feb. 25, 1958, CCH Av. Law Rep. §22,160.01.
[30] Order Serial No. 13066, Oct. 27, 1958.
[31] Press release, CAB 60–10, April 29, 1960; *Traffic World,* CV (May 7, 1960), 125.

period the rate of return set in the general investigation.[32] This decision emerged in November 1960 and settled some, though not all, of the problems associated with standards for reasonable air fares.[33] It set a return on the industry's investment (after taxes but before interest) of 10.5 percent. This allegedly represents the weighted average of the rates of return needed by the Big Four (10.25 percent) and the smaller eight trunks (11.125) in order to maintain access to the capital markets — the conventional "cost of capital" approach to setting rates of return for public utilities. The assumed capital structure (mixture of debt and equity) underlying this rate of return was that currently prevailing in the industry.[34] The decision did not discuss the problem of setting fares for the industry to yield the large and small firms the rates of return fed into the weighted average, nor for that matter did it discuss the dispersion of profit rates for individual carriers that would surround such a warranted rate for the entire industry. All it did was to deny that the Civil Aeronautics Act required the establishment of a normal rate of return for the weakest firm and to defend the weighted average as a justifiable compromise.[35] For the capital base to which this rate of return was to be applied, the Board switched from its previous base of total capitalization (net worth plus long-term debt) to depreciated used and useful assets. It did not exclude cash deposits with aircraft manufacturers for new equipment (an issue in the proceedings), but this change did in principle relieve air travelers of the burden of providing a normal rate of return on such facilities as the Miami television station owned by National Airlines.[36] Depreciation standards were announced for figuring costs and profits for rate-making purposes, standards somewhat less conservative than the carriers had historically favored. The rates of return to be allowed under these conditions were described as "not minimum returns below which confiscation would result" and "above the minimum returns but within the broad range of reasonableness." [37] An economic evaluation will be deferred until Part Four of this study.

[32] *Traffic World,* CV (June 25, 1960), 197–198.
[33] Order Serial No. E-16068, Nov. 25, 1960.
[34] *Ibid.,* pp. 12–32.
[35] *Ibid.,* pp. 72–77.
[36] *Ibid.,* pp. 33–41.
[37] *Ibid.,* p. 76.

The general passenger-fare investigation had sought more than a recipe for testing the lawfulness of particular fare levels. There had also been much testimony in the early hearings on the airlines' actual and prospective cost and revenue levels and how the Board should weigh past, current, and prospective conditions in setting fares. On this matter the investigation came to nothing. The actual results of 1957 and 1958 had borne little relation to the forecasts either of the carriers or of the Board's staff. The transition to jet aircraft made future cost levels highly uncertain. It also discouraged the Board about the possibility of setting "standard" load factors for the industry. In sum, the Board failed to adopt standards because of the inadequacy of the record before it and abandoned any hope of a mechanical rule for relating legal fare levels to past or projected data. It even refused to say anything specific about how long the set rates would be allowed to stand without revision. There was no reference to the old "good years and bad" philosophy.[38] Thus, from this lengthy proceeding, the Board seems to have drawn a fairly definite method for evaluating the reasonableness of carrier earnings but no definite standard for setting and adjusting the fare level to achieve this rate of return.

A decision on the rate of return for local-service carriers, handed down just a few months before, had followed very similar lines.[39] The rate, based on a cost-of-capital approach, was to be 5.5 percent on debt capital and a spectacular 21.35 percent on equity. The latter resulted from boosting the current earnings-price ratio on equity of the smaller eight trunks by 50 percent, a procedure the decision attempted to justify only in general terms.[40] Because of extremely high debt ratios (around 75 percent) in the local-service segment which it wished to see lowered, the Board was faced with a dilemma on setting a standard debt-equity ratio. Applying the debt and equity rates of return to its desired debt ratio (55 percent) would give significant windfalls to the carriers' stockholders. Applying these rates to the industry's actual debt ratio would make it difficult to increase the carriers' equity base without diluting existing equities. To avoid these two

[38] *Ibid.*, pp. 42–52, 70–71.
[39] Order Serial No. E-15696, Rate of Return Local Service Carriers Investigation, Docket No. 8404, Aug 26, 1960.
[40] *Ibid.*, pp. 2–5.

pitfalls the Board decided to set each carrier's rate of return separately on the basis of its current actual-debt ratio, subject to a ceiling on its over-all rate of return of 12.75 percent and a floor of 9 percent.[41] Concerning the setting of mail pay for past periods of time, in which case the government becomes the risk bearer, the Board allowed only a 7 percent rate of return compared to the maximum 12.75 percent for the prospective setting of mail pay or fares. The considerable difference is one of the many indications of the weight the Board has put on "risk" factors to justify spectacularly high rates of return in the air-transport industry.

A red thread running through this narrative has been the Board's fear of any action that might, even indirectly, yield low rates of return for the carriers. There are many other instances of its nervousness about any fare proposals or situations that could lead to substantial general price competition among the carriers. This was apparent, for example, in its handling of air-freight rates in the years 1947–1949. In 1947 significant competition in freight rates broke out between the uncertified cargo airlines and the certified trunks; the former were operating as scheduled common carriers pending action on their applications for certificates of public convenience and necessity. The certified carriers started the episode by filing tariffs 25 percent lower than those previously in force; the noncertified carriers responded by filing rates 30 percent lower. The certified carriers filed another round of reductions, at which point the noncertified cargo lines appealed to the Board to investigate the lawfulness of the certified carriers' tariffs on the grounds that they represented service below cost and rested on the receipt of air-mail subsidy.[42] In its first decision on the problem, the Board refused the requested suspension on several grounds. It was not clear that much undercutting was actually involved. What did exist was not necessarily undesirable. Not enough was known of costs on an experimental service to pass on the charge of service below cost. Carriers on service-mail rates cannot be said to be offering subsidized com-

---

[41] *Ibid.*, pp. 6–13. This solution was possible because the local-service carriers do not by and large compete directly and because the mail-pay rate, including a subsidy element, can be set for each of them independent of the others.

[42] Air Freight Forwarder Association et al., Motions, Docket No. 3152, 8 CAB 469 (1947).

petition. In any case, the Board instituted an investigation of the general structure of freight rates, which it found to be unsystematic and disorderly. Soon after, the certified trunklines filed further reductions. Without finding them unlawful, the Board declared that competition should not be permitted to increase and insisted on maintaining the status quo until its investigation was complete.[43] It finally turned out, in the Board's estimation, that prevailing freight rates did not cover current or prospective costs of the service, and consequently a schedule of minimum rates was set.[44]

Another illustration of the Civil Aeronautics Board's occasional temptation to act to avert price competition was in an order allowing the trunk carriers to form a committee to deal with the Department of Defense in securing military transport business. Competition for this traffic had become more intense as the major carriers retired large piston-engine transports from domestic service and made them available for special military contracts. The Board expressed concern that the carriers had been making "bids at uneconomically low rates" and hoped that a common negotiating committee would alter the situation.[45]

As we shall see, there have been many other Board decisions directly or marginally related to pricing that reflect a desire to halt any tendency toward lower air fares. Despite its complete authority over the level of fares, the Board has often been unable to shake the fear that price rivalry might somehow get "out of hand."

DISCRIMINATION AND FARE STRUCTURE

Any economist approaching the history of public regulation of transportation rate structures with a theoretical definition of price discrimination in mind is immediately struck by the spottiness and selectivity with which the regulators act. Many sorts of discrimination are theoretically possible in transportation

[43] Suspension and Investigation, Air Freight Tariffs, Docket No. 3170, 8 CAB 621, p. 622 (1947).
[44] Air Freight Rate Investigation, Docket No. 1705 et al., 9 CAB 340 (1948).
[45] Order Serial No. E-14439, Sept. 13, 1959. The order restricted the collusion to carriage of individually ticketed passengers or individually waybilled cargo as a protection to the supplemental carriers, whose authority to seek military contracts was shortly thereafter extended in Order Serial No. E-14484 and E-14485.

services, even though it is often useful broadly to classify them into discrimination between places and between types of customers served. Discrimination can occur because the same charges are extracted for services having different marginal costs as well as because different users pay different amounts for services having identical marginal costs.[46] Laws inhibit discrimination because it is popularly perceived to be unfair, and popular perceptions of price discrimination are highly selective at best. Some forms of discrimination are banned entirely while others are tolerated or even encouraged and required. Some pricing phenomena are branded discriminatory and banned even though they do not or at least may not meet the economist's definition of price discrimination. The regulatory bodies that proceed to enforce statutes banning undue and unjust preference or discrimination, guided by this kind of vague statutory instruction and legislative intent, naturally come up with somewhat uneven results.

The Civil Aeronautics Act is no exception to this pattern. It requires that the carriers maintain "just and reasonable individual and joint rates" and that:

No air carrier or foreign air carrier shall make, give, or cause any undue or unreasonable preference or advantage to any particular person, port, locality, or description of traffic in air transportation in any respect whatsoever or subject any particular person, port, locality, or description of traffic in air transportation to any unjust discrimination or any undue or unreasonable prejudice or disadvantage in any respect whatsoever.[47]

In principle, no form of discrimination would seem to lie beyond the reach of the statute. Indeed, the restriction is not tied to price discrimination but relates to any form of discrimination in service or in the terms of carriage. The question is how to interpret what is "unreasonable," "undue," or "unjust," and how to judge what falls under the headings of discrimination, prejudice, or disadvantage.

The easiest way to describe the Board's handling of discrimination and the fare structure is first to exclude those areas where fairly clear-cut attitudes prevail. One of these, not surprisingly, involves cases of discrimination among persons not based on any

---

[46] See Jack Hirshleifer, "Peak Loads and Efficient Pricing: Comment," *Quarterly Journal of Economics*, LXXI (Aug. 1958), 457–458.

[47] Civil Aeronautics Act, sec. 404 (b); Federal Aviation Act, 72 Stat. 760, 49 U.S.C.A. 1374.

objective and external criteria of selection. Two cases, both decided on June 5, 1950, illustrate this. In an enforcement proceeding against Seaboard & Western Airlines, an air-freight carrier, the company was ordered to cease and desist practices that gave certain customers under contract more favorable rates than others and that discriminated by prejudicial application of the privilege of accumulating shipments over time to secure lower quantity rates.[48] In an enforcement proceeding against Viking Air Transport Co. for numerous alleged violations of the Board's restrictions upon "nonscheduled" carriers, the Board found that Viking had at times charged and received greater and less fares than those provided for in its published tariffs. This was done in contracts for carriage arranged with the United States Immigration and Naturalization Service, not involving service which the Board would recognize as a separate or different type.[49]

Another area in which it has maintained a clear-cut position has been where different charges on comparable routes or services by a carrier have been the result of competitive necessity. In *Air Freight Forwarder Association, et al.,* the Board refused to see discrimination in selective air-freight rate cuts made by the certified cargo carriers in meeting competition from noncertified airlines. It cited rulings to this effect by the Interstate Commerce Commission which had received the approval of the courts.[50] And in *Tour Basing Fares,* the Board reversed the holding of its hearing examiner that discrimination must be inferred only from "factors directly relating to the carriage" in question. Citing Supreme Court authority, the Board declared that the presence of competition was at least one factor external to the particular carriage which might have to be considered. Nevertheless, in this case competitive and other factors were held not to be substantial enough to warrant the proposed discrimination between regular travelers on Latin American routes and those buying special package tours.[51]

Military Tender Investigation, a case dealing with the certified

---

[48] Investigation of Seaboard and Western Airlines, Inc., Docket No. 3346, 11 CAB 372, pp. 381–384 (1950).

[49] Viking Airlines, Aero-Van Express Corporation, and Viking Air Transport Company, Inc. — Noncertificated Operations, Docket No. 3447, 11 CAB 401, p. 411 (1950).

[50] Motions, 8 CAB 469, p. 471 (1947).

[51] Tour Basing Fares, Dockets No. 4443 and 4480, 14 CAB 257, p. 258 (1951).

airlines' discounts to official military traffic, recently raised almost the same points. The Board disagreed with the hearing examiner, who had refused in passing on the reasonableness of the discrimination to look beyond the "conditions related to the actual carriage." It was willing to infer the competitive necessity of the discount from the fact that, before the 10 percent discount on military traffic was adopted in 1949, the airlines had been almost shut out of this market; even with the discount in force, they still had a smaller share of total official military traffic moving by air or rail than they did of all public air and rail passenger travel. The discount, which was held to have *some* cost basis, was allowed.[52] A case that conclusively shows the effectiveness of competitive necessity in justifying a discrimination is *Free and Reduced-Rate Transportation,* in which the Board denied a domestic carrier the right permitted to international carriers to offer free transportation to travel agents. The international lines faced the competitive pressure of similar privileges given by steamships; the domestic lines did not.[53]

One immediately notices that the "competitive necessity" involved in all of these cases arises from competition offered by agencies selling surface transportation. Would the Board let the same justification support a price discrimination used by one air carrier as a competitive weapon against another? The Board's habit of keeping floors under carrier prices and profits points to a negative answer, and in the *Pacific Northwest-Alaska Tariff Investigation,* with such an issue before it, the Board performed according to expectation. Two different discriminations were involved. One was the common faring of Portland and Seattle on air-freight shipments to and from Alaska. This practice of charging identical fares over different distances, which had not been shown to harm Seattle, the shorter-haul city from Alaska, was held justified because surface common carriers also followed it.[54] At issue in the same case was Alaska Airlines' common faring of Fairbanks and Anchorage on passenger flights from Seattle. This

[52] Certificated Air Carrier Military Tender Investigation, Docket No. 9036, decided Feb. 25, 1959, CCH Av. Law Rep. §22,248.01.
[53] Free and Reduced-Rate Transportation Case, Docket No. 2737 et al., 14 CAB 481, pp. 483–484 (1951).
[54] Pacific Northwest-Alaska Tariff Investigation — Supplemental Opinion and Order on Reconsideration, Docket No. 5067 et al., 18 CAB 481, p. 482 (1954).

gave the carrier a competitive advantage in the Seattle–Anchorage market because it could offer at no extra fare an indirect passage via Fairbanks with stopover privileges there. Even though there was no evidence that significant competitive diversion of passengers had been occurring, the Board disallowed the common-faring practice, holding that "we would be unrealistic if we closed our eyes to a dangerous potential." [55]

The Board, then, has approved price discrimination shown to rest firmly on competition with other forms of transportation. It has disapproved discrimination based on arbitrary classifications of customers. However, most of the discrimination cases before the Board are not settled on these simple principles. They turn instead on the meaning which the Board has established for the statutory terms of "unreasonableness," "discrimination," and "prejudice." In hanging a scaffold of meaning on them the Board has set several independent tests which all discriminatory tariffs must pass. To complicate matters further, many of the fare-structure decisions have clearly been influenced by factors not receiving judicial notice in the decisions, and numerous important fare-structure changes have gone into effect without a resulting formal Board opinion.

The most restrictive of these tests, and perhaps the most surprising, is the one which the Board applies to determine whether a tariff is "unjust and unreasonable." The tariff is cast out on these grounds if the Board thinks that it will reduce the profits of either the carrier submitting the tariff or the certified industry as a whole.[56] The Board usually has not been willing to let carriers exercise their own judgment on the feasibility of such price experiments, even where there was no threat of competitive diversion from other air carriers.[57] In most of the discrimination cases involving possible competitive ramifications among the air carriers, the Board has been equally unwilling to leave the verdict to the market mechanism. When the carriers in the New York–

[55] 18 CAB 481, p. 484 (1954).

[56] For a good discussion of the extent to which the Board's desires to assist the industry in maximizing profits controlled the decisions in discrimination cases, see Lucile S. Keyes, "Passenger Fare Policies of the Civil Aeronautics Board," *Journal of Air Law and Commerce*, XVIII (Winter 1951), 46–77.

[57] Investigation of Reduced Excess-Baggage Charges, Docket No. 4330, 12 CAB 75 (1950); The Hawaiian Common Fares Case, Docket No. 3762, 10 CAB 921, pp. 923–924 (1949).

Miami market filed summer-excursion fares for 1950, they were not in agreement over whether these fares had contributed to industry profits in the previous summer when they had first been tried. The Board examined the results in detail and found that they appeared to have been unprofitable and therefore were now to be rejected as unreasonable.[58] In several cases a major issue has been whether a particular carrier's tariff would impair industry profits once it had been met by other carriers; the Board has not rejected fare-structure experiments as unreasonable on this ground, but several divided opinions have resulted.[59] In one of these cases the Board approved of Capital's proposed changes in the family-fare plan. It declared uncharacteristically that "great weight must be accorded the self-interest of the carrier in initiating promotional plans which we expect to be profitable." And it gave little weight to American Airlines' attempt to show that its profits would be hurt by Capital's revised tariff. But here it is hard not to suspect that the Board was influenced by the fact that Capital was in financial difficulty while American was financially one of the strongest of the carriers.[60]

Testing for unprofitability under the rubric of unreasonableness is always a major feature in airline price-discrimination cases, but other tests also seem to be applied regularly. Tariffs can also be unlawful if, in any one of several ways, they are unduly discriminatory or prejudicial. A tariff can fail (1) if it involves selling nearly identical services at different prices, (the "like and contemporaneous service" test), (2) if it involves selling the same service at different prices to nearly identical persons or groups (the "rule of equality" test), or (3) if it denies a city or area fares commensurate with its locational advantage (the "undue prejudice" test). The major puzzles for the Board in the "like and contemporaneous service" situation have come in cases involving coach and excursion fares. General rules are hard to deduce from these. A summer-excursion fare was rejected as

---

[58] Summer Excursion Fares Case, Docket No. 4166, 11 CAB 218, p. 222 (1950).

[59] National Airlines, Inc., DC-6 Daylight Coach Case, Docket No. 4786 et al., 14 CAB 331 (1951); Capital Family Plan Case, Docket No. 8229 et al., decided Oct. 11, 1957, CCH Av. Law Rep. §22,083.01.

[60] Capital Family Plan Case, CCH Av. Law Rep. §22,083.01.

being like and contemporaneous with standard fare services,[61] but a daytime coach service in the most modern equipment was approved because of minor differences in the passenger service provided on the flight.[62] In more recent cases the "like and contemporaneous service" test has evolved into an avowedly cost-based test: two services are presumed to be like and contemporaneous unless the carrier can show that a significant cost difference exists.[63] In one relatively straightforward case, the Board found no unjust discrimination in the fact that accompanied children were carried at substantial discounts while unaccompanied children had to travel on full-fare tickets. It determined that unaccompanied children required greater passenger-service costs than adult passengers, so that in fact a cost difference refuted the possibility that children *en famille* were enjoying an unwarranted preference.[64]

The case which has occasioned the most thorough discussion of cost differences as a test of whether two services are like and contemporaneous is *Capital Group Student Fares*. The Board first had found these fares to be unjustly discriminatory. Capital Airlines had made no attempt to show that significant cost savings resulted from handling student groups as compared to equal numbers of regular passengers. When the Board refused to accept the carrier's argument that a general social policy in favor of students justified the discrimination, no grounds remained for approving the tariff.[65] When the proceeding was reopened, Capital proposed a round-trip fare of 160 percent of the regular first-class fare for members of groups of twenty-five or more students; there was a seven-day limit to the duration of the trips. The tariff was temporary and experimental, a fact which the Board said had something to do with its decision to approve it. Capital was found to have sustained the burden of showing "substantial

---

[61] Summer Excursion Fares Case, p. 223; Investigation of Braniff Airways Excursion Fares, Docket No. 4435, 12 CAB 227, pp. 230–231 (1950).

[62] National Airlines, Inc., DC-6 Daylight Coach Case, 14 CAB 331, p. 332 (1951).

[63] This sort of analysis has been applied in testing both special fares and also special classes of service; the latter are discussed below, pp. 233–237.

[64] Investigation of Full Adult Fares for Unaccompanied Children, Docket No. 7299, 24 CAB 408 (1956).

[65] Capital Group Student Fares — Group Educational Excursion Fares, Docket No. 8456, decided July 31, 1957, CCH Av. Law Rep. §22,065.01.

cost savings." The Board chose to accept Capital's judgment, though the estimates were hotly contested by Delta Air Lines, an intervener in the proceeding.[66] This case returned before the Board for still a third hearing when American Airlines sought reconsideration on five different grounds, notably because Capital had not shown that the cost saving on members of student groups was proportional to the fare discount offered. The Board rejected this contention, which in economic terms amounts to an argument that "discriminations" can be approved only where cost differences render them no discriminations at all. In doing so it called attention to the objectives it sought to further by permitting essentially discriminatory pricing — furthering air carriers in their competition with surface transportation, stimulating new types of airline business in the face of "deceleration in the rate of traffic growth," and the like.[67]

Given the Board's general outlook, this decision is quite proper. Its view of price discrimination is heavily colored by its interest in promoting the gross and net revenues of the air carriers — maximizing the profits to be won by at least certain types of price discriminations. In theory the profitable use of price discrimination consists in setting different profit margins for sales to different groups of customers. Intrinsically it depends on demand (elasticity) differences, and the presence or absence of cost (level) differences is unimportant. Hence, if the "like and contemporaneous service" rule were held to require a price proportional to cost for each class of service, it would exclude many sorts of discrimination that the Board clearly wants to permit. Conversely, since the Board has other grounds for excluding undesirable discriminations, it is hard to see the rule as anything more than a cloak for deciding cases on grounds the Board would prefer not to mention.

A slightly vaguer requirement which the Board imposes on price discrimination, the "rule of equality" or test of reasonably equal treatment, has had its major use in the group-fare cases. The Board has held that offering a reduced fare to a two-

[66] Capital Group Student Fares — Reopened Proceeding, decided March 20, 1958, CCH Av. Law Rep. §22,166.01.
[67] Capital Group Student Fares — Supplemental Opinion and Order, decided Sept. 5, 1958, CCH Av. Law Rep. §22,197.01. See also Certificated Air Carrier Military Tender Investigation, CCH Av. Law Rep. §22,248.03.

person group is an unwarranted discrimination against the single traveler and has suggested that an eligible group should consist of not less than fifteen persons.[68] A two-person group does not differ enough from a one-person "group" to waive the rule of equal treatment — unless the two-person group is a family. The Board has regularly approved family-fare plans, although with some misgiving. It has conceded that the family-fare plan "approaches the outer limits for which reduced fares may properly be approved under the 'rule of equality.' "[69] Not only must the classes of customers identified in discriminatory fare arrangements differ satisfactorily from one another, but also the classes must be defined broadly enough to exclude no closely related subclasses. Thus group fares must be available to *any* applying group.[70] The Board has repeatedly asserted its concern for equal treatment and has insisted that it would permit departures "only when an extraordinarily important and serious business interest of the carrier or of air carriers generally was involved."[71] Furthermore, with the exception of the family-fare plan, it has generally rejected pleas for discriminations that would seem to violate its rule of equality (or the "like and contemporaneous service" test, or both) even though they offer the prospect of increased profits and are in common use elsewhere in the economy.[72] Thus, at least compared to the conduct typical in other transport regulatory agencies, the Board has been fairly tight-fisted in permitting discrimination for persons or groups. But it has refused to face up to the ultimate problem of interclass equity raised by price discrimination — that, in the absence of special cost conditions, creating a discrimination in favor of one class of traffic normally tends to shift a heavier burden on the others. The examiner's decision squarely raised this objection in *Military Tender Investi-*

[68] Free and Reduced-Rate Transportation Case, Docket No. 2737 et al., 14 CAB 481, p. 489 (1951); Group Excursion Fare Investigation, Docket No. 7913, decided April 9, 1957, CCH Av. Law Rep. §22,040.01.

[69] Group Excursion Fare Investigation, CCH Av. Law Rep. §22,040.01. See also Capital Family Plan Case, CCH Av. Law. Rep. §22,083.01.

[70] Free and Reduced-Rate Transportation Case, 14 CAB 481, p. 489 (1951).

[71] *Ibid.,* p. 483

[72] Investigation of Full Adult Fares for Unaccompanied Children, CCH Av. Law Rep. §22,05.03 (*cf.* the dissent by J. P. Adams); Capital Group Student Fares — Group Educational Excursion Fares, CCH Av. Law Rep. §22,065.01. *Cf.* Group Excursion Fare Investigation, CCH Av. Law Rep. §22,040.01.

gation, but the Board, bent on aiding the carriers in their competition with surface transport, refused directly to consider the argument.[73]

The final test for the Board's passing on price discriminations has been used in very few cases. It is the test of undue preference or prejudice, words taken from the Act which the Board has chosen to apply to discriminations among places. The one case in which this sort of discrimination was rejected on the ground of undue prejudice was *Hawaiian Common Fares,* in which the Board found an undue preference given to the more distant of the islands by the practice of charging identical fares to all Hawaiian points from the United States mainland.[74] Other cases involving common fares have arisen, but the undue-preference test has not since been applied in this way. The Hawaiian case involved proposed fares with no competitive ramifications. The two other common-fare cases in which a similar decision might have been written actually went the other way: the air carriers had adopted common-faring practices with a venerable history in other forms of transportation, and the Board was not willing to upset them.[75]

Viewed in broad perspective, the Board's decisions in discrimination cases are only a small part of the story of its control, or lack of control, of the industry's fare structure. Probably the most important feature of the fare structure is its "taper" — the way fares in cents per passenger-mile vary with the distance of the journey. As we shall see later, airline fares started out more or less based on a flat rate per mile with no taper. This meant, in the days of subsidy to all carriers, that the smaller airlines with shorter routes normally had larger commercial losses and received a higher rate of subsidy. The Board recognized no particular problem in this situation until the end of direct subsidy in the

[73] Certificated Air Carrier Military Tender Investigation, CCH Av. Law Rep. §22,248.05.

[74] 10 CAB 921, pp. 924–925 (1949).

[75] West Coast Common Fares Case, Docket No. 4586, 15 CAB 90 (1952); Pacific Northwest-Alaska Tariff Investigation — Supplemental Opinion and Order on Reconsideration, Docket No. 5067 et al., 18 CAB 481, p. 482 (1954). In the former case, the Board declared: "The natural result of this long history of common fares is that the economy of west coast cities, intermediate points as well as major terminals, has become geared to the concept that all will compete equally insofar as the more important passenger rates from the east are concerned" (p. 92).

early 1950s left it to regulate a group of carriers with sharply unequal levels of profitability. The first dollar-a-ticket increase was an initial step, and the abortive general passenger-fare investigation which followed it was supposed to go into the problem. During the second general fare investigation another dollar-a-ticket increase was granted as an emergency measure without any specific justification in terms of its impact on the taper of air fares. At the close of this investigation another fare increase involved a third dollar a ticket, again justified only in terms of its impact on the general fare level. From the Board's own statements one has no way of knowing whether or not the fare structure with regard to distance has come into some sort of proper adjustment. Theoretically, the Board has committed itself to holding a full investigation of the general fare structure. Key members of the staff, however, are pessimistic about such an investigation because the issues would expand indefinitely and the resulting record would be too incomplete, too diffuse, or too stale to warrant any real reforms. They feel that the Board is condemned to the *ad hoc* approach represented by the dollar-a-ticket increases. There have been a few less consequential actions by the Board relating to the distance taper of fares, mostly concerned with whether certain surcharges should have a taper. The Board at first suspended United's dollar surcharge over the coach fare on its "Custom Coach" flights because this surcharge was independent of distance.[76] The surcharges filed by most carriers on turbojet aircraft did bear a rough distance taper, and the Board required those which did not to conform to this pattern.[77]

Another important aspect of the fare structure which the Board has controlled rather loosely has been the differential fares among classes of service. When coach service was first introduced a decade ago, the Board showed some interest in American Airlines' idea of pricing so that, at a given load factor, airplanes in coach service on a route would yield the same net revenue as those in first-class service; that is, the fare difference would just offset the difference in seating density. This would be quite close to a nondiscriminatory pricing pattern. This standard, enforced

[76] Order Serial No. E-12291, March 27, 1958; E-12411, April 25, 1958; E-12976, Sept. 16, 1958.
[77] Order Serial No. E-14825, Jan. 13, 1960.

for a time, later partially disappeared from view as the Board alternately pressed for higher coach fares to maximize profits and lower ones to develop traffic. The Board resisted only the carriers' most drastic moves to provide first-class service at coach prices or coach service at first-class prices. Recently following the lead of United Air Lines, a group of east-west long-haul carriers, the most profitable segment of the industry, applied for as much as a 17 percent increase in long-haul coach fares on jet aircraft. This would have moved coach fares to about 75 percent of first class, compared to a level of roughly two thirds implied by the old equivalent-density standard. It would have given the carriers in question an 8 percent over-all fare increase on what were already their most profitable runs. Not only was it approved by the Board over an objection from the Administrator of General Services, but it was approved without formal hearings, in response to the carriers' complaint that, without a narrowing of the differential, too many business travelers would switch to coach sections of the jets.[78] Was such a narrowing of the differential discriminatory? If not, should it not have been narrowed by reducing first-class fares somewhat? Is the differential based on cost differences, or should it be? The Board's apparent failure to inquire into these questions in its haste to aid an increase in industry profit rates typifies its lack of meaningful standards for controlling the fare structure and its lack of continuous scrutiny of the general fare level.

The handling of surcharges has been subject to similar uncertainties. National Airlines, in first introducing domestic jet service, charged first-class fares in the coach compartment and a surcharge on first-class seats. The Board suspended the former feature, but not until the introductory season was past, and the proceeding was dismissed without prejudice because National indicated that it did not wish to use this pattern in the future.[79] When American Airlines later filed identical surcharges on coach and first-class service, the Board at first approved the first-class surcharge but rejected the coach surcharge on the basis of the old seating-density standard; seating in jet coach compartments was

---

[78] Order Serial No. E-15894, Oct. 7, 1960. See also *Traffic World,* CVI (Oct. 8, 1960), 121.
[79] Order Serial No. E-13232, Dec. 4, 1958.

comparable in density to that in piston-engine coaches. However, American, supported by several other trunklines, petitioned for reconsideration, threatening not to use the first-class surcharge unless it could employ one for coach service as well. The Board gave in, arguing weakly that the jet coach service had a higher quality in speed and comfort that warranted the higher price.[80]

A final important class of decisions on fare structure that has had rather casual consideration from the Board has been that dealing with pricing new varieties of coach service. It approved a 25 percent reduction in off-peak, off-season flights in the New York–Miami and related east-coast markets on the grounds that, even at the resulting low (three cents a mile) fares, the carriers would cover out-of-pocket costs.[81] This night-coach service operated only on certain nights of the week. Later, when Northeast Airlines asked to extend it to all nights of the week because of the great shift in load factors that had occurred, the Board heeded the pleas of Northeast's rivals and suspended this revision.[82] Here the Board's fear of the competitive impact of proliferating classes of service seems to have come into play.[83] This force was only partly responsible for its rejection of an effort by Continental Air Lines to create a new low-priced brand of coach service; here the complicating factor was that Continental offered this as part of a package that involved increasing the fare on regular coach and first-class travel. The Board, sharply divided, could agree on no course but rejection of the whole package.[84] Again, the picture is one of intermittent control of the fare structure, laced with the Board's fears of contributing to excessive competition.

CONCLUSION

The Civil Aeronautics Board sometimes inspects closely the price discriminations appearing in tariff filings, seeking to make sure that such devices will tend to raise industry traffic and

[80] Order Serial No. E-13395, Jan. 16, 1959; E-13417, Jan. 22, 1959.

[81] Order Serial No. E-13821, May 1, 1959. See also *Traffic World,* CIII (April 25, 1959), 131.

[82] Order Serial No. E-14292, July 30, 1959; E-14434, Sept. 8, 1959. See also *Traffic World,* CIV (Sept. 5, 1959), 100.

[83] As it did in the rejection of a Northern Consolidated Airlines tariff in Order Serial No. E-13829, May 5, 1959.

[84] Order Serial No. E-13037, Sept. 30, 1958.

profits and, especially, that they will not cut individual carriers' profits or set off something resembling price competition. The other tests the Board applies in such cases all operate as constraints on profit maximization through price discrimination, and they are based on largely noneconomic values and criteria. The Board's rulings on issues of discrimination have touched only those forms that have come into its line of vision, and these have appeared usually because they bore some relation to the competitive marketing strategies of the carriers. It has ignored the many possible discriminations in the carriers' fare structure, such as those between coach and first-class passengers, long-haul and short-haul passengers, peak-season and off-season passengers, and so forth. Considering all of the agency's decisions on pricing, the overriding concern has been with "sound economic conditions." Regulation has been sporadic and has operated without any apparent clear-cut standards. Furthermore, the Board generally has been without the cost and demand information necessary for knowing the consequences of various pricing alternatives, and it has been without the accounting control to see that what cost information it did have could be reliably interpreted.

The Board's control of the general fare level has been at least as incomplete. One authority declares that "the Board has not initiated price policy or pricing actions except where a policy vacuum existed . . . or where there was an irreconcilable conflict among industry groups." [85] The fact that the *General Passenger Fare Investigation* case settled some of the crucial issues involved in regulating the fare level as many as twenty-two years after the Board came into being tells part of the story. That it did not settle very many of them tells the rest. Like other regulatory agencies, the Civil Aeronautics Board seeks to find the appropriate level of prices by allowing an appropriate margin of profit. What of the level of cost on which this profit margin floats? What of the incentives provided to the carriers for lower costs and the possibility of lower prices to the public? Issues such as these the Board has never openly faced.

[85] Cherington, pp. 5, 448–450.

8 Regulation of Entry, Exit, and Collusion

Since the Civil Aeronautics Board has never felt a strong obligation to maintain legalistic consistency in its decisions, cases of a type that comes up only now and then are much less likely to show a consistent pattern than those often appearing before the Board. Such individual cases will reflect instead the Board's membership and its major concerns at particular moments in time. In no field is this more true than in the Board's decisions on entry into and exit from the domestic airline industry.

ENTRY INTO DOMESTIC AIR TRANSPORT

The Board's policy toward the entry of new trunkline carriers is easy to summarize: none has been certified since the "grandfather" carriers. New carriers have been admitted to special segments of the industry: Pacific Northwest–Alaska and New York–Puerto Rico, for example. The large irregular carriers of the postwar years were allowed a constrained, wraithlike existence. The local-service carriers are now being permitted to creep into some trunkline markets. But no carrier has come in through the front door to full-fledged trunk status. The basic reasoning is simple. The Board has always had reasons for wanting to expand the route structures of some carriers already certified, to cut their subsidy requirements, to improve their profitability, or to increase their size. Admitting a new carrier to a profitable route structure would erase the opportunity for an underprivileged trunk to move into such routes. It would dissipate profits that could serve to cut the subsidy bill or shore up the position of a marginally profitable firm or maintain unprofitable service on a thin route. The only reason any entry has been permitted is to further the Board's goals of promoting and developing air transportation.

In view of the gallonage of ink already spilled over the Board's entry policies,[1] the cases that support these generalizations will

---

[1] For example, Lucile S. Keyes, *Federal Control of Entry into Air Transportation,* and "A Reconsideration of Federal Control of Entry into Air Transportation," *Journal of Air Law and Commerce,* XXII (Spring 1955), 192–202;

be noted very briefly. There were numerous early cases offering the Board a choice between an existing carrier and a new one for a particular route. The award always went to the grandfather carrier. The same results appear in more recent cases. Supplemental carriers have sought regular certification as coach specialists in both the St. Louis–Florida and the Chicago–Florida markets. Although expansion of coach service had been accepted by this time as a goal in the Board's route decisions, certified carriers were chosen instead. Furthermore, in contrast to the elaborate analyses the Board often undertakes in choosing among certified carriers, these applicants were dismissed with the brief findings that they would create excessive diversion if admitted *along with* an additional grandfather carrier.[2] The Board's attitudes were controlled by its desire to expand the route systems of the smaller certified carriers and, at least at times, to control the profit level or the subsidy requirements of the trunk industry.

Though the Board has kept out new trunks in line with attaining "sound economic conditions," it has sometimes sought to admit new carriers to achieve its promotional objectives. An excellent example is the Board's policy on local-service carriers. An investigation made during World War II suggested that the prospects were not encouraging for local air service to be provided at a reasonable cost to the government. The service would be an experiment that could succeed only "by taking advantage of every possible economy." New carriers were to be given temporary life to pursue this goal.[3] Other experiments for which the Board has chosen new carriers have been all-cargo service, helicopter service, all-expense air tours, and specialized coach service between continental United States and Puerto Rico and Alaska. In each instance the Board has viewed the proposed service as sufficiently novel and sufficiently uncertain to require the attention of a new "specialist" carrier whose life hangs on the success of the experiment.

H. K. Maclay and W. C. Burt, "Entry of New Carriers into Domestic Trunkline Air Transportation," *Journal of Air Law and Commerce,* XXII (Spring 1955), 131–156; C. R. Cherington, "The Essential Role of Large Irregular Air Carriers," *Journal of Air Law and Commerce,* XIX (Autumn 1952), 411–422.

[2] Great Lakes-Southeast Service Case, Docket No. 2396 et al., decided Sept. 30, 1958, CCH Av. Law Rep. §22,211.02.

[3] Investigation of Local, Feeder, and Pick-up Air Service, Docket No. 857, 6 CAB 1 (1944).

The specialist doctrine has been used by the Board now and then in route cases and has not proved easy to apply consistently. It has been even less manageable in certification cases. The cases mentioned so far suggest that a new carrier will never be picked to supply a standard service but will always be chosen for a completely novel and risky one. What if the contemplated service has some new and pioneering elements but also treads on the market interests of the established carriers? This is precisely the dilemma which the nonscheduled air-coach operators have posed for nearly two decades. No other issue in its history has involved the Board in more troublesome political pressures or so well illustrated the gaps and weaknesses of the Board's regulatory policies. The long story of the "nonskeds" reveals more about the political setting of the Board's decision making than it does about control of entry into air transport, and as such it will be treated later in Chapter 12. The point to be noted here is the Board's effort to enforce the specialist doctrine and to make the nonscheduled coach operators a separate segment of the air-transport industry. Unwilling to admit the nonskeds to regular trunkline status, and unable or unwilling to dispose of them entirely, the Board has sought to keep them in a special status for fifteen years, in the face of growing evidence that the special status is not a viable one.

The irregular carriers had grown up after World War II through an exemption created by the Board before the war under provisions of the Civil Aeronautics Act that allowed the Board to exempt from certification requirements those classes of carriers for whom the economic regulations of Title IV would be onerous. The Board in its early days was swamped with applications for certificates of public convenience and necessity by the grandfather carriers and others seeking entry to the industry. Yet the wording of the act was such that a number of small-scale air-taxi operators and others flying unscheduled services from a fixed base would have been put out of business without some action on the part of the Board. Thus an exemption was created for nonscheduled operations making it unnecessary to obtain individual Board authorizations. At this time all such firms used single-engine planes and in no way competed with the certified carriers. After the war, although trunkline profits were low, there was excess demand and high profits to be made on heavily traveled

long-haul routes. Under the old exemption for nonscheduled
operations, a number of firms using war-surplus aircraft entered
the industry. Charging lower fares than the certified industry
and appealing to price-conscious customers traveling for personal
reasons, they expanded their operations until in the year ending
September 30, 1951, they flew 6.7 percent as many revenue
passenger-miles as the certified airlines. The Board opened a
proceeding in July 1944 on the exemption regulation for nonscheduled operators, but it was only after the record was developed in the case that the postwar expansion of the long-haul
nonskeds became apparent. The Board ultimately made no change
in the existing exemption for nonscheduled operations other than
imposing a registration requirement, but it did try to indicate
more precisely the limits of the meaning of "nonscheduled" and
expressed the hope that the number of borderline cases would
diminish as experience grew.[4]

This hope fairly soon proved fruitless for a great number of
reasons. The sort of irregular air service which the Board contemplated does not tend to be particularly profitable — or at least
it is much less profitable than a regular route operation in dense,
long-haul domestic passenger markets. The irregular coach operators had every incentive to evade the Board's regulations and run
a regular route service. Lacking sufficient enforcement personnel
and having many other problems besides this one, the Board
finally admitted the impossibility of keeping the irregular carriers
irregular under its rules. On June 10, 1947, it amended section
292.1 of its economic regulations, distinguishing between large
and small irregular carriers in language obviously intended to
restrict the large ones. A year later it instituted a general investigation and froze all applications for letters of registration
under the old exemption rule. On December 10, 1948, a revised
section 292.1 was issued withdrawing the blanket exemption.
Hereafter the large irregular carriers would be required to secure
individual exemptions from the certification requirement of the
act. The Board saw this as the only way to enforce its concept of

[4] Investigation of Nonscheduled Air Services, Docket No. 1501, 6 CAB 1049
(1946); Page Airways, Inc., Investigation, Docket No. 1896, 6 CAB 1061
(1946); Trans-Marine Airlines, Inc., Investigation of Activities, Docket No.
1967, 6 CAB 1071 (1946). See also Keyes, *Federal Control of Entry into Air
Transportation,* chap. 5.

nonscheduled operations and to sort out the violators offering a regular route service.[5]

While these efforts to enforce its concept of the noncertified coach carrier went on, the applications of twenty-one of the nonskeds for certification proceeded in a case, *Transcontinental Coach-Type Service*. Only four of these survived the heavy costs of pursuing such an application to final decision, and all were rejected. The Board found no evidence that the proposed regular coach services differed significantly from those which certified carriers could provide, though the latter had not done so aggressively up to that time. The specialist doctrine was thus not applicable. Coach service provided on a charter or irregular basis was a specialist function; coach service on a regular scheduled basis was not. With this shaky distinction accepted, the only basis for certifying the nonskeds would be a need for point-to-point competition in major markets. This the Board could not find. The implicit underlying argument was that it wished to maintain the prevailing volume of unprofitable service in thin markets and yet continue the reduction of public subsidy. Supernormal profits in the rich markets where the nonskeds sought to operate were necessary to subsidize loss operations. The Board ignored the possibility of removing the need for rich routes to subsidize thin ones by means of fare-structure adjustments.[6] Even the partial dissent by Member J. P. Adams questioned only part of this implicit reasoning — the insistence on continuing the reduction of total subsidy and the assumption that the trunkline operators were now ready and willing to extend coach service.[7]

With full entry into trunkline service denied the irregulars, the Board began a long and twisting proceeding aimed at giving the nonskeds individual exemptions to the certification procedure, as provided in the 1948 revision of section 292.1 of the economic regulations. When this proceeding finally concluded in 1959,[8] the

[5] For an account of these moves, see J. P. Moore and K. R. Hahn, "Regulation of Irregular Air Carriers," *Cornell Law Quarterly*, XXXV (Fall 1949), 48–76.

[6] Transcontinental Coach-Type Service Case, Docket No. 3397 et al., 14 CAB 720 (1951).

[7] *Ibid.*, pp. 728–730.

[8] For a biased but useful account of this proceeding, see William V. Henzey, "CAB's Whitewash of Non-Sked Operators Imperils Structure of Airline System," *American Aviation*, XIX (Dec. 5, 1955), 80–81.

Board decided to give the survivors special certificates of public convenience and necessity rather than exemptions; this was the traditional method, and the "stability, dignity, and protection of a certificate" was warranted for carriers found to be essential parts of the national transportation network. Each of the approved supplemental carriers receiving a certificate was permitted a maximum of ten trips per month between any given pair of points. The twenty-six certificates initially issued were all temporary, twelve running for five years and fourteen for two years.[9] The trunks, which fought this case to the bitter end, contended that this solution was inconsistent with the act. They held that certificates could not be issued limiting the number of trips, that they had to be route authorizations stated in terms of terminals and intermediate points, and that public convenience and necessity could not be proved for a whole class of carriers at once. The Board sought to answer each point in its opinion, but it was hard to avoid the feeling that the trunks had the stronger legal argument. And indeed they did succeed in getting the supplemental carriers' certificates overturned in the courts.[10] Congress hastily acted to keep this decision from putting the supplementals out of business until the Board could come up with some other expedient. The irregular carriers were in as uncertain a position as ever. Even the ten-trip authorization did not seem to provide them a viable operating arrangement.

The nonsked experience seems to imply that the Board will not permit direct entry of new trunklines. At any rate, it has not in the past and seems unlikely to do so in the future. A Board that is "conservative" in outlook surely will not do so. One that is "liberal" is likely to pursue the goal of equalizing the relative strength of existing carriers, a procedure at odds with the admission of new ones. The only effective kind of entry into domestic air transport is likely to be by the roundabout method of entry in a specialist role that later dissolves into open competition with the established trunk carriers. This has been happening to

[9] Large Irregular Air Carrier Investigation, Docket No. 5132 et al., decided Jan. 28, 1959, CCH Av. Law Rep. §22,247. See also, Large Irregular Air Carrier Investigation — Supplemental Opinion and Order, Docket No. 5132, 22 CAB 838 (1955).

[10] United Air Lines, Inc. v. Civil Aeronautics Board, 278 F.2d 446 (1960). See also *Traffic World,* CV (April 16, 1960), 138–139.

some degree with the local-service carriers and is likely to continue. Advances in helicopter technology could open the possibility for the existing metropolitan helicopter airlines to enter dense short-haul markets. The admission of Alaska and Hawaii as states removes the legal distinction between routes to these areas and mainland routes; Pan American World Airways[11] and the two specialized Alaska carriers now have "domestic" routes.

To the economist concerned with allocative efficiency, the important thing about the Board's control of entry is not the possible past injustices to the irregular coach operators so much as it is the maintenance of a reservoir of potential entrants to domestic trunkline routes. Viewed in this light, the Board's historic antipathy to direct entry into trunkline status looks less reprehensible and less menacing for the future. This is especially true since the threat of entry often seems nearly as effective a check on an industry's market conduct as does periodic actual entry. The airline industry is no exception to this. At an early stage in the nonsked exemption proceedings, the Board used the threat of easier treatment of the irregular carriers as a club to induce the certified trunks to cut their coach fares from 4.5 to 4 cents a mile.[12] The trunks have long been suspicious of the local-service carriers and have tried to circumscribe their operations. When "feeder" air

[11] Pan American's route system gives it an enormous incentive to seek domestic routes, since it operates its overseas routes from a number of bases on the periphery of the United States without any routes directly linking these bases. This surely complicates the scheduling of planes into bases for maintenance and forces a number of ferry flights for maintenance purposes which an airline with an integrated route pattern could manage on commercial schedules. Pan American has made at least three major formal efforts to solve this problem. An application for an extensive domestic route structure was turned down in Pan American Airways, Inc. — Domestic Route Case, Docket No. 1803, 11 CAB 852 (1950). It was denied the privilege of carrying international passengers traveling beyond Miami free of charge on ferry flights from New York to Miami in Pan American Ferry Flight Case, Docket No. 5477, 18 CAB 214 (1953). More recently, Pan American succeeded in reaching agreements with National Airlines giving Pan American options covering 35 percent of National's common stock. Voting rights held on the stock actually exchanged between the carriers were to remain with a trustee until 1966, but Pan American thereby had at least potential future entry into the domestic market via National's routes. (See Carl Rieser, "George T. Baker's Feud with the World," *Fortune,* LXI [March 1960], 212.) The Board, however, frustrated this by ordering divestiture of the stock interest in Order Serial No. 15541, July 14, 1960 (Pan American-National Agreement Investigation, Docket No. 9921 et al.).

[12] *Aviation Week,* LXI (March 10, 1952), 64.

service was first contemplated, the trunks sought to pre-empt the field, only to be turned away by the Board on other grounds. There have been some conspicuous feuds between trunks and local-service carriers with actual or suspected ambitions to become full-fledged trunkline competitors.[13]

EXIT FROM DOMESTIC AIR TRANSPORT

Firms can disappear from domestic passenger transport through merger, bankruptcy, or suspension of their certificates by the Board. The Board has never faced the problem of exit by a bankrupt carrier in its pure form, though the recent difficulties of Capital Airlines presented the Board with a merger as an alternative to a bankruptcy. A number of cases involving mergers have been heard, along with a few involving the suspension of temporary certificates held by local-service carriers.

Most of the Board's discussion in many decisions on mergers[14] deals with two matters which are not of much pertinence here. One is the provision of protective labor conditions to guard the rights and seniority of the personnel of the carrier being absorbed. The other is the valuation of the assets of the disappearing carrier as they are to appear on the books of the absorbing carrier, a matter that is important to the Board for preventing inflation of the capital structure on which a return is allowed. The Board started out by showing some enthusiasm for preventing the purchase price of a merging carrier from containing any franchise value for the publicly conferred certificate of convenience and necessity. However, it soon encountered a case in which an acquisition could occur only on payment of something over the value of the tangible assets involved.[15] Subsequently, the Board

[13] See, for example, William J. Coughlin, "Bonanza Strikes Gold on Coast," *Aviation Week*, LVII (Oct. 13, 1952), 92–96.

[14] For analysis of these cases see Louis E. Black, Jr., "Realignment of the Domestic Airline Route Pattern," *Journal of Air Law and Commerce*, XV (Autumn 1948), 409–433; Paul D. Zook, "Recasting the Air Route Pattern by Airline Consolidations and Mergers," *Journal of Air Law and Commerce*, XXI (Summer 1954), 293–311; A. J. Thomas, Jr., *Economic Regulation of Scheduled Air Transport, National and International* (Buffalo, 1951), pp. 148–153.

[15] Acquisition of Mayflower Airlines, Inc., by Northeast Airlines, Inc. — Supplemental Opinion, Docket No. 1083, 6 CAB 139 (1944). Also see the supplemental opinion in the TWA-Marquette merger, Marquette Airlines, Inc. — Certificate of Public Convenience and Necessity; Acquisition by TWA, Docket No. 7–401(E)1, 3 CAB 111 (1941).

has allowed any price set in arm's-length bargaining between the parties, though it has implied that a clearly extreme price for intangibles might be disallowed. However, the purchased assets could go into the investment base for rate-making purposes only to the extent of the original cost less allowable depreciation.[16] In one contrary case the Board, yielding to its periodic wish to promote mergers, permitted a small write-up as an incentive to advance a merger that it could not order directly.[17] It also recognized, in the United-Western route-transfer case, that when earnings are controlled for the whole industry and not for individual firms, as with unsubsidized trunklines, controlling the capital transactions of individual carriers becomes less important.[18]

The Civil Aeronautics Act directs the Board to disapprove mergers if they tend to create a monopoly and thereby restrain competition or jeopardize another carrier. Thus mergers might be turned down either because they restrict competition in particular markets or areas or because they give a carrier a position of dominance in size over its rivals. Both prospects have been grounds for disallowing mergers. However, the wording of the statute is even more restrictive: approved mergers must be found to be in the public interest. Thus an agreement could be disallowed because it conferred no significant benefits, even in the absence of monopoly or "bigness" considerations.

Largely because of the particular mergers that have come up for the Board's approval, only two of these three sets of criteria have been very much developed — the extent to which a merger may promote bigness or dominance and the extent to which a merger must furnish certain advantages for the public interest. In several cases the Board has held that the creation of some point-to-point monopoly is not a sufficient basis for rejecting a merger.[19] But only two domestic mergers have been allowed to

[16] See, for example, Colonial-Eastern Acquisition Case, Docket No. 6998, 23 CAB 500, p. 523 (1956).

[17] West Coast-Empire Merger Case, Docket No. 5220, 15 CAB 971 (1952); see also Zook, pp. 301–311. The Board's willingness to make an exception in this case probably also reflected the fact that it had previously disallowed a merger agreement involving West Coast Airlines, after having encouraged the carrier to seek such a merger.

[18] United Air Lines, Inc. — Western Air Lines, Inc., Acquisition of Air Carrier Property, Docket No. 2839, 8 CAB 298, pp. 320–321 (1947).

[19] For example, Marine Airways, Alaska Air Transport, Inc. — Consolidation, Docket No. 358, 3 CAB 315, p. 319 (1942).

take place, despite some reduction in point-to-point competition. One was the absorption of Mid-Continent Airlines by Braniff, in which the ills of eliminating competition between Kansas City and Houston were found to be offset by the improved service which the combined carrier could offer.[20] Recently the Board allowed a large merger between United Air Lines and Capital Airlines that reduced competition in a number of markets, but this was a special case which it declared would have no standing as a general precedent. With Capital on the verge of bankruptcy and threatened with foreclosure by Vickers Aircraft, the Board felt that it had to invoke the "failing business doctrine" because the prospect of the carrier's rehabilitation was remote. Although the decision formally excluded rehabilitation through public subsidy because lengthy and time-consuming proceedings would be required, in effect it was saying that sufficient subsidy to revitalize the carrier was a political impossibility.[21]

More proposed airline mergers have raised the threat of bigness or dominance than that of point-to-point monopoly. A merger between United and Western was turned down in 1940 because the combined carrier would have offered east-west service from all four major west-coast cities, while its transcontinental rivals served only two. Furthermore, the elimination of Western's independent north-south route would have destroyed the competitive check of connecting service to United's monopoly of north-south service along the coast.[22] The American–Mid-Continent merger case also elicited from the Board an explicit discussion of its objections to allowing a carrier to become dominant in a region.[23] Two interveners, Braniff and Delta, argued that by absorbing Mid-Continent, a north-south line running at right angles to American's transcontinental route, American would get control

[20] Braniff–Mid-Continent Merger Case, Docket No. 5376, 15 CAB 708, p. 735 (1952).

[21] United-Capital Merger Case, Docket No. 11699, decided April 3, 1961, Order No. E-16605, pp. 2–14.

[22] United Air Lines Transport Corporation — Acquisition of Western Air Express Corporation, Docket No. 270, 1 CAA 739, pp. 745–747 (1940). For a similar decision in a case involving small Alaskan carriers, see Acquisition of Cordova Air Service, Inc., by Alaska Airlines, Docket No. 930, 4 CAB 708, p. 712 (1944).

[23] American Airlines, Inc., Acquisition of Control of Mid-Continent Airlines, Inc., Docket No. 2068, 7 CAB 365 (1946).

of the connecting traffic originating on Mid-Continent's routes. Instead of delivering traffic impartially to American and other connecting carriers, Mid-Continent's routes would be operated to favor the transfer of connecting passengers to American's other flights. The Board did not analyze this prospect in great detail, but did find that this diversion "would be inconsistent with sound economic conditions in air transportation." [24] In the tangled Eastern-Colonial merger, the Board made a somewhat similar finding. Merger of Colonial with Eastern Air Lines rather than with National Airlines would be preferable because less diversion from other carriers would result. This finding was made despite Eastern's being much larger than National.[25]

Another twist has been given to the "bigness" objection to mergers among the local-service carriers. Two large end-on combinations of local-service carriers have been rejected because of the sheer geographic coverage of the resulting carrier and the potential competition it could offer the trunklines; a third merger nearly went down for the same reason. This objection first turned up in Member Josh Lee's dissent from the Board's approval of the merger of Arizona and Monarch Airlines into what became Frontier Airlines.[26] The majority approved the merger because Arizona had not gathered enough capital to get into operation on its own. But Lee felt that the decision pointed toward creating a series of second-string trunklines on perpetual subsidy. A year later the majority took this position when it was handed a merger proposal between Southwest Airways and West Coast Airlines.[27] These two carriers, put together, would have comprised a local-service system covering the whole west coast and serving its four largest cities. United and Western, as interveners, objected violently. The Board noted that the merged carrier could not provide effective competition with the trunks without further legal action to secure skip-stop authority, but it still desired to "remove the fear expressed by the trunk lines in this case." A recent merger

[24] *Ibid.*, pp. 378–381.
[25] Eastern-Colonial, Acquisition of Assets, National-Colonial Integration Investigation — Supplemental Opinion, Dockets No. 5569, 5666, 18 CAB 781 (1954).
[26] Arizona-Monarch Merger, Docket No. 3977 et al., 11 CAB 246, p. 255 (1950).
[27] Southwest-West Coast Merger Case, Docket No. 4405, 14 CAB 356 (1951)

proposal between North Central and Lake Central Airlines was rejected on the same grounds. North Central operates northwest of Chicago and Detroit, Lake Central in the Great Lakes states. The combined carrier would have five thousand miles of routes and serve eighty cities; it "would take on characteristics akin to a trunk-line carrier and pose the kind of threat to existing trunk lines which was of concern to the Board when it denied approval of the proposed merger in the *Southwest-West Coast Merger Case*."[28] Summarizing these cases, the Board has been fairly hard on merger proposals containing the threat of bigness. Bigness here is to be interpreted as a potential increase of competition with other carriers rather than as the dominance of absolute size in any broader sense. The Board gives a very sympathetic ear to airline interveners who fear the competitive threat of a merged carrier.

Beyond the tests of bigness and monopoly in merger cases, there remains the requirement that some affirmative public interest must be shown. One goal the Board has always found to be in the public interest is a reduction in the subsidy bill. Most of the local-service merger cases mention specific estimates of the annual saving expected; and, in the absence of "bigness" problems, this is a sufficient showing of public interest.[29] In other cases the gain in the public interest lay in "route integration," here referring generally to the offering of significant, new single-carrier service. This advantage had to do with the Board's approval of the Braniff–Mid-Continent, Delta–Chicago & Southern, and Continental–Pioneer mergers.[30] It is notable that no other airlines objected seriously in any of these three cases. Conversely, a lack of route integration has been either a main or a subsidiary reason for turning down several mergers. It was one of the main grounds

[28] North Central-Lake Central Acquisition Case, Docket No. 5770 et al., decided July 9, 1957, CCH Av. Law Rep. §22,057.01.

[29] Monarch-Challenger Merger Case, Docket No. 4129, 11 CAB 33 (1949) — granted over the objections of Continental and Inland before the Southwest-West Coast case; West Coast-Empire Merger Case, Docket No. 5220, 15 CAB 971 (1952); *cf.* Southwest-West Coast Merger Case, 14 CAB 356, p. 357 (1951). Eliminating a subsidized trunkline also lay behind the Eastern-Colonial case.

[30] Braniff–Mid-Continent Merger Case, Docket No. 5376, 15 CAB 708, p. 733 (1952); Delta–Chicago and Southern Merger Case, 16 CAB 647, pp. 690–691 (1952); Continental–Pioneer Acquisition Case, Docket No. 6457 et al., 20 CAB 323, pp. 332, 364 (1955).

for rejecting a merger between National and Caribbean-Atlantic, a carrier based in Puerto Rico whose routes nowhere touched National's.[31] Lack of integration was mentioned largely as a make-weight in rejecting the American–Mid-Continent, Southwest–West Coast, and North Central–Lake Central combinations.

Drawing these matters together, the Board's decisions on mergers seem to have been dominated by the presence or absence of objections from other carriers and the Board's current degree of concern with bolstering carrier revenues. The only merger that reduced competition in many city-pair markets, United-Capital, came in very special circumstances and was designated by the Board as having no significance as a precedent. The finding of public interest has never had much independent weight except when the Board has been eager to cut subsidy requirements. Thus, a merger to which the Board had no objection on other grounds would probably survive the public-interest test, since some additional through service will nearly always result. Viewed from a distance, the Board's standards in merger cases seem somewhat unsatisfactory — indeed, more unsatisfactory than the results they have produced. Elimination of point-to-point competition is important, yet the Board can normally find other carriers wanting entrance to a route if it is of major commercial significance. Avoiding sprawling local-service systems to prevent competition with the trunks seems unimportant because the Board controls all the operating rights needed to effect such competition; the objective of avoiding the inefficient spreading of managerial attention makes more sense, but the Board has never established this as more than a vague possibility. The impact of mergers on the total number of airlines in the industry would hardly seem to be something the Board could ignore, particularly with formal entry into the trunkline industry so effectively closed. Only in the last few years has the Board had its first taste of the problems that can arise in dealing with an industry consisting of an absolutely small number of carriers. Yet it is again showing some enthusiasm for mergers, with no apparent attention to the threat which a shrinking number of carriers poses for the effectiveness of regula-

[31] National–Caribbean-Atlantic Control Case, Docket No. 1907 et al., 6 CAB 671, pp. 676–677 (1946). The Board also objected to an unreasonable purchase price and the fact that the transaction had been illegally completed before its approval.

tion and thereby for the "public interest." According to complaints from the carriers, the mere fact that approval must be secured in a formal proceeding is a deterrent. Noting that the Board has taken, on the average, eleven months to decide merger cases since 1938, one trade publication asserted that "signing of a merger agreement can be corporate suicide if government approval is not gained in a reasonable time" because of problems of employee morale, the time and opportunities for maneuver given to minority stockholders, and the chances given to competing carriers during the period of uncertainty.[32] The carriers naturally would prefer more freedom in consummating merger agreements, but if the industry is tending to shrink to an undesirably small total number of carriers, the procedural blocks to mergers might have their virtues.

Exit from the air-transport industry has occurred not only through merger but also through the Board's occasional failure to renew temporary certificates or its application of its subsidy policies. It has disposed of three local-service carriers by refusal to renew — Florida Airways, Mid-West Airlines, and Wiggins Airlines. Ostensibly these were allowed to lapse on objective criteria — the high ratio of mail pay to commercial revenue of these three as compared to the other local-service carriers. However, only the Florida Airways decision was straightforward and unanimous.[33] The other two cases involved local-service carriers which had been using single-engine aircraft and experiencing very high subsidy requirements. Both, however, proposed to operate DC-3s on an expanded route system at a more favorable ratio of noncommercial to commercial revenue. The Board majority in both of these 1952 cases weighted the cost comparisons against the carriers. In the case of Mid-West, the prospective *first-year* results of its expanded operation were compared to the *current* results of the other local-service carriers.[34] The failure to renew the Wiggins certificate rested mostly on examination of past financial results rather than of the proposed DC-3 operation.[35]

[32] "Will Red Tape Strangle Mergers?" *Airlift,* XXIII (Feb. 1960), 21.

[33] Florida Airways, Inc., Certificate Extension, Docket No. 3511, 10 CAB 93 (1949).

[34] Mid-West Certificate Renewal Case, Docket No. 4052 et al., 15 CAB 424 (1952).

[35] Wiggins Renewal Investigation Case, Docket No. 5055 et al., 16 CAB 483 (1952).

At the time of the Wiggins and Mid-West decisions, the Board had a relatively conservative majority and also apparently felt itself under considerable pressure to cut or at least control the subsidy bill. The statute gives no guidance on such matters except the general "public interest" standard. Thus it is natural that decisions on renewing carrier certificates and other matters heavily affecting the subsidy requirements would reflect the current opinions of the Board's majority and of its influential critics.

For the sake of completeness, we should note here the proceedings instituted by the Board in the late 1940s that looked toward the elimination of carriers from certain routes and possibly the dismemberment of a few carriers. The final decisions in these cases came several years later, when economic conditions in the industry had improved greatly and when the Board was no longer under such heavy fire from outside critics (see Chapter 12). Hence, only one of these final decisions argued the substantive issues of the case at very great length. This was *Through Service Investigation,* dealing with the Twin Cities–Detroit–Washington markets.[36] Even here, there was not much analysis except that of the improvement in the carriers' traffic volume and financial condition since the proceeding had begun.

In addition to outright mergers, from time to time the Board has had to pass on agreements that would give one carrier partial control of another or otherwise affect the independence of a carrier's management. A stock-ownership arrangement that *might* have brought TWA and Northeast Airlines under common control was nullified by requiring that shares controlling Northeast go into a voting trust.[37] The Board approved, on the other hand, an arrangement that clearly brought Northeast and a supplemental carrier, Transocean, temporarily under the control of the same holding company. Calling this its first case dealing directly with common control of two airlines, the Board found the agreement in the public interest for several reasons. Transocean had submitted to five-year control by Atlas Corporation in return for aid which staved off bankruptcy for Transocean. It was felt

[36] Through Service Investigation Twin Cities–Washington–Detroit–Washington, Docket No. 3661, 16 CAB 6 (1952).

[37] Hughes-TWA-Atlas-Northeast Airlines Possible Common Control Case — Order on Reconsideration, Docket No. 8235, decided Aug. 29, 1958, CCH Av. Law Rep. §22,196.

that these facts, plus the absence of actual competition and the near absence of potential competition between the two carriers, placed the agreement in the public interest.[38] In a much more important case, an agreement was rejected that would ultimately have given voting control of National Airlines to Pan American World Airways. The two carriers had agreed on an exchange of stock that would have given Pan American a 25 to 36 percent interest in National. This would have been the largest single block of National stock (and more than that held by its present management), and the Board saw that Pan American would have gained effective control after a voting trust expired in 1966. In finding the agreement adverse to the public interest, the Board focused not on National's loss of independence but on the probable outcome of Pan American's entry into National's domestic routes. Having rejected Pan American's efforts to obtain domestic routes several times before, the Board now declined to let such a result come about indirectly. The Board has always feared the unleashing of the competitive power of Pan American, with its considerable resources and high profits on its international service.[39] Thus the grounds for deciding this case were hardly typical of a situation of merger or combined control, except as they reinforced the American–Mid-Continent decision in suggesting the Board's desire for avoiding the impact of "bigness" on competitive balance.

Thus, in this case as in the outright merger cases, the Board has tried to prevent both the direct monopolization of city-pair markets and also the rise of the "dominance" it felt might lead to monopoly.[40] Nonetheless, viewing broadly the Board's regulation of entry and exit in air transportation, a disturbing pattern appears. There has been no direct entry into competition with the domestic trunk carriers. At the same time there has been a normal attrition of existing trunks through merger. Furthermore, the originally unbalanced character of the industry and the rapid changes that can occur in the profitability of various carriers' operations make periodic disappearances quite likely. As I shall

[38] Transocean-Atlas Case — Control and Interlocking Relationships, Dockets No. 8943 and 10337, decided Aug. 21, 1959, CCH Av. Law Rep. §22,300.01.

[39] Order Serial No. E-15541, July 14, 1960, esp. pp. 7–11.

[40] For similar conclusions, see Keyes, *Federal Control of Entry into Air Transportation,* pp. 253–271.

argue below, in dealing with an air-transport industry of so few carriers, problems of oligopolistic interdependence can make the Board's task of effective regulation very difficult. This interdependence can grow even in such periods as the 1950s, when the degree of concentration in the typical city-pair market was decreasing. But the Board has not cut itself off from a supply of potential entrants to the domestic trunk industry. Furthermore, it has recognized some of the undesirable consequences of having few firms in the industry. (Contrast its vivid consciousness of the drawbacks of having one firm or few firms in the city-pair market.) But, in connection with its policies regulating the number of trunk carriers, it has not fully faced the problem of how to decide the best total number and size distribution of firms for the industry.

REGULATION OF CARRIER AGREEMENTS

The Board's control of effective rivalry in the domestic air-transport industry depends not only on its regulation of the number of firms but also on its policy toward collusion and joint action. Here the Board also has a reasonable amount of power through the requirement of the act that all agreements between carriers be submitted for its approval. Thousands of agreements have been put into effect, most dealing with such minor matters as joint use of certain facilities at airports. However, among these agreements is also the articles of association for the Air Transport Association, the domestic industry's principal trade association. The Board has investigated certain intercarrier agreements having a definite collusive air to them. Most of these inquiries have come in the past decade, not because of increased activity among the carriers but rather because of a stiffening of Board attitudes on such matters.

Although the Board by and large has been easy-going in its treatment of collusive activities among the carriers, one fairly clear pattern emerges. It has allowed collusion on matters where joint-profit maximizing efforts by the carriers were consistent with its own goals of the moment. It has been less generous where agreements could tend to subvert its regulatory efforts.

Several conspicuous developments of the last few years support these generalizations. Consider the Mutual Aid Strike Pact of

1958, an agreement initially among five domestic trunks and Pan American for profit sharing among struck and operating lines in the event of labor disturbances. The airline trade unions entered vigorous protests against this agreement; so did the supplemental or irregular carriers, especially against the feature whereby struck carriers would try to channel business to operating members of the pact.[41] The Board proceeded cautiously. It denied permission to a group of the supplementals to fly over the routes of struck members of the pact, but it also ordered more information to be submitted on how payments among the carriers were to be calculated and how the traffic was to be routed to other members.[42] When the agreement was finally approved a few months later, the provision for rerouting traffic was eliminated and membership had to be open to other carriers.[43] Thus the Board ruled out features of the agreement that might cause strife within the industry, but it let stand the basic pact as a form of collusion against the bargaining power of organized labor.[44]

Equally revealing is the Board's dispute with the military agencies over whether to permit open competitive bidding for military charters, a competition which had carried transatlantic rates down to one third of the regular commercial level. First came the decision in *Military Tender Investigation,* a Board-instituted review of the discriminatory nature of a long-standing 10 percent discount granted by the airlines to military personnel traveling at government expense. Reversing its hearing examiner, the Board found competitive pressure from other transport agencies to justify the resulting discrimination.[45] A few weeks later, the Board proposed an amendment to its economic regulations concerning rates for military traffic that would have established a minimum rate calculated to yield a normal rate of return. Later,

[41] *Traffic World,* CII (Nov. 15, 1958), 97–98.

[42] Order Serial No. E-13308, Dec. 22, 1958; E-13321, January 2, 1959. See also *Traffic World,* CIII (Jan. 3, 1959), 62; CII (Dec. 27, 1958), 81.

[43] Six Carrier Mutual Aid Pact, Docket No. 9977, decided May 20, 1959, CCH Av. Law Rep. §22,269.

[44] This was a split decision, as was the order by which the Board refused reconsideration. See Order Serial No. E-14563, October 19, 1959.

[45] The discount had other features as well and derived from an agreement between the military agencies and the Air Traffic Conference, a wing of the Air Transport Association. See Certificated Air Carrier Military Tender Investigation, Docket No. 9036, decided Feb. 25, 1959, CCH Av. Law Rep. §22,248.

under heavy pressure from the Defense Department and the Sub-committee on Military Operations of the House Committee on Government Operations, the Board withdrew the proposal while registering its continued alarm over "an increasingly unhealthy rate situation." [46] It also issued a decision approving a four-carrier negotiating committee to deal with the government agencies, hoping that the committee could get government purchase of air transportation to augment the Military Air Transport Service on a remunerative contractual basis and end the continuous open bidding for business.[47] The Board recognized the antitrust implications of the committee and imposed requirements limiting the scope of its negotiations and stipulating that any authorized carrier could join. It extended the life of this negotiating committee three times, but finally it lapsed in August 1960, apparently without reaching any agreements with Defense officials.[48]

Counterexamples of the Board's limiting of carrier collusion against "outsiders" are very hard to find. On the surface, one such case seems to be a 1959 decision forcing the Air Traffic Conference to relax its restrictions on persons or firms allowed to become ticket agencies.[49] There are two reasons for discounting this decision, however. First, the airlines' handling of travel agencies had come under heavy fire three years earlier from the Celler Committee, and the Board probably felt that some action was politically desirable. Second, the decision did not touch the basic machinery whereby the carriers collusively established the commissions to be permitted agents on ticket sales. This seems never to have been up for formal Board consideration.

In contrast to this generosity toward collusion aimed at vic-

[46] *Traffic World,* CIII (March 21, 1959), 88; CAB, Statement Concerning Rates for Military Traffic, June 11, 1959, CCH Av. Law Rep. §23,334. Another factor that was surely relevant to the Board's backing down was a lack of unity among the certified carriers on the proposed regulation.

[47] Northwest Airlines, Inc., Pan American Airways, Inc., Seaboard & Western Airlines, Inc., and Trans World Airlines, Inc. — In the Matter of an Agreement Concerning Government Air Transportation Requirements, Agreement CAB No. 13434, decided Aug. 29, 1959, CCH Av. Law Rep. §22,301.

[48] CAB, answers to questions submitted by Senator Estes Kefauver, chairman, Anti-Trust and Monopoly Subcommittee, Senate Committee on the Judiciary. Reprinted in *Traffic World,* CVI (Nov. 26, 1960), 115–120.

[49] ATC Agency Resolution Investigation, Docket No. 8300 et al., decided June 10, 1959, CCH Av. Law Rep. §22,282. Orders Serial No. E-14647, Nov. 12, 1959; E-14924, Feb. 15, 1960.

tims outside the Board's scope of interest, the last few years have seen much hostility to collusion that could run counter to the Board's own objectives. For one thing, the carriers must seek permission from the Board for group discussions of proposed changes in the general level of fares. This has not been handed out very liberally.

One of the Board's first major cases in this area was *Air Freight Tariff Agreement*, decided in 1951 but based on an agreement initially filed in 1946.[50] The Board objected to two provisions relating to the method of forming and changing air-freight tariffs. One was a requirement that, before filing a new tariff with the Board, at least fifteen days' advance notice must be given to the certified industry through the common tariff agent. The Board required this to be put on a voluntary basis. It also objected to a provision calling for discussion of changes in competitive local (not joint) rates, holding that such discussions "must inevitably tend toward the discouragement of individual rate-making based upon competitive considerations." Such discussions could take place only with special Board permission. When this decision was handed down, similar provisions appeared in a passenger-tariff agreement that had been previously filed. The carriers amended this on their own to bring it into line with the *Air Freight Tariff* decision.[51]

At the time of the fare adjustments in the late 1940s, meetings involving the Board and industry representatives seem to have been a common way of planning formal proposals for general fare changes. However, in the 1950s the atmosphere changed rather sharply. In May 1954, with the mark of the 1953–54 recession freshly imprinted on the carriers' profit records, the president of the Air Transport Association made an informal presentation before the Board of the industry's alleged woes. No formal proposals for general fare changes were then before the Board. However, it responded that a rate change on the basis of such short-run evidence would be premature. This view rested on the dismissal of the first *General Passenger Fare* case, in which the Board had committed itself to maintaining stable fares in the

---

[50] Air Freight Tariff Agreement Case, Docket No. 2719 et al., 14 CAB 424 (1951). See also Cherington, pp. 128–132.

[51] Cherington, p. 132.

absence of compelling contrary trends.[52] Weeks later the Board turned down a request from the carriers to hold formal discussions of their financial problems on the ground that no overwhelming need had been demonstrated. Carrier spokesmen grumbled considerably over this order, which seemed to imply that the carriers could make common cause only if the Board had already decided there was some chance of its accepting the proposal they might come up with.[53] In 1958 the Board again substantially denied a request of the Air Transport Association for joint consultation on fares with regard to discounts, stop-over privileges, and circuitous routings. (The request was granted only on the minor item of rounding fares to even-dollar amounts.) Member Chan Gurney dissented, feeling that the Board should be more generous in allowing discussion that might lead to "improvement and simplification of many parts of the fare structure which has remained untouched for these many years. It is obvious that the carriers cannot approach these improvements individually because of the numerous joint rates involved." He felt that the Board should not restrict industry-wide meetings because it held the power of approval over any agreements reached — perhaps a narrow view of the function such meetings might perform.[54]

In 1959 the Board took another step toward a tough attitude on community of interest among the airlines. Over loud protest from the carriers, it instituted a comprehensive investigation of the Air Transport Association. The mildly phrased initiating order made no allegations and justified itself merely by citing the Board's need for information on the activities of the association. It soon reaffirmed this order over an appeal for dismissal from the airlines.[55] At about the same time, the Board instituted a new rule that trade associations could participate in its proceedings only on motion or by the Board's initiative *and* where partici-

---

[52] *American Aviation,* XVIII (June 21, 1954), 28.

[53] W. V. Henzey, "Airlines Again Ask CAB for Authority to Discuss Financial Problem," *American Aviation,* XVIII (Aug. 2, 1954), 36.

[54] Order Serial No. E-12790, July 13, 1958; E-13021, Sept. 12, 1958. See also *Traffic World,* CII (Sept. 20, 1958), 105; CII (July 19, 1958), 96.

[55] Order Serial No. E-13597, March 10, 1959; Air Transport Association of America — In the matter of an inspection and review in the activities of ATA and its instrumentalities, Docket No. 10281, decided June 10, 1959, CCH Av. Law Rep. §22,280.

pation would serve certain specified ends — such as speaking for
the interest of the association (in contrast to its members), chan-
neling information (not opinions) to the Board, or representing
members at their formal request.[56] Also, substantial new reporting
requirements have been imposed on the agency. The inspection
of the association's files was suspended after some 40 percent of
the available documents had been seen, pending court rulings on
certain aspects of the inquiry.[57]

How much conviction lay behind it in the first place? The
Board was certainly under some pressure to conduct the inquiry.
The Celler Committee had been highly critical of the generally
close relations between the Board and the association. Furthermore, the Board's investigation was part of a three-pronged
attack on the association involving a Justice Department inquiry
into possible antitrust violations and a Treasury inquiry into its
tax-exempt status. It was not clear to what extent these investigations were coordinated or, indeed, where the initiative lay. A
trade magazine close to the association speculated:

Why the drive against ATA at this time? Doubtless one major reason is
to justify CAB's contention that ATA should not be a party in CAB proceedings, that it has overstepped its bounds as a trade association and is
participating in many activities without authority or approval of all of
its members.[58]

These instances of the Board's regulation of carrier agreements
and industry meetings are fairly representative of the whole
pattern. Starting with the earlier years, it has been shown that the
Board has never permitted the carriers to form overt agreements
not to compete. Though it has approved concerted action on fares
by the domestic carriers in a few instances, it never sanctioned the
sort of collusive rate making common in other regulated industries
and has been wary about approving arrangements that would lead
in this direction.[59] This confirms the suggestion made above that
the Board's attitude toward overt collusion and agreement among
the carriers has been a fairly consistent one. It has condoned

[56] *Traffic World,* CIII (June 20, 1959), 98.
[57] *Traffic World,* CVI (Nov. 26, 1960), 116.
[58] Editorial, "How Far Does Federal Authority Go?" *Airlift,* XXII (April
1959), 7. See also *Traffic World,* CIII (April 4, 1959), 96.
[59] Keyes, *Federal Control of Entry into Air Transportation,* pp. 282–292.

nearly all common-cause pacts directed toward the carriers' handling of their mutual problems or common enemies, permitting some activities that probably would not have survived the scrutiny of antitrust officials in an unregulated industry. However, in the 1950s the Board grew increasingly suspicious of common actions that might effectively exploit the airlines' customers or frustrate the Board's regulatory efforts.

9 Entry into City-Pair Markets

Decisions in route cases, like those dealing with air fares and price discrimination, must be studied with close reference to the time at which they were made. Although the carriers' desires for new routes have fluctuated greatly, the fluctuations of the Board's attitudes have played the controlling role, especially in route cases involving requests to establish competitive service. Just as with regard to the general passenger-fare level, at times the Board has seemed to bend in the face of outside pressure to modify its attitude toward competitive route authorizations and noncompetitive route extensions into thin territory.

A definite set of political-economic forces seems to control these shifts in the Board's attitude. The mechanism is quite simple for noncompetitive route authorizations. New routes without competitive ramifications, usually for subsidized carriers, have always been uneventful for the Board, though the cases are time-consuming and awkward. The main problem has been balancing the intrinsic worth and developmental prospects of the extra service against the extra subsidy it is likely to entail. Where this balance is struck depends largely on the amount of pressure on the Board to cut subsidy requirements. In the first years of the Eisenhower administration, this pressure was heavy and the Board was correspondingly tight with new route authorizations; in the later 1950s, faced with growing congressional support for the local-service carriers, as manifested by the legislation requiring their permanent certification, the Board grew bolder with route extensions between city-pairs not previously served.[1]

The dynamics of the decisions involving competitive route authorizations are more complicated. When industry profits have risen above normal levels, the carriers have sought new competitive routes and the Board has been willing to grant them. On the

[1] On noncompetitive route extensions in the Board's early years, see Keyes, *Federal Control of Entry into Air Transportation*, pp. 108–15.

other hand, the Board's critics have often blamed periods of subnormal profits or sharply rising subsidies on "excessive competition" authorized by the Board. It has apparently heeded such pressures and sharply cut down the extension of point-to-point competition until the profit slump was well past.

Because of these shifts in the economic environment, the standards controlling the Board's judgment have seemed to change frequently. These changes occurred independently of turnover in personnel and often without any alteration in the composition of the Board's majority. Even so, it will be convenient to key the following discussion to only two major phases of policy in route cases — the period before 1951, the time when the need for subsidy began to attenuate, and that after 1951. Two aspects of the Board's decisions in route cases have major market implications and therefore demand close analysis. What is the standard used to decide whether the public interest calls for the contemplated service extension? What is the standard used to select the carrier to provide any service deemed necessary? [2]

COMPETITION AMONG SUBSIDIZED CARRIERS

The Board took over regulation of the air-transport industry at a time when the subsidy arrangements had been inadequate to the scope of operations. It was immediately faced with a rising subsidy bill, and hence not unnaturally it began with conservative standards for judging the need for expanded service. Applications for entirely new routes were approved only where the resulting increase in public subsidy and the prospects for ultimate self-sufficiency were not out of line with conditions on existing routes.[3] The conservatism of the Board's calculations of the cost of new services is illustrated by its habit of looking at the average and not at the (much lower) incremental costs of service over new

---

[2] Sources which discuss the route cases before 1951 and upon which the following section draws are: Howard C. Westwood, "Choice of the Air Carrier for New Air Transport Routes, Part I," *George Washington Law Review,* XVI (Dec. 1947), 1–103, and "Part II," XVI (Feb. 1948), 159–237; A. J. Thomas, Jr., *Economic Regulation of Scheduled Air Transport, National and International* (Buffalo, 1951).

[3] CAB, *Annual Report* (Washington, 1941), p. 14; United Research, Inc., *Federal Regulation of the Domestic Air Transport Industry* (Cambridge, Mass., 1959), p. 47.

routes.[4] Where connecting carriers served a route or market, the Board was often willing to settle for connecting service rather than through service, even while recognizing that connecting schedules are freely variable in the short run and hence not a firm basis for testing the need for permanent extra service.[5] A general declaration in the Board's first major case dealing with the extension of domestic service called attention to Congress' wish to avoid "the duplication of transportation facilities and services, the wasteful competitive practices, such as the operation of nonproductive routes." [6]

However, the Board also moved early to recognize a responsibility for using subsidy to extend air service, especially where no adequate surface carriage existed and where complementary business development would occur.[7] Also, as Westwood's study of the early route cases shows, it soon began to move toward a disposition favoring competitive service wherever the market would support it. Two ideas seemed to propel the members' thinking in this direction. One was that the prospects for rapid growth of the industry, becoming evident with the onset of World War II, would render city-pair markets increasingly able to support duplicating service. The other was that, in such a fluid situation, it was better to lean on the market as a regulatory force rather than on its own guesswork.[8] The Board at first had held that it would not allow competition where substantial subsidy

[4] For example, National Airlines, Inc., et al. — Certificates of Public Convenience and Necessity (Daytona Beach–Jacksonville Operation), Docket No. 5–401(B)–1 et al., 1 CAA 612, p. 623 (1940); Braniff Airways, Inc., et al. Certificate of Public Convenience and Necessity (Houston–Memphis–Louisville Route), Docket No. 1–401(B)–1 et al., 2 CAB 353, pp. 374–375 (1940).

[5] Eastern Air Lines, Inc. — Memphis–Greenville Operation, Docket No. 423, 4 CAB 429, pp. 431, 436 (1943); National Airlines, Inc., et al., Daytona Beach–Jacksonville Operation, 1 CAA 612, pp. 617, 636 (1940); Braniff Airways, Inc., et al. — Houston–Memphis–Louisville Route, 2 CAB 353, pp. 377–378 (1940); Northwest Airlines, Inc., et al. — Certificate of Public Convenience and Necessity (Additional Service to Canada), Docket No. 327 et al., 2 CAB 627, p. 637 (1941).

[6] Northwest Airlines, Inc. — Certificate of Public Convenience and Necessity (Duluth–Twin Cities Operation), Dockets No. 131, 232, 1 CAA 573, p. 578 (1940).

[7] Continental Air Lines, Inc. — Amendment of Certificate of Public Convenience and Necessity (Roswell–Hobbs–Carlsbad Operation), Dockets No. 265, 285, 1 CAA 598, p. 610 (1940).

[8] Westwood, pp. 167–172; Braniff Airways, Inc., et al., Houston–Memphis–Louisville Route, 2 CAB 353, p. 386 (1940).

would be required,[9] but even this concern faded from view as war-time traffic conditions made many routes profitable at commercially compensatory mail rates.[10] The Board's acceptance of a "competitive presumption" became more and more evident in 1943, reaching full flower in the supplemental opinion given in the *North-South California Services* case. Here Western Air Lines was certified to provide service between San Francisco and Los Angeles in competition with United and TWA, even though the Board could cite no specific benefits, such as single-carrier beyond-terminal service, to follow from such an action.[11] It denied that the justification for competition depends on the inability or unwillingness of an existing carrier to provide service. Further, "it would seem to be a sound principle that, since competition in itself presents an incentive to improved service and technological development, there would be a strong, although not conclusive, presumption in favor of competition on any route which offered sufficient traffic to support competing services without unreasonable increase of total operating cost." [12]

This presumption controlled the Board's discussion of the need for additional service over a period of a year or so but, as Westwood has shown, it eventually fell into a state of confusion (not, surprisingly, because of changes in Board membership) which continued until the large wave of postwar route cases had run out. In *Additional Service to Boston,* the "competitive presumption" doctrine began to wobble, for there it was stated not in the clear form of the preceding cases but rather as something to be applied in context of "all the factors and circumstances surrounding the case." [13] Finally, in a split decision denying the extension of Western Air Lines from San Francisco to Portland and Seattle,

[9] Northwest Airlines, Inc., et al. — Additional Service to Canada, 2 CAB 627, pp. 641, 652 (1941).

[10] See Continental Air Lines, Inc., et al., Denver–Kansas City Service, Docket No. 2–401–B–4, 4 CAB 1, p. 9 (1942).

[11] Transcontinental & Western Air, Inc., et al., Additional North-South California Services — Supplemental Opinion, Docket No. 314 et al., 4 CAB 373, p. 377 (1943).

[12] Transcontinental & Western Air, Inc., et al., Additional North-South California Services — Supplemental Opinion, 4 CAB 373, p. 375 (1943). See also Colonial Airlines, Inc., et al., Atlantic Seaboard Operation — Supplemental Opinion, Docket No. 445 et al., 4 CAB 552, p. 555 (1944).

[13] Northeast Airlines, Inc., et al., Additional Service to Boston, Docket No. 13–401–B–1, 4 CAB 686, p. 690 (1944). See Westwood, pp. 193–208.

the competitive presumption was effectively reversed. The Board in effect held that competitive service would not be authorized *merely* because the traffic is sufficient to support it.[14] In the pure competitive-presumption cases the Board seemed to hold just the opposite view.[15] There is no pattern in the remaining route cases of the late 1940s. Financial conditions in the airline industry deteriorated in the years after the war as anticipation of traffic growth — a key underpinning of the competitive presumption — was revised sharply downward. The Board came under heavy fire for allowing "wasteful excessive competition," and cases bearing any mark of the competitive-presumption doctrine became fewer and fewer. In their place were cases like *Cincinnati–New York Additional Service,* in which the Board not only gave no consideration to the ability of the market to support competition but also refused to permit the applicants to establish a need for competition on the basis of a lack of turnabout service and high load factors. The Board felt that "there is no reason for believing that, as equipment is available, additional service will not be provided by the carriers presently authorized to serve this traffic." [16] In those postwar cases which saw competitive service authorized, one could argue that it grew solely from the Board's feeling that the potential benefits of single-carrier through service were large relative to the amount of competition and potential revenue diversion.[17] In short, the competitive presumption had largely disappeared or, at the very least, the potential virtues of competitive service had become but one argument for adding a new carrier to a particular route.

The other factors considered by the Board when passing on applications for new routes are somewhat overshadowed by the rise and fall of the competitive presumption, but they were im-

[14] West Coast Case, Docket No. 250 et al., 6 CAB 961, pp. 969–970, 1005 (1946). See also Braniff Airways, Inc., et al., Memphis–Oklahoma City–El Paso Service, Docket No. 503, 6 CAB 169, pp. 172–173 (1944).

[15] See, for example, Transcontinental & Western Air, Inc., et al., Additional North-South California Services — Supplemental Opinion, p. 376.

[16] Transcontinental & Western Air, Inc., et al., Cincinnati–New York Additional Service, Docket No. 221, 8 CAB 152, p. 160 (1947). See also Great Lakes Area Case, Docket No. 535 et al., 8 CAB 360, pp. 366–367, 373 (1947); Middle Atlantic Area Case, Docket No. 674 et al. 9 CAB 131, pp. 137–138, 142 (1948).

[17] For example, Boston–New York–Atlanta–New Orleans Case, Docket No. 730 et al., 9 CAB 38 (1948).

portant in certain cases. Only two of these regularly carried much weight. One was the amount of new single-carrier service resulting from a proposed route extension; the other was the diversion of operating revenues from air carriers that would face new rivals as a result of a proposed extension.

Nearly all of the route cases of this period contain elaborate estimates of the revenue subject to diversion by a proposed route expansion. The Board periodically indicated that such diversion (a necessary result of effective competition) was usually to be viewed as undesirable, even though it "is not the controlling consideration where the new service offers substantial advantages to the public." [18] Diversion was usually measured as a percentage of gross operating revenues of the threatened carrier. With other things constant, a threat of greater diversion increased the chances that the Board would turn down the proposed extension. During World War II the discussions of diversion had an air of unreality because the Board was planning the route structure for the unknown postwar period and had only outdated prewar data as a basis for its findings. But in the postwar years the discussions of diversion grew more concrete and more influential, especially with regard to the choice of a carrier to provide service. In a sense, the discussion of diversion versus the benefits of route extension replaced the moribund competitive presumption. This was not an unreasonable change, since the analysis of potential diversion is essentially an extension and quantification of the analysis of the ability of a market to support additional carriers, which is implicit in the competitive presumption. Where the amount of diversion is small, relatively small amounts of public benefit will offset it. Where the diversion is large, the Board clearly felt it must find substantial public benefit to justify competitive service.[19]

What were the public benefits which the Board stacked up against what it considered the drawbacks of diversion? Only one of them — additional single-carrier service — was handled precisely, by estimating from air-traffic surveys the number of

[18] Eastern Air Lines, Inc., et al., Additional Washington Service, Docket No. 9–401–B–2, 4 CAB 325, p. 330 (1943); Northwest Airlines, Inc., et al., Detroit–Washington Service, Docket No. 679, 8 CAB 487, p. 516 (1947).

[19] Northwest Airlines, Inc., et al., Detroit–Washington Service, pp. 518–520.

travelers who would be able to complete their journeys on a single airline as a result of a given route extension. Other types of public benefits often mentioned included either specialized short-haul commuter service or specialized through service, more active efforts at traffic promotion and development, and the like. Among the inadequacies of existing service on a potential competitive route were inadequate peak capacity, poor quality of service, and so forth. In one case, the high fares charged by the existing carrier were mentioned.[20] Westwood rightly concludes that none of these factors was typically considered in a thorough fashion.[21] They often seemed to function only as makeweights in decisions reached on other grounds. Thus, on days when the competitive presumption was not operating, the Board would wink at substantial evidence of inadequate service. One example is *Additional Air Service in Texas,* a case in which American Airlines' service between the west coast and Dallas/Ft. Worth was held to be adequate, even though passengers unable to get space in 1940 were shown to be 17.9 percent of those who actually flew.[22] The test of the need for service in the wave of route cases decided at and after the end of World War II was by and large one of whether the social gains from new single-carrier service would exceed the alleged losses from revenue diversion. How the Board was estimating these is neither a precise nor a describable process. Nor, in the opinion of dissenting members in several cases, were the estimates performed with much consistency.[23]

As we turn to those portions of the pre-1951 route cases dealing with the choice of a carrier to provide needed service, the conditions of minimizing revenue diversion and maximizing single-carrier service again play a major role. However, other factors also appear: an explicit preference for smaller and weaker carriers in potentially profitable routes and a "specialist doctrine" associating particular carriers with specialized abilities for serving either short-haul or long-haul traffic.

[20] Eastern Air Lines, Inc., et al., Great Lakes to Florida Service, Docket No. 570 et al. 6 CAB 429, pp. 435–436 (1945).

[21] Westwood, pp. 209–211.

[22] Continental Air Lines, Inc., et al., Additional Air Service in Texas, Docket No. 2–401–B–2, 4 CAB 215, p. 236 (1943).

[23] See, for example, Landis' dissent in the Detroit–Washington case, 8 CAB 487, p. 524 (1947).

In many of these cases the choice of a carrier also depends on the showing of a need for competitive service. If the Board sees potential diversion from established carriers as a major argument against adding competitive service, it will not find a need for competition unless the applicant will be a weak competitor and divert only a moderate amount of traffic.[24] Conversely, where the Board wishes to introduce strong competitive pressure into a market, a carrier potentially able to carve out a large market share is chosen.[25] Alternatively, where diversion is seen as a threat, the Board often injects a competitive carrier into a market but hobbles it by means of a long-haul or closed-door restriction. The former requires a carrier to serve a city-pair market only on flights originating or terminating at (or beyond) some distant point. This limits the flights the newcomer can profitably place in the city-pair market to those that can draw sufficient traffic to and from the distant point. The closed-door restriction is more stringent still: it forbids an airline to carry passengers between two points even though each point can receive service to and from other cities on its route. Because of the Board's concern with diversion and its application of such restrictions, it is possible to explain the choice of a carrier in many cases where diversion is an issue only if one reviews simultaneously the "need" and "choice of carrier" aspects of the case.

The goal of creating more single-carrier service was a strong factor in the Board's early route cases, a weaker one thereafter. Up to the entry of the United States into World War II, route cases often were decided solely on the grounds of which carrier could provide single-carrier through service to the largest number of passengers.[26] Even later, when other considerations had become much more important in controlling the choice of carrier, the goal of maximum single-carrier service played a residual role. An excellent example is the 1944 decision in the *Memphis–Oklahoma*

[24] For example, the choice of Continental Air Lines for a Denver–Kansas City route in Continental Air Lines, Inc., et al., Denver–Kansas City Service, p. 19.
[25] Braniff Airways, Inc., et al., Houston-Memphis-Louisville Route, p. 386.
[26] For example, Northwest Airlines, Inc., et al. — Certificate of Public Convenience and Necessity (Additional Service to Canada), pp. 653–654; Transcontinental & Western Air, Inc., et al. — Certificate of Public Convenience and Necessity (Reading Operation), Docket No. 380, 2 CAB 667, pp. 672–673 (1941).

City–El Paso case. Of the four applicants for a Memphis–Oklahoma City route, American was first ruled out (on the grounds of need for a regional carrier specializing in short-haul activities) ; of the remaining three smaller carriers, Braniff was selected for its ability to provide the maximum single-carrier and single-plane service.[27]

In the route cases decided after the moratorium at the outset of World War II, the Board began to realize that maximizing single-carrier service involved some unhappy consequences. Used to allot any important route, the principle would normally favor the largest carrier applying, since it would tend to have connecting service from any one city to a large number of other traffic points. And the carrier offering the most single-carrier service will often be the one diverting the most business from other carriers. In a very important statement in the 1942 *Denver–Kansas City* case, the Board squarely announced that maximum single-carrier service could not be the controlling element because, if it were, "all cases would be decided for large carriers as against small carriers." Both maximum single-carrier service and the goal of selecting the applicant with the lowest costs might have to be sacrificed to "the requirements of the development of an economically sound air transportation system." [28] This statement, though anticipated in numerous previous decisions,[29] marks the rise of an objective that has continually dominated the Board's choice-of-carrier decisions since — the strengthening of relatively small carriers. Westwood has traced the development of this notion, which had its roots in goals of helping smaller carriers spread their overhead across a larger traffic volume and which gradually developed into a diffuse democratic ideology that the Board should act, wherever possible, to reduce the disparities of size and profitability among the certified carriers.[30] The doctrine

[27] Braniff Airways, Inc., et al., Memphis–Oklahoma City–El Paso Service, p. 181.

[28] Continental Air Lines Inc., et al., Denver–Kansas City Service, p. 18. See also Western Air Lines, Inc., et al., Denver–Los Angeles Service, Docket No. 519 et al., 6 CAB 199, pp. 209–211 (1944).

[29] For example, National Airlines, Inc., et al., Daytona Beach–Jacksonville Operation, 1 CAA 612, p. 631 (1940) — smaller carrier chosen because opposite choice would create more diversion; Northwest Airlines, Inc., et al., Additional Service to Canada, p. 633 — plea of Northwest for entry into New York to create "balanced competition" in the industry considered but rejected.

[30] Westwood, pp. 61–95.

was phrased in terms of "strengthening" smaller carriers and gratifying their "need" for new routes. However, it was applied not to relieve the special problems of the smaller carriers but for the simpler purpose of making them larger.[31]

The dominant role, from 1944 to the present, of the goal of strengthening deserving carriers can be seen from the way in which other factors in the decisions are used to lead to the same conclusions. One of these factors is the Board's concept of a carrier as a specialist. Numerous awards of short-haul routes were made to the smaller carriers after World War II because, lacking transcontinental hauls, they could be called specialists in short-haul operations.[32] The Board has used the specialist doctrine for other purposes, such as the choice of new carriers rather than existing trunklines to offer experimental local air service. But it has not let the doctrine develop an independent life: Pan American, for instance, failed in a bid for a spectacular network of domestic lang-haul routes which it sought on the grounds of specialization.[33]

Another element in route decisions that has been overshadowed by considerations of carrier strengthening is the role of minimizing cost in choosing airlines to provide needed service. Although the Board has claimed that in all route cases it gives some attention to the comparative cost estimates of the applicants,[34] it is hard to find evidence that costs are considered at all. Until rather recently, the larger carriers have had substantial cost advantages, and in 1942 the Board recognized that always choosing the lowest-cost carrier had the unwanted implication of making the large larger.[35] Thereafter, considerations of comparative costs largely disappeared from discussions in which carrier strengthening played a role. The analysis of potential diversion in route cases also operates in a way that is generally consistent with the strengthening goal. A new carrier that offers a small threat of

[31] For example, Colonial Airlines, Inc., et al., Atlantic Seaboard Operation — Supplemental Opinion, Docket No. 445, 4 CAB 552 (1944).

[32] For example, Braniff Airways, Inc., et al., Memphis–Oklahoma City–El Paso Service, p. 181. See Westwood, pp. 24–46.

[33] Pan American Airways, Inc. — Domestic Route Case, Docket No. 1803, 11 CAB 852, p. 860 (1950). The existing domestic carriers made elaborate claims that they would be demolished by competition from Pan American (p. 927).

[34] Additional Service to Latin America, Docket No. 525 et al., 6 CAB 857, p. 900 (1946).

[35] Continental Air Lines, Inc., et al., Denver–Kansas City Service, p. 18.

diversion on a route is generally a "weak" one in the Board's estimation. In several cases a small carrier was chosen over a larger one to minimize diversion of revenue, and one feels that in the absence of that consideration the need of the smaller carrier for strengthening would have yielded the same result.[36]

After the collapse of the postwar bubble of airline prosperity, the goal of strengthening weak carriers receded along with the competitive presumption. The Board in some cases showed no interest in strengthening carriers where any threat of revenue diversion, or increased need for subsidy, arose.[37] However, the doctrine remained important in many ways. Where a need for competitive service was found, the preference still was for the carrier in greatest need of strengthening. Thus Pennsylvania-Central (later Capital) was chosen over American Airlines for service from the Twin Cities and Milwaukee to the east; deciding the other way — to maximize single-carrier service — would mean "throttling forever the growth of the smaller carriers" and in this instance deny Pennsylvania-Central "an important source of traffic." [38] Also, if the Board was now less willing to expand a weak carrier in order to strengthen it, it was more willing to deny competitive service in order to protect a weak carrier.[39] Finally, the financial crisis began to color the Board's analysis of diversion and carrier strengthening to the extent of making the choice of carrier in at least one case fall to the one with the worst short-term financial crisis, although the customary analysis of diversion and strengthening would have pointed to the other.[40]

By the late 1940s, route cases were coming before the Board less frequently, and it was swamped with pressures of air-fare adjustments, the nonsked problem, and political attacks on the volume of air-carrier subsidy. Into the early 1950s the few route

[36] For example, Transcontinental & Western Air, Inc., et al., Detroit–Memphis Service, Docket No. 303 et al., 6 CAB 117, p. 127 (1944) ; Western Air Lines, Inc., et al., Denver–Los Angeles Service, p. 210.

[37] Great Lakes Area Case, p. 368.

[38] North Central Case, Twin Cities Service — Supplemental Opinion, Docket No. 415 et al., 8 CAB 477, p. 479 (1947).

[39] Great Lakes Area Case, pp. 369–370 (denial of a Cleveland–St. Louis–Omaha route to United Air Lines to avoid small diversion from Continental Air Lines).

[40] Kansas City–Memphis–Florida Case, Docket No. 1051 et al., 8 CAB 554, pp. 569, 571–572 (1947).

cases decided are characterized by split decisions and wildly vacillating standards; the only common element evidenced is the strong interest in cutting subsidy and increasing carrier profits. By 1947 some members of the Board had been showing general dissatisfaction with the program of strengthening small carriers and with competition in the industry generally.[41] A few years later, a string of decisions either turned down service extensions entirely or openly awarded new service rights to the financially strongest carrier applying.[42] Nothing shows the shifting character of the Board's route decisions so well as the perambulations of the *Southern Service to the West* case. In the opening decision (1951), all applications for route extensions were denied because of the threat of excessive diversion, and the majority bowed to the charges of excessive competition then coming from congressional critics. Equipment interchanges between carriers were substituted for route extensions.[43] Later in the same year, the Board reconsidered one of the interchanges which had worked out badly, and it gave Continental Air Lines a restricted route extension designed to have the minimum competitive effect.[44] The case's next appearance was in 1952, when a shifted majority of the Board granted an interchange proposal that competed with the major interchange approved in the case's first hearing. The acrimonious dissent in this three-to-two decision charges "competition for competition's sake," and complains that the new service is "largely duplicative" and will raise subsidy requirements for one carrier.[45] The year 1953 brought more changes in Board membership and another shift in the majority in this

[41] Member Young's dissent in North Central Case, Twin Cities Service — Supplemental Opinion, pp. 483–484.

[42] Transcontinental & Western Air, Inc.–Delta Air Lines, Inc., Interchange Agreement (Reopened Proceeding), Docket No. 2346, 10 CAB 527 (1949); Mid-Continent Airlines, Inc., Alternate Kansas City–New Orleans Operation, Docket No. 1956 et al., 11 CAB 4 (1949); Milwaukee–Chicago–New York Restriction Case, Docket No. 1789 et al., 11 CAB 310 (1950); Service to Toronto, Dockets, No. 3853 and 4032, 12 CAB 305 (1950).

[43] Southern Service to the West Case, Docket No. 1102 et al., 12 CAB 518 (1951).

[44] Southern Service to the West Case — Supplemental Opinion on Reconsideration, 14 CAB 310 (1951).

[45] Southern Service to the West Case — Supplemental Opinion, 15 CAB 94 (1952).

case. The competing interchange approved the year before was dismantled.[46] By this time, however, the Board was about to settle down to a new round of major route cases.

ROUTE CASES IN THE 1950s

In the 1950s the environment of the Board's route cases changed considerably and, with it, the apparent weight put on certain of the criteria for deciding such cases. The most important of the environmental changes, as the Board itself recognized in *Southwest-Northeast Service,* is the disappearance of the subsidy guaranteeing normal profits to the trunk carriers and the consequent fading of the Board's concern over competitive conduct that might raise the total subsidy bill. As the Board stated, "We are no longer faced with the problem of heavy subsidy support for our trunkline carriers — which was a factor which necessarily inhibited the award of competitive services and, at an earlier date, made the question of diversion of particular importance." [47] The other central concern of the Board in route cases in earlier years was the strengthening of relatively weak carriers, and this now came even more to the fore. The subsidy problem concerned the need of the entire industry for revenue; the problem of weak and strong carriers referred to differences among the airlines. A direct need for competitive certification would be required only when a relatively weak carrier faced competition. Subordinate to strengthening weak carriers, a wide variety of goals have been pursued in the route cases of the past decade. Coach service became accepted by the Board as something to be promoted enthusiastically, making the ability or incentive to provide it a strong point in awarding a new route. Maximum single-plane and single-carrier service retained general favor. A pliable doctrine of historic interest came to cover certain considerations of efficiency, such as minimizing duplicating terminal facilities.

The route cases of the 1950s fall broadly into two classes: one group alters the competitive patterns in major trunk markets, and the other group deals similarly with the local-service carriers. The trunk cases have dealt mostly with competitive routes; the

[46] Reopened Southern Service to the West Case, Docket No. 1102 et al., 18 CAB 234 (1953). See especially the dissents in this decision.

[47] Southwest-Northeast Service Case, Docket No. 2355 et al., 22 CAB 52, p. 75 (1955).

local-service cases have granted noncompetitive extensions into small towns and thinner routes, but also have created some competition among the locals. They involve substitution of local-service for trunk carriers in many markets and have hinted at a future source of competitive market regulation in the occasional granting of opportunities for the locals to compete on an equal footing with the trunks.

As one would expect, the standards of "need" in these two categories of cases are not at all similar and afford no fruitful comparisons. However, the problem of choice of carrier, one which appears frequently in local-service cases and almost continuously in the trunk-competition cases, is treated in essentially the same way in both classes.

Since the trunks became commercially self-sufficient, the "competitive presumption" doctrine has been in complete control in cases affecting them. The Board often has made no elaborate attempt to show a specific public need for competitive service and indeed has asserted that no such showing is necessary. In *Southwest-Northeast Service,* which saw Braniff and Delta placed in competition with Eastern and American on major routes between Texas and New York, the Board stated that it did not need to find whether existing service failed to meet "minimum standards of legal adequacy." It satisfied itself that the markets involved were of sufficient size to support competitive carriers and, hence, allowed the inference of need to rest on a presumption of the superiority of competitive over noncompetitive service.[48] Also, in *Denver Service,* the Board declared: "We cannot accept the contention that the Board, in awarding a new route, must find a need for every new service which may be offered as a result thereof. Such a contention is at war with consistent Board practice since the promulgation of the Act." [49] As many times as this principle has been stated in Board cases of recent years, it still occasionally draws a dissent from one of the members. One such case is *Intra-Area Cargo.* There the issue before the Board was a modification of the special form of the certificates given to east-west cargo airlines, which did not define their routes between

[48] Southwest-Northeast Service Case, p. 56 and *passim*.

[49] Denver Service Case — Supplemental Opinion and Order on Reconsideration, Docket No. 1841 et al., 22 CAB 1178, p. 1306 (1955).

particular cities but between areas covering numerous cities. The proposed amendment was to permit carriage among cities within an area as well as between areas. This the Board did on the basis solely of the need of the carriers for strengthening; the public interest in the changed arrangement was not even discussed, and this drew a dissent from Chan Gurney.[50]

The most important test of the competitive-presumption doctrine in recent years has occurred in cases in which competition between trunks and local-service carriers or among local-service carriers is contemplated. At the beginning of the 1950s, the Board adhered to the position that all routes should be characterized either as trunk or feeder routes, that the local-service carriers should be confined to feeder or local routes, and that there should be no competition among them. Gradually, irregularly, and with a conscious effort not to create substantial precedents, the Board has moved toward permitting limited competition between trunks and local-service carriers and away from the fiction that all routes are intrinsically either trunk or local-service in character.[51] In only one case has a local-service carrier been selected on its own merits for unrestricted service in a major market (Mohawk as a competitor with American between New York and Syracuse);[52] the Board took considerable pains to make this case seem more of a special instance than it really was.[53] The main ground for the

[50] Intra-Area Cargo Case, Docket No. 8258 et al., decided Jan. 16, 1959, CCH Av. Law Rep. §22,232.02.

[51] As the Board has progressively relaxed the requirement that each local-service flight stop at every point on the route, the trunks have periodically complained that the resulting "skip-stop authority" moves the local-service carriers closer and closer to providing competitive through service between terminals. The Board has often put off these complaints with assurances that it holds the power to restrict the locals from competitive service; at the same time it has granted them effective authority to offer limited competition. See All American Airways, Inc., Atlantic City–New York/Newark Extension Case, Docket No. 4015 et al., 14 CAB 59 (1951); West Coast Certificate Renewal Case, Docket No. 3966 et al., 15 CAB 349 (1952); Reopened Bonanza Renewal Case, Docket No. 5773 et al., decided May 3, 1957, CCH Av. Law Rep. §22,047; Reopened Bonanza Renewal Case — Supplemental Opinion and Order on Reconsideration, Docket No. 5773 et al., decided Aug. 15, 1957, CCH Av. Law Rep. §22,068; South Central Area Local Service Case, Docket No. 7935 et al., decided March 20, 1959, CCH Av. Law Rep. §22,255.04.

[52] Syracuse-New York City Case, Docket No. 6179 et al., 24 CAB 770 (1957).

[53] See Frontier Route No. 93 Renewal Case, Docket No. 4522 et al., 16 CAB 948, p. 950 (1953); Erie–Detroit Service Case, Docket No. 6927 et al., 24 CAB 523, pp. 525–527 (1956); Seven States Area Investigation, Docket No. 7454 et al., decided Dec. 8, 1958, CCH Av. Law Rep. §22,226.02, 22,226.14, 22,226.20.

award to Mohawk was the old specialist doctrine — Mohawk would provide turnabout commuter service while American would specialize in long-haul traffic from Syracuse. Yet this same form of the specialist doctrine has justified both restricted and unrestricted local-service competition in numerous other cases.[54] Skip-stop authority has been granted abundantly in recent years; and, with most of the local-service carriers spoiling to take on the trunks in competitive markets, this has meant some pursuit by the locals of through traffic even where they are hampered by restrictions of one or two intermediate stops. But because the Board has consciously avoided forming any general policy on this matter, the results of any particular case tend to be rather unpredictable.[55]

How does the competitive presumption work in trunkline-competition cases? Whether or not the Board explicitly denies the requirement of showing a need for service, it is satisfied with indicating the size (and often the growth potential) of the market in question and its ability to absorb the services of additional carriers. An outstanding example is the portion of the *Great Lakes-Southeast Service* case dealing with the Chicago–Miami market, in which the Board merely alluded to the fact that this city-pair "is by far the largest two-carrier market in the country" and pointed to the continuing growth of vacation and industrial activity in Florida.[56] The same test of need by market size (relative to the present number of carriers) and market growth appears in several cases where more specific deficiencies of existing service are also discussed.[57] Conversely, the Board has decided against adding a competitive carrier in cases where the primary factor seems to be the apparent lack of sufficient traffic to yield profitable operations for more than the present number of carriers at

[54] Denver–Grand Junction Nonstop Case, Docket No. 9173, decided June 25, 1958, CCH Av. Law Rep. §22,186.01, and cases cited in note 51 above.

[55] In Service to Trenton Case, Docket No. 6435 et al., 20 CAB 290, pp. 294–297 (1955), Member J. P. Adams called attention to the resulting confused situation and argued that Board's policy on competition between trunks and local-service carriers should be re-examined.

[56] Great Lakes-Southeast Service Case, Docket No. 2396 et al., decided Sept. 30, 1958, CCH Av. Law Rep. §22,211.02.

[57] For example, New York–Florida Case, Docket No. 3051 et al., 24 CAB 94, p. 98 (1956); Application of Tucson Airport Authority, Docket No. 5564, 23 CAB 772, p. 774 (1956); New York–San Francisco Nonstop Service Case, Docket No. 9214 et al., decided Sept. 2, 1959, CCH Av. Law Rep. §22,304.01.

existing fares. In recent years most markets found too small to sustain competitive carriers have been local-service markets, where the decision was scarcely a hard one to make. One, however, was the significant Cincinnati–New York market, which the Board found would not support Eastern Air Lines on top of two other Big Four carriers, TWA and American. In a petition for reconsideration, Eastern argued that the Cincinnati–New York market, with two nonstop carriers, had many of the characteristics of the New York–St. Louis market, where in the same case the Board had raised the unrestricted carriers to three. The Board's rebuttal was an outright size comparison: the New York–St. Louis market involved 29 percent more passengers and 96 percent more passenger-miles than Cincinnati–New York.[58] There is, nonetheless, no set of cases which will yield a precise definition of the minimum market size required to support additional competitive service. Naturally such a threshold could not be defined simply in terms of volume of passengers or passenger-miles without considering the city-pair network in which the market is embedded. The Board paradoxically used this fact to defend its failure to define the minimum market size; the decision "must turn upon all the surrounding facts and circumstances."[59]

One thing that one immediately notices about the route cases in which the size of the market is the major or sole evidence of the need for additional service is that the incumbent carriers are nearly always members of the Big Four or other trunklines with good market positions and financial strength. Conversely, the mere size of the market usually will not justify another airline when a relatively weak carrier's most important market is on the block. In *Chicago–Milwaukee–Twin Cities,* the Board declared that the Chicago–Twin Cities market could sustain another carrier. Next came a documentation of the inadequacy of existing services that in itself made a strong case for a competing carrier. Chicago–Twin Cities was the major monopoly market of Northwest Airlines, counted a relatively weak carrier; the Board placed in competition with it Capital Airlines, another carrier which the Board clearly wished to strengthen and yet which would not pose

---

[58] Eastern Route Consolidation Case — Supplemental Opinion and Order on Reconsideration, Docket No. 3292 et al., decided July 23, 1957, CCH Av. Law Rep. §22,062.02.

[59] Southwest-Northeast Service Case, p. 75.

too much of a threat to Northwest. In the same proceeding, Northwest received the first single-carrier nonstop authorization between Twin Cities and Milwaukee, on the one hand, and Miami, on the other.[60] In a petition for reconsideration, Eastern pointed out that the market-size test could be used to show that Northwest's new Twin Cities/Milwaukee–Miami market would support not one but two unrestricted carriers. This contention the Board rejected without detailed analysis, holding that the carrier had "not established error in the Board's findings." [61] It refused to allow Eastern to eliminate an intermediate stop between Florida and points north of Chicago.

The mere showing of a market large enough to support further competition will not suffice, then, when an established carrier is one the Board currently feels needs strengthening or at least protection from increased competition. What more tangible marks of inadequate service has the Board noted in the cases of the past decade? One that appears quite frequently is the growth of traffic in a market as compared to similar markets. As we have seen, the Board's affection for competition rests entirely on its nonprice consequences; among these, market development and promotion are especially favored. Thus inadequate traffic development is one of the first faults sought in a noncompetitive market. In ending Eastern Air Lines' monopoly of the St. Louis–Florida market, the Board remarked that the growth of traffic had lagged behind that of the Florida traffic from several major metropolitan cities in the same general geographic area as St. Louis. In terms of relative population, Indianapolis, Pittsburgh, Cleveland, Cincinnati, and Louisville had developed considerably more traffic to Florida. The Board felt that this "must to a large extent be attributed to the inferior pattern of service which Eastern for many years has offered . . . and to the lack of effective competition." [62] In the majority of such route cases more precise deficiencies are named. Nonstop competition to western Texas cities

[60] Chicago–Milwaukee–Twin Cities Case, Docket No. 3207 et al., decided May 19, 1959, CCH Av. Law Rep. §22,270.01.
[61] Chicago–Milwaukee–Twin Cities Case — Supplemental Opinion and Order on Reconsideration, decided Sept. 15, 1959, CCH Av. Law Rep. §22,307.02.
[62] St. Louis-Southeast Service Case, Docket No. 7735, decided Sept. 30, 1958, CCH Av. Law Rep. §22,210.01. For a similar analysis, see Eastern Route Consolidation Case, Docket No. 3292 et al., decided April 1, 1957, CCH Av. Law Rep. §22,037.01.

from Dallas was found necessary because the existing carrier's
service had not expanded to match the growth in traffic:

Despite the fact that from 1950 to 1956 the Amarillo-Dallas traffic
doubled, Braniff still offers only one nonstop flight with Convair equipment as it did in 1950, and the quality of Braniff's service during that
period has actually deteriorated, since three of the five flights Braniff has
continued to provide . . . now require longer travel time.[63]

Frequently the main service deficiency stressed by the Board is
inadequate total capacity for the market in question. Often the
Board infers this lack from the persistence of high load factors,
implying that at times of peak travel some passengers probably
cannot get reservations. Sometimes, when considering a city-pair
market that tends to have relatively great fluctuations between
peak and off-peak travel volumes, the Board will deduce service
inadequacy from the fact that excess demand exists in peak
periods even if load factors over peak and off-peak periods are
not especially high. A case in which high load factors played an
important (if controversial) part in establishing a need for increased competition was *New York–San Francisco Nonstop
Service.* Here the unduly high load factors on transcontinental
nonstop flights in one past period were used as part of the justification for removing a requirement that American Airlines flights
between New York and San Francisco stop at Chicago.[64] The
problem of inadequate service for peak loads has been mentioned
in some cases in the same breath with excessive load factors. In
others, such as *New York–Florida,* peak loads have been viewed
as a separate problem. The Board recited at some length the facts
of the extended waiting lists common for New York–Miami
flights at peak season and the reduced on-time reliability and inconvenience for passengers that resulted when the two carriers

[63] Dallas to the West Service Case, Docket No. 7596 et al., decided Feb. 11,
1959, CCH Av. Law Rep. §22,239.01.

[64] New York–San Francisco Nonstop Service Case, §22,239.01. See also Northwest Airlines, Pittsburgh–Cleveland and Detroit Restriction Case and New
York–Chicago Service Case, Docket No. 4294 et al., 23 CAB 943, p. 945 (1956),
in which Capital's high load factors were cited as one ground for giving Northwest unrestricted rights to serve the Pittsburgh–Detroit and Pittsburgh–Cleveland markets. American's high load factors were cited as indicating a need for
competitive service in Application of Tucson Airport Authority, p. 775.

then serving the market attempted to meet this demand by excessively tight scheduling.[65] Inadequate service for daily as well as for seasonal peaks is mentioned, as when, in *Chicago–Milwaukee–Twin Cities,* the Board spoke of inadequate "schedules offered at peak travel hours of the day."[66]

Still other service deficiencies are recognized by the Board as tending to establish a need for competing air service. After some hesitation, in 1952 the Board took the view that a large amount of coach service was a desirable thing. Since then, the underdevelopment of coach travel in a market has been cited fairly regularly as a reason for adding another carrier.[67] The failure of a carrier to offer adequate turnabout service in a market has led the Board to certify a competing carrier.[68] Once in a while the Board will mention the inferiority of the equipment used in a market by an established carrier as a reason for certifying competition,[69] though this is a dangerous argument. For reasons discussed elsewhere, inferiority of equipment and smallness tend to go together, encouraging the expansion of only the large carriers.

Just because the Board will use these inadequacies in service to support a new route authorization, it does not follow that a carrier has much chance of persuading the Board that its competitive services are needed where the deficiencies are present. Eastern Air Lines discovered this in its unsuccessful pursuit of Cincinnati–New York authorization; it had argued that the load factors of TWA and American in this market were higher than those in Eastern's markets, where new competition had recently been installed.[70] This is another indication of the double standard employed in the showing of a need for additional service and the

[65] New York–Florida Case, pp. 174–176.

[66] CCH Av. Law Rep. §22,270.01.

[67] For example, Chicago–Milwaukee–Twin Cities Case, CCH Av. Law Rep. §22,270.01; New York–San Francisco Nonstop Service Case, CCH Av. Law Rep. §22,304.01.

[68] Turnabout or shuttle service between two terminals is viewed as desirable because it eliminates delays owing to aircraft arriving late from other points on a route. See Syracuse–New York City Case, Docket No. 6179 et al., 24 CAB 770, pp. 773–774 (1957).

[69] For example, Chicago–Milwaukee–Twin Cities Case.

[70] Eastern Route Consolidation Case — Supplemental Opinion and Order on Reconsideration, CCH Av. Law Rep. §22,602.02. There are many similar examples.

extent to which considerations of competitive balance control the Board's decisions (TWA has been treated as a weak carrier because of poor profits).

It follows then that the Board can add nothing to the logic of its own position by measuring the probable diversion from existing carriers as a factor in evaluating the need for competition. In cases where diversion might loom as a serious threat, the Board will automatically apply the stiff test of inadequacy of competitive service. Indeed, elaborate discussions and measurements of traffic diversion are rare in the route cases of the last decade, except in the local-service cases and where they have some bearing on the choice of a new competitive carrier. Where diversion is mentioned at all, it is usually in an aside declaring that the public benefits from further competition will outweigh the undesirable effects of any diversion.[71] In *Great Lakes-Southeast Service,* the Board declared: "The diversionary impact on an existing carrier must seriously affect its financial position before it could justify withholding authorization of needed competitive services." [72] Here the identification of significant diversion with harm to a relatively weak carrier is perfectly clear. An interesting borderline case with regard to the value placed on diversion is *New York–San Francisco Nonstop Service.* This was one of the few of the great route cases in the latter 1950s in which the Board has had to deal openly with the problem of the maximum number of carriers a market will support. Many of the arguments of United and TWA against the removal of a one-stop restriction on American's transcontinental service rested on detailed calculations of schedules and the possibilities of efficient use of high-capacity jet aircraft with an extra, fully competitive carrier present. The majority in a three-to-two decision admitted that United and TWA would face substantial diversion but held that the public benefits of additional competition would outweigh it. The minor-

---

[71] See, for example, Northwest Airlines, Pittsburgh–Cleveland and Detroit Restriction Case and New York–Chicago Service Case, p. 945. An alternative means of laying the diversion problem to rest was taken in the Southwest-Northeast Service Case, p. 75, where the Board minimized the threat of substantial diversion from Eastern and American by noting that it would "be at least in part offset by normal traffic growth in the markets involved."

[72] CCH Av. Law Rep. §22,211.02.

ity, however, felt that the resulting diversion might seriously injure the incumbent carriers.[73]

We turn now to the criteria the Board employed over the past decade in the choice of a carrier to be added where the need for competitive service was shown. One criterion dominated all others — the need of the various applicants for strengthening. Because the trunk carriers were going off subsidy, it grew less important to protect the profits of strong carriers and much more important to equalize (at the going fare structure) the relative profitability and absolute size of the trunks. Only in the local-service cases has the need-for-strengthening criterion meshed with the goal of subsidy reduction, and then other aspects of strengthening a carrier's operations have often overshadowed the consideration of cutting the flow of subsidy payments.

The dominance of the goal of strengthening is best seen in the aggregate results of the recent route cases. Other than a few awards to TWA, practically nothing has gone to the Big Four carriers, excepting the removal of a few certificate restrictions of the long-haul or closed-door type. The specific wording of the Board's decisions sometimes recognizes the dominance of this objective. This is true of the selection of Capital for service between the Twin Cities and Chicago, the choice of Northwest over Eastern for unrestricted service between Pittsburgh, on the one hand, and Cleveland and Detroit, on the other, the grant of Texas–New York routes to Braniff and Delta, and many other cases.[74] At other times, the choice of a small or weak carrier in a route case is justified on the basis of improvement of subordinate operating factors, such as reduction in the seasonality of the carrier's demand, or on the basis of the rather diffuse "historic interest" doctrine, discussed below. The goal of bolstering weak carriers has been allowed to override some immediate and tangible service improvement. Thus the majority in the *Southwest-Northeast* decision selected Braniff for major competitive routes, although the two minority members complained forcefully of the carrier's lack of qualifications for developing the new routes.

[73] New York–San Francisco Nonstop Service Case, CCH Av. Law Rep. §22,304.01.
[74] Northwest Airlines, Pittsburgh–Cleveland and Detroit Restriction case, pp 945–946; Southwest-Northeast Service Case, pp. 56–59.

Similarly, Capital has been selected for several major routes, although the Board recognized that it was inexperienced in long-haul operations and in recent years had furnished relatively little coach service.[75] The *New York–Florida* case shows how far the Board will let the "strengthening" goal control a decision on choice of carrier.[76] Here the weakest of the trunk carriers, Northeast Airlines, was picked for the highly lucrative New York–Miami route over Delta, Capital, and Pan American. This was a three-to-two decision, with the minority favoring Delta on the ground that that carrier was much better qualified to serve the public interest. The majority's choice of Northeast rested very heavily on its alleged need for the route. The carrier was the last of the trunklines to go off subsidy, due to its network of local-service routes in New England and the difficult climatic conditions it faced there. It had not been treated generously in route cases in the past. Finally, there was virtually no other direction in which its routes might be extended, and without this award it would be permanently doomed to the role of a local-service carrier. The majority had to skirt a variety of factors weighing against Northeast's selection. They denied that, given its first major long-haul route, Northeast would probably tend to neglect its short-haul and low-density New England routes, though this tendency has been noted in almost every local-service area case for years. They also had to develop various *ad hoc* arguments to counter the facts that Northeast's best airplanes, DC-6Bs, were inferior in passenger appeal to the DC-7s already in general use on the New York–Miami route and that Northeast had previously failed in an attempt to establish itself in a major market (New York–Boston).

With the "strengthening" goal so dominant in the Board's decisions, it seems desirable to review the troubles a carrier must have in order to be found "weak." In the 1940s, the Board's concern was to improve the weak carriers' relative size and profitability. A weak carrier was then a small one or one with intrinsically unprofitable routes; these two conditions always appeared to-

[75] Southwest-Northeast Service Case, pp. 59–63, 95–97; Chicago–Milwaukee–Twin Cities Case, CCH Av. Law Rep. §22,270.01; Great Lakes-Southeast Service Case, CCH Av. Law Rep. §22,211.04 (regarding the choice of Capital over National for a Buffalo–Miami service).

[76] New York–Florida Case, Docket No. 3051 et al., 24 CAB 94 (1956).

gether, and there was no problem of distinguishing between them. The same general test is still applied to determine worthiness for route charity, as the New York–Miami award to Northeast makes clear. However, with the departure of the trunk carriers from need-subsidy status in the 1950s, a new element has come into use as a test of need — a carrier's short-term financial condition. Thus, in the *United Restriction* case, the Board examiner had ruled against lifting the "Boise restriction" which prevented United Airlines from offering nonstop Seattle/Portland–Chicago service in competition with Northwest Airlines. The Board reversed its examiner, largely because, after the hearings on the case, Northwest had started to earn a fairly substantial profit.[77] Similar hints can be found in several of the cases involving Capital Airlines in the mid-1950s. Thus, in relaxing a closed-door restriction on Eastern's service between Pittsburgh and Akron, Cleveland, and Detroit, the Board declared that "in view of Capital's vastly improved condition" the wasteful restriction was no longer justified.[78] A carrier which the Board will seek to strengthen, then, may be not only a small one, or one with intrinsically unprofitable routes, but also one which for any reason has temporarily encountered trouble. As we shall see, this constitutes a major shift in the pattern of incentives which the Board places before the carriers.

Critics of the Board's decisions in route cases often register shock on discovering that, despite the vital role given to the goal of strengthening weak carriers, the Board does little to assure itself that an award will strengthen a carrier rather than exhaust its resources in the fight for a market share. There are two things to be said against this criticism. First, the attitude of the Board is consistent with a general outlook pervading much of its regulatory activity: the pursuit of its objectives through creating incentives rather than through attempting to create or order particular results. Thus the small carrier is placed in the large market not for the service improvements it may promise, but rather for the incentive thus generated to fight actively for a market share and the incentive for improvements which its arrival

[77] United Restriction Case — Supplemental Opinion, Docket No. 2190, 21 CAB 767, p. 769 (1955).

[78] Northwest Airlines, Pittsburgh–Cleveland and Detroit Restriction Case and New York–Chicago Service Case, p. 947.

will create for its competitors. Second, by avoiding inspection of the probable results of attempting to strengthen a small carrier, the Board ducks some difficult problems of oligopolistic rivalry. In a life-or-death struggle, the large carrier has many advantages. The size and flexibility of its fleet of aircraft let it blanket a market with schedules. Its profits and reserves from its historically strong route system give it access to the most attractive aircraft available and to financial reserves to stave off temporary losses. Finally, the small carrier is denied the weapon of price and some forms of product competition by the Board, and perhaps by the nature of the oligopolistic market if not by the Board. In short, if the Board publicly entertained doubts about the ability of small or weak carriers to establish themselves in large competitive markets, these doubts would tend to be self-validating because established carriers *could* often prevent successful market entry. The Board undoubtedly realizes this dilemma, as we can see from various decisions. The *Southwest-Northeast* decision specifically takes up the charge that route extensions may weaken small carriers and counters by arguing that, unless they are given equality of competitive opportunity, their problems of achieving equipment parity and equal competitive strength with larger carriers will be even more troublesome.[79]

There are three other types of considerations that seem to influence the Board's decision on choice of carrier in route cases. These are: (1) certain features of public service influenced directly by the award, (2) various factors which cut the operating costs of the carrier granted the extension, and (3) the reduction of the aggregate cost of carrier subsidy to the government, which now takes a role partly independent of that of the need of carriers for strengthening.

Taking up these groups in turn, one of the more important public-service considerations is the old one of maximizing the supporting or connecting traffic that will receive single-carrier

---

[79] Southwest-Northeast Service Case, pp. 56–59. See also Syracuse–New York City Case, p. 777, in which the Board notes the problem the entrant carrier, Mohawk, will have in competing with American Airlines' Lockheed Electras: "We see no reason to bar Mohawk from this route on the bare assumption that . . . Mohawk will be incapable of meeting the resulting changes in competitive conditions."

service as a result of the award. This objective, it will be recalled, was pursued extensively by the Board in its early years, before the goal of equalizing carrier strength and opportunities gained ascendancy.[80] This goal does not yet pervade the local-service route decisions, in which the rivals do not differ greatly in strength. The local airline able to provide the most connecting traffic often has a strong case for selection. In *Erie–Detroit Service,* both Mohawk and Allegheny were granted extensions from Erie to Detroit in preference to Lake Central and North Central because each of the former pair would service large amounts of connecting traffic.[81] Many other local-service cases involve the same criterion.[82] Such cases usually contain elaborate analyses of the extent of community of interest among the points involved, and the Board receives ample information about what route pattern is likely to maximize connecting or supporting traffic. Thus in *Seven States Area Investigation,* where community-of-interest data governed many choices among the local-service carriers involved, the Board declared that the "need of a carrier for route strengthening is only one of the many public interest factors." [83]

But there are also instances in which the goal of carrier strengthening has caused the Board to reject the carrier able to provide the most connecting service.[84] In the major trunkline cases involving competitive route authorizations, the general rule is that maximization of single-carrier connecting traffic has no significant weight. Thus, in awarding National a Miami–Houston route in preference to Eastern, the Board said: "As we have frequently observed, if single-carrier service were the criterion for

[80] See pp. 199–200.

[81] Erie–Detroit Service Case, Docket No. 6927 et al., 24 CAB 523 (1956).

[82] For example, Seven States Area Investigation, Docket No. 7454 et al., decided Dec. 8, 1958, CCH Av. Law Rep. §22,226.21; Lima–Detroit Service Case, Docket No. 7480 et al., 24 CAB 432 (1957); Montana Local Service Case — Supplemental Opinion, Docket No. 6293 et al., decided July 29, 1959, CCH Av. Law Rep. §22,296.02.

[83] CCH Av. Law Rep. §22,226.12. See also, South Central Area Local Service Case, Docket No. 7935 et al., decided March 20, 1959, CCH Av. Law Rep. §22,255.07.

[84] For instance, the choice of Bonanza over Frontier for a Salt Lake City–Phoenix route in Service to Phoenix Case, Docket No. 6247 et al., decided Sept. 27, 1957, CCH Av. Law Rep. §22,079.02.

selection of carrier, new routes would inevitably go to the largest carrier applying." [85] Furthermore, when necessary, the Board has subordinated the advantages of single-carrier service by noting the relatively slight disadvantage to the traveler who must deal with connecting carriers.[86] Usually, when the maximizing of connecting traffic serves as a reason for the choice of a carrier, it is consistent with the goal of strengthening.[87] The consideration of improved service to connecting or beyond-segment traffic can, however, be sufficiently important to warrant the choice of a carrier in relatively less need of strengthening. Two similar instances of this were the selection of TWA over National for a St. Louis–Miami extension and the selection of Northwest over National for a third carrier in the Chicago-Miami market.[88] Both decisions allowed single-carrier service between points west of the Mississippi River and the Florida resort cities. In the award to TWA the Board laid great stress on the provisions of single-carrier and single-plane service to Florida from Los Angeles, San Francisco, and Kansas City,[89] while the award to Northwest would afford single-carrier service to beyond-segment traffic from

---

[85] Florida–Texas Service Case, Docket No. 5701 et al., 24 CAB 308, p. 317 (1956).

[86] Thus, in selecting Capital over Delta in the Norfolk–Atlanta Nonstop Investigation, Docket No. 6647 et al., 21 CAB 295, p. 296 (1955), the Board disposed of the single-carrier service argument favoring Delta by counting the number of connecting flights at Atlanta that would be available to passengers from Norfolk using Capital's proposed schedules. An even more extreme method of averting the single-carrier argument was taken by the Board in Panama City, Florida–Atlanta Investigation, Docket No. 7233 et al., 23 CAB 459, pp. 460–462 (1956); here the Board, denying that connecting service was a serious inconvenience, picked a local-service carrier, Southern, over Eastern and National, partly on the argument that Southern would provide connections at Atlanta in the sole interest of giving the best service to all passengers, rather than trying to feed them into the longer-haul routes of either Eastern or National, as the trunks would have been motivated to do were they given this stub-end route.

[87] For instance, the choice of Capital over National for Buffalo–Miami service, Great Lakes-Southeast Service Case, CCH Av. Law Rep. §22,211.04.

[88] St. Louis-Southeast Service Case, CCH Av. Law Rep. §22,210.02; Great Lakes-Southeast Service Case, CCH Av. Law Rep. §22,211.02.

[89] Thus TWA received permission effectively to fly a one-stop southern transcontinental run. The Board rejected the pleas of other carriers for consolidation of this proceeding with the Southern Transcontinental Case (Docket No. 7984 et al.) on the technical ground that the applications for consolidation had not been timely, but was forced as a result of a circuit court decision to reconsider the award.

Milwaukee, the Twin Cities, and the Pacific Northwest. It should be kept in mind that the benefits to beyond-segment traffic in these two cases were very clear-cut, since the losing carrier, National, could service no traffic flow beyond the terminal cities of St. Louis and Chicago. Furthermore, though National is a smaller carrier than either Northwest or TWA, its financial position was somewhat stronger than either of them at the time the awards were made. And in the Chicago–Miami market there is specific evidence that the goal of carrier strengthening was in the Board's mind when it rejected the applications of United and TWA for the same service on just that basis.[90]

Several less important direct public-service factors play a role in the choice of a carrier in route cases. Around 1955, when the Board became satisfied with the success of the air-coach experiment and when carrier profits were generally high, apparent willingness to increase coach service began to emerge as a basis for granting awards. Possibly the first appearance of this new outlook was in *Reopened Milwaukee–Chicago–New York Restriction,* a case in which TWA's reputation as a coach operator was important in getting it a nonstop authorization for Cleveland–New York, a market which had previously had no coach service.[91] A year later, the goal of expanding coach service played a role in gaining access for TWA to the Tucson market.[92] Other recent decisions suggest, however, that a carrier's willingness to provide coach service is unlikely to be an overriding reason for its selection. The Board has continued to deny the applications of all the supplemental carriers to provide a specialized low-cost coach service.[93] Furthermore, it has been willing to put a financially weak carrier furnishing little coach service into a market where a main cause of the existing service inadequacy was found to be a shortage of coach seats.[94] The rationale in this case was that the competition offered by the newcomer would induce the in-

[90] Great Lakes-Southeast Service Case, CCH Av. Law Rep. §22,211.02.

[91] Reopened Milwaukee–Chicago–New York Restriction Case (Cleveland–New York Nonstop Service) — Supplemental Opinion, Docket No. 1789 et al., 21 CAB 760, pp. 761–763 (1955).

[92] Application of Tucson Airport Authority, p. 774.

[93] St. Louis-Southeast Service Case, CCH Av. Law Rep. §22,210.02; Great Lakes-Southeast Service Case, CCH Av. Law Rep. §22,211.02.

[94] Chicago–Milwaukee–Twin Cities Case, CCH Av. Law Rep. 22,270.01.

cumbent monopoly carrier to raise its volume of coach service, a conjecture which, as the Board noted in a supplementary opinion, was later borne out by experience.[95]

Beyond the two considerations of public service already discussed, maximization of one-carrier connecting traffic and encouragement of coach service, minor public-service factors occasionally influence the choice of carrier. One example would be the Board's refusal to substitute a local-service carrier, Bonanza, for United on the intermediate points of a thin route between Salt Lake City and Reno because Bonanza's unpressurized DC-3s would be uncomfortable at the high altitudes required on the route.[96]

A number of factors affecting the operating efficiency of various carriers also affect the Board's choice of carriers. Some of these are rather particular matters dealing with route structure or route integration. Thus the Board will sometimes extend into a strong traffic-generating point a carrier's route that presently terminates at a small or weak point. This tends to relieve the carrier of the problem of low load factors at the weak end of the route and allows it to offer more flights to the intermediate points. In extending National Airlines' route from New Orleans to Houston, the Board noted that this should improve its schedules to the intermediate segments Tampa–Miami and Jacksonville–New Orleans.[97] The same sort of consideration has been the basis for noncompetitive extensions of the local-service carriers into larger cities in the last few years' round of local-service area cases. Another type of route factor that may be important is the granting of a segment to a carrier which can conveniently serve both points on a single long-haul flight. An example was Eastern's receipt of a Chattanooga–Birmingham authorization so that both points could be served on flights to or from Houston or New Orleans.[98] This was granted even though it meant competition for Capital Airlines in a thin market. On the other hand, carriers are frequently denied awards of segments that would clearly improve their route structure or operational flexibility but at the

[95] Chicago–Milwaukee–Twin Cities Case — Supplemental Opinion and Order on Reconsideration, CCH Av. Law Rep. §22,307.01.

[96] Pacific Northwest Local Air Service Case, Docket No. 5463 et al., decided May 28, 1959, CCH Av. Law Rep. §22,272.06.

[97] Florida–Texas Service Case, 24 CAB 308 (1956).

[98] St. Louis–Southeast Service Case, CCH Av. Law Rep. §22,210.03.

same time threaten to divert excessive traffic from weaker competitive carriers. Thus United and TWA were denied the removal of restrictions preventing them from furnishing shuttle or turnabout service in the Chicago–Washington market because of the threat to Capital, although the Board conceded that their operations would gain "greater flexibility" thereby.[99] Another operating factor which has influenced the Board is granting routes so as to reduce the seasonality of the demand facing individual carriers. Carriers serving the Florida vacation markets have excess capacity in the summer; others, especially the east-west transcontinentals, have excess capacity in the winter. Reducing the seasonality of a carrier's total demand pattern has been mentioned frequently in connection with the granting of routes to the Florida vacation cities to Northeast, Capital, Northwest, and TWA, and in denials of north-south route extensions to Eastern, National, and Delta.[100] Again, however, this operating factor is never controlling; it has done little to gratify the desires of Pan American for a New York–Miami domestic segment or those of Eastern for an east-west transcontinental haul.

These examples by no means indicate the full variety of considerations that come before the Board under the general heading of "route integration." Such matters can be involved as the possibility of increasing the utilization of a carrier's planes or adapting its route structure more closely to the fleet it owns, increasing its average load factors by rearranging the city-pairs it serves on its route segments, and the like. The Board has discussed these matters at length in opinions only in some of the local-service cases. All of them seem to be viewed as genuinely desirable goals but distinctly expendable when more important considerations, such as those of competitive balance, are present.[101]

[99] Great Lakes-Southeast Service Case, CCH Av. Law Rep. §22,211.07. See also, St. Louis-Southeast Service Case, CCH Av. Law Rep. §22,210.03 — denial of St. Louis–Birmingham rights to Eastern to protect TWA's new St. Louis-Southeast route; Service to Phoenix Case, CCH Av. Law Rep. §22,079.01 — termination of Western's Denver–Phoenix route at San Diego rather than Los Angeles to protect Continental's Denver–Los Angeles service.

[100] New York–Florida Case, p. 102; St. Louis-Southeast Service Case; Great Lakes-Southeast Service Case; Chicago–Milwaukee–Twin Cities Case.

[101] Eastern Air Lines has plied the Board in proceedings on the major route cases with pleas for route extensions based on operating factors, but with no success. To no avail, Eastern pointed to its available reserves of new equipment

Though its name would not imply so, the "historic interest" doctrine that has appeared in many recent decisions often boils down to an operating-factor advantage for a particular carrier. The exact meaning of "historic interest," however, has vacillated wildly from case to case, and some analysis is necessary. Sometimes a carrier's appeal for a route on grounds of historic interest seems to mean nothing more than that it has been operating in the general area in question.[102] This has weight with the Board only where no other significant factor is present.[103] In other cases the Board has cited historic interest in lifting a restriction on a carrier's certificate (such as an intermediate stop requirement) which had cut into a share it once held in a market.[104] Frequently the historic-interest doctrine has been a makeweight argument where some other consideration, such as strengthening a relatively weak carrier, dominated the result.[105] A special variant on this makeweight usage of the doctrine was introduced for the cases which brought new carriers from the north into the Florida vacation cities. The newcomers were held to have an overriding historic interest because they were identified with the *source* of the Florida-bound vacation traffic; this struck the Board as a more noble calling than being historically identified with the goal of

---

in Southwest–Northeast Service Case — Supplemental Opinion and Order on Reconsideration, Docket No. 2355 et al., 23 CAB 42, p. 43 (1956).

[102] For example, Delta's application for St. Louis–Miami service in St. Louis–Southeast Service Case, CCH Av. Law Rep. §22,210.02.

[103] This was somewhat the situation in the Board's selection of Trans-Texas over Southern for a Memphis–Houston local-service route, although considerations of maximum single-plane service also indicated Trans-Texas. See South Central Area Local Service Case, Docket No. 7935, decided March 20, 1959, CCH Av. Law Rep. §22,255.01, 22,255.02.

[104] Eastern Route Consolidation Case — Supplemental Opinion and Order on Reconsideration, CCH Av. Law Rep. §22,062.01; New York–San Francisco Nonstop Service Case, CCH Av. Law Rep. §22,304.04. In the latter case, the Board declared: "This Board has consistently recognized historic interest in a market as a factor of importance in carrier selection, and where as here the historic interest is as sizeable and as long standing as American's, we are impelled to give it great weight."

[105] Northwest Airlines, Pittsburgh–Cleveland and Detroit Restriction Case and New York–Chicago Service Case, p. 945 — Northwest over Eastern for unrestricted service from Pittsburgh to Akron, Cleveland, and Detroit; Service to Phoenix Case, CCH Av. Law Rep. §22,079.02 — Bonanza over Frontier for a Salt Lake City–Phoenix segment.

the vacationers' journeys, though obviously the argument could be worked out either way.[106]

How, then, can the historic-interest doctrine be said to center on an operating factor? The one stable meaning that the doctrine has had when used affirmatively by the Board is that the chosen carrier already has stations at many or all cities on the segment in question, so that the extra investment in ground facilities resulting from the award is minimized. The Board had this in mind when it removed restrictions preventing New York–San Francisco nonstop service by American Airlines rather than putting Northwest onto the route for the first time,[107] as well as in several other trunkline-competition[108] and local-service[109] cases. As one would expect, this operating advantage in choosing established carriers is often sacrificed to goals of carriers strengthening. In the *Florida–Texas Service* case, Eastern invoked, to no avail, the historic-interest doctrine because it had been established in the area first and because it had facilities at more of the cities in question than did its rival, National.[110] The conclusion remains that operating factors seldom control the choice of a carrier in trunkline route cases. Any doubts about this are dispelled by the fact that the Board's decisions contain almost no significant dis-

[106] For example, Chicago–Milwaukee–Twin Cities Case, CCH Av. Law Rep. §22,270.22 — Northwest over Eastern and Delta; Great Lakes-Southeast Service Case, CCH Av. Law Rep. §22,211.04 — Capital over National for Buffalo–Miami market.

[107] New York–San Francisco Nonstop Service Case, CCH Av. Law Rep. §22,304.04. For an earlier instance, see Great Lakes Area Case, Docket No. 535 et al., 8 CAB 360, p. 371 (1947).

[108] Chicago–Milwaukee–Twin Cities Case, CCH Av. Law Rep. §22,270.01 — Capital over Eastern for Chicago–Twin Cities market; Syracuse–New York City Case, p. 772 — Mohawk over Eastern for New York–Syracuse nonstop.

[109] Southeast Area Local Service Case — Interim Service to Huntsville and Anniston, Ala., and Elgin Air Force Base and Melbourne, Fla., Docket No. 7038 et al., decided Sept. 29, 1958, CCH Av. Law Rep. §22,206.02; Seven States Area Investigation, CCH Av. Law Rep. §22,226.21. *Cf.* Reopened Bonanza Renewal Case, Docket No. 5773 et al., decided May 3, 1957, CCH Av. Law Rep. §22,047.01, on choice of Bonanza over Southwest for a Los Angeles-Las Vegas segment.

[110] Florida–Texas Service Case, p. 318. Of the latter point, the Board said: "While this is a relevant factor, it does not loom large in the circumstances of this case, for both carriers are capable of conducting the operation on a profitable basis, and the establishment of a new station at Houston will not entail any special problems for National."

cussion of the ultimate measure of operating advantages — minimizing the cost of providing whatever level of service is desired. The only references are in local-service cases, and there the focus is normally not upon the total costs of providing service but upon costs to the government in subsidy payments.

Among the factors that can influence the choice of a carrier in route cases, only one remains to be considered — that of minimizing or controlling the cost to the government. This is still a significant factor in many local-service authorizations, though the Board's handling of it has been in a state of flux throughout the past decade. Subsidy minimization in the selection of carriers is an issue not only when the Board must choose among local-service carriers but in many related types of cases as well. Should a trunk carrier be allowed to pass on a loss point to a local-service carrier? Should a trunk be forced to hand a profitable station over to a local-service carrier, raising the latter's profits and cutting its subsidy? Should a local-service carrier receive the operating authority to provide limited-stop service between major terminals, giving it a chance at presumably profitable long-haul traffic? As we look briefly at all of these types of decisions, we shall see that minimizing subsidy has played a significantly decreasing role in these choice-of-carrier decisions through much of the 1950s but that there have been a few signs of reversal of the trend recently.

In the early 1950s the Board's concern with controlling and minimizing subsidies was generally high, reaching a peak with the Eisenhower administration's promises to restore the country to a state of fiscal grace. The Board tried to get the local-service carriers into profitable routes, even in cases where it involved ousting trunk carriers reluctant to sacrifice their own profits. Possibly the most striking of these cases is *Southwest Renewal — United Suspension,* in which United Air Lines was suspended at four California cities in favor of Southwest, the corporate predecessor of Pacific Air Lines. United would lose $150,000 in profits as a result of the suspensions; Southwest and West Coast, a connecting local-service carrier, would gain an estimated $207,500 "which would ultimately revert to the Government in the form of reduced subsidy mail-pay requirements." The Board emphasized that the suspension was temporary but also that, if the device achieved its objective, it might be used elsewhere.[111] A few months later, in *Piedmont Certificate Renewal*,[112] the examiner recommended suspending American Airlines at three Virginia cities, substituting Piedmont Aviation, which could probably thereby cut its mail-pay requirements. The Board went along with two of these recommended suspensions but turned down the third, Roanoke, because it would inconvenience too many long-haul passengers. In a case involving local-service routes in Arizona, TWA was permitted to suspend service at Winslow at a considerable saving, but American was not allowed to drop Douglas, although it could cut a $13,000 to $15,000 annual out-of-pocket loss by doing so. The alternative would have been to place Douglas on a thin local-service segment, costing the government $220,000 a year. The examiner in the case reminded a reluctant American Airlines of its petition in the *Transcontinental Coach-type Service* case, where the carrier had emphasized its public-spirited willingness to serve such loss points.[113]

Still another sort of decision from the 1952–53 period typifying the Board's efforts to select carriers for routes in a way to minimize subsidy requirements was *Mid-West Certificate Renewal*. Here a divided Board failed to renew the temporary certificate of a local-service carrier which had been operating unsuccessfully with single-engine aircraft, but which sought to serve an extended system with DC-3s at a cost to the government not out of line with that of other local-service operations. The Board turned down this request on standards which, as dissenting member J. P. Adams pointed out, were not consistent with earlier cases. Proceedings were instituted to transfer Mid-West's former cities to trunkline carriers, United and Mid-Continent.[114]

[111] Southwest Renewal — United Suspension Case, Docket No. 3718 et al., 15 CAB 61, pp. 68–73 (1952). In the same case, United was denied its request to suspend service at Salinas; United could allegedly have saved $54,000 annually if it were granted, since a whole flight could be eliminated. However, the transfer of Salinas to Southwest would not have contributed to the latter's net revenue and so was not permitted (p. 74).

[112] Docket No. 4762 et al., 15 CAB 736, p. 740 (1952).

[113] Frontier Route No. 93 Renewal Case, Docket No. 4522 et al., 16 CAB 948, pp. 950, 971–974 (1953).

[114] Mid-West Certificate Renewal Case, Docket No. 4052 et al., 15 CAB 424, pp. 427–428, 432, 433 (1952). Adams also charged that the majority had given little thought to the difficulties of adding nine small cities to the routes of Mid-Continent, a weak carrier freshly merged with Braniff Airways.

Choice-of-carrier decisions dominated by the Board's concern with cutting the cost of subsidy continued to be common through 1953. Braniff was displaced from a route between Rockford, Illinois, and Milwaukee to give Ozark Airlines, a local-service carrier, a strong northern terminal to a route from St. Louis.[115] In a case involving service between Klamath Falls and Medford, Oregon, the Board was faced with the following three alternatives: (1) service by United Air Lines, offering ample through service beyond Medford at no cost to the government; (2) service by both Southwest and West Coast, involving equivalent through service but substantial subsidy cost; (3) service by Southwest Airlines alone, probably reaping some profit but offering Klamath Falls passengers much less single-carrier service beyond Medford. The Board chose the third solution.[116] Finally, United was suspended at Rock Springs, Wyoming, to leave Frontier as the sole carrier, over United's vigorous protests.[117]

In 1954 and after, these considerations of subsidy minimization seemed to wane in influence. This switch coincided with a show of considerable congressional support for the local-service carriers: they secured a committee report favoring award to them of permanent rather than temporary certificates of public convenience and necessity in 1954, and passage of a bill to this effect in 1955.[118] Examination of the Board's decisions strongly suggests that this congressional sentiment was also taken as a green light for substantial increases in the subsidy bill for the local-service carriers, and the goal of subsidy minimization (for the local-service carriers, at least) abruptly dropped from the picture. There are cases after 1953 in which the same sort of results are reached, but in each case special circumstances are at issue.[119] One was *Route No. 106 Renewal,* in which the Board sought a

---

[115] North Central Route Investigation Case, Reopened, Docket No. 4603 et al., 17 CAB 106 (1953).

[116] Klamath Falls–Medford Service Case, Docket No. 4191 et al., 17 CAB 713 (1953).

[117] Suspension of United Air Lines, Inc., at Rock Springs, Wyo., Docket No. 5995, 18 CAB 147 (1953). United contested this suspension (which had been first ordered on Feb. 17, 1950, in Order Serial No. E–3914) before the courts, but the Board's authority to order it was upheld in United Air Lines, Inc., v. Civil Aeronautics Board, 198 F.2d 100 (1952).

[118] See below, pp. 285–286.

[119] Pacific Northwest Local Air Service Case, CCH Av. Law Rep. §22,272.06.

way to secure service over the Chicago–Sioux City route of the defunct Mid-West Airlines. This case gave the Board trouble because the cities involved were of marginal trunkline size, but certain difficulties of route integration (principally a weak terminal at Sioux City) existed. The Board's first decision was to carve the route up and parcel its cities out to United and Braniff, although a local-service carrier, Ozark, actively sought it. Two members dissented, principally on the ground that Route No. 106 had been designated as a local-service segment and that the Board's earlier policy of rigid segregation of trunk and local-service routes should be maintained.[120] United and Braniff sought reconsideration, indicating that no solution handing the route over to trunk carriers would be acceptable. The Board changed its mind and gave the route to Ozark, declaring:

> In our original plan, we sought to attain two objectives: (1) the improvement in service, and (2) a reduction in subsidy. Under our present plan, we cannot attain the second objective. But since the service advantages offered by the present plan are so far superior to those of the original plan, we think it is in the public interest for us to forego the hoped-for reduction in subsidy.[121]

Member J. P. Adams, normally a supporter of local-service extensions, dissented vigorously from this reversal. He held that the revised solution was operationally illogical, involved competition between a trunk and a local-service carrier in some extremely thin markets, and would bear a heavy subsidy burden. The only party to benefit from the change was United Air Lines. Furthermore, he explicitly warned his colleagues that congressional pressure for permanent certification was not necessarily the same thing as congressional willingness to pay an increased subsidy bill.[122]

This warning, however, was soon forgotten, and Adams left the Board not long after. The concern with subsidy minimization has tended to disappear from local-service cases. The Board set up an extremely liberal standard for making experimental extensions of local air service to marginal points. In matters directly

[120] Route No. 106 Renewal Case and Ozark Certificate Renewal Case, Docket No. 6050 et al. and 5988 et al., 20 CAB 160, pp. 167–170, 179–180 (1954).

[121] Route No. 106 Renewal Case and Ozark Certificate Renewal Case — Supplemental Opinion, 21 CAB 86, pp. 89–91 (1955).

[122] *Ibid.*, pp. 96–98, 101–103.

involving choice of carrier, it has given the trunk carriers virtually a blank check for wholesale abandonment of the weaker money-losing points on their systems and has handed these cities over to the local-service carriers. Practically every major local-service case in the late 1950s permitted trunk carriers to shed a few such points.[123] Usually the Board seems to assume that, although the discarded point did not make money for the trunk, it will do so for the local-service carrier, or at least offer a good chance of doing so. This is doubtless true in a number of cases, since the trunks have shifted primarily to four-engine equipment that is efficient only on relatively long-haul high-density operations while the local-service carriers have upgraded their fleets to include comfortable and efficient postwar two-engine planes.[124] But the noteworthy fact is that the Board has seldom been much concerned with establishing whether or not subsidy would be increased by these substitutions. In most cases trunk service to the points at which suspension is sought has been reduced to a single round-trip daily, often at an inconvenient hour. The Board can and often does point to the improved service the local-service substitute will offer in terms of more frequent and better-timed flights.[125] This same service improvement is noted in placating cities irate over losing the prestige associated with service by one of the major trunk carriers. In the few recent cases in which a trunk has been put out of a market in favor of a local-service carrier, the reason has appeared to be not a desire of the Board to minimize subsidy requirements but rather a wish to extend and aggrandize the route structures of the local-service carriers.[126] An especially interesting case is *Duluth–Chicago Service Investigation.* Here the Board substituted North Central for North-

---

[123] As a randomly chosen example, see Montana Local Service Case, Docket No. 6293 et al., decided July 2, 1959, CCH Av. Law Rep. §22,290.02, 22,290.05.

[124] This transformation of the route structure is discussed later, Chapter 11.

[125] Occasionally a member will dissent from a local-service carrier substitution on the ground that it does nothing but let the trunkline off the hook. See, for example, Minetti's dissent in the Montana Local Service Case, and Pacific Northwest Local Service Case — Supplemental Opinion, Docket No. 5463 et al., decided July 30, 1959, CCH Av. Law Rep. §22,297.01, in which Durfee and Minetti dissented from substitution of West Coast for United at Bellingham, Washington. The majority's regular position, however, has been that described in the text.

[126] For example, see Seven States Area Investigation, CCH Av. Law Rep. §22,226.04 (substitution of Frontier for Braniff at Lincoln, Nebraska).

west at Duluth; the trunk carrier protested, although it had previously stopped serving the city. This decision was reaffirmed on a reconsideration, even though North Central's subsidy requirements had increased in the meantime and Northwest had pressed this heavily as an argument for restoring Duluth to its own routes.[127]

Recently in the local-service cases the goal of minimizing subsidy has had only the occasional role of causing the Board to base its selection of one local-service carrier over another on the resulting lower costs or lower subsidy bill.[128] But in this guise subsidy minimization must compete with the other criteria for carrier selection — strengthening the carriers' route structures, maximizing single-carrier connecting traffic, and the like. Now it seldom emerges as a controlling element.

CONCLUSION

The Board has devoted enormous time and effort to deciding which of the existing certified carriers shall fly what routes. So much has been said above about the details that it is well to recall the broad features. The Board has nearly always believed in promoting rivalry in city-pair markets to secure the virtues of competition: service improvement and market development. Granting competitive route extensions has also had the advantage of strengthening weak carriers. During the 1940s this struck the Board as the democratic thing to do; in the 1950s it took on a new urgency with the desire to equalize the commercial profitability of the various trunks' route systems. The limits on the Board's extension of city-pair competition have been of several sorts. The most tangible is its current reaction to the willingness of Congress to authorize subsidies to air carriers. Equally important has been a fear of the destruction of "sound economic conditions" in the industry. A much vaguer limit has been the Board's feeling about how many carriers can occupy a given market without resultant inefficient operations. Certain features of the process of route

[127] Duluth–Chicago Service Investigation, Docket No. 7122 et al., decided Sept. 27, 1959, CCH Av. Law Rep. §22,080.01; Duluth–Chicago Service Investigation — Opinion and Order Denying Petitions for Reconsideration, Docket No. 7122, decided April 1, 1958, CCH Av. Law Rep. §22,167.01.

[128] Kanab-Page-Glen Canyon Area Investigation, Docket No. 9185 et al., decided Feb. 6, 1959, CCH Av. Law Rep. §22,238.01.

awards have gone on without any critical examination from the
Board. It has never asked whether or not such detailed control
of the maximum number of carriers in a city-pair market is
necessary to avert "destructive competition." It has never really
enforced the promises the carriers have made in seeking entry to
a route. It has never cast a dispassionate, retrospective eye over
the consequences of using route awards to change the size and
profitability distribution of firms in the air industry.

The handling of route cases has broadly rested on the Board's
commendable general philosophy of regulating the industry's
conduct and performance by manipulating the incentives facing
individual firms. Thus, as the following chapter will argue, route
cases are actually one of the Board's main tools for controlling
the quality of the service offered by the airlines. The incentives
created are those growing from the fear of point-to-point competition as well as the results of actual competition. However, the
process also destroys some incentives. If a weak carrier will be
made strong through route extensions, an airline has less incentive
for avoiding courses of action that could get it into financial
trouble. A large or strong one, having nothing to gain in route
cases, might feel freer about defying the Board. Specifically, a
large carrier would have little to lose from actions that might
drive a smaller rival to bankruptcy or merger.

How much has the Board changed the industry's route network
from what would have been produced by market forces? Probably
the answer is, much less than the Board has generally thought.
Even with the Board's control of entry to the industry and its
subsidy arrangements, it is hard to point to any group of air
routes that has for long had many less than the maximum number of carriers that could occupy it efficiently, though there were
major exceptions in some of the prime markets of the Big Four
before the mid-1950s. The route systems created by the Board's
decisions do have some inefficiencies — patterns lacking links
that could be efficiently served, patterns with seasonal imbalance,
patterns of routes requiring sharply differing types of planes or
service. But it must be remembered that the Board has very
seldom forced on carriers any routes they did not ask for, so
there is some ground for thinking that route extensions have not
involved serious commercial inefficiencies even where the best

choice has not been made. Furthermore, route extensions by the Board have not been timed so differently from what commercial considerations would indicate. The major increases in competitive service came during the periods of rapid traffic expansion following World War II and during the prosperous 1950s. The removal of the trunk carriers from subsidy induced a rationalization of their route structure, with small cities and thin segments eliminated and small aircraft largely dropped from their fleets. The Board indeed has passively permitted this, finding the prospective subsidy cost of placing these points on local-service routes reasonable enough to bear. In short, the Board's control of point-to-point competition loses importance when its net significance is weighed in this way. It has seemed crucial to the Board mainly because of its prohibition of the entry of new carriers to the industry, its policy on carrier subsidy, and its serious delay in ironing out the industry's fare structure.

In March 1961, the Board decided the last of the great competitive route-extension cases, *Southern Transcontinental Service*.[129] This decision ran true to the form of its predecessors of the past decade, but it also contained words which form a requiem for the whole series. It granted somewhat less extensive authorizations than the Board's examiner had recommended, recognizing "the effect which the use of [the] jet aircraft, with its greatly expanded capacity, will have on the needs of individual markets and limiting duplicating service to those markets which we fully expect will produce a volume of traffic sufficient to support more than one carrier." [130] There will be no more of these cases in the foreseeable future. It may be that, once economic conditions in the airlines have fully adjusted to jet aircraft and profits have recovered from the heavy initial depreciation and adaptation costs, route cases will again come before the Board. If so, the same sort of balancing of goals that we have seen is likely to rule the new decisions.

[129] Southern Transcontinental Service Case, Docket No. 7984 et al., decided March 13, 1961, Order Serial No. E–16500.
[130] *Ibid.*, p. 5.

10 Regulation of Product Competition and Quality

Controlling product competition and the quality of service is a task which the Civil Aeronautics Board has never undertaken gladly. Its heavy reliance upon point-to-point competition between established carriers has been motivated in large part by a belief that such competition is the best possible spur to product and service improvement. The Board has viewed almost any amount of *price* competition — no matter how little — as too much. It has feared product rivalry much less, although it has felt dismay over certain types of service competition. These attitudes explain the nature of the rather few and sporadic decisions on product competition. They have been either moves to curb what the Board feared might become destructive product competition or, recently, efforts to jar the carriers into service improvements which competition had failed to induce. Another recent development is the consideration of a rising number of formal complaints from cities feeling that they have received inadequate air service.

CONTROLLING PRODUCT COMPETITION

Of the sporadic cases dealing directly with the quality or adequacy of service, the most important variety until recently has been those in which the Board sought to keep the carriers from offering "too much" service and engaging in excessive product competition. From the approval of the first coach tariffs in the certified industry until well into the 1950s, the Board undertook a series of actions to control the quality of coach service and to make sure that it was strongly differentiated from first-class operations.[1] The development of coach service came immediately after a period in which the Board had faced rapidly mounting mail-pay requirements and when it was preoccupied with finding ways of increasing carrier revenues. The stamp of these concerns

---

[1] See Paul W. Cherington, *Airline Price Policy;* CAB Policy Statement on Coach Services of Certificated Domestic Air Carriers, Dec. 6, 1951, CCH Av. Law Rep. §23,128; CAB Policy Statement on Coach Services of Certificated Domestic Air Carriers, Oct. 5, 1953, CCH Av. Law Rep. §23,173.

can be seen in its order suspending a proposal by United Air Lines for DC-4 coach service with relatively low seating density. Entering the coach market late, United attempted to steal a march on its transcontinental competitors and defended its position with the argument that high seating densities were unsafe.[2] The reasons the Board named for why such service might be "unjust or unreasonable, unjustly discriminatory, or unduly preferential" were: "(1) it will initiate a trend to lesser seating with resulting higher costs . . . or at least reverse the trend to greater seating with lower costs; (2) it may approach first-class seating configurations closely enough to result in unjust discrimination; (3) United's fares for this coach service might become unjust and unreasonable because they did not contribute to the carrier's profits."[3] The standards obviously are the same as those employed by the Board in price-discrimination cases, with the terms "unreasonable," "discrimination," and "preference" having the same meaning. To limit the competitive impact of coach service the Board was even willing to deny Capital Airlines, the domestic coach innovator, the fruits of its innovation. Capital had originally been certified between New York and Chicago subject to a two-stop requirement that was relaxed to one-stop for the coach experiment. When TWA and American introduced nonstop coach service in this market, the Board put Capital back under a two-stop requirement, and when United entered the nonstop coach field Capital was forced to withdraw entirely.[4]

The Board's extensive efforts to control the maximum quality of coach service in the early 1950s were made through statements of policy and suspensions of offending tariffs rather than through formal decisions. Hence they established no standards or tests for new classes of service or changes in service quality. However, in more recent years, several service cases of the same type have reached formal decisions. Three of these dealt with competitive service improvements introduced by the three large transcontinen-

---

[2] It should be pointed out that there is no conclusive evidence of bad faith on United's part, though this interpretation of its actions was made in many quarters. See *Aviation Week,* LVIII (Jan. 12, 1953), 18.

[3] Board Order Serial No. E–7126, Feb. 3, 1953. For other cases of the Board's rejecting airline efforts to use better aircraft in coach service, see *Aviation Week,* L (April 18, 1949), 50.

[4] *Aviation Week,* LVII (Dec. 15, 1952), 82.

tal carriers. The fourth similarly dealt with the results of product competition in the Pacific Northwest–Alaska market. The first of the cases involving the transcontinental carriers was the suspension of United's "Custom Coach" plan, a coach service operated with the most modern DC-7 equipment at a slight surcharge over regular coach service. Coming to this case at a time when carrier profits were high and the general outlook bright, the Board approved it in a decision that ignored all the factors that one would normally expect to receive close inspection. A detailed description of the extra frills of the proposed service occupies much of the decision, with merely casual mention of the fact that costs will be raised as a result, and there is no study of the relation between prospective changes in cost and revenue for the carrier. Bureau counsel raised the issue of whether this change in Board policy on coach service would not lead to unprofitable service improvement in the coach field. The Board, however, denied that any change was contemplated or that the profit impact deserved extensive consideration. Approval "only reflects our belief that the traveling public should have the opportunity to select an additional and different type of service than has been available in the past — a service fitting in somewhere between ordinary coach and first-class service." [5] No doubt the reason the decision contains so little discussion of the competitive impact of custom coach is that the competitive countermoves of TWA and American were already known and in effect. TWA had had mixed-class service in its newest Constellation aircraft since 1955, and American installed a deluxe coach service even before United. Thus the *Custom Coach* decision in effect affirmed this whole round of product strategies. It is quite likely that the Board would have preferred to stop the new strategies but was unable to do so. This is because TWA's introduction of two-class flights, the earliest of these moves, involved for TWA nothing more than using on its domestic runs the two-class aircraft it already had for its international service. This the Board felt unprepared to refuse because of the obvious cost penalty for the carrier, providing a striking

[5] United Custom Coach — Suspension and Investigation, Docket Nos. 8625 and 8697, decided Oct. 15, 1957, CCH Av. Law Rep. §22,084. See discussion in A. J. Gellman, "The Regulation of Competition in United States Domestic Air Transportation: A Judicial Survey and Analysis — II. Competition and Specific Civil Aeronautics Board Policy," *Journal of Air Law and Commerce*, XXV (Spring 1958), 158–160.

illustration of the way that competitive effects can spill over from a more to a less product-competitive segment of air transport.[6]

About a year later came the other two service cases involving the transcontinental carriers — the *TWA Siesta Sleeper Seat* decision and a case involving American Airlines' application to use first-class configuration aircraft in coach service. These later cases bear no resemblance to *Custom Coach*. Two good reasons for the change lie in circumstances outside the actual decisions. First, it must be noted that, before these 1958 decisions and after the *Custom Coach* decision, the impact of the 1957–58 recession had been felt in the industry and the Board had had to grant a 6.6 percent general interim fare increase. Second, these two decisions had as their setting a new series of competitive product strategies of the transcontinental Big Three, and this time the Board decided to put a stop to the whole cycle.

TWA had been suffering from having slower equipment than its transcontinental competitors, United and American, and its share of first-class transcontinental traffic had fallen from 36 percent in 1950 to 10 percent in 1956. An attempted solution was to increase passenger comfort with the "Siesta Sleeper Seat," a seat that would nearly flatten out for sleeping and was sold by TWA at a surcharge on its transatlantic route. TWA urged that competitive pressure justified the change in its first-class service, but representatives of United and American stated that the innovation would force them to retaliate. They and Bureau counsel argued that the service constituted an unfair advantage to TWA's domestic first-class passengers in comparison to its domestic tourist and international first-class traffic. Producing seat-miles in the Siesta Sleeper configuration would cost TWA 37.5 percent more than regular first-class seats because many fewer could be installed in the plane. Clearly the adoption of this device by all transcontinental carriers would have cut heavily into their profits. Faced with this thorny situation, the Board reversed its hearing examiner and decided that the sleeper service could be offered by TWA only if a surcharge of at least 20 percent were attached. It feared that the innovation, as competitive pressures worked themselves out, would destroy the carefully kept distinction be-

---

[6] *Department of Commerce and Related Agencies Appropriations for 1958,* hearings, U.S. House of Representatives, Committee on Appropriations, Subcommittee, 85th Cong., 1st sess. (Washington, 1957), p. 943.

tween coach and first-class service and cut into carrier profits enough to force a general fare increase.

It is essential to note that TWA does not seek to justify the offering of sleeper-seat service at prevailing first-class fares on the ground that such service will promote new air traffic. Rather, it contends that it is offering such service almost exclusively because of competitive considerations . . . The evidence shows that if all three carriers . . . were to operate a sleeper-seat service the nonstop transcontinental market would be uneconomical for each.[7]

Here one sees by implication the same tests of unreasonableness and discrimination that appeared in the price-discrimination cases, along with the same concern for restraining competitive market strategies that might pull down the general profit level for the industry. Very similar is the *American Airlines Off-Peak Coach Service* case, decided less than a month later. In response to TWA's sleeper-seat proposal,[8] American had sought permission to operate aircraft in first-class seating configuration in transcontinental service between 10 P.M. and 4 A.M. The Board pointed to its standing policy of allowing the use of first-class aircraft in coach service only in off-peak hours and noted its earlier finding that there were no significant peaks in transcontinental movements. American had tried to show that the service would indeed be off-peak, but the Board noted that the burden of proof lay on the carrier and felt that it had not been sustained.[9] It agreed with American that the introduction of jet aircraft would tend to create more of a night-time slack period in transcontinental demand but said it did not make enough difference to change the conclusion.[10] Finally, American sought to combat the charge that the service would be unduly discriminatory to first-class passengers by pointing to other instances of off-peak coach service that was "like and contemporaneous" with first-class flights, but the Board simply noted that these instances were not part of the

[7] Trans World Airlines Siesta Sleeper Seat Service, Docket No. 9063 et al., decided Nov. 20, 1958, CCH Av. Law Rep. §22,219.01.

[8] The American proposal was filed 20 days after the hearing examiner decided in favor of the TWA Siesta Seat proposal and before the Board's decision. [*Aviation Week,* LXIX (Dec. 1, 1958), 37–38.] This made it inevitable that the Board would either approve or disapprove both proposals.

[9] American Airlines Off-Peak Coach Service, Docket No. 9591 et al., decided Dec. 16, 1958, CCH Av. Law Rep. §22,229.01.

[10] *Ibid.,* §22,229.02.

present proceeding.[11] In this case and the *Siesta Seat* decision, competitive effects were not considered openly, but undoubtedly they lay in the background.

There is another area of product rivalry in which the Board has recently come to fear the results of excessive service to the public — such as overscheduling flights in particular markets, which tends to reduce the carriers' load factors and raise their cost per *revenue* passenger-mile. Though it has not yet tried to act beyond moral suasion, the Board has been seriously concerned with its lack of control in this area, and understandably so. In short-haul high-density markets, large numbers of flights are a powerful marketing weapon for a carrier, attracting traffic both from other forms of transportation and from other carriers.[12] Furthermore, the resulting cost increase for the carrier is a completely controllable one. If the marketing strategy of "mass scheduling" does not pay off in extra profits, the carrier can appeal to the Board for higher fares to cover the extra costs. If the Board is unsympathetic, then the extra schedules can be canceled. Little or nothing is lost, and much may be gained either in increased market share or fare level. In both of the general fare cases of 1957–58, the Board lectured the carriers sternly on the virtues of maintaining reasonable load factors. Turning down requests for 6 percent fare increases in the 1957 *Suspended Passenger Fare Increase* case, the Board asserted that load factors were controllable by the carriers except during the first impact of a new competitor on a route:

We wish to make it clear that management has the obligation to tailor schedules to the need of the market once sufficient experience has been gained to determine the need.[13]

The Board was in the difficult position of instructing the carriers that, after a reasonable period of time, everyone (or someone) should give way gracefully so that the capacity in the market would yield a normal load factor. The dilemma is seen in another passage from the decision:

Competition has been added only where the traffic potential warranted it and . . . the added service would be beneficial to the air transportation

[11] *Ibid.,* §22,229.03.
[12] See Chapter 2 above.
[13] Suspended Passenger Fare Increase Case, CCH Av. Law Rep. §22,077.03.

industry as a whole. In fact, the new route awards are in many cases essential if some of the smaller carriers are to withstand successfully the impact of the coming jet age. Certainly the Board cannot ignore the objectives of its route awards and permit them to be nullified through excessive scheduling to be financed by higher fares. Where a carrier has preexisting plans for expansion of equipment and services which are in conflict with route actions taken by the Board the carrier must reshape its plans.[14]

A few months later, when the Board granted a general fare increase of one dollar per ticket plus 4 percent, it noted that load factors were not formally a part of the proceeding but declared:

Both the Board and the air-carriers are fully aware of the adverse effects declining load factors can have on earnings. It is therefore incumbent upon management to take such measures as are necessary to maintain reasonable load factors. In most instances this means tailoring capacity to meet the needs of traffic.[15]

Noting the way in which the growth of the industry's capacity had recently outstripped the growth of its markets, the Board voiced a more definite threat:

If the carriers' reports continue to reveal increases in capacity well beyond increases in traffic, it is apparent that even if reported earnings were to deteriorate further, we would find it most difficult to favorably consider any request for fare revision without a searching review of the load factor problem.[16]

General Passenger Fare Investigation again raised the issue of load-factor control. Though Bureau counsel recommended the adoption of definite load-factor standards, the hearing examiner was not willing to go along.[17] His decision concludes that a load-factor standard for setting fares would probably be of no help in ending competitive load-factor reductions. Carrier witnesses convinced him that, where increased schedules in a particular market seem desirable to meet competition, no airline would be deterred by the impact its move would have on the industry's general load factor. Again, the regulatory authority was up against

---

[14] *Ibid.*
[15] Trans World Airlines, Inc. — ("Interim Fare Increases"), CCH Av. Law Rep. §22,160.02.
[16] *Ibid.*, §22,160.03.
[17] Initial Decision, General Passenger Fare Investigation, Docket No. 8008, pp. 102–124 (mimeographed copy).

the fact that it could not control load factors without blunting one of the carriers' major tools of market penetration and rivalry.[18]

PROMOTING BETTER SERVICE

Cases in which the main issue before the Board was improving rather than restraining product quality have been very rare until recently. The Board has been greatly concerned with providing incentives for product improvement but has seen fit to do so by indirect means.

Route cases have made up much of the regulatory activity of the Board, and it has used competitive route certifications as its major means for securing high-quality service. In a small way this reflects the limitations of the Civil Aeronautics Act, which requires the certified carriers to provide adequate and efficient service but which seems to deny the Board power to regulate the volume of schedules flown, surely the main factor that makes a service adequate or inadequate.[19] With or without this provision, the Board's general philosophy of manipulating incentives rather than business conduct would cause it to prefer to promote service standards through intercarrier rivalry rather than by direct action.

Aside from their obvious impact on the affected city-pair segments, how do the Board's route authorizations work as a stimulus to service improvement? As the Board itself has recognized, the service improvements adopted under competitive pressure in one market will often spread to other markets served by the same carriers. There are also some features of the way in which route cases are decided that surely affect the quality of carrier service beyond that directly touched by the decisions. As we saw in Chapter 9, service inadequacies are one factor cited by the Board in showing a need for additional carriers. True, their presence is not crucial to the decision in all cases. The Big Four trunklines could reasonably conclude from recent route cases that no amount of effort at service improvement would sway the Board from

---

[18] In its final decision the Board also refrained from setting any load-factor standard but left the door open to doing so in the future. See Order Serial No. E–16068, Nov. 25, 1960, pp. 42–54.

[19] Civil Aeronautics Act, sections 401(f), 404(a); Federal Aviation Act, 72 Stat. 754, 760, 49 U.S.C.A. 1371, 1374.

adding competitive service in those of their markets large enough to support it. For the smaller trunks and the local-service carriers, however, the quality of service provided seems to make some difference to the Board in deciding whether to add competition. Continuous efforts at service improvement, therefore, may be viewed by them as a means of keeping the wolf of competition from the door. There is still another way in which the Board's handling of route cases tends to furnish a continuous incentive for carriers to maintain the quality of service, even in monopoly market segments or those where the number of carriers has not changed recently. Decisions in route cases often note that existing carriers have moved to rectify the inadequacies in their service after a route proceeding has been opened. If the Board would accept such improvements as a basis for not adding competitors, the carriers would have a relatively easy time of neutralizing the Board's efforts to promote the quality of service through point-to-point competition. However, the Board does not operate in this way. Rectifying service inadequacies to deter a competitive route award has in no significant case caused the Board to stay its decision to add competing service.[20] A carrier which fears that one of its markets may attract would-be competitors cannot skimp on service until the threat is actually in sight.

There is another class of Board decisions that has had a very marked effect on product competition in the industry though ostensibly dealing with other matters: the Board's decisions on fare differentials for different types of aircraft. It has permitted cream-skimming surcharges on unusual new equipment — the pressurized four-engine planes after World War II and the turbojet aircraft more recently — and has also permitted the carriers to remove these surcharges at will. Even more important, in the one case to reach a formal decision, the Board refused to permit a carrier with inferior equipment to charge a lower fare. This was

[20] The only prominent exception to this finding is the New York–Florida Case — Supplemental Opinion and Order on Reconsideration, Docket No. 3051 et al. Capital Airlines had previously been certified to offer service between Winston-Salem and Greensboro–High Point, but at the time of the original *New York–Florida* decision it had not been inaugurated. "We did not believe that it was necessary or desirable to require the cities to wait upon Capital's convenience in inaugurating the needed new service." Hence National Airlines was certificated for the route. However, Capital had either begun service or made definite plans to do so, and since the market would not support two additional carriers the award to National was rescinded.

in *States-Alaska Fare,* wherein Alaska Airlines sought to charge a lower fare for service between Seattle and Fairbanks for its DC-4 flights than Pan American did for DC-6B equipment. Alaska Airlines' package involved other minor service deteriorations (cold meals, no carpeting or magazines, and such) that involved no significant cost saving but tended to put the service into a different class.[21] The Board found that the differential was not warranted either by value-of-service or by cost considerations (the DC-6B was not more costly to operate than the DC-4). Thus the Board reached its crucial conclusion: "We believe that a fare differential would lessen the incentive of the carriers to introduce better equipment and thereby discourage the development of a sound air transportation system." [22] In 1949 the Board had rejected a similar proposal by Northwest Airlines to set fares of six cents per mile on its best equipment (Boeing Stratocruisers), five cents on its DC-4s and Martins, and four cents on coach flights. This would have affected fares on Northwest's entire system. It was objected to by four major carriers and suspended by the Board, and never came to a formal decision.[23] Thus, in its actions on fare differentials, the Board has allowed the carrier with new and superior equipment to set a differential if it desires to do so for short-run profit-maximizing purposes. However, it forbids the carrier with older or inferior equipment to set a differential to protect its market position. These policies create an overwhelming incentive for carriers to acquire equipment as modern or as appealing as any used by their direct competitors. Nor is this case the only one reflecting the Board's uniform unwillingness to discourage the trunk carriers in any moves to secure and utilize new equipment. In a split decision it voted approval of a Reconstruction Finance Corporation loan to assist Northwest Airlines in buying a new aircraft of questionable efficiency.[24] It gave quick

---

[21] States-Alaska Fare Case, Docket No. 6328 et al., 21 CAB 354, pp. 356–58 (1955).

[22] *Ibid.,* p. 361. Member J. P. Adams, dissenting from this portion of the decision, indicated just the issue that is involved. Refusing to allow lower fares on older equipment means putting "serviceable and entirely safe, but nevertheless outmoded, aircraft" out of service rather than utilizing them "under certain profitable and practical conditions" (p. 370).

[23] *Aviation Week,* LI (Aug. 29, 1949), 35; LI (Oct. 10, 1949), 50.

[24] Northwest Airlines, Inc. — Reconstruction Finance Corporation Loan, Report of the Civil Aeronautics Board, 10 CAB 683 (1949). See also *Aviation Week,* LI (Sept. 12, 1949), 47–48.

approval to National Airlines' lease of Pan American turbojet aircraft, though this might have been disapproved on several grounds.[25] The Board's uniformly favorable attitude toward the use of new types of equipment,[26] coupled with its extensive hostility toward competitive market strategies of carriers with older equipment (consider the *States-Alaska Fares, Siesta Sleeper Seat,* and *Transcontinental Coach Service* decisions), gives a powerful spur to continual re-equipment with the newest aircraft. The carrier suffering equipment inferiority has all major avenues to protecting its market position blocked except that one.

Compared to the Board's handling of route awards and fare differentials, the cases dealing directly with product quality are relatively unimportant. In periods when the Board has been mainly concerned with carrier solvency, it has not acted to promote service standards. Thus, in one of the "grandfather certificate" cases in the Board's first year of life, it held that a carrier's service is not legally "inadequate and inefficient" even if run at a loss with high costs and inadequate capital, so long as the service to the public is, "for example, reasonably safe, comfortable, expeditious, convenient, and dependable." [27] Again, before the dawn of the competitive presumption, the Board suggested that where the existing carrier "on a long range basis and in normal times" can furnish adequate service, any temporary inadequacies should be removed by proceedings under the relevant sections of the Civil Aeronautics Act rather than by adding competitive carriers.[28]

[25] Ranging more broadly among policy pronouncements by Board members, one can trace a continuing interest in the development of new aircraft. See, for example, "Higher Subsidies for More Planes," *Aviation Week,* LIV (March 5, 1951), 39; "Policy for '52?", *Aviation Week,* LIV (May 21, 1951), 68; F. L. Moore, "C.A.B. Proposes Jet Transport Subsidy Plan," *Aviation Week,* LVI (May 19, 1952), 12–13. This enthusiasm has been restrained only when new equipment seemed likely to involve an unacceptable increase in subsidy requirements.

[26] As a qualifying exception, in the early 1950s at least some Board members were seriously concerned about overinvestment in equipment by the carriers and sought authority for the Board to control it directly. Such authority was not granted, however, and these views did not influence the Board's later actions. See *Aviation Week,* LIV (March 26, 1951), 16; LVIII (Jan. 26, 1953), 77; LVIII (April 13, 1953), 90.

[27] Marquette Airlines, Inc. — Certificate of Public Convenience and Necessity, Docket No. 7–401–E–1, 1 CAA 301, p. 309 (1939).

[28] Continental Air Lines, Inc., et al., Additional Air Service in Texas, Docket No. 2–401–B–2 et al., 2 CAB 215, pp. 236, 239–240 (1943).

The 1950 *Through Service Proceeding* was a Board-instituted investigation of the adequacy of connecting service for passengers traveling between points southeast of Memphis and St. Louis, on the one hand, and points north and west of these cities as far as Denver, on the other. It led to the approval of two voluntary interchange proposals, but it also postponed the installation of one-carrier through service.[29] The Board has investigated the reasonableness of the free-baggage allowance and excess-baggage charges.[30] It has criticized carriers for advertising elapsed flight times shorter than could normally be provided and has installed a reporting requirement so that some moral suasion could be used to get all carriers to maintain reasonable on-time performance.[31] It has had under way a rule-making procedure to control overbooking, the carriers' practice of sometimes making more reservations on a flight than the number of seats available as a hedge against late cancellations and no-shows. Specific cases on overbooking have involved National Airlines and Eastern Air Lines.[32] Recently an examiner's initial decision in the *New York Short-Haul Coach Investigation* has recommended a standard of minimum adequacy of coach service which, if accepted by the Board, might be applied to many large, short-haul city-pair markets.[33] This and other adequacy-of-service investigations discussed below will undoubtedly be challenged by the carriers in the courts. If they survive, they may herald a tightening of the patchwork surveillance of the airlines' product which the Board has maintained in past years; they would be a great improvement over the ineffectual brawling with the carriers that followed the Board's efforts to get such changes in the past.[34]

[29] Through Service Proceeding, Docket No. 3426 et al., 12 CAB 266 (1950).

[30] Free Baggage Allowance and Excess Baggage Charges, Docket No. 7912, decided Feb. 5, 1959, CCH Av. Law Rep. §22,237.01.

[31] See National Airlines, Inc., Unrealistic Schedules, Enforcement Proceedings, Docket No. 9223, decided June 24, 1959, CCH Av. Law Rep. §22,286.01; *American Aviation*, XIX (May 7, 1956), 83; it backed away, however, from enforcing a general rule requiring on-time performance standards to be met.

[32] Order Serial No. E–15614, Aug. 4, 1960, National Airlines, Inc., Enforcement Proceeding, Docket No. 8761. See also Order Serial No. E–14962, Feb. 26, 1960.

[33] Initial Decision, New York Short-haul Coach Investigation, Docket No. 9973 (as reported in *Wall Street Journal*, Dec. 15, 1960, p. 4). See also L. L. Doty, "Carriers Dispute Board's Coach Stand," *Aviation Week*, LXXII (March 14, 1960), 38–39.

[34] For example, *Aviation Week*, LVIII (June 8, 1953), 22; LVIII (June 22, 1953), 96; LIX (Nov. 16, 1953), 103.

The last few years have brought an entirely new type of case dealing with alleged service inadequacies — complaints from cities about the general adequacy of the service provided them. These complaints have their origin in sections 404(a) and 404(b) of the act, respectively requiring carriers to furnish service upon reasonable request and banning unreasonable preference or advantage to "any particular person, port, locality." [35] A forerunner of such cases was the 1952 *Philadelphia-Transatlantic Service* case. Philadelphia had had transatlantic service since 1945, but it had been very lightly used and Pan American sought to abandon it. Philadelphia complained of the superior service given New York and Boston, but the Board still gave permission to suspend service:

> Assuming, without deciding, that the amount of service afforded a community may raise a question of undue or unreasonable preference or prejudice under the terms of section 404(b) of the Act, we think it clear on the facts of this case that neither New York nor Boston was unduly preferred by the provision of greater service.[36]

Yet another predecessor was *Niagara Falls Airport,* in which American Airlines was denied the right to serve Niagara Falls solely through the Buffalo airport and informally ordered to increase its service at Niagara Falls. The examiner's initial decision had found American's service formally inadequate, but the Board granted the carrier's contention that this was not an issue in the proceeding.[37] Thus in the *Philadelphia* and *Niagara Falls* cases the Board shied away from legal rulings on both complaints of discrimination and inadequacy. But in a recent series of cases[38]

[35] There have also been route cases, under section 401(h) of the Civil Aeronautics Act, having their origin in the complaints of particular cities. See Tucson Airport Authority — Application for Designation of Tucson as an Intermediate Point on Route No. 2, CCH Av. Law Rep. §21,977; Service to Phoenix Case, CCH Av. Law Rep. §22,079.

[36] Philadelphia-Transatlantic Service Case, Docket No. 4228 et al., 15 CAB 148, p. 152 (1952).

[37] Niagara Falls Airport Case, Docket No. 6125, 18 CAB 693 (1954). The informal order was sufficient to produce the desired improvement. A year after the decision, the *Official Airline Guide* showed that American had replaced its single multiple-stop Boston–Chicago round trip with the desired two daily round trips to New York.

[38] Reopened Charleston–Columbus Case, Docket No. 6346 et al., decided Jan. 16, 1958, CCH Av. Law Rep. §22,153; Fort Worth Investigation — Adequacy of Service, Docket No. 7382, decided Sept. 23, 1958, CCH Av. Law Rep.

the Board has had to tangle head-on with both types. It has conceded that cities may seek relief for felt inadequacies of service and recently began granting some of their requests.

There have been two lines of attack taken by the complaining cities. One, which nicely exposes the motivation involved, is to argue the existence of discrimination or prejudice — a section 404(b) violation — because a rival city receives superior air service. This was the sole issue in the *Reopened Charleston–Columbus* case. Eastern Air Lines' routes were being altered in a way to provide direct service to Columbus and Toledo from Charlotte, but not from Greensboro–High Point. Greensboro lost nothing, but Charlotte gained more service. Greensboro charged that it was being subjected to unreasonable discrimination; and when the Board's initial opinion ignored the charge, Greensboro secured an appelate court verdict requiring that it receive a plain answer to its charge and finding that the issue was relevant to the Board's ultimate assessment of public convenience and necessity.[39] After rehearing the case, the Board reaffirmed its original decision, finding that there was no need for service from Greensboro to the Ohio points; that service by Eastern to Greensboro would mean substantial diversion from local-service carrier Piedmont; that Charlotte had superior need and traffic potential; and that even if traffic potential were identical geographical factors could justify such discrimination. The Board refused to act as a "umpire between two cities" and pointed to the far broader considerations underlying the public interest.[40]

A few months later, hearing Fort Worth's complaint of service inferior to that of its rival, Dallas, the Board refused to take a charitable view of the charge of discrimination and reaffirmed its unwillingness to arbitrate among the hopes and desires of the

---

§22,205; Toledo Adequacy of Service Investigation, Docket No. 8851, decided Nov. 10, 1959, CCH Av. Law Rep. §22,325; Flint–Grand Rapids Adequacy of Service Investigation, Docket No. 9177; Washington–Baltimore Adequacy of Service Investigation, Docket No. 8148. On these cases generally, see "Adequacy of Domestic Airline Service: The Community's Role in a Changing Industry," *Yale Law Journal,* LXVIII (May 1959), 1199–1244.

[39] Greensboro–High Point Airport Authority v. Civil Aeronautics Board, 231 F.2d 517 (1956). The Board's initial decision was in Charleston–Columbus Case, Docket No. 6346 et al., 19 CAB 731 (1955).

[40] Reopened Charleston–Columbus Case, CCH Av. Law Rep. §22,153.01.

nation's chambers of commerce.[41] It held that any sort of dissimilarities in economic structure and traffic potential of two cities could rule out direct comparison of the air services offered them, no matter how close together they might be. Further, the Dallas and Fort Worth airports were only twelve miles apart, and Fort Worth's claim of discrimination could not be evaluated without noting the convenience of nearby Dallas service. There was another angle, however, to Fort Worth's complaint. The city claimed not only that it suffered discrimination but also that its air service was generally inadequate, a violation of section 404(a) of the act. The Board found that inadequacy could not be determined with regard to a city's total air service but only by inspection of particular city-pair markets. Furthermore, the adequacy of service in a city-pair market served by more than one carrier could be evaluated only by inspecting the schedules provided by all authorized carriers. Thus Braniff was excused for providing no single-plane Fort Worth–New York service because of the adequacy of American's.

At this point, cities unhappy with the quality of their air service had made little headway in securing findings of discrimination or inadequacy. Three recent cases, however, have changed the situation drastically and point to a number of failings in a city's air service which may cause the Board to find inadequacy and order improvements by the carriers certified for service. These are *Washington–Baltimore Adequacy of Service Investigation, Toledo Adequacy of Service Investigation,* and *Flint–Grand Rapids Adequacy of Service Investigation.*[42] The Baltimore case offered facts

[41] Fort Worth Investigation, CCH Av. Law Rep. §22,205.04. In New York–San Francisco Nonstop, the Board faced the same sort of appeal from the city and county of San Francisco (and many related interests) based on rivalry with Los Angeles. In denying reconsideration of the expanded service authorized in the case, the Board denied that it had been influenced by the "hard sell" of the city and of American Airlines, but the neutral observer is likely to have doubts. See New York–San Francisco Nonstop Service Case — Opinion and Order Denying and Dismissing Portions of Petitions for Reconsideration, Docket No. 9214 et al., decided Nov. 19, 1959, CCH Av. Law Rep. §22,333. This case was remanded by court action for hearings on the issue of undue influence.

[42] Washington–Baltimore Adequacy of Service Investigation, Docket No. 8148, decided April 29, 1960, Order Serial No. E–15162; Toledo Adequacy of Service Investigation, Docket No. 8851, decided Nov. 10, 1959, CCH Av. Law Rep. §22,325.01; Flint–Grand Rapids Adequacy of Service Investigation, Docket No. 9177, decided April 29, 1960, Order Serial No. E–15161.

superficially similar to the Fort Worth situation. Baltimore is located near Washington, which received vastly superior air service at least until jet service to Washington began to operate through the Baltimore airport. The carriers had evidently counted on Baltimore air passengers' willingness to journey to the Washington airport to make connections. However, the driving time between the two airports was more than one hour, not fifteen minutes as in the case of Dallas to Fort Worth. Furthermore, the air traffic generated at the Baltimore airport was grossly beneath what the city's size and economic activity would have indicated. Turning to particular city-pair markets involving Baltimore, the Board found three sorts of conditions to involve service inadequacy. The first of these was the absence of single-plane service to cities where an average of ten passengers were exchanged daily with Baltimore.[43] In identifying the markets that had been short-changed by this test, the Board adjusted Baltimore traffic statistics upward to allow for Baltimore passengers who had gone to Washington to secure flights. The Board found two other sources of inadequacy: the use of unpressurized aircraft (DC-3s and DC-4s) in first-class service and inconvenient departure times.[44] Numerous markets failed to meet these tests of adequate service, and the Board singled out particular certified carriers, sometimes arbitrarily, to provide the warranted service improvements.[45]

The *Flint* case was decided the same day as the *Baltimore* investigation. Here Capital Airlines was found to be providing inadequate service in four city-pair markets and was ordered to provide single-plane service with no more than two intermediate stops. The Board declared that "service is adequate when it is provided in such quantity and quality as to satisfy the reasonable

[43] The hearing examiner had adopted this criterion on the basis of a showing by Baltimore witnesses that 60 percent of all city-pairs currently receiving through-plane service exchanged less than ten passengers daily. He held that either single-plane service should be provided in markets where ten or more passengers were exchanged or at least that this standard is "of major importance" in evaluating the adequacy of service (Initial Decision, p. 57, and Appendices K, L).

[44] Order Serial No. E–15162, pp. 24–25.

[45] American Airlines had argued that the Board lacked the power to pick among nonperforming competing carriers in a market to order expansions of service. The Board rejected this, suggesting that since it had the power to order adequate service by all carriers it could certainly order it from any one of them (E–15162, p. 27).

needs of a community for both local and through transportation to its principal points of interest" and without the regular inconvenience of insufficient seats or the necessity to travel to nearby cities.[46] Thus inadequate capacity (high load factors), often mentioned in the route cases, became an indicator of inadequacy of service. Poor on-time performance was also found to be a form of service inadequacy, even though the Board made no formal attempt to cure it.

The *Toledo* case holds interest not because it adds to the substance of the measures of inadequacy indicated in the *Baltimore* and *Flint* decisions, but because of its handling of the test of inadequacy in a market served by more than one carrier. Toledo complained of the service by Capital and United to four major cities. United offered no coach schedules, Capital no through-plane service at all. The striking point about the case is the logic by which the Board ordered Capital to provide two round-trip coach flights for one year in the markets at issue. Capital had been the latecomer to the Toledo market, selected in the *New York–Chicago* case over two rivals to provide the maximum of effective competition with United. In accepting this award, the Board held that Capital had "assumed the primary obligation to compete in these markets," and the hearing examiner remarked that "a carrier should not be permitted, with impunity, to mislead a regulatory body by extending false promises of rendering improved service." [47] The Board sharply distinguished this case from the *Fort Worth* decision, which would at first seem inconsistent with the onus of the *Toledo* order. One difference was the original purpose of certifying Capital for the Toledo market. The other lay in "all the facts and circumstances" of the two cases, presumably referring to the availability to Fort Worth travelers of good service at nearby Dallas.

Several interesting features lie just below the surface of the *Baltimore, Flint,* and *Toledo* cases. First, the profitability of the service extensions under consideration was not an issue in any of them. In both the *Baltimore* and *Flint* decisions the carriers declined to submit cost information, attempting to place the burden of proof on the complainants to show that the extensions would

---

[46] Order Serial No. E–15161, p. 8.
[47] Toledo Adequacy of Service Investigation, Initial Decision, p. 22.

be profitable. The Board declined to permit this strategy, and indeed declared that it did not need to show that any of the service extensions ordered would be profitable.[48] In the *Toledo* case, costs of the extension of coach service by Capital were discussed in the examiner's decision, but only to the extent of finding that incremental rather than average costs should be used in evaluating the profit or loss which the service would involve. Further, much was said about the obligation of carriers to use profits from lucrative markets to subsidize those of lesser profitability.[49] However, the orders were not designed to force permanent extensions of unprofitable service; rather they were intended to force the carriers to test the profitability of the services ordered — experiments which the spur of competition had failed to induce. Paradoxically, the *Flint* and *Toledo* decisions recognized that certain features of these cases showed that part of the troubles complained of resulted from competitive pressures. Capital Airlines, short on aircraft competitive with those of its major rivals, had sought to maintain acceptable market shares in its largest markets at the expense of substantial deteriorations of service in smaller markets.[50] Capital was not the first carrier to follow this strategy. Possibly the carrier viewed this as a short-run profit-maximizing strategy; certainly as a long-run maximizing one. Chronic overscheduling in highly competitive markets, which has bothered the Board a good deal recently, essentially means accepting substantially lower load factors (and presumably lower short-run profits) in these markets than the same carriers would in relatively noncompetitive ones. Thus the Board's decisions in *Baltimore, Flint,* and *Toledo* are a direct attack on the overscheduling problem and perhaps more effective than the lectures delivered to the carriers in the 1957 and 1958 cases on fare increases. Such cases must be some embarrassment to a carrier mindful of its public image. In the *Baltimore* decision, the Board employed an objective standard of adequate service, resembling that for extension of air service for the local-service carriers' "use it or lose it" authorizations. Such a standard of ade-

---

[48] Flint–Grand Rapids Adequacy of Service Investigation, Order Serial No. E–15161, pp. 11–12.

[49] Toledo Adequacy of Service Investigation, Initial Decision, pp. 22–23.

[50] The examiner's Initial Decision in the *Toledo* case (*ibid.*, pp. 15–18) traces this in detail.

quate service is fairly easy to apply, so the Board can police more markets than if it has to weigh the reasonableness of its standards in each particular case. Furthermore, with an objective standard in force, the carriers can hardly ignore informal pressure to meet it. Though the economist at first glance is likely to think of the adequacy-of-service cases as a lawyer's paradise[51] and as an inefficient way of tampering with the market mechanism, there is a problem here, in fact, of oligopolistic conduct in major markets. It has assumed major proportions, and the only obvious solution[52] would seem to lie in a broader revision of the Board's powers and policies on entry into city-pair markets.

CONCLUSION

The Board's regulation of the airlines' product strongly resembles its regulation of price. The Board has certain fixed policies on the product which the airlines offer the traveler — for instance, its battery of incentives to use the most modern available aircraft and its restrictions of "unfair practices" such as deceptive scheduling, substitution of inferior aircraft, and the like. (The safety regulations administered by the Federal Aviation Agency apply a similar form of product regulation.) The Board also draws the line at certain extreme differences, or certain lacks of difference, between classes of air service. These policies add up to only a loose direct control over the product offered by the airlines, and the Board's most powerful direct influence on product comes from the restrictions on entry of the Civil Aeronautics Act and the Board's own historic policies on competition in city-pair markets. The same statements apply to the Board's control of the carriers' prices and profits — controls on price discrimination used mainly to avert price competition; loose and imprecise controls exercised over the fares and profits of the industry; the Board's reliance placed mainly on indirect pressures through its policies on entry and competitive certification.

Chapter 9 presented the evidence that the Board has placed

[51] A suspicion that is amply confirmed by reading "Adequacy of Domestic Airline Service," especially pp. 1214–1215, 1230, 1233–1234.

[52] The Board has announced a broader inquiry into standards of adequate service which would cover other policy problems as well. See *Traffic World*, CVII (May 13, 1961), 130–131, and also CVII (May 6, 1961), 124–125 — complaint of Oakland about inadequate service.

much of its faith in direct point-to-point competition to insure the quality of air service. It has justified this faith by a belief that oligopoly, rather than monopoly, will yield the traveler the best service at the existing fares and promote the choice of air travel in preference to other means. The economist would see virtues of a different sort in a policy of making the most point-to-point competition consistent with minimum costs. He would emphasize optimizing the allocation of airline resources among city-pair markets, introducing an appropriate structure of fares, producing an appropriate variety of classes of service, and installing incentives for the improvement of service and for marketing innovations. Only on the last one of these four does he join hands with the Civil Aeronautics Board, but, for whichever set of reasons, the Board is right in counting on the control of market structure to obtain the conduct and performance it wishes.

Despite its use of entry into city-pair markets to promote competition, the Board chronically gets cold feet when market conduct takes a competitive turn. The Board has comprehensive powers to control price rivalry and many forms of product rivalry, and the industry's market structure is unlikely to produce "destructive competition" (that is, predatory conduct to exclude rivals). Nevertheless, it has been unwilling to allow either price or product competition to flourish, and this has had important consequences. For the firm wishing to make a competitive move, many changes of price and product may be good substitutes. The Board controls price rivalry completely but only some forms of product rivalry. When its policies suppress most of those forms of rivalry which it can control, market rivalry turns to those dimensions of product rivalry which it does not control. These take the form, principally, of offering the most desirable aircraft (of which the Board approves), providing a large volume of flights (about which the Board has doubts), and installing minor lures ranging from elegant downtown ticket offices to free goods for customers. These forms of rivalry tend to adjust the structure of costs to the reigning structure of prices so that normal profits result.[53] Where the Board's controls over price and product tend

---

[53] Some airline employees' unions are aware of this and have urged the carriers to deflate the quality of their service on the theory that the unions could then capture the extra profits that would result. See *American Aviation*, XXII (Nov. 3, 1958), 55.

to make dense long-haul markets relatively profitable, there is a natural tendency toward the erosion of the quality of service in thinner short-haul markets. The recent rash of adequacy-of-service cases is probably a reflection of this, though such a conclusion should wait upon more information on the profitability of the extra service sought. The economist viewing these restrictions on the industry's conduct in adjusting price and product is left uncertain about how well adapted output is to demand. There is no way of knowing whether adjustments banned or discouraged by the Board would in fact go too far, and require market-induced corrections, or whether they would indeed be a step in the right direction. The only certainty is that the industry's whole balance of costs, prices, and products is subject to influences that steer it away from a market-determined solution.

11 Control of Carrier Subsidies, Costs, and Profits

Public subsidy to an industry yields some combination of two results: higher-than-normal profits and the employment of more resources than market demand and cost conditions warrant. As will be shown in Part Four, profits in the air-transport industry have not been more than normal. Hence public regulation has succeeded in its goal of inducing the industry to provide more service than market forces would warrant. For allocation of the economy's scarce resources, then, the most important consequence of the subsidy provisions of the Civil Aeronautics Act has been the offering of direct air service in city-pair markets in which it could not earn a normal return under monopolistic pricing. This fact, however, is not so important when we view subsidy administration by the Civil Aeronautics Board as an influence on the market conduct of the industry. This chapter deals instead with the method of administering carrier subsidies and the pattern of incentives it has produced in the industry. Subsidy to air transport takes two essentially different forms. One is the provision of service inputs to the industry at no cost or at subnormal returns. Examples are free federal airways, navigation aids and weather information, and airport facilities provided by local governments at charges not covering costs — flat or fixed subsidy. The other is "need" subsidy — subsidy designed to fill the gap between individual carriers' commercial revenues and their costs, including a normal return on investment. The former type has little influence on market conduct per se so long as it does not discriminate among the carriers benefited. It will be largely ignored in this chapter. The latter has had far-reaching influence on the industry's conduct.

The importance of the Board's administration of carrier subsidies is declining. Since the early 1950s the trunk carriers, earning most of the industry's revenues, have not received cost-covering or need subsidy. Still, the local-service carriers, helicopter operators, and other smaller segments of the industry continue to receive this kind of subsidy. Subsidy was a very important feature in regulating the trunks before the early 1950s. Furthermore, it is extremely useful to compare the control wielded by the Board over airline managements with and without a need subsidy in effect.[1]

SETTING AIRLINE SUBSIDY

By the terms of section 406 of the Civil Aeronautics Act, subsidy payments have always been handed the air carriers in association with payments for carrying mail. Before the act was passed in 1938, the Post Office had been in direct charge of buying the services of commercial aviation, often with a free hand in the amount of subsidy to be given.[2] This system persisted after 1938, with the Post Office appropriations including whatever volume of subsidy the Board decided to grant. After a considerable political dispute in the early 1950s (discussed in the next chapter), this arrangement was changed so that the Board had to extract the subsidy money from Congress itself. Also, its awards of mail pay to the carriers began to indicate what portion was subsidy and what was supposed to be purely compensatory payment for carrying the mail. Overtly, the Board's procedure has been to decide how much air service should be provided in route cases and certification proceedings; then in mail-pay proceedings it would award whatever sums were needed to cover the net cost of this warranted service.

But there is little in the mail-pay cases themselves to control the volume of the air service offered, and, broadly speaking, the Board's practice has been to authorize as much service as a politically acceptable level of subsidy would finance.[3] Thus in its

[1] For secondary sources treating the development of air-mail pay in some detail, see Gilbert L. Gifford, "The Evolution of Air Mail Rate Making," *Journal of Air Law and Commerce,* XII (Summer 1955), 298–342; John H. Frederick, *Commercial Air Transportation* (4th ed.; Homewood, 1955), chap. 8; Nelson L. Smith, "Regulation of Returns to Transportation Agencies," *Law and Contemporary Problems,* XXIV (Autumn 1959), 702–732; J. J. O'Connell, Jr., "Air Mail Pay under the Civil Aeronautics Act," *Indiana Law Journal,* XXV (Fall 1949), 27–41.

[2] See Paul T. David, *The Economics of Air Mail Transportation* (Washington, 1934); Claude E. Puffer, *Air Transportation* (Philadelphia, 1941); Lucile S. Keyes, *Federal Control of Entry into Air Transportation.*

[3] As was emphasized in Chapter 7, because subsidy makes up the deficiencies in commercial revenue, the Board's fare proceedings also affect the volume of subsidy. However, this connection was so little realized by the Board (or so little exploited) while the trunks were still on subsidy that it needs little attention here.

early years it granted new trunkline routes in thin territory when it seemed that they could be operated at no greater subsidy than routes covered in the "grandfather" certificates. The presumption was that Congress had legislated the permanent certification of the latter and so would approve of the former at the same unit cost.[4] In the 1950s a series of route cases that promised a sharp increase in subsidy to the local-service carriers followed a series of measures passed by Congress indicating strong political support for the local airlines.[5] If the Board tries to gear its decisions on the volume of subsidy to what is politically feasible, why did it get into so much trouble in the late 1940s, drawing charges of favoring the trunk carriers and of creating excessive competition? This outburst was largely due to bad forecasting by the Board. Temporary certifications of local-service carriers and many route extensions for the trunks had been granted during World War II. They rested on extravagant estimates of the postwar traffic and profits of the airlines, and the Board expected the subsidy cost to be much less than it actually turned out to be.[6] As the actual results of the postwar years appeared, the Board cut back sharply on trunk route extensions and reversed its own policies on certifying the local-service carriers. It made some effort to shut off new certifications and to give new local-service routes to the more profitable of the trunks.[7]

The Board's normal procedure in setting subsidy is to fix it in absolute amount over an indefinite future period for the individual carrier. These "closed" rates can, however, be reopened on petition either of the Board or the carrier. A carrier on an "open" rate has the prospect of getting a subsidy in the future to guarantee it a normal rate of return through the open period, until

[4] Keyes, p. 115; Keyes, "National Policy Toward Commercial Aviation — Some Basic Problems," *Journal of Air Law and Commerce,* XVI (Summer 1949), 281. See, for example, Continental Air Lines, Inc. — Amendment of Certificate of Public Convenience and Necessity (Roswell–Hobbs–Carlsbad Operation), Docket No. 265, 1 CAA 598 (1940).

[5] Donald J. Frederick, "Forecast: Locals' Subsidy Bill Going Up," *American Aviation,* XII (July 28, 1958), 53.

[6] Keyes, "National Policy Toward Commercial Aviation," pp. 283, 288; Dole A. Anderson, "Airline Self-Sufficiency and the Local Air Service Problem," *Journal of Air Law and Commerce,* XXI (Winter 1954), 5.

[7] Paul D. Zook, "The Certification of Local and Feeder Air Carriers," *Southwestern Law Journal,* VII (Spring 1953), 185–207; Great Lakes Area Case, Docket No. 535 et al., 8 CAB 360, pp. 384–389 (1947).

a final rate is again set by the Board. There is no recapture of a carrier's earnings under a closed rate, and the courts have held that subsidy cannot be extended to cover losses before the rate is reopened. Consequently, the carrier on a closed rate would tend to have all the normal incentives to maximize profits or minimize costs. A carrier on an open rate, however, has no such direct incentive. The Board, which gives a good deal of attention to incentives, has thus always tried to keep the subsidized carriers on closed rates.[8] It has had only modest success. Normal procedural requirements mean a significant delay between the reopening of a rate and its closing, and this problem has been made worse because the economic conditions for all carriers tend to change in the same direction at a given time; if any exist at all, the Board is then likely to get swamped with open mail rates. In mid-1958 only two of the local-service carriers and one of the three helicopter lines were on final rates, and most of the others had been on open rates for two years or more.[9]

Although the *General Passenger Fare* and *Local Service Rate of Return* cases have only recently established the Board's procedure for allowing profits in fare cases, such procedures have been a settled matter in mail-pay cases. The Board sidestepped the classic valuation controversies of the older public-utility industries: it rejected fair-value procedures[10] and settled on a cost-of-capital approach to the control of profits based on allowing a normal return on the airlines' actual total capitalization.[11] This avoided the absurdities of valuation by reproduction cost and the lesser problems of other standards based on physical valuation, but it also meant guaranteeing a return on capital which the airlines might not be devoting to air service. Income from nonoperating assets, of course, would be deducted to figure net subsidy requirements, but the problem is that including these assets in the rate base meant guaranteeing a normal rate of return on them.[12] Until recently the Civil Aeronautics Board followed the

[8] See O'Connell, pp. 31–32.

[9] F. P. Kimball, "For Locals, Inefficiency Can Pay Off," *American Aviation,* XXII (Aug. 11, 1958), 54.

[10] American Airlines, Inc., Mail Rate Proceeding, Docket No. 334 et al., 4 CAB 770, p. 788 (1942).

[11] Gifford, pp. 300–302, 335–336.

[12] See Order Serial No. E–16068, Nov. 25, 1960, General Passenger Fare Investigation, Docket No. 8008, pp. 33–35. Here the Board decided to switch to

practice of most other regulatory agencies in setting the allowable rate of return in very casual fashion, usually at 7 percent on total capital for past periods and 8 percent for future periods. There have been a few exceptions of higher rates of return allowed in setting future mail rates for carriers facing such uncertainties as re-equipment.[13] About a decade ago the Board turned to a special procedure for setting rates of return for the local-service carriers. The trouble was that, as their fleets of pre-World War II DC-3 aircraft came to be almost fully depreciated, their investment base sank to an extremely low level. Keeping the same rate of return meant a very low rate of profit on sales. The Board, feeling this to be undesirable, began setting a floor under the profit rate on sales in the form of a minimum return per plane-mile.[14] Recently, this problem has disappeared as the investment bases of the subsidized carriers have increased with the purchase of new equipment. Anticipating the outcome of the *Local Service Rate of Return* case, in 1958 the Board began allowing higher rates of return for future periods to the local-service carriers. In that year the Board allowed a 9.5 percent rate of return for Mohawk Airlines on the grounds that this was the lowest rate of return advocated by any party in the rate-of-return case.[15] This same rate was used in other local-service cases before the final decision in the rate-of-return case, which set a still higher rate of 12.75 percent maximum, 9 percent minimum, based on a breathtaking allowance of 21.35 percent rate of return on equity capital.[16]

Until 1951 air-carrier subsidy and payment for carrying mail were handled together. Since that time the Board has treated them separately, setting the "service rate" for carrying air mail and the subsidy level for carriers still receiving subsidy in separate

---

a different base of depreciated used and useful assets, essentially an "original cost" approach in terms of traditional methods of public-utility valuation.

[13] For example, Pan American-Grace Airways, Inc. — Mail Rates, Docket No. 716, 3 CAB 550, pp. 563–565 (1942).

[14] This minimum return first appeared in Trans-Texas Airways, Mail Rates, Docket No. 2931, 12 CAB 101 (1950). The device was used in a number of later final mail-rate cases, with the minimum return varying from 1.8 to 2.34 cents per plane-mile, eventually settling around 2 cents. See Gotch and Crawford, *Promise . . . Progress . . . Performance Without Profit, A Report on the Earnings Experience of the Local Service Airlines* (Washington, 1956), p. 28.

[15] See *Aviation Week*, LXIX (Sept. 8, 1958), 44–45.

[16] Order Serial No. E–15696, Rate of Return Local Service Carriers Investigation, Docket No. 8404, decided Aug. 26, 1960, pp. 1–3.

proceedings. The practices used to allow a rate of return on investment pertain to the subsidy-mail pay cases before the 1951 change, but only to the subsidy cases since then. Service rates on air mail have been set in two important cases, one decided in 1951 and one in 1955.[17] Determined to set a service mail rate on the basis of the cost of service, the Board found itself facing a problem of joint costs. To oversimplify somewhat, a plane flying between two cities can carry a certain number of passengers and a certain volume of mail, express, and freight. To the extent that these maximum proportions cannot be varied, passenger transport and cargo (mail and goods) transport are true joint products. There is no theoretically right way of allocating the joint costs of operating the flight between them. After a reasonably good assignment of the direct costs of passenger, mail, and freight services, the remaining joint costs were treated in the 1951 decision by assuming that all freight and express services were by-products, except to the extent that they actually produced revenue in excess of their direct costs. This meant dividing the joint costs between air mail and passenger traffic, excluding family-fare passengers whose discounts required them to travel at off-peak times. In the 1954 proceedings (which reached a final decision in 1955) the allocation of joint costs was given a more complicated basis. The net effect was to make the cost of air-mail carriage to the government a little less than it would have been under the 1951 system, but a little more than if joint costs were allocated to all types of air service on a straight revenue ton-mile basis.

In both of the decisions an 8 percent rate of return was allowed the carriers as compensation for carrying mail. In the 1951 case the actual charge to the Post Office per ton-mile was figured by grouping carriers with similar cost levels and setting a different line-haul charge for each group. This soon caused trouble, for it meant asking the Post Office to pay different charges for the same service when two carriers in different cost groups competed between the same pair of cities. After some grumbling, the Post Office adopted a policy of choosing the lower cost carrier, normally the larger one. Before the 1954–55 revision of the service mail-pay

---

[17] American Airlines, Inc., et al., Mail Rates, Docket No. 2849 et al., 14 CAB 558 (1951); American Airlines, Inc., Domestic Trunklines, Service Mail Rates, Docket No. 6599 et al., 21 CAB 8 (1955). For an analysis of these cases, see Gifford, pp. 314–333.

scheme, the Board had adopted several stopgap measures to keep some carriers from losing their air-mail revenues entirely. In that revision it came up with a final solution. This was a two-part rate, with a fixed line-haul charge that was the same for all carriers and a terminal charge that varied inversely with the size of the dispatching city. This produced relatively larger revenues for the higher-cost carriers operating from smaller cities and yet fixed the same charge for any two carriers operating between a given pair of cities. Periodically the charge is made that the Board's "service" mail rates actually contain an element of subsidy by covering more than the true cost of the service. Though this allegation will be considered again in Part Four, it is worth noting here that the service rate depends strongly on the decision made about allocating joint costs. Economically speaking, a "service" rate resting on cost could only be identified as lying within upper and lower limits set by extreme allocations of the joint costs.

EFFECTS OF MAIL-PAY ARRANGEMENTS

The preceding paragraphs have told briefly how the Board sets the volume of air carrier subsidy and distributes it to the airlines. Now we turn to the impact of these methods on the incentives to the carriers' managements. There is the obvious question of the extent to which a subsidy to guarantee normal profits removes the incentive to minimize costs. Beyond that, there are subtle but far-reaching problems of the impact of subsidy on the pattern of competition among the carriers.

The Board has great potential control over the costs, and thereby the operations, of carriers receiving direct subsidy. The Civil Aeronautics Act requires only a return to cover costs incurred under "honest, economical, and efficient management." The last two words have given the Board the power to disallow airline expenditures for many things not meeting its approval, outright inefficiency among them. Frequently these disallowances have aimed at controlling the volume of service provided by the carriers. At times they have sought to punish bad managerial judgment by withholding subsidy to cover mistakes. And sometimes they have sought to control competitive product-improvement expenditures. Table 25 presents a classification of the most

Table 25. Types and amounts of carrier expenses disallowed by Civil Aeronautics Board in local-service mail-pay cases, 1947–1955

Type of expenses	Amount
Disallowed mileage flown	$506,984
Disallowed maintenance in excess of $34 per flying hour	214,387
Disallowed flying operations and maintenance expenses on excessive aircraft	120,927
Disallowed general and administrative expenses exceeding 13.5 percent of other cash costs	106,142
Disallowed ground and indirect expenses by comparison with other carriers	38,590
Disallowed traffic and sales expenses by comparison with other carriers	58,418
Disallowed legal fees above cost level	75,837
Disallowed president's salary	58,329
Disallowed depreciation on aircraft value in excess of prescribed acquisition cost	107,494
Disallowed depreciation through adjusted service life and residual values	343,623
Total	$1,630,731

Source: Gotch and Crawford, *Promise . . . Progress . . . Performance without Profit, A Report on the Earnings Experience of the Local Service Airlines* (Washington, D.C., 1956), table 24.

important types of disallowances in local-service mail-pay cases through 1955. It shows several important features of the Board's disallowance practices. First of all, the largest single item, disallowed mileage, and the related one of disallowed operation expenses for excessive aircraft indicate the Board's concern with controlling promotional expansions of service by the local airlines, and thereby with controlling the level of subsidy to carriers. Mechanical standards have been developed, through comparisons of costs within carrier groups, to disallow excessive general and administrative expenses and excess maintenance. Smaller amounts have been deleted for unsupported expense items, charity contributions, and the like, on the basis of managerial second-guessing.[18]

Since 1948 the Board has used a sliding-scale arrangement for disallowing excessive flights by local-service carriers. Two round

[18] Gotch and Crawford, pp. 44–45. See also O'Connell, pp. 32–36, and Harvey C. Bunke, "Commercial Aviation and the Civil Aeronautics Act of 1938," *Southern Economic Journal*, XX (April 1954), 358.

trips daily over a route have been the normal amount. Extra schedules must generate enough revenue to guarantee that an increasing portion of total operating expenses is covered by total commercial revenue. This system has been changed on occasion but still has one essential feature: an increasing portion of average (not marginal) costs must be covered if flights over a segment are increased. Thus it creates a potent incentive for the local carriers not to add schedules. In theory, an extra flight scheduled over a route can increase a carrier's profits *after* subsidy only if the flights previously scheduled have met some standard of maximum loss, even if the extra flight is profitable in itself.[19]

One important control of expenses has been over the aircraft purchased by local-service carriers. Pioneer Air Lines, a prosperous Texas local-service carrier, began in the early 1950s to convert its fleet from DC-3s to the larger postwar Martin 2–0–2 aircraft. Because Pioneer's routes were lightly traveled, by trunkline standards, the change brought initially higher cost per revenue passenger-mile and an initially higher subsidy requirement. Pioneer's request for more subsidy reached the Board during an economy drive, and the excess expenses of the Martins were disallowed. The carrier sought to recover its DC-3s but never got over the financial shock and eventually disappeared by merger with Continental Air Lines.[20] The Pioneer case was not a major precedent. In 1954 the Board warned a subsidized trunkline, Braniff, that increased costs resulting from what it thought was an unjustifiably large purchase of new aircraft would not be covered by subsidy. However, it also approved purchase of new aircraft on a more cautious basis by another local-service carrier, Southwest Airways.[21] By 1958, a decade of fairly high profits for the trunk carriers and strong congressional support for the local-service airlines had changed the picture, and the Board indicated

[19] Gotch and Crawford, pp. 35–40; Piedmont Aviation, Inc., Mail Rates, Docket No. 6363, 19 CAB 241 (1954); *Aviation Week,* LXXII (Feb. 8, 1960), 43, and LXXI (Aug. 10, 1959), 40.

[20] Pioneer Air Lines, Inc., Mail Rates, Docket No. 5499, 17 CAB 499 (1953); Pioneer Air Lines, Inc., Mail Rates, Docket No. 6375, 18 CAB 561 (1954). But in another case the Board backed away from taking the responsibility to assert that the carrier was not "fit, willing, and able" to render service under these circumstances; see Pioneer Air Lines, Inc., Amended Certificate, Docket No. 5500, 18 CAB 11 (1953).

[21] *Aviation Week,* LX (June 14, 1954), 92; LXI (Oct. 25, 1954), 101.

its general willingness to support the subsidized local carriers in switching from DC-3s to better aircraft if this was done at a reasonable pace.[22]

These patterns of cost regulation in the local-service industry are fairly similar to the way in which the trunks were handled. The more important trunks, however, were off subsidy by the early 1950s, and the harried Board of the late 1940s exercised rather little control of allowable costs. There were occasional dramatic moves, such as the disallowance of $2.6 million of past costs that Colonial Airlines had allegedly incurred through improper management.[23] Generally, however, enough excuses for high costs were open to a carrier, and the Board's efforts to disallow the expenses stemming from inefficiency were not very effective. Further, it has been suggested that the extent of disallowances for a carrier was often in proportion to its financial ability to stand them, so that the least prosperous and possibly least efficient carriers got the easiest treatment.[24] Many instances make even the outsider suspicious of the worth of the Board's direct control over the subsidized carriers' costs, such as the small amount of field auditing of reported expenses the Board has done. In 1956 the House Appropriations Committee badgered the Board members about an audit report of the Comptroller General questioning the 1950 *Big Four Final Mail Rate* proceeding and other uses of carriers' cost information. Cost information submitted to the Board proved impossible to reconcile with the carriers' annual reports. The audit found a considerable amount of expensing items that should have been capitalized and claimed that one trunk had hidden $1.6 million of investment as current costs in a single year.[25] A year earlier the same committee questioned the Board on its failure to make a thorough audit of the international

[22] Mohawk Airlines, Inc. — Temporary Mail Rates — Order to Show Cause, Docket No. 7277, decided Jan. 24, 1958, CCH Av. Law Rep. §22,161; Mohawk Airlines, Inc. — Mail Rates, Docket No. 7277, decided May 20, 1959, CCH Av. Law Rep. §22,272.

[23] *Aviation Week,* LV (Oct. 22, 1951), 68–69.

[24] Bunke, p. 358.

[25] See "Audit Report to the Congress of the United States on Civil Aeronautics Board, October, 1955," reprinted in *Department of Commerce and Related Agencies Appropriations for 1957,* hearings, U.S. House of Representatives, Committee on Appropriations, Subcommittee, 84th Cong., 2nd sess. (Washington, 1956), pp. 754–811.

carriers' costs and had cut the Board's request for appropriations except to provide more funds for field auditing. Another factor that casts suspicion on the Board's control of carrier costs and efficiency is the rather variable practices used in deciding whether various kinds of nonoperating revenues have to be counted as offsets to subsidy requirements.[26] Court decisions have forced the Board to offset subsidy by the amount of some nonoperating revenues, and recently it has taken a more severe and more consistent stand in requiring offsetting.[27]

Other actions by the Board to control efficiency and managerial actions affecting profits have had just as little success. For example, court decisions have given the Board control over the carrier's accounting practices only for rate-making purposes. Thus the Board can control depreciation of equipment as it affects the profits discussed in rate cases, but not as it affects the profits the carriers impute to themselves or proclaim to the general public.[28] Also, the Board could not prevent the allegedly gross mismanagement of one of the largest airlines, TWA. In a 1950 case it was unable to avert further control of the carrier by Howard Hughes, although the decision contained pages of evidence suggesting that Hughes's procrastination in the early postwar period had been responsible for many of the carrier's difficulties.[29]

Despite the weakness of its direct control of costs, the Civil Aeronautics Board deserves a good mark for at least a substantial effort at administering need subsidy without eliminating the pressure on managements to minimize costs. It has tried to keep the carriers on closed rates and thus not on cost-plus operation. Its troubles in doing this grow largely out of the general slowness of its formal proceedings, which is in turn a function of the Board's small staff and the constraints of due process. It has tried to disallow improper expenses. Opinions differ on how effec-

[26] This variability is shown by R. J. Rasenberger, "Legislative and Administrative Control of Air Carrier Subsidy," *George Washington Law Review,* XXV (March 1957), 416–420.

[27] Capital Gains Proceeding, Docket No. 7902, decided Aug. 1, 1958, CCH Av. Law Rep. §22,191.

[28] Alaska Airlines, Inc. v. Civil Aeronautics Board, 257 F.2d 229 (1958), cert. denied, 358 U.S. 881 (1958).

[29] Trans World Airlines, Inc., Further Control by Hughes Tool Company, Docket No. 2796, 12 CAB 192 (1950).

tively this has been done.[30] At least for the local-service carriers, disallowances up to 1956 had in effect cut their cumulative profits in half. One can conclude that the Board probably did as well as possible, given its statutory instructions. Critics of the Board have urged many times that it should change its formal arrangements in order to give subsidy as the fixed contractual payment for providing an agreed pattern of air service. This would entirely eliminate the "need" of particular corporate entities. The Board has announced a move in this direction. It started in 1961 to subsidize the local-service carriers, according to various operating factors for the industry as a whole rather than for individual carriers. The local airlines are divided into four groups according to the size of their route systems. Subsidy is based on group characteristics, so that cost cutting by one carrier will raise its own profits rather than cut its subsidy.[31] The Board may finally have found a way to avoid undesirable incentives in administering subsidy.

In a many-faceted industry such as air transport, the subsidy provisions affect many incentives facing carrier managements other than those for cost minimization. Imagine a firm selling services in many markets. Its selling prices are fixed by public authority and it receives public subsidy. Some of the markets are competitive and yield profits. Others, in which it is the sole seller, yield either trivial profits or commercial losses. The subsidy is fixed rather than being set retroactively, but the fixed rate is changed frequently toward yielding normal profits in future periods. What would such a firm do that an unsubsidized firm, finding itself in the same situation, would not do? The most obvious prediction is that the subsidized firm would have no reason for giving up its unprofitable markets. Indeed, if it maximizes total profits (and not the internal rate of return), it would seek to offer as much unprofitable service as it could. Each new money-losing market would mean more equipment and a larger investment base on which to earn a normal rate of return. Of course, the same could be said for increasing its share of the profitable competitive markets. Efforts to gain a larger share of these mar-

[30] *Cf.* Bunke, p. 358, and D. W. Bluestone, "The Problem of Competition among Domestic Trunk Airlines," *Journal of Air Law and Commerce,* XXI (Winter 1954), 62.

[31] *Wall Street Journal,* Dec. 29, 1960, p. 4.

kets, if successful, would yield temporary profits until over-all subsidy was adjusted downward. On the other hand, reduced profits due to the increased costs of a brisk competitive struggle in a potentially profitable market would yield temporary losses until subsidy is adjusted upward. What the balance of these two possibilities is one cannot say, and the final answer seems to be that the profit incentive for expansion into unprofitable monopoly markets is not clearly greater or less than that for expansion on the same scale into competitive markets. The psychic income of a quiet life cuts one way, the psychic income of besting one's rivals, the other. But this indeterminacy disappears if we change the assumptions slightly and consider a subsidized firm which believes that the growth of markets and cost-cutting innovations will remove it from subsidy in the near future. Then it will have an enormous incentive to pursue larger shares of more lucrative markets while still receiving subsidy, for such an action could have an enormous payoff in the future at no present cost. (The Civil Aeronautics Board maintained the position through the 1940s that subsidy to the trunk carriers was only a transitional form of aid.)

With this we may contrast the unsubsidized firm in the same market situation. It would have every incentive to abandon all unprofitable markets except those in a developmental phase. Depending on its time horizon and many other factors, it would have a motive to fight for a bigger market share in the profitable markets. Indeed, under a variety of short-run conditions, it might abandon marginally profitable monopoly markets to concentrate its attention on profitable competitive markets.

There are other effects of need subsidy on incentives. The subsidized firm would face a different distribution of payoffs in deciding whether to innovate. The distribution would certainly have more of a central tendency than for the unsubsidized firm. It might be biased toward positive returns, if the regulatory authority handling subsidy covered the losses from innovations that fail but allowed capture of some of the profits of successful innovation. Thus there is some possibility for the subsidized firm to be bolder at innovating, especially with marketing innovations that could provoke retaliation from rivals.

Now suppose that the subsidized firm has some say in the

process that sets the prices it charges. Unless some set of prices existed that would boost it out of subsidized status into greater-than-normal commercial profits, it would have no incentive to worry about prices either way. To the extent that such an incentive existed, however, it would be to secure low prices, which would raise its volume of sales (unless demand were completely inelastic) and thereby its investment base and total allowable profits. There would be no strong incentive for the firm to consider changing prices to alter differential rates of commercial return in its various markets. The contrasting, profit-maximizing, pricing decisions of an unsubsidized firm are well known. They would identify an appropriate price in every market that could be profitably served at *some* price.

Jumping ahead of the story somewhat, these predictions are strikingly accurate for the air-transport industry — both for its behavior under subsidy and the adjustments made by firms that have gone off subsidy. Before the early 1950s, the trunk carriers actively sought extension into thin territory as well as greater shares of profitable markets. Since their over-all systems became commercially profitable in the 1950s, most, though not all, of them have been shedding unprofitable markets at a brisk rate.[32] Marginally profitable monopoly markets have sometimes been jetisoned to allow concentration on a struggle for larger competitive markets. Subsidized carriers may have been more willing to undertake marketing innovations than others. Finally, there has been a slowly growing consciousness of the problem of efficient pricing, especially in the sense of "fare structure" — setting prices in different city-pair markets so that they bear an appropriate relation to one another. The pricing of the local-service carriers remaining on subsidy in the 1950s contrasts to the unsubsidized trunks. The former have favored low fares and the Board has had to prod them to take general increases. They have been willing to take almost any new markets offered to them and in many other ways have shown behavior strikingly similar to that of the trunks in their years of need subsidy.

---

[32] For figures on this, see *Permanent Certificates for Local Service Air Carriers,* hearings on S. 651, U.S. Senate, Committee on Interstate and Foreign Commerce, Subcommittee, 84th Cong., 1st sess. (Washington, 1955), pp. 118–120.

CARRIER SUBSIDY AND OTHER BOARD POLICIES

As previous chapters have suggested, the Civil Aeronautics Board's function of paying subsidy to the airlines has had an enormous impact on other types of decisions. Though there have been many deviations from the trend, the Board's general objective has been to make some progress toward eliminating subsidy for any given group of carriers while maintaining air service over the most extensive route network possible. When the trunks were on need subsidy, this meant that it was largely the Board, not the carriers, that pressed for general fare increases and fought price competition in the profitable markets. With somewhat mixed motives, the Board also fought entry of new firms into the commercially profitable markets, the creation of coach service, and other product-strategy moves having the same effect as price cuts. At the same time the Board did not have to worry about differences in the various carriers' levels of cost and efficiency, and indeed the route extensions granted to the smaller trunks in the 1940s were aimed not so much at getting them up to minimum efficient scale as at doing the "democratic" thing. The Board and the carrier managements were jointly responsible for the airlines' profits. This reduced the managements' responsibility and distracted the Board from consideration of its ultimate goals of air development and service. The Board was left to mull over such questions as whether it should try to manipulate subsidy to compel mergers, route abandonments, and service deteriorations which would cut the subsidy bill but which it lacked the power to order directly.[33]

Under conditions of need subsidy to all carriers, the notion of "excess competition" had a perfectly sensible meaning for the Board — rivalry in potentially profitable markets that cut heavily

[33] See O'Connell, p. 36; Keyes, "National Policy Toward Commercial Aviation," pp. 287–288; Keyes, "A Reconsideration of Federal Control of Entry into Air Transportation," *Journal of Air Law and Commerce,* XXII (Spring 1955), 194–195. Many articles in the *Journal of Air Law and Commerce* a decade ago reflected this concern over the volume of subsidy and the way it colored the Board's other regulatory decisions. See, for example, James M. Landis, "Air Routes under the Civil Aeronautics Act," XV (Summer 1948), 295–302; Paul W. Cherington, "Objectives and Strategies for Airline Pricing," XVIII (Summer 1951), 253–265; H. A. Jones and F. Davis, "The 'Air Coach' Experiment and National Air Transport Policy," XVII (Winter 1950), 1–21.

into the carriers' commercial profits and raised the subsidy bill. With subsidy used to cover the costs of the airlines rather than directly to set a pattern of service over unprofitable routes, the Board could not have let competitive motives rage unchecked. There is strong evidence that this outlook persisted in the Board's thinking after most of the trunks became commercially self-sufficient. Removal of the subsidy prop restored the normal self-correcting mechanism present in unregulated industries when oligopolistic rivalry forces profits below normal. It also created a normal incentive for recognition of the oligopolistic mutual dependence of the carriers, which now promised a payoff that was missing when a gain of commercial monopoly profits in one market meant only a cut of loss-covering subsidy in another. In short, the shift of the trunks away from need-subsidy status tended to change the incentives governing conduct from "too much competition" toward "too much monopoly." Yet one could argue from many of the Board's decisions on fares and product competition in the 1950s that there was no recognition of how the departure from subsidy largely solved the "problem" of competition.[34]

However, no sooner is this pervasive influence of the Board's subsidy function recognized than the caution must be inserted not to make too much of it. The Board often tends to bend its rules and to sacrifice other objectives to protect the corporate existence of particular airlines. Some critics have blamed this protective policy on the "need" provisions of the mail-pay section of the act.[35] But it might be wiser to focus on the certification features of the act. The certified carrier accepts a legal obligation to offer service over stated routes upon reasonable request. Inevitably, the regulatory authority assumes some obligation to protect the certified firm from commercial threats to its perform-

[34] Again, the literature of the industry reflects this failure to see the change in carrier motivation. Partly this stemmed from poor analysis; partly it was because the carriers' spokesmen saw their advantage in the Board's keeping its old outlook. See Anderson, pp. 6, 13, and Stuart G. Tipton and Stanley Gewirtz, "The Effect of Regulated Competition on the Air Transport Industry," *Journal of Air Law and Commerce*, XXII (Spring 1955), 157–191.

[35] United Research, Inc., *Federal Regulation of the Domestic Air Transport Industry* (Cambridge, Mass., 1959), pp. 86–92, 111–112, and *passim*. This excellent document perhaps leans too heavily on Mrs. Keyes's arguments of a decade earlier.

ance of this service.[36] The airlines, with or without subsidy, operate under such a certification system. Subsidy procedures have been proposed which would not wed the giver of subsidy to particular recipient firms, and indeed the Civil Aeronautics Board has been recently moving in the direction of viewing the local-service subsidy as the payment made to secure service over unprofitable routes rather than as a payment to keep particular firms profitable. But a certificate is given to a particular firm for a particular service; the regulator is seldom certain that the service will again be provided if the firm fails. Here would seem to lie a major source of the solicitude of the Board for the welfare of the airlines it regulates.

[36] Horace Gray used this fact as the basis for his attack on the "public utility" concept. See H. M. Gray, "The Passing of the Public Utility Concept," *Journal of Land and Public Utility Economics*, XVI (Feb. 1940), 8–20.

12 The Political Environment of Civil Aeronautics Board Policy

A regulatory agency, in purest theory, is something like a perpetual-motion machine. It is set running initially by a statute which assigns it a set of objectives and provides powers and tools appropriate to achieving them. From there on, subject to judicial restraint on its substantive or procedural excesses of authority, the agency is on its own. Reality anything but matches this picture. In matters of both procedure and substance, a thousand facts of life prevent such agencies from leading this sort of rarefied existence.

The Board faces a small number of air carriers that appear before it daily in case after case, presenting their problems, wishes, and attitudes in legal briefs and arguments. Further pressure comes from trade publications in the air-transport industry, which issue editorial comment on the Board's decisions and in effect judge the Board's actions from the airlines' point of view. More sporadic pressure comes from the other organs of the federal government. The Board is theoretically a child of Congress, exercising regulatory powers delegated by the legislature. But Congress never speaks with a single voice to tell the Board whether or not it is correctly carrying out the legislative will. There have been no significant changes of the major provisions of the Civil Aeronautics Act since its passage in 1938. Particular congressional committees, however, have repeatedly brought heavy pressure on the Board to modify its policies. The House and Senate Appropriations Committees, controlling the agency's lifeblood of funds, have often pressed it for major changes in policies, including some only indirectly related to its budgetary requirements. The House and Senate Interstate and Foreign Commerce Committees, particularly the latter, have also been a major source of influence on Board policies because the Board needs their good will to get desired changes in its statutory powers and duties and to fight off unwanted ones. Other committees have at times put strong pressure on the Board through generating adverse publicity, thereby weakening the Board's reserve of "good will" all along the line. The Senate Select Committee on Small Business and the Anti-Monopoly Subcommittee of the House Committee on the Judiciary at times have played this role.

Within the executive branch, the Board has faced the influence of the President and occasionally other executive agencies, principally the Department of Commerce. The President may review decisions affecting the routes of the international air carriers and thus has direct authority in this field.[1] This is not the case with the domestic industry. Still, because the terms of Civil Aeronautics Board members expire after six years and require presidential reappointment, the President or members of his staff can exert much influence on decisions affecting domestic carriers by threatening not to reappoint or by actually dropping members who have voted consistently the "wrong way." The Department of Commerce is the only other arm of the executive branch that regularly poses problems of political relations for the Board. These problems arise because of the department's general orientation toward the welfare of business and, more particularly, because it has long harbored desires to take over some of the Board's functions, having succeeded in detaching the Civil Aeronautics Authority before World War II. Commerce Department attitudes have typically tended to support "sound economic conditions" (higher profits) in the air-transport industry, the reduction of subsidy, the merger of smaller carriers, and the restriction of competition.

A full-scale analysis of the impact of political pressures on the Board's decisions would be an overwhelming task. The one thorough analysis, Basil Mott's study of the decision to separate carrier subsidy from air-mail pay, is a lengthy piece of detective work.[2] This chapter will attempt a broad and relatively impres-

---

[1] This control and its uses were critically discussed in 1958 before the Harris Committee. See *Investigation of Regulatory Commissions and Agencies,* hearings, U.S. House of Representatives, Committee on Interstate and Foreign Commerce, Subcommittee, 85th Cong., 2nd sess. (Washington, 1958), part 1, pp. 14–73.

[2] See Basil J. F. Mott, Jr., "The Effect of Political Interest Groups on C.A.B. Policies," *Journal of Air Law and Commerce,* XIX (Autumn 1952), 379–410. A number of Inter-University Case Program studies deal with aviation policy, but the only one concerning the domestic carriers is Emmette S. Redford, *The General Passenger Fare Investigation,* ICP Case Series No. 56 (University, Ala., 1960).

sionistic sketch of the extent to which political pressure has left a visible mark on the Board's decisions and will make a rough estimate of the limits which various influence groups can set on the Board's actions. As the preceding chapters have indicated, some types of cases before the Board appear with relative frequency, and no one case has overwhelming implications for the whole domestic airline industry. Other sorts of decisions appear less frequently, and individual cases are both more important to the industry at large and less amenable to affording decisions on the basis of precedent. These, as one would expect, reflect outside pressures to a much greater degree. The handling of the irregular coach carriers in the decade after World War II, the decision to separate carrier subsidy from payments for carrying air mail, the comings and goings of the general passenger-fare investigation, the major switches in policy on new competitive route awards and on the treatment of the local-service carriers — these are the types of decisions that bear marks of political pressures upon the Board. This is true not only for the obvious reason that groups able to influence the Board care more about these decisions, but also because the Board is always under pressure to complete relatively routine work and thus is apt to put off matters which, though fundamental, can be postponed.

THE BOARD AND OTHER ORGANS OF GOVERNMENT

The Board survived its first years of operation and then World War II without facing any very serious pressures from other segments of the federal government. The late 1940s, however, were to be a different story. Three areas of Board policy toward the domestic carriers became major centers of controversy. One was the combination of expanded point-to-point carrier competition and rapidly increasing mail pay that brought a hail of charges that the Board had fostered "excessive competition." Later this charge gave way to demands that the Board abandon its policy of refusing to unscramble the element of subsidy from the total payment for carrying air mail. The third major issue was the Board's policy toward the irregular or nonscheduled airlines which had sprung from the heap of surplus transport aircraft available at the end of World War II.

The background of these policies lies in the pressures and preoccupations of the Board's early years. It was swamped at the outset with applications for certificates of public convenience and necessity by the "grandfather" carriers and others seeking entry to the industry. After the exigencies of the first war years were past, the Board set out to deal with a huge backlog of new route applications. As was seen above, the optimistic outlook of the carriers for the postwar period, the rise of the "competitive presumption," and the desire to give profitable routes to the smaller carriers[3] conspired with the complete lack of reliable predictions of postwar costs and revenues to draw the Board into a haphazard but enthusiastic awarding of new routes.

The postwar period was hardly under way when things began to go badly for the certified industry and the Board. At first, with their fleets only partly restored after the war, the airlines were deluged with traffic. They lacked the equipment and the managerial efficiency to deal with this, and booming business went hand in hand with deteriorating service and rising costs.[4] Later, the phasing in of new types of aircraft led to temporarily higher costs. The attendant crashes and groundings frightened away enough customers to accentuate the slippage in traffic growth that occurred naturally as the economy returned to normal. The Board was swamped with requests for increased mail pay and with problems of adjusting the fare level upward. At the same time that the certified industry was losing money (even after mail-pay subsidies), a few heavily traveled long-haul routes were yielding significant profits. Into these routes moved the nonscheduled airlines, cutting into the profits earned there by the subsidized trunks and thus raising the aggregate cost of subsidy to the government. For a time the Board tried imposing regulations that limited the ability of the "nonskeds" to divert profitable traffic from the trunks,[5] but they proved unenforceable. It complained that no sooner was one flagrant violator of the irregular-service

[3] The solicitude for small carriers was itself partly a result of pressure from these carriers and a minority of the House Committee on Interstate and Foreign Commerce. See H. C. Westwood, "Choice of Air Carrier for New Air Transport Routes," *George Washington Law Review,* XVI (Feb. 1948), 179–180.

[4] See "What's Wrong with the Airlines?" *Fortune,* XXXIV (August 1946), 73–78.

[5] For a more comprehensive discussion of this situation, see pp. 169–174 above and the references cited there.

requirement put out of business than its planes and personnel turned up with a new corporate identity.[6] Finally, according to charges of the certified carriers, at least some members of the Board were in no hurry to curtail the competitive, low-fare service furnished by these carriers.[7]

The Board had its first taste of postwar troubles in 1946 as the House Committee on Interstate and Foreign Commerce issued a report recording complaints about air-carrier subsidy from other segments of the transportation industry. In the following year, the Republican 80th Congress met at a time of air-carrier deficits, crashes, and poor service. The commerce committees in both houses investigated the air-safety problem and the Department of Commerce criticized the carriers and the Civil Aeronautics Board for overselling and overexpanding air transport. In March 1947, the Board issued its decision in the *American President Lines* case reaffirming its stiff policy against the entry of surface carriers into air transportation.[8] The steamship companies, then voicing willingness to operate international air routes without subsidy, brought further attention to the issue of subsidy as they aired their grievances before the House Committee on Interstate and Foreign Commerce. The Senate commerce committee was friendlier to the Board at this time and refrained from a proposed investigation of airline finance, but some members wanted to look into the subsidy issue.

By mid-1947, discontent with conditions in the airline industry had given rise to two separate investigations — the Presidential Air Policy Commission and the Congressional Aviation Policy Board. Both were given general hunting licenses into matters affecting federal influence on civil and military air transport.[9] A little later, in August, a cautious statement emerged from the Air Coordinating Committee suggesting the direction in which governmental opinion on air-transport regulation was moving.

[6] *Air-line Industry Investigation,* hearings pursuant to S. Res. 50, U.S. Senate, Committee on Interstate and Foreign Commerce, 81st Cong., 1st sess. (Washington, 1949), pp. 496–497.

[7] Testimony of Robert Ramspeck (of the Air Transport Association), *ibid.,* p. 384.

[8] American President Lines, Ltd., et al., Petition, Docket No. 2411, 7 CAB 799 (1947).

[9] For the respective enabling documents, see *Journal of Air Law and Commerce.* XIV (Summer 1947), 364–366.

(This committee, which occasionally has played a major role in air-transport policy, arose in 1945 as a liaison group of the military, the aviation agencies, and the Departments of State and Commerce, with the Post Office, Bureau of the Budget, Treasury, and Federal Communications Commission added later.[10]) Competition was found desirable as long as it was "constructive in character." It was suggested that, as the postwar situation proceeded, "it may become desirable to permit mergers, abandonment or reassignment of routes or liquidation of a carrier." [11] Early in 1948 the investigatory reports emerged from the Congressional Aviation Policy Board and the Presidential Air Policy Commission. Neither was heavily critical of the Board, but both implied that something should be done about the situation of losses and rising subsidy requirements. And during 1948 several congressional hearings and statements voiced sentiments for getting the volume of air-mail subsidy out into the open. Later in 1948 the Board, under a new chairman, began to crack down on the noncertified coach carriers, requiring them to apply for individual exemptions to operate. Furthermore, there was some dispute among segments of the Board's staff on how to proceed with the short-term pressures of the mail-rate cases and the longer-run matter of a cost study of air-mail service. Speaking of this period in testimony before the Senate commerce committee, the chairman of the board of Chicago and Southern Air Lines declared:

The answer you get so often when you talk to the staff or to the Board is, "We have got to have mergers, we have got to reduce the number of carriers, we have to find all the ways we can of getting the carriers off this subsidy because Congress is adamant on the subject." Apparently you have succeeded, here on the Hill, in generating an atmosphere which is very restrictive in its impact upon that Board.[12]

The next year, 1949, brought heavier pressures of all sorts upon the Board. Enforcement of the regulations on nonscheduled air-

---

[10] See George A. Brownell, "The Air Coordinating Committee: A Problem in Federal Staff Work," *Journal of Air Law and Commerce,* XIV (Autumn 1947), 405–435.

[11] Air Coordinating Committee, "A Statement of Certain Policies of the Executive Branch of the Government in the General Field of Aviation," reprinted in *Journal of Air Law and Commerce,* XIV (Summer 1947), 367.

[12] *Air-line Industry Investigation,* p. 484.

lines was beginning to raise significant public criticism for stifling small business. The powerful Senate and House Appropriations Committees were objecting to the granting of retroactive subsidy to cover the costs of grounding defective aircraft types earlier in the postwar period and to the size of the salaries of some airline executives.[13] Pushed by the Senate committee, Senator Edwin C. Johnson of the Senate Interstate and Foreign Commerce Committee opened a large investigation into the financial condition of the airlines, which heard all of the groups that were then in opposition to the Board's policies. A Hoover Commission reorganization proposal asked for the Department of Commerce to work out over-all route programs and "balanced promotional programs for land, sea, and air transportation." The ever-threatening commerce department had wanted more than this — control of sea and air subsidy programs, for which it had argued in order to gain general control over the policies of the respective regulatory boards.[14] With the air-mail subsidy under fire from many sides and the House Appropriations Committee gnawing at the Board's budget request, the Board was forced to retreat from its unwillingness to separate mail pay into its subsidy and compensatory elements. It was not possible to give way gracefully on this issue, and, largely because of it, the Board's relations with the Senate Interstate and Foreign Commerce Committee and the House Appropriations Committee deteriorated steadily.[15] Only with the departure of Board Chairman J. J. O'Connell in mid-1950 were these relations patched up. No bill dealing with subsidy separation ever got through both houses of Congress, but by 1950 even the carriers were pinning their hopes on subsidy separation by the Board (rather than someone else). In October 1951, the Board finally issued an administrative separation of subsidy from mail pay.

This by no means quieted the clamor over subsidies. President Truman's 1952 budget message deplored air-carrier subsidies and urged congressional action on subsidy separation. Suspicion of the sort of separation the Board might produce on its own was behind strong moves in both houses to pass subsidy separation that year,

[13] *Aviation Week,* L (April 18, 1949), 13–14, 46–47.
[14] *Aviation Week,* LI (Sept. 5, 1949), 38.
[15] See, for example, *Aviation Week,* LI (Nov. 21, 1949), 48–49.

but the bill died because no agreement could be reached on a particular plan. The following year, 1953, saw the problem of subsidy legislation rise again. In the Senate, nineteen members supported a bill introduced by Senator John F. Kennedy requiring separation on the basis of cost of service plus a fair return.[16] The Post Office was strongly set on getting arrangements that would produce a lower mail rate, including a resort to competitive bidding if necessary,[17] but the administrative subsidy separation proved acceptable to enough people to take the steam out of legislative action.

Meanwhile, a number of other influences came to bear on Board policy. In response to the findings of the Congressional Aviation Policy Board and the Presidential Air Policy Commission, the Board opened investigations of the route structures of National,[18] Northeast, and Western, having in mind the possibility of dismembering these carriers and parceling their routes out to other airlines. It also issued orders for investigation of the competitive situation in several major markets (Detroit–New York, Detroit–Washington, Chicago–Washington, Minneapolis–Washington) and announced that a general study of the domestic route pattern was under way. It warned that attention would be given to "possible corrective action which may be achieved by mergers, consolidations, interchanges, or suspensions." [19]

At this same time, 1948–49, the Board's differences with the nonscheduled airlines came to a head. This was partly an accident of timing, partly the result of pressures on the Board to eliminate the rising subsidy bill and the unprofitable condition of the certified industry. The Board's difficulties in confining the nonskeds to irregular service had grown more and more vexing. By the end of 1948 it was willing to admit defeat as long as the irregular carriers held a blanket exemption from the Board's

[16] *Aviation Week,* LVIII (March 30, 1953), 26.

[17] Lee Moore, "P. O. Wants to Cut Airmail Rates," *Aviation Week,* LVIII (May 25, 1953), 17.

[18] There was another twist to the investigation of National, for it had been shut down by a ten-month pilots' strike. The airline charged that the Air Line Pilots Association had worked through AFL President William Green to have the White House pressure the Board into ordering the probe. See *Aviation Week,* L (Jan. 17, 1949), 55.

[19] CAB, "Statement of Policy for Economic Program in 1949," Feb. 26, 1949, CCH Av. Law Rep. §23,075.

certification requirement and general economic regulations. A staff memorandum to the Board, dated September 16, 1948, and considered by several congressional investigators,[20] dealt with various ways of treating the nonskeds in order to enable the Board to enforce its concept of their "specialist" function. The Board chose to require each irregular carrier to apply for individual exemption from certification, which would be granted only to carriers that had been living within the law of the Board's requirements. This change became effective in May 1949. A year later, along with decisions granting two such applications for exemption and denying eleven others, the Board issued a clarifying statement. The exemptions would contain a restriction on the exempted irregulars' scheduling to a maximum of eight flights per month in any city-pair market and to three in one direction in certain designated major markets; this was dubbed the three-and-eight requirement.[21] It is well to keep in mind that the substance of the role which the Board wished to assign the irregular carriers had not changed up to this point. We still see stepped-up attempts to enforce the original notion of an irregular or call-and-demand service. This effort to enforce its own regulations was fast getting the Board into trouble with a new set of congressional and public critics — those supporting small business.

The potent political support the irregular carriers could muster was apparent in the 1949 hearings before the Senate Interstate and Foreign Commerce Committee, where Senator Wayne Morse and others came forward to testify in their behalf. The defense department was also a general supporter of the nonskeds because of their military-charter activities. The nonskeds had tried to convince the Department of Justice that questionable activities were afoot, and a Justice representative at one hearing before the Board took a strong position in defense of the irregulars.[22] By 1951 the Senate Select Committee on Small Business had taken up the cause and was actively opposing the Board's efforts

[20] For example, *Monopoly Problems in Regulated Industries — Airlines,* hearings, U.S. House of Representatives, Committee on the Judiciary, 84th Cong., 2nd sess. (Washington, 1957), II, 1008–1022.

[21] These policies are analyzed at length by Lucile S. Keyes, *Federal Control of Entry into Air Transportation,* pp. 176–205.

[22] *Aviation Week,* L (March 7, 1949), 39–40.

to enforce its requirements of irregular service. On March 1, 1951, the Board adopted an amendment to its economic regulations extending the three-and-eight rule to those irregular carriers whose applications for individual exemptions had not been processed. The Small Business Committee, chaired by Senator John Sparkman, protested vigorously, and successive stays of the order were granted.[23] Later this order was scuttled by a court injunction. Near the end of 1951 the Board issued a decision rejecting the applications of four of the irregular carriers for certificates of public convenience and necessity. In doing so, it paid unprecedented lip service to the promotional desirability of low-fare air service. However, it found that the certified carriers could provide low-cost coach service as efficiently as the nonskeds and were moving progressively toward doing it. And the Board insisted that the profits which restricted entry permitted the certified carriers to earn in major markets were necessary to subsidize unprofitable services.[24] The Board also opened an investigation into the possibility of some form of supplemental operating authority for the irregulars. The Small Business Committee noted with satisfaction that "the Board had accepted in principle the Committee's recommendation." [25] The new investigation left open the possibility that the committee's request for more liberal operating authority (fourteen or fifteen flights a month per city-pair market) might be accepted, and the pressure was substantially eased.

The Board, however, had been under heavy fire from many sources and had made concessions accordingly. Besides the attacks of the Small Business Committee, a committee chaired by Senator Paul H. Douglas, investigating business influence in government, had taken the Board to task for being too friendly with the certified carriers.[26] Probably these congressional pressures, along with the traffic and profit upswing due to the Korean War and the decision in the *Transcontinental Coach-type Service* case, explain the Board's mid-1951 shift from actively opposing low-

[23] *Annual Report,* U.S. Senate, Select Committee on Small Business, Report No. 1068, 82nd Cong., 2nd sess. (Washington, 1952), pp. 243–244.
[24] Transcontinental Coach-Type Service Case, Docket No. 3397 et al., 14 CAB 720 (1951). See Chapter 10 above.
[25] Select Committee on Small Business, *Annual Report.* p. 251.
[26] *Aviation Week,* LIV (March 26, 1951), 13.

fare coach service to urging the certified carriers to expand it. Also important, of course, was the fact that by this time the Board had collected data which suggested that, on balance, low-fare services contributed to the carriers' net revenues.[27]

It is useful to review the range of pressures which the Board faced from the postwar period up to 1951. On the one hand, there were forces which opposed either the low profits of the airlines or the rising subsidies they were receiving, or both. The House and Senate Appropriations Committees and the Department of Commerce were the centers of these attitudes. The congressional commerce committees and the Post Office also joined this camp. Those policies of the Board which drew the most fire from these groups were the competitive route extensions that took place around the end of World War II and the Board's reluctance to distinguish outright subsidy from mail pay. On the other hand, the Small Business Committee and other groups interested in small business and consumer welfare were irate at the Board's treatment of the nonscheduled airlines and its reluctance to expand coach service, as was the Department of Defense.[28] The Board felt it necessary to placate both groups, and yet their demands were largely inconsistent. The latter group ultimately was satisfied on only one point — the expansion of coach service — and that only when the Board became convinced that no serious sacrifice of carrier profits would result. The former group, whose outlook more or less coincided with that of the Board's majority in those years, was more amply gratified. Its pressure relaxed once the commitment to subsidy separation was made and the Korean War improved the carriers' profits, but its impact died out slowly. At the beginning of 1951 the Board issued its first decision in the *Southern Service to the West* case.[29] A four-man majority denied all applications for route extensions in the southwestern part of the United States on grounds of excessive diversion and the threat of increased subsidy requirements or draining the monopoly revenues earned from the relatively profitable routes. Due respect

[27] See Paul W. Cherington, *Airline Price Policy*, pp. 91–99.

[28] Ten years later the Board again collided with the defense department over the Board's desire to set a floor under bids submitted by both regular and supplemental carriers for military charters See pp 186–187.

[29] Southern Service to the West Case, Docket No. 1102 et al., 12 CAB 518 (1951).

was paid to the opponents of excessive competition. The goal of "competition to the extent necessary" is "no mandate to seek competition merely for the sake of having competition." Rising profits, the decision stated, should not obscure the need for an adequate profitability cushion to withstand recessions. Moreover (for the Small Business Committee), "a relatively good earning position at a given time may suggest the need for giving serious consideration to the possibilities of reducing transportation rates and fares rather than the need for expanding competitive services."[30] *Southern Service to the West* indeed had something for everybody. Later that year the investigations begun in 1948 and 1949 into the route structures of weak carriers were dropped without action.[31] The investigation of the efficiency of operations of the Big Four carriers was merged into the *Big Four Mail Rate* case and dropped when that case was settled. The *Large Irregular Air Carrier Investigation* was started upon its long procedural course. The major conflicts of attitude which had assailed the Board's political relations for six years were at least partly dissolved.

In the period from 1953 to the present, pressures on the Board have been less patterned. Still, several major turns in Board policy in recent years have had a direct relation to the prevailing political climate. The Eisenhower administration did somewhat more than its predecessors to try to swing Civil Aeronautics Board policies into line with its own general economic philosophy. The forays of congressional committees and particular congressmen and the balance of power among various congressional groups continued to be important to the environment of Board decision making.

Up to 1955 the Board acted boldly to eliminate the remaining sources of the subsidy requirements. One of the most dramatic incidents was the Board's decision to scuttle Pioneer Air Lines, economically among the most promising of the local-service carriers, by refusing to support its switch from DC-3s to more

---

[30] Southern Service to the West Case, pp. 532–534. *Cf.* Josh Lee's dissent, especially p. 586.

[31] National Airlines, Inc., Route Investigation, Docket No. 3500 et al., 12 CAB 798 (1951); Investigation of Routes and Operations of Western Air Lines, Inc., Docket No. 2911, 12 CAB 892 (1951).

modern Martin aircraft.[32] Another significant decision of the 1952 period is *Mid-West Certificate Renewal*.[33] Mid-West had been operating with inefficiently small, single-engine equipment, but proposed an expanded operation using DC-3s. The majority, deciding against the carrier, compared its prospective first-year results with those of other going local-service carriers. However, if the Board had taken the more promotionally minded approach of comparing the prospective first-year result of Mid-West's expanded operation with the first-year results of other local-service carriers, such a decision would have been hard to justify.[34]

The Eisenhower administration's views received a formal airing in 1954 when the Air Coordinating Committee responded to a Presidential request for a comprehensive view of aviation policy.[35] The report showed a strong concern for the reduction of subsidy and withdrawing the right of carriers to return to subsidy. It strongly favored allowing only those unprofitable services that could be carried by profits from richer markets and took a favorable view of mergers and reductions of route competition that would promote this objective. It suggested that the local-service carriers should either be eliminated or strengthened. Necessary but unprofitable services should be given to profitable trunklines.[36] The Air Coordinating Committee report reflected the attitude of the Department of Commerce.[37] Just after the President ordered preparation of the report, R. B. Murray, Jr., Under-Secretary of Commerce for Transportation and Chairman of the Air Coordinating Committee, had made a speech voicing almost exactly the same policy suggestions the report was later to contain.[38] However, the report also directly reflected the thinking

[32] See pp. 261–262.

[33] Mid-West Certificate Renewal Case, Docket No. 4052 et al., 15 CAB 424 (1952).

[34] See J. P. Adams' dissent, p. 433.

[35] U.S. Air Coordinating Committee, *Civil Air Policy* (May 1954).

[36] *Ibid.*, pp. 6–25.

[37] The Department of Commerce has maintained through the 1950s a consistent record of favoring measures likely to cut the government's subsidy cost or raise the carriers' profits. For instance, it appeared before the Board to urge approval of an agreement among the carriers on pooling profits between carriers shut down by strikes and those still operating; see *Traffic World*, CIII (Jan. 17, 1959), 15.

[38] Eric Bramley, "Murray Calls for Sweeping Policy Changes," *American Aviation*, XVII (Sept. 28, 1953), 19.

of a majority of the Board at the time, and several acrimonious split decisions shortly after saw it put partly into effect. In *Route No. 106 Renewal*, a Chicago–Sioux City route consisting of cities of marginal trunkline size was carved up and handed over to United and Braniff rather than being converted into a strong local-service segment.[39] The Board majority gave noncommital approval to the merger between Continental and Pioneer, while Josh Lee's barbed dissent declared: "The majority's decision constitutes a further implementation of the policy of abolishing feeder carriers, a policy which this same majority of three supported in the Air Coordinating Committee report." [40] Other fruits of the committee's attitude were tentative efforts toward handing over part of the operations of Southwest Airways to United and the informal pressure that apparently was put on Colonial, a struggling, subsidized "grandfather" carrier, to find a merger partner.

These cases are not solely the result of the administration's influence on the Board, since a majority of the Board's members were in basic agreement with this attitude until 1955. The Air Coordinating Committee report strengthened the hand of this majority but probably made little long-run difference for the handling of route cases, for a shift in the Board's membership which brought Ross Rizley to the chairmanship coincided with a series of route extensions which were scarcely what the committee had had in mind.

Of the isolated interferences of the White House into the regulatory processes of the Board, probably no other has been so important as an alleged intervention to force the Board to raise air fares. In late 1957, the Board was proceeding with its general fare investigation over repeated demands of the carriers for an emergency fare increase. The White House, apparently

[39] Route No. 106 Renewal Case and Ozark Certificate Renewal Case, Docket Nos. 6050 et al. and 598 et al., 20 CAB 160 (1954). This decision was complicated by operational traits of the route in question which led Member Adams to favor the trunk solution even though normally he was a local-service supporter. Later, when United Air Lines proved unwilling to provide the service for which it was here certified, the Board tried still a different solution; see Route No. 106 Renewal Case and Ozark Certificate Renewal Case, Docket Nos. 6050 et al. and 5988 et al., 21 CAB 86 (1955).

[40] Continental-Pioneer Acquisition Case, Docket No. 6457 et al., 20 CAB 323, p. 335 (1955).

worried over the airlines' ability to complete the purchase of jet equipment, intervened to force the Board to grant a 6.6 percent interim increase.[41]

Of course, there is no way of telling how common such episodes as this have been, but the nature of the President's regular channels of authority over the Board gives us some idea. One such channel covers all international route awards, which must be submitted for Presidential approval. The political tugging and hauling that go on over these routes has become notorious, especially the activities of Pan American World Airways, called by a *Fortune* writer "pound for pound the best political infighter on earth." [42] The actual process of awarding international routes is outside the scope of the present study, but the flurries that result have often spilled over and affected the regulation of domestic transport. For instance, the scandal resulting from a Pan American-Northwest tussle for White House favor for a Pacific Northwest-Hawaii route allegedly led to the appointment of Ross Rizley to the Board, an appointment that was probably crucial to the course which competitive route awards took from 1955 on. Also, this provision of the act requires Presidential approval when a domestic carrier with international stub-end routes is involved in a merger. Thus when both Eastern and National were after Colonial Airlines, a small carrier with routes into Canada, Eastern's ultimate success was due not to Board policy but rather to the White House stamp of approval.[43] Since nine of the domestic trunks and one local-service carrier have international routes, this sort of situation could well emerge again.

The most enduring channel of White House communication to the Board lies in the Presidential power to appoint members or to threaten not to reappoint them. The latter power especially has been used in rather rough-handed fashion. A writer in an airline trade magazine declared:

[41] *Time,* LXXI (Feb. 3, 1958), 74. This report was confirmed in confidential interviews.

[42] Dero A. Saunders, "The Airlines' Flight from Reality," *Fortune,* LIII (Feb. 1956), 218–219.

[43] For an account of the maneuvers involved, see William V. Henzey, "Colonial-Eastern Merger Believed Near," *American Aviation,* XIX (Jan. 30, 1956), 67–68. This incident also seems to have had some impact on the selection of one new Board member.

Josh Lee, whose term came to an end Dec. 31, reportedly was advised on several occasions that his job could be saved by voting the "right way" on several pending matters. But this type of activity reached the degrading stage in December when one member . . . "broke down" under the strain of threats to his personal future right before Christmas.[44]

The failure of President Eisenhower to reappoint J. P. Adams to the Board was described as a favor to the Secretary of Commerce, and the complaint was often heard during the last decade that the administration's failure to notify Board members until the last minute whether or not they would be reappointed, then delaying in filling the vacancy upon failing to reappoint, often left the Board short of members, stopping business and threatening tie votes.[45]

Turning to congressional pressures on the Board in recent years, the Select Committee on Small Business kept up its fire on the issue of the irregular carriers. In 1953 it recommended a more liberal operating authority in the form of a temporary regulation, allowing fourteen round trips monthly between any pair of points, and urged that a few irregulars be given temporary exemptions for regular route services in certain markets. It also called for the expediting of the *Large Irregular Air Carriers* investigation. Senator Johnson of the Aviation Subcommittee of the Senate Interstate and Foreign Commerce Committee promptly attacked the report as more "propagandizing than a calm and logical appraisal of actual conditions." [46] The small-business pressures on the Board in favor of the coach operators were probably less strong now because they found little support within the Republican administration, despite the fact that Presidential Assistant Sherman Adams was later disclosed to have intervened in favor of a large irregular-carrier group embroiled in an enforcement proceeding.[47] Relations with the congressional commerce

[44] William V. Henzey, "CAB Record Puts Administration on Spot," *American Aviation*, XIX (Jan. 16, 1956), 84.

[45] Robert F. Bendiner, "The Rise and Fall of the Nonskeds," *The Reporter*, XVI (May 30, 1957), 33; William V. Henzey, "Outgoing CAB Members Get Rough Deal," *American Aviation*, XX (Jan. 14, 1957), 30.

[46] *American Aviation*, XVII (Aug. 17, 1953), 15.

[47] In the Harris Committee's inquiry into influence in the regulatory agencies. For the text of letters between Adams and Murray Chotiner, representative of North American Airlines, see Bernard Schwartz, *The Professor and the Commissions* (New York, 1959), pp. 223–225.

committees were generally friendly during the period. In 1954 the Senate commerce committee held extended hearings on an omnibus revision of the Civil Aeronautics Act introduced by Senator Patrick McCarran. The bill would have reunited the economic- and safety-regulation functions in a seven-man Civil Aeronautics Authority, the situation which had existed before 1940. It would have made many less important changes, including removal of the Board's authority to exempt carriers from the certificate requirements while giving it much more flexibility in the types of certificates it could grant. These hearings evoked no particular enthusiasm or controversy, except when Under-Secretary of Commerce Murray appeared to defend his Air Coordinating Committee views and tangled with two Democratic members of the committee, Senators Monroney and Smathers.[48] In 1955 strong congressional support for the local-service carriers and the friendship of the commerce groups was largely responsible for legislation giving them permanent certification. The commerce committees and Congress generally continued to give the Board more help than it asked for by passing two bills to give financial aid to the local airlines in the next two years. In 1960, the Senate commerce committee was reported in support of a bill introduced by Senator Jennings Randolph that would have interfered with the Board's route-case procedures by making mandatory the suspension of trunks on thin routes and the substitution of local-service carriers.[49] The appropriations committees were sometimes troublesome but not consistently hostile to the Board in the 1950s. The usual pattern was for the Board to face some hostility and a trimming of its budget request from the House; friendlier treatment and some restoration from the Senate. The House committee was critical about subsidy to the international carriers, and in 1954 it began a campaign that succeeded in forcing the Board to do more careful field auditing in connection with setting the amount of subsidy. In subsequent years the House committee attacked the Board for failing to press general fare investigation, and some personal animosity appeared among members of the

---

[48] *Revision of Civil Aeronautics Act,* hearings on S. 2647, U.S. Senate, Committee on Interstate and Foreign Commerce, 83rd Cong., 2nd sess. (Washington, 1954).

[49] *Aviation Week,* LXXII (June 27, 1960), 50.

committee and of the Board and its staff.[50] By 1959 subsidy to the local-service carriers was growing rapidly due to enlargement of their route systems in the "area" cases. The House appropriations committee became quite hostile to this and cut one request for supplemental appropriations. The Board seemed, as in the late 1940s, to have overestimated its ability to procure subsidy funds.

By far the Board's most significant brush with a congressional committee in the 1950s came with the 1956 inquiry of the Antimonopoly Subcommittee of the House Judiciary Committee into monopoly problems in regulated industries. The attack which Representative Emanuel Celler and his staff mounted against the Board covered many features of regulation of the domestic industry, but the most important objection was to the Board's policies on regulation of fares and the scope of activities permitted the trade associations. The Board members were attacked for the 1953 decision to suspend the first general fare investigation. No one would defend it. When it turned out that there was strong evidence that airline pressure might have secured this dismissal, and that the Board chairman at the time of the hearings did not know that the dismissal contemplated continuing staff studies of the fare problem, the Board had little choice but to reinstitute the general investigation. Indeed, one of the trade publications suggested a year later that, when the Board turned down a request for a 6 percent fare increase, the five carriers that did not file for this increase refrained for fear that the imminent report of the Antitrust Subcommittee would mean a certain denial.[51] Somewhat later the Board instituted an investigation into the activities of the Air Transport Association, probably also a reflection of the Celler Committee's inquiry, although suspicion of this agency seemed to have been growing within the Board for several years.[52] This committee's inquiry and its aftermath

[50] See, for example, *Department of Commerce and Related Agencies Appropriations for 1958,* hearings, U.S. House of Representatives, Committee on Appropriations, Subcommittee, 85th Cong., 1st sess. (Washington, 1957), pp. 901, 910, 932.

[51] *American Aviation,* XXI (July 1, 1957), 56. See also, William V. Henzey, "Profits Shrink . . . Sharp Decline in Net Operating Income Poses Threat to Jet-age Financing," *American Aviation,* XX (April 22, 1957), 32.

[52] Order Serial No. E-13597, March 10, 1959.

is a good demonstration of the impact which a single hard-breathing investigation can have on the policies of regulatory agencies.

Growing numbers of individual congressmen have been pressing the Board for satisfaction on individual requests. The Board's recent investigation of the carriers' charges for excess baggage, for example, is alleged to have been started as a result of insistence within the Senate. By far the most common congressional demand, however, has been for extended service in route cases, particularly the large local-service area cases. With air transportation becoming a staple commodity, especially for the business world, cities have become more and more concerned with getting the most air service possible. As a trade magazine remarked, "Congressmen often have a hard time explaining lack of local air service to constituents." The result is that many congressmen have appeared in most of the route cases. The Board has tried to use relatively objective standards, such as the "use it or lose it" rules for local service extensions developed in the *Seven States Area Investigation*. But these have not solved all the problems of relations with congressmen, and some industry observers feel that the Board has erred by bending occasionally to congressional whims. No doubt such arm's-length decision making is much more easily said than done.

CARRIER INFLUENCE ON THE BOARD

The influence of the carriers upon the Board is hard to describe because of the close relation they necessarily have with it. They plead cases before the Board daily in routine proceedings and continually confer informally with members of the Board and its staff on all kinds of things. Their "influence" becomes conceptually a very difficult thing to pinpoint. There is no shortage of hypotheses about the "cliental" relation that allegedly develops between a regulatory agency and the firms it regulates. Regulatory commissions are said to go through a life cycle, ending in a morally decrepit state in which they function to protect the firms they originally set out to regulate.

None of these notions is of much help in explaining the relations between the Civil Aeronautics Board and the certified carriers. The Board's regulatory vigor has certainly fluctuated over time, but there is no clear trend toward more and more willingness to accept the industry's outlook. Also, one proves nothing by pointing out periods when the Board has appeared relatively friendly toward the carriers' efforts to maximize profits. The Civil Aeronautics Act offered the Board a set of partly conflicting objectives. Some of these are largely consistent with maximum profits for the industry; some are not. Reasonable men can differ about which objectives are best pursued. At times the Board majority has set its sights almost exclusively on maintaining "sound economic conditions" in the industry, much to the carriers' delight. But this scarcely proves that the Board has been unduly swayed. Consider even such a suspicious matter as the long war of attrition with the irregular carriers. The Board and the carriers honestly believed at the time that service on thinner routes should be maintained, that it involved a loss for the trunklines, and that this loss could be covered only by the profits from long-haul, high-density routes wherein the irregular carriers sought to operate. No responsible congressional voice ever suggested that the Board should certify the nonskeds (or otherwise liberalize their operating authority) and *also* permit either an increase of subsidy or extensive abandonment of service on thin routes. The Board knew it would run into disastrous opposition if either of the latter effects appeared. The nonsked policy can be explained by the Board's concept of its statutory objectives and the actual and potential congressional pressures it faced. A "plot theory" is possible but unnecessary.

The influence of the carriers on the Board's decisions is perhaps best approached by asking the following questions: How does the Board deal procedurally with the carriers and their efforts to influence it? Can the carriers marshal indirect pressure (for example, through Congress) to sway the Board's decisions? Have the carriers ever succeeded in getting the Board to change well-defined policies? Have the carriers appeared to influence Board decisions by forcing it to consider things outside the record in particular dockets before it? Isolated examples support a positive answer to each of these questions, but on balance the Board has not catered to the airlines' wishes in ways that cannot be squared with its statutory objectives.

First of all, there is no denying that representatives of the carriers circulate freely among members of the Board and its staff and continually represent their point of view both in formal proceedings and informal contact. Louis J. Hector, a dissident ex-member, has written:

> The whole system of adjudication by commissioners as practiced today inevitably raises suspicions of *ex parte* influence. Commissioners circulate more or less freely in the industry they regulate. As a part of this, there develops the social intercourse which is normal in business, executive or legislative life. When some of the groups in the industry then enter into a litigated case, the same commissioner climbs on the bench and is supposed suddenly to become a judge. But everyone knows that he really has no chance to familiarize himself with the record and that the oral argument and briefs which only summarize the case are about all he will ever learn about it. It is obvious that under such circumstances, memories of casual conversations, tid-bits of information picked up here and there, trade-press editorials, and congressional or Executive views or desires, can exert a powerful influence.[53]

Apparently the Board frequently holds meetings with representatives of a particular carrier or group of carriers to discuss matters which are of interest to the airlines but which are not currently at any stage of formal proceedings. "When such a meeting is arranged," the Board has indicated in a formal statement, "it is not publicly announced, and the attendance usually is limited to those who request the meeting."[54] The carriers' efforts to influence the Board are no doubt systematic and substantial.[55] A new member of the Board receives an elaborate welcome from the carriers, characterized by a former member as "hanging a halo around his neck."

Despite these long-standing pressures, the Board's relations with the carriers' representatives seem to have become, if anything, even more formal over time. Former members of the staff have indicated that a major autonomous change came about in

---

[53] Louis J. Hector, "Problems of the C.A.B. and the Independent Regulatory Commissions," *Yale Law Journal*, LXIX (May 1960), 959. Hector's final quoted sentence continues with a more debatable clause: "which they would not have on judges intimately familiar with the record."

[54] Answers to questions submitted by Senator Estes Kefauver, chairman, Anti-Trust and Monopoly Subcommittee. Reprinted in *Traffic World*, CVI (Nov. 26, 1960), 118.

[55] *Department of Commerce and Related Agencies Appropriations for 1957*, hearings, U.S. House of Representatives, Committee on Appropriations, Subcommittee, 84th Cong., 2nd sess. (Washington, 1956), pp. 858–859.

the early 1950s, a time when complaints about business interference in government were being aired everywhere. Before then,
many matters were worked out in informal conferences with
carrier representatives. No one worried much about the propriety
of speaking to representatives of some carriers while those of
others were absent. However, reform sentiment came from within
the General Counsel's office, and relations with the carriers have
come to be on a more formal arm's-length basis.[56] It is easy to
see this by comparing the pattern of developments in the general
fare-increase filings of the late 1940s with those since 1956. The
former were normally worked out in off-the-record meetings
between Board members and the carriers and entered formally
as identical filings by all airlines. Since then, formal filings have
gone in as uncoordinated "trial balloons," and the Board apparently has decided on its own what it would permit.

Such is the evidence on contacts of the carriers with the Board.
There are almost no stories of obvious influence peddling. Congressional investigators have produced only a few cases of Board
personnel's accepting of lavish hospitality from the airlines, and
none of these has been tied to the outcome of proceedings before
the Board. The investigators have wasted much of their fire on
an innocent target, the custom of Board members or staff to go
on free inaugural flights provided for assorted dignitaries by airlines introducing new routes or equipment. These seem quite consistent with the Board's promotional function and in any case are
hardly the road to ruin. However, the carriers have at times
succeeded in "reaching" the Board on very important matters.
One isolated but glaring instance was Member Harmar Denny's
decision in early 1953 to change his vote and permit dismissal of
the general fare investigation. A newly appointed member of the
Board, Denny first supported continuation of the inquiry but
later reversed it after a visit from Stuart G. Tipton of the Air
Transport Association. A lengthy inquiry by the Celler Committee
in 1956 did not prove conclusively that Tipton talked Denny
into changing his vote, but any other explanation is hard to defend.[57] In major route cases the carriers often try and probably

[56] One former staff member feels that this change does not bring a clear net
gain in regulatory effectiveness. If the carriers now find it less easy to get at
Board personnel, it is also now harder for the regulators to get at the carriers.
[57] See above, pp. 146–148.

sometimes succeed in the effort to influence the Board by producing favorable witnesses. Much of this goes on in the local-service area cases, with a dozen or more congressmen sometimes appearing in one proceeding. The game is played with special vigor by the chief trunklines. In the *Southern Transcontinental* case, National, Braniff, and Delta complained that Eastern had been campaigning for local support after the close of the hearings.[58] Most dramatic of all was *New York–San Francisco Nonstop Service,* in which American Airlines sought to get a one-stop restriction lifted. In November 1957, American's president appeared in San Francisco to urge civil leaders to "keep hammering" on behalf of its request.[59] The hammering took the form of numerous pleas from San Francisco's mayor and other officials, members of Congress, and the Port of New York Authority. Many of the San Francisco communications could have been submitted formally but were not, and thus were not served on United and TWA as parties to the proceeding. The decision went in American's favor three to two, with one rather surprising affirmative vote. The losers petitioned for reconsideration and were denied, but a circuit court remanded the case to the Board for reconsideration.[60]

There are other aspects of the Board's decisions that suggest a friendly attitude toward the regulated carriers and an unfriendly one toward their enemies. There is a disturbing aspect in the Board's handling of the irregular carriers, even if one recognizes the possible consistency of these policies with the Board's broader objectives. For instance, in partially dissenting from an enforcement proceeding against North American Airlines, the largest of the irregulars, Member Joseph P. Adams condemned the majority for refusing even to meet with the carrier's officers or consider some penalty other than the most drastic possible — revocation of its letter of registration.[61] Spokesmen for the irregular carriers contrasted this approach bitterly to the cordial service

[58] *Aviation Week,* LXXII (Jan. 25, 1960), 45.

[59] New York–San Francisco Nonstop Service Case — Opinion and Order Denying and Dismissing Portions of Petitions for Reconsideration, Docket No. 9214 et al., decided Nov. 19, 1959, CCH Av. Law Rep. §22,333.02.

[60] *Airlift,* XXIV (June 1960), 18.

[61] Compliance Proceeding, Twentieth Century Air Lines, Inc., et al., Docket No. 6000, 21 CAB 133, pp. 148–152 (1955).

sometimes given to the certified carriers. An example, apparently an isolated one, was an exemption authority granted to American Airlines for nonstop service from New York or Washington to Mexico City. American wanted this quickly and quietly in order to meet competition from Air France, and the Board granted it by a three-to-two vote without requiring the usual notice to potential interveners.[62] Another phenomenon that might be taken as evidence of successful influencing by the carriers is the Board's willingness to permit collusive action to advance the industry's interests against outside groups. It approved, with one dissenting vote, the carriers' mutual-aid strike pact, a device aimed at returning to struck carriers the profits on traffic diverted to their competitors.[63] It took alarm at active price competition among the carriers in bidding for military charters and approved a cleaned-up version of a committee of certified carriers to bargain with the defense establishment for stabler arrangements.[64] Yet another instance of the Board's friendliness toward the certified carriers is its former willingness to rely on the carriers' accounts rather than insist on its own field audits.[65] And final evidence of this good will lies in the Board's willingness to undo its "Sherman doctrine" on their behalf. In a 1954 case the Board announced that it would not approve agreements between the carriers put into effect before its permission was secured unless the *status quo ante* was first restored.[66] Yet it has waived this requirement in all cases where it would have worked significant hardship on the carriers involved.[67]

[62] Order Serial No. E-8055, Docket No. 6510, Jan. 24, 1954. See also *Revision of Civil Aeronautics Act,* pp. 839, 854–855.

[63] Six Carrier Mutual Aid Pact, Docket No. 9977, decided May 20, 1959, CCH Av. Law Rep. §22,269.

[64] Northwest Airlines, Inc., Pan American Airways, Inc., Seaboard & Western Airlines, Inc., and Trans World Airlines, Inc. — In the Matter of an Agreement Concerning Government Air Transportation Requirements, Agreement CAB No. 13434, decided Aug. 28, 1959, CCH Av. Law Rep. §22,301.

[65] See "Audit Report to the Congress of the United States on Civil Aeronautics Board, October, 1955," reprinted in *Department of Commerce and Related Agencies Appropriations for 1957,* pp. 754–811.

[66] Charles C. Sherman and Edna K. Sherman — Interlocking Relationship and Stock Ownership in Airline Transport Carriers, Inc., and California Central Airlines, Docket No. 4109, 15 CAB 876, p. 881 (1952).

[67] For example, Resort Refinancing Case, Docket No. 8687, decided April 9, 1958, CCH Av. Law Rep. §22,171.02.

Many important Board decisions reflect an implicit bargaining process with the carriers. For instance, when the Board dismissed the first general passenger-fare investigation, the trade press took the view that the Board's price for this favor was a more energetic extension of air-coach service.[68] There is also a great deal of evidence that the Board got the trunks to agree to cooperate with the experimental certification of local-service carriers by elaborate promises that these would never be permitted to come into full competitive status. This came to light in the mid-1950s as the Board fought a delaying action to restrain congressional enthusiasm for giving permanent certificates to the local airlines.[69] The reason for these actions throws much light on the Board's relations with the carriers: its limited legal powers and the procedural restraints on its operations cause the Board to depend on a certain amount of good will from the airlines in order to achieve its objectives. The carriers could make life a good deal harder for the Board than it is; for instance, they seem unwilling to oppose the Board's budget before the appropriations committees, though such a strategy might well be effective.

Though the evidence is entirely circumstantial, the carriers and the Air Transport Association seem to maintain good relations with Congress. The local-service carriers have been particularly successful in getting favorable legislation with or without Board approval. They gained passage of bills providing for their permanent certification, followed by guaranteed-loan and capital-gains bills (the latter letting them retain capital gains for purchase of new flight equipment). It has also been suggested that the locals secured heavy congressional support in getting the Board partially to reverse its *Pioneer Mail Rate* policy on re-equipment, and also that they stirred congressional attacks upon the Board for at least one decision benefiting a trunk carrier at the expense of a local airline.[70] Congress, particularly members of the commerce committees, has actively defended the general interests of the air carriers against such threats as the expansion of the Military

[68] *Aviation Week,* LVIII (May 25, 1953), 96.
[69] *Permanent Certificates for Local Service Air Carriers,* hearings on S. 651, U.S. Senate, Committee on Interstate and Foreign Commerce, 84th Cong., 1st sess. (Washington, 1955), p. 206.
[70] See William V. Henzey, "Locals to Get Aid in Buying New Fleets," *American Aviation,* XIX (Feb. 13, 1956), 92.

Air Transport Service (MATS) and the passing of legislation to bar the trunklines from returning to a subsidized status. Also, one must note the Civil Aeronautics Board's chronic lack of success in getting such extensions of its power as control over carriers' accounting, international fare regulation, and viable enforcement powers against violations of its regulations.

Access to the White House is probably much less important for the domestic carriers than is access to Congress. However, there are at least two allegations that the former route has been successfully used. One is the 1958 interim fare increase discussed above. The other is the claim of Bernard Schwartz that, through intervention by the Air Transport Association, the White House demanded review and later rejection of the international aspects of the *Large Irregular Air Carriers* decision.[71]

THE PATTERN OF PRESSURES

The pattern of regulation formed by the Civil Aeronautics Board is to some degree always affected by the political environment in which the Board operates. The choice of members by the President is a direct political control, even though the Board did not show a neat swing from Democratic to Republican policy preferences in the past decade. The relations of the Board with congressional committees (not Congress as a whole) are the next most conspicuous political influence. The Board feels a strong and continuing dependence on the good will of the Senate and House commerce and appropriations committees. These committees thereby hold a substantial power to bend Board policy toward their views or the views of their majorities or dominant members. Other congressional committees can shift the Board's policies from time to time, either by focusing the light of unfavorable publicity on the Board or by gaining the sympathy of the committees upon which the Board is directly dependent. The certified air carriers have done rather well at winning the favor of these same crucial committees, so that the Board can expect that any action which is highly noxious to the carriers will cause trouble with Congress. There have also been congressmen who would defend the Board's position against the certified carriers, but they have not been in "strong" positions or shown a continuing

[71] Schwartz, p. 218.

interest. Furthermore, many congressional liberals have been at odds with the Board over its policies on nonscheduled carriers and other matters. Within the administrative branch, the historic use made of the Presidential power to grant or withhold reappointment has disrupted the Board's work periodically and probably produced some sensitivity to Executive preferences on policy. Another ongoing influence within the executive branch is the Department of Commerce position, which has varied over time on details but which has generally pressed the Board to be more sympathetic to the interests of the managements of the certified carriers. The other agency pressures on the Board have also been relatively stable. The congressional appropriations committees are to a varying degree hostile to the Board's role of giving subsidies. The commerce committees are normally friendly both toward its efforts to promote and advance air transport and toward its aid of the weaker firms in the certified industry. The attitudes of the Post Office and Defense agencies and the antitrust authorities and committees have similarly been predictable over long periods.

The direct political influence of the carriers upon the Board is not easy to define and does not take simple forms. There are certainly many minor actions or policies which one can read as bearing the mark of favor to these carriers. Generally this has taken the form of what Samuel P. Huntington calls "ameliorative clientalism" — doing favors for the regulated firms which have no serious adverse effects on organized outside interests.[72] But this has been true of the Board's major policies only where these policies can also be called a plausible interpretation of "public interest" as defined in the law. Many actions that look like favoritism are entirely consistent with the Civil Aeronautics Act's instruction to identify the public interest with "the encouragement and development" of the air-transport industry. Has the Board done favors for the carriers to advance the promotional objectives of the act, or has it used the promotional objectives to indulge its dotage upon the airlines? Obviously there is no way of deciding which view is right, but some critics seem a bit unfair in assuming away the former interpretation.[73] As Ross Rizley,

[72] Samuel P. Huntington, "Clientalism: A Study in Administrative Politics" (unpublished dissertation, Harvard University, 1950), chap. 2.

[73] For example, Marver H. Bernstein in *Regulating Business by Independent*

whose name is anathema to the carriers, has pointed out, the problem created by pressures from the carriers and others is not so much that they succeed as that they necessarily distort the Board's perspective on issues before it and make a reasoned evaluation harder.[74]

A second reason why the "cliental" relation between the Board and the carriers should not be overstressed is that part of it is forced on the Board by the statutory and judicial requirements of due process. An example is the "Ashbacker doctrine," which requires comparative consideration of mutually exclusive applications. It creates enormous difficulties for the Board in route cases, where each carrier typically applies for a somewhat different pattern of routes, making mutual exclusivity extremely hard to determine. The Board's attention is drawn from the need for additional service, competitive or noncompetitive, between various points and planning an efficient and rational transport network; it must decide instead complicated questions of which carrier will provide which service. The issues and the record in such cases tend to grow all out of manageable proportions,[75] and the Board ends up by appearing to spend all its efforts picking among carriers rather than contemplating the public interest.

The unfortunate truth is that procedural safeguards for businesses subject to government regulation almost necessarily inflict a certain amount of clientalism upon the regulators. Absolute regulatory efficiency requires more autarchy for the regulators than American society is willing to grant, and efficiency and due process act, to some extent, as substitutes. Though there is no reason why a dictatorial regulatory commission would not succumb to clientalism, there is no avoiding the fact that full procedural rights tend strongly to promote it.

I have argued that either the Board's emphasis on promotional

---

Commission (Princeton, 1955), chap. 6, and his testimony in *Monopoly Problems in Regulated Industries — Airlines,* pp. 59ff.

[74] Ross Rizley, "Some Personal Reflections After Eight Months as Chairman of the Civil Aeronautics Board," *Journal of Air Law and Commerce,* XXII (Autumn 1955), 450.

[75] *Ibid.,* pp. 448–450. See, however, "The Ashbacker Rule and the CAB: Cumbersome Procedure v. Public Interest," *Virginia Law Review,* XLIV (Nov. 1958), 1147–1165, which points out that the courts have been fairly generous in allowing the Board freedom in determining mutual exclusivity.

objectives of the act or the procedural restraints under which it operates is at least capable of explaining many of the appearances of "clientalism." But perhaps the most important consequence of the Board's political relations with the carriers is an unwillingness to "rock the boat." It has not been willing to reform minor public injustices at the cost of major annoyance to the carriers. It has not sought out bold and imaginative policies, with chances of great success but also with chances of great failure and strong repercussions in the industry. It has not tried to stir public discussion of the "public interest" in air-transport policy as an alternative to taking a plausible public-interest view that has never diverged too far from the interests of the carrier managements themselves. The organizational pressures on the members of regulatory bodies all work to discourage drastic or imaginative action. There is no good argument against the principle of unripe time. But the cliental relation of the regulators to the regulated is certainly a key factor in assuring this built-in conservatism.

CONCLUSION

The preceding chapters have begun from the unstated hypothesis that the Board's decisions in each substantive field make up a unified and consistent body of decisions based on definite principles. The hypothesis was only modestly confirmed. In certain areas, such as the route cases, one can conclude by arguing that the results could be the product of a single mind drawing upon a clear-cut preference map. In others, such as fare decisions, no significant consistency exists, and each decision seems very much the result of general conditions at the time it was reached rather than of the record before the Board. This chapter has aimed mainly at illuminating decision-making areas of the latter type. The timing and substance of policies on such important things as the irregular airlines, passenger fares, and the treatment of the local-service carriers are explainable only with reference to the political environment in which the Board works. The conclusion so far, then, has been that the Civil Aeronautics Board's role can be explained in terms of its statutory powers and objectives and the public environment in which it operates. How much unexplained variance remains to be attributed to the whims or the "creative statesmanship" of individual members of the Board? Such a question is too vague to warrant extended study, but a rough answer would be, "not much." Probably the main reason for this is that Board turnover has been very high. The political forces working on the Board's decisions also affect the selection of new members. Some have acted differently from their backers' expectations. But, in general, the dominant forces acting on the Board have kept new appointments in tune with the current balance of pressures it faces.

PART III

MARKET CONDUCT

13 Airline Policies toward Investment and Expansion

The study of an industry's market conduct normally covers two areas of business decision making: the way in which firms set and adjust their prices (or terms of sale) and the qualities or varieties of the product they offer for sale. Occasionally other features take on importance: buying arrangements in the case of monopsony or oligopsony; policies and strategies for handling patents; the use of tying arrangements, exclusive-dealing contracts, and the like. Explanation of each of these lines of activity requires a knowledge of the way in which firms independently make calculations of policy and of the resulting patterns of rivalry, coalition, or collusion that appear when their strategies interact in the market.

The market conduct of the domestic airlines must be outlined in rather an odd way because of a technological difference in conduct between airlines and most other industries. A toothpaste buyer is utterly unconcerned with the nature and appearance of the capital goods which produce his dentifrice. The air traveler bases his choice among airlines on the nature of the capital goods producing the service more than on anything else. By far the most important aspects of market conduct in the airlines are those surrounding the carriers' decisions on investing in aircraft and on the use of these airplanes in product competition. These decisions set the quality of the industry's market performance, and they absorb much of the attention of carrier managements. Pricing and price policy, normally the outstanding features of market conduct, here take a lesser role. Few carrier managements hold to anything like a constant price policy over time. There are no steady patterns of price leadership and the like.

An airline's managerial organization chart reflects this relative emphasis. The larger airlines, particularly, have extensive engineering staffs that devote attention to the design and characteristics of available new aircraft, often working closely with aircraft manufacturers during their development. The top executives of the airlines, who in the past have typically been one-time pilots, are always heavily involved in investment planning and aircraft purchase. The day-to-day market strategies of the carriers turn mainly on scheduling the use of aircraft and on related features of passenger service. Normally a scheduling committee of relatively high-level executives has direct charge of planning the flights. Often the only airline personnel continuously concerned with pricing are those involved in the complex technical matters of tariff construction, interline agreements and such. Their activities have little to do with the kind of pricing that is interesting for present purposes, since their job is to maintain orderly conditions in the interrelated network of point-to-point fares — a difficult problem but not a broadly significant one. Few airlines seem to maintain employees who consistently deal with pricing for the broader objective of carrying out profit maximization or other objectives of top management.[1]

Equipment-purchase decisions set the framework within which the short-run decisions about production (and, occasionally, price) adjustment take place. Thus they will be discussed first among the major phases of market conduct. Closely related to the investment decision is another type of planning discussed in this chapter — where and when to seek expansion into new markets.

DECISIONS ON PURCHASE OF AIRCRAFT

It is useful to divide the carrier's decision to purchase new aircraft into two aspects — the choice among available aircraft and the decision on how large a fleet to order. The layman might suppose that the choice among competing aircraft designs rests entirely on technical analysis and evaluation. Great amounts of scientific data are indeed involved but are far from being the sole thing considered, and they are certainly not always the controlling factor.[2] First of all, airlines must frequently make their choices

---

[1] For descriptions of airline-management organization, see J. H. Frederick, *Commercial Air Transportation,* chap. 13; Paul W. Cherington, *Airline Price Policy,* pp. 24–30; Perrin Stryker, "United *vs.* American: There's More Than One Way to Run an Airline," *Fortune,* LXIII (Feb. 1961), 96–101 +.

[2] For descriptions of the process of decision, see J. A. Stern, "Airline Planning for Jets," *Canadian Aeronautical Journal,* IV (April 1958), 117–120; J. T. Dyment, "Selection of the Vickers Vanguard by Trans-Canada Air Lines," *Canadian Aeronautical Journal,* IV (May 1958), 149–155; A. E. Ades, "Airline Evaluation of Transport Aircraft," *Canadian Aeronautical Journal,* II (Oct. 1956), 277–283.

of aircraft not among established operating types, but among designs on paper or experimental prototypes. Typically an aircraft manufacturer goes ahead with plans to produce a plane only when he has enough firm orders to insure him no worse than a bearable loss. The major decision an airline makes is the commitment to purchase a new plane which will compose much of its fleet, thereby bolstering the backlog of orders that will bring the plane into production. When a carrier orders a plane which is already in commercial service, it is usually augmenting a previous order for the same plane or else making a belated entry into competitive status.

The operating costs and characteristics of an airplane can be calculated from its design specifications, even though no prototype has ever actually flown. Indeed, there exists a standard formula, developed and periodically revised by the Air Transport Association, which all manufacturers, United States and foreign, use to compute costs when offering a design to the airlines. The formula, however, does not yield completely trustworthy information. It appears to have had a rather poor record in forecasting the costs for aircraft that have actually gone into operation. Even if this were not so, the coefficients of the formula rest on some sort of average experience of the airlines and thus could give the wrong answer for the route system of a particular air carrier. Furthermore, airline executives have suggested that the manufacturers' estimates are "biased due to their overenthusiasm for selling their equipment." [3] All carriers, therefore, make some modifications of these standard costs in their own calculations, and the larger carriers with extensive engineering staffs make elaborate estimates of projected performance over their own routes. Many of the planning studies that will be needed, if and when a given plane goes into service for a carrier, are done when its purchase is considered — flight operations, passenger service, and maintenance functions. Mechanical, communication, and instrument systems are reviewed and specifications for them are written into the purchase contract. "The ideal of the selection process is to obtain an aircraft which meets the requirements of

[3] An Eastern Air Lines executive in Transcript of Hearings before Examiner, General Passenger Fare Investigation, Docket No. 8008, p. 8570.

both sales and operating personnel while insuring minimum operating costs on both an airplane and seat-mile basis." [4]

But this careful process involves many uncertainties, for prospective operating cost and performance characteristics are not the only factors the prospective aircraft buyer considers. As the average automobile buyer does, he worries about the future availability of spare parts and service. In rejecting a foreign design, a major airline's president once remarked that parts supplies from manufacturers on his doorstep were enough of a problem, let alone those from a manufacturer four thousand miles away. Also, in choosing among unproved designs, it is clear that manufacturers' reputations and past experience are major factors.[5] For example, some pilots feel that Douglas' aircraft normally have handling characteristics superior to those of other makers, and this and similar impressions have great weight in aircraft selection. More intangible yet are airline executives' ideas on the passenger acceptance that a new design will meet. Though airlines still worry about people's fear of flying, they have come to the conclusion that the flying public is generally eager to try a new aircraft. Several of the demand forecasts prepared for the last general passenger-fare investigation contained a "jet stimulation factor" of 5 or 10 percent to cover the extra journeys that would be made in the new, faster, and more comfortable aircraft.[6] But, the airline management still has the problem of deciding just which design might have the most appeal. Will passengers greatly prefer a plane with large windows to one with small windows? Will a slight disadvantage in speed seriously hamper a design's chances as a competitive tool? The industry seems to rely heavily on folklore for answers to such questions. It has been quite seriously believed in the industry that Americans would be reluctant to fly in an airplane not built in the United States. It has been thought that

[4] Stern, p. 117; Dyment, p. 151.

[5] "No one knows just how good the final result will be before the aircraft actually flies . . . The past experience of the manufacturer, in meeting and overcoming the passenger comfort problems, bears very heavily with us in airplane selection." Ades, p. 278.

[6] See, for example, United Air Lines, Inc., "Estimated Results of Nonstop Jet Operations San Francisco/Oakland–New York with and without American Airlines," Exhibit No. U-110, New York–San Francisco Nonstop Case, Docket No. 9214, p. 3. United puts the jet-stimulation factor at 12 percent for segments greater than 2000 miles, 10 percent between 1000 and 2000 miles, and 5 percent under 1000 miles.

the public would strongly prefer a four-engine plane to a two-engine plane on grounds of safety (although engine failure is almost never the cause of an accident). Both of these beliefs have recently been fading, but other conjectures of this sort still can play a decisive role in aircraft purchases.

How does competitive marketing affect the carriers' initial investment decisions? A better plane is not a more profitable one for a carrier if it is delivered after important competitors have instituted equipment with a strong appeal to the public. Furthermore, competition considerations affecting choice of plane also affect the choice of seating configuration and other appointments that must be planned far in advance. Equipment decisions keyed solely to competitive strategy are not hard to find. In the early 1950s National Airlines ordered what was probably an inefficiently small fleet of DC-7s to meet competition from Eastern Air Lines' best Constellation aircraft.[7] And Western Air Lines secured long-range Boeing 707s to use on its short-haul routes to meet competition from United Air Lines, though Western complained that the purchase was for competitive reasons only and that its average stage length was only 40 percent of those of its principal jet competitors.[8] For other insights into the working of competitive factors in the selection of aircraft, let us review the story of the carriers' problems in choosing turbine equipment in the 1950s.

By the 1950s, a pattern in the purchase of equipment was rather well established. Leadership fell to the large airlines,[9] the Big Four and, especially, Pan American, the dominant international carrier. The high levels of fares (maintained by cartel agreements) in international travel, coupled with the national-prestige motives influencing most foreign carriers, mean that product and quality competition is even more fierce there than in the American domestic market.[10] Thus Pan American, with its abundant

[7] *Aviation Week,* LVI (March 10, 1952), 7.

[8] *Airlift,* XXIV (Aug. 1960), 20.

[9] For instance, in 1936 American Airlines had been first to place the DC-3 in service, followed quickly by TWA, United, and Eastern. See *Monopoly Problems in Regulated Industries — Airlines,* U.S. House of Representatives, II, 787. For good general coverage of the equipment situation to 1949, see F. W. Gill and G. L. Bates, *Airline Competition* (Boston, 1949), chap. 2.

[10] See A. H. Fox, "Fare-Fixing in Air Transport," *Three Banks Review,* no. 35 (Sept. 1957), pp. 23–35. For an example of international equipment rivalry affecting a domestic carrier, see *Aviation Week,* LI (Aug. 22, 1949), 43.

foreign competition, great size, and substantial profitability, was frequently the first carrier to order a new design. It had been the first to order the Republic Rainbow, a high-performance design that never reached the stage of production. American Airlines had followed with an order for the Rainbow, and in the same round of activity United and Northwest ordered the Boeing Stratocruiser, also a long-range luxury aircraft.[11] Northwest faced some rivalry from Pan American. The smaller airlines had not been under much pressure before the 1950s; the weakest among them operated almost entirely noncompetitive routes.

The early 1950s were the scene of the first decisions that would bring the airlines into the "jet age." In 1951, the first commercial jet, the British de Havilland Comet I, was in service with British Overseas Airways Corporation.[12] The American aircraft manufacturers were already thinking of jet designs, and the airlines, especially American and United, had been working with manufacturers Douglas, Lockheed, and Boeing on various types of jet plans.[13] Lockheed had tried unsuccessfully to sell American Airlines a design it claimed would operate at lower costs than the reigning Douglas DC-6.[14] A trade magazine guessed that the first American carrier to place a jet order would be one of the large international lines, either Pan American or TWA, but American Airlines was also supposed to have given Douglas a verbal commitment on the DC-8 jet.[15] At this time everyone seemed to think that commercial jets could not be operated economically for some time to come. The president of National Airlines declared: "We do not plan to buy jet transports until one is available with which we can make money, unless we are forced into purchasing uneconomical equipment by the competition." American's president voiced the view that United States airlines should wait for a jet with lower costs than the Douglas DC-6B and with a transcon-

[11] Pan American Airways, Inc. — Domestic Route Case, Docket No. 1803, 11 CAB 852 (1950).

[12] As early as 1949, the chairman of the Senate commerce committee, Senator Edwin C. Johnson, said he had been informed that several United States airlines would purchase the British jet; see *Aviation Week,* LI (Aug. 29, 1949), 31.

[13] Transcript of Hearings before Examiner, General Passenger Fare Investigation, p. 5417.

[14] *Aviation Week,* LIV (June 18, 1951), 83.

[15] *Aviation Week,* LVI (June 30, 1952), 7.

tinental range, specifications not met by the Comet I.[16] A break came in October 1952, when Pan American closed a deal (later held in abeyance) to buy three Comets of advanced design from de Havilland. It was noted that this would put severe pressure on Eastern Air Lines, competing with Pan American on a New York–San Juan route.[17] And, indeed, at the same time Eastern Air Lines was negotiating for Comets. President Rickenbacker announced "to the startled British and the world in press conferences" that he would have a large fleet of Comet IIIs if he could get adequate deliveries in 1956. It turned out that Rickenbacker had been bluffing, but by this time the domestic aircraft manufacturers had hastened their jet designs and Boeing announced that its prototype was under construction. This may have been precisely Rickenbacker's purpose.[18] Thus the scene was set. Sure of international competition with jet aircraft, Pan American had immediately plunged in with a token order.

Its long-haul routes were well suited to jet operation, and the high level of international fares made Pan American less concerned about the costs of jet operation. Moreover, as a *Fortune* writer put it: "The probable underlying reason why Pan Am made the first move . . . is that Pan Am *likes* to be first — a penchant that has led it to operate as many as six or eight different breeds of equipment at once." [19] It was clear that the other United States international carriers, TWA and Northwest, would sooner or later have to follow suit. But TWA and Northwest, unlike Pan American, also had very substantial domestic routes. Any new equipment they purchased would surely be used on their prime domestic routes, drawing the purely domestic carriers into the cycle. Whether because of this specific threat or a more general unwillingness to be caught with less than the most appealing equipment available, the major domestic lines were already in a quandary over what to do about jet aircraft.

During 1953 and 1954 a bad state of nerves prevailed in the domestic industry. The executives of the transcontinental Big

[16] John McDonald, "Jet Airliners: Year of Decision," *Fortune,* XLVII (April 1953), 246.

[17] *Aviation Week,* LVII (Oct. 27, 1952), 13–14.

[18] McDonald, pp. 244, 246; *Aviation Week,* LVII (Sept. 15, 1952), 79–80.

[19] Dero A. Saunders, "The Airlines' Flight from Reality," *Fortune,* p. 217.

Three, American, TWA, and United, judged the prospective cost
of operating the Comet III to be high despite its passenger appeal
and felt that, although one of them with high load factors might
make money by operating it, all could not do so.[20] Also, the
relatively high-cost DC-7 and the corresponding Lockheed Constellation series were just going into service, and any rush to
order the British jet could lead to a capital loss on these planes
with no assurance that a profitable aircraft would be gained in
return. In the end, mutual interdependence prevailed, and no
orders were placed. However, in mid-1954 Capital Airlines dis-
turbed the domestic tranquility by placing a large order for the
first British turboprop aircraft, the Vickers Viscount. Capital had
had difficulty in modernizing its fleet. Against substantial competition from DC-6s, Constellations, and pressurized two-engine
planes, it still had mainly unpressurized DC-3s and DC-4s. The
order for a very large Viscount fleet gave Capital the combined
advantages of a great equipment superiority over its competitors
and a fleet standardized on one aircraft. Capital felt that the
Viscount would have a substantial passenger appeal over piston-
powered aircraft and that after the Viscount's introduction it
would be at least three years before a competitive American turboprop appeared.[21] This move was expected by the industry to speed
the development of an American turboprop and generally brought
closer the big round of orders for American-made jets.

The year 1955 brought the crucial decisions that set the equipment situation for the carriers for the decade to follow. In June,
American Airlines, which competed with Capital Airlines on
several important routes, placed the first order for Lockheed's
large long-range turboprop, the Electra. By this time Boeing had
been claiming substantially lower seat-mile costs for its entry
than existing piston planes could offer, and a military decision
clearing the way for Boeing to produce its 707 jet (a revamped
military tanker) had brought the date of availability for commercial service much closer. Douglas Aircraft had a design for the
DC-8, and several more British jet designs were being discussed.

[20] McDonald, p. 248; *Aviation Week,* LVIII (Feb. 2, 1953), 92, and LIX
(Nov. 23, 1953), 88.
[21] William D. Perreault, "British Invade U.S. Market with Viscount," *American Aviation,* XVIII (June 21, 1954), 17–18; *Aviation Week,* LXIII (July 4,
1955), 81.

United Air Lines had long since made clear that it would order a jet as soon as a satisfactory model was found. By August, a trade magazine declared that:

> It is a foregone conclusion that several airline orders are imminent, and that the first to be placed could touch off an avalanche of buying that may involve a major share of the market in a brief period . . .
>
> As a result, airline officials now bent on buying jets find themselves faced with a perplexing choice. Instead of the normal competition between airplane designs, such factors as delivery dates, state of development and the producer's past history with transports are moving to the fore as deciding issues.[22]

At this point all eyes focused on four airlines — American, Eastern, United, and Pan American. (TWA was playing an uncertain lone-wolf role through the actions of its capricious major stockholder, Howard Hughes.) Apparently President Patterson of United led a substantial effort to get these carriers to agree to order a single airplane. There were numerous reasons for United to make such a move. It was not clear that both the Boeing 707 and Douglas DC-8 would actually be produced in commercial quantities, and a scattering of orders for each would have produced an awkward situation. Pooled purchases would probably allow the chosen manufacturer to offer a lower price. Finally, United, traditionally skilled in the ways of service competition, seemed to feel that it could manage well enough if all of its major competitors had the same equipment. The presidents of American and Pan American were reported to be in day-to-day discussions to resolve some sort of pooling agreement. It was likely that TWA would refuse to go along with the pool and thereby have a unique aircraft as well as a substantial delivery data advantage (if the pool settled on Douglas, as it presumably would have). However, the pool did not come off.[23]

The choice between jets clearly rested on imponderables for all four of the big carriers. The Boeing prototype had been flying for a year and offered an earlier delivery date. However, the Boeing was a replastered military aircraft whereas the Douglas had been designed from the start for commercial use, and airline

---

[22] Joseph S. Murphy, "AF Go-Ahead on 707 Spurs New Jet Race," *American Aviation*, XIX (Aug. 1, 1955), 21. See also *American Aviation*, XVIII (Aug. 30, 1954), 20; Saunders, p. 217.

[23] *American Aviation*, XIX (Aug. 29, 1955), 63; XIX (Sept. 12, 1955), 84.

engineers apparently felt that this fact plus Douglas' greater commercial experience was bound to mean hidden penalties for the Boeing. It was Pan American that resolved these doubts by ordering *both* jets — twenty-five DC-8s and twenty Boeing 707s — thus assuring a lead over its international competitors in introducing both planes. With this guarantee that both planes would be produced, United made a quick decision for Douglas, ordering thirty DC-8s. This left open the possibility for American to introduce domestic jet service by ordering the 707, which it promptly did, bargaining design modifications and a price concession from Boeing and starting a "speed race" by claiming that a faster transcontinental schedule could be maintained with the 707.[24] Other airlines fell into line fairly quickly. In December, National placed an order for the Douglas plane; its major competitor, Eastern, had long before ordered a large fleet of Electras. A competitor of American, Continental Air Lines, ordered Boeings. Another round of orders came in March and April of 1956. TWA finally got around to ordering Boeing planes, getting a time lead in jet service over United but not over American or its international competitor, Pan American. Braniff, Delta, and Eastern followed.[25]

Later decisions in the jet race were less dramatic but no less heavily keyed to considerations of market rivalry. For example, by mid-1956 it was clear to Capital Airlines that it would face competition from Electra turboprops and probably also a medium-range jet produced by Convair. Capital decided to make another bold move to avoid return to a status of equipment inferiority by placing an order for British Comet jets, a deal which later fell through owing to financing difficulties.[26] A similar problem later

[24] William V. Henzey, "PAA Orders Both Boeing and Douglas Jets," *American Aviation,* XIX (Oct. 24, 1955), 158–160; Fred S. Hunter, "Pan American's Jet Strategy Gives It Big Competitive Edge," *American Aviation,* XIX (Nov. 7, 1955), 82; Anthony Vandyk, "Jet Race Quickens; UAL Orders 30 DC8's," *American Aviation,* XIX (Nov. 7, 1955), 23–24; William V. Henzey, "American Makes Bid for Lead in Jet Race with $165-Million Order for 30 707s," *American Aviation,* XIX (Nov. 21, 1955), 19; "Remarks by the Hon. Louis J. Hector, Member, Civil Aeronautics Board, before the New York Society of Security Analysts," New York, Nov. 28, 1956 (mimeographed); *Time,* LXXII (Nov. 17, 1958), 88.

[25] United Air Lines, Inc., "Chronology of Domestic Carriers' Initial Jet Orders," Exhibit No. U-5, New York–San Francisco Nonstop Case, Docket No. 9214, p. 1.

[26] *Aviation Week,* LXV (July 23, 1956), 38.

faced Northeast Airlines in deciding how to stretch its slender borrowing ability over its various equipment requirements. By 1960 it had acquired a Viscount fleet and established a successful operation in the Boston–New York–Washington market. It was trying to keep a foot in the Boston–New York–Miami market, using DC-6Bs entirely in coach service. The carrier's executives expressed a wish for more Viscounts to augment the successful commuter operation among the northeastern cities; but Florida "is a jet market" and they felt that the first duty was to find jet equipment that could win a market position there.[27] The president of Northwest stated that the carrier was seriously considering ordering medium-range jets rather than the intercontinental models that would be best for its combined transcontinental and intercontinental system because of a one-year difference in delivery dates; competitive pressure made this difference crucial.[28]

Though the evidence is hard to pin down, it is clear that large carriers have advantages over small ones. As was mentioned above, a prospective big customer can usually influence the specifications of a new design to his liking. Furthermore, he has substantial advantages in playing the game of strategies and coalitions about new designs. For instance, Howard Hughes, in an effort to overcome TWA's lag in ordering jets, tried to corner the market for jet engines.[29] Although this move was unsuccessful, it was still one which only a large carrier could contemplate. Another good example of the advantages of bigness in this area is the agreement made between Eastern and American to allocate between them the early deliveries of the Lockheed Electra. Rickenbacker of Eastern confessed under crossexamination in the following passage from the transcript of the *Southern Transcontinental* case:

Q. What I wanted to ask you was whether you had some kind of an option or right to purchase the Lockheed Electra aircraft for some period of time before you actually committed yourself to them.

A. [Rickenbacker] It was a commitment, as I remember it. We had a commitment for 40 of them. American had a commitment for 35.

[27] Glenn Garrison, "Northeast Keys Future Success to Jets," *Aviation Week,* LXXII (Feb. 1, 1960), 32.

[28] Transcript of Hearings before Examiner, General Passenger Fare Investigation, pp. 6401–6404.

[29] C. J. V. Murphy and T. A. Wise, "The Problem of Howard Hughes," *Fortune,* LIX (Jan. 1959), 166.

O. You mean Lockheed gave you a first refusal on a certain number of airplanes?

A. Both of us — American and Eastern. In fact, we were to have one-and-one until a certain period down the road.

Q. There was a time when you had the right to tell Lockheed how many you would take, wasn't there?

A. That time is always.

Q. Without penalty, I mean.

A. No.

Q. Is it a fact that you insisted and made a condition of your order that Lockheed would not give concurrent delivery to your major competitors?

A. No, because we had agreed on that between Lockheed, American and ourselves. They were a part of it . . . We were to get one and they were to get one, and that was to go on until we got up around the twenty-some mark. I have forgotten what it is. And in turn, then others came in with positions, and they held out certain positions for other operators.[30]

In another case, the senior vice-president and treasurer of National Airlines testified that in 1955, when the Electra was first publicly presented:

National's President talked with Lockheed about buying Electras and was told that Eastern and American had all the deliveries tied up. He endeavored to induce Lockheed to give National a couple of early deliveries simultaneously with Eastern's deliveries. He was informed that Eastern had ordered forty Electras and had insisted that National not be given any until theirs were in operation for several months. On December 9, 1955 we signed our contract for the purchase of twelve Electras with options for eight more and took the best delivery we could get. The first Electra was to be delivered in April, 1959. Eastern's were . . . delayed until about November, 1958.[31]

Several persons close to the industry have said that such instances are not uncommon, but they are rather hard to document.

Reflecting on the equipment orders of the 1950s, competitive considerations heavily dominated both the timing of the orders and the choice among competing aircraft designs. Substantial

[30] Transcript of Hearings before Examiner, Southern Transcontinental Case, Docket No. 7984, pp. 8953–8955. The actual pattern of Electra deliveries did not resemble the pattern Rickenbacker described of one to Eastern, one to American, and so on, apparently because American decided on a modification which held up its deliveries.

[31] National Airlines, Inc., "Testimony of J. C. Brawner," Exhibit No. NAL-A, Pan American-National Agreements Investigation, Docket No. 9921, pp. 1–2.

point-to-point competition makes it impossible for a carrier to stand equipment inferiority for very long in the absence of price differentials.[32] Thus the possibility arises that considerations of efficiency and of marketing strategy in picking aircraft may not point in the same direction. The disadvantage of the smaller carrier appears to be substantial in getting early delivery of a new plane. Its position is not hopeless, though — witness Delta's recent introduction of the Convair 880 medium-range jet. The matter is primarily one of finance. It seems likely that a smaller carrier with equal access to loanable funds could probably operate in the equipment market with as much freedom as the Big Four. This is particularly true now, with several competing designs of each aircraft type available.

Now, what of the matter of the *size* of the order placed for whatever planes are chosen? The ability to offer a large variety of flight times, depending on a proportionally large fleet of aircraft, is a prime competitive tool. A carrier wanting a larger market share would tend to order a large fleet relative to its existing market position. Conversely, efficient joint monopolistic exploitation of the market would require conscious parallel action to keep purchases down.

The first thing to be said is that, as with choosing airplane designs, evidence shows that determination of the size of equipment orders generally rests on rather imprecise calculations. This was especially so in the 1940s, when no one had the vaguest idea of how to forecast future demand for air transportation in general,

[32] Evidence supporting this point will be discussed later, although it is common knowledge within the industry. Consider this passage from a Board document: "The history of equipment purchases leaves little doubt that the stimulus of competition has been in the forefront of the factors influencing airline management in its constant search for new equipment. Thus, new equipment has traditionally been placed in operation first on the most competitive segments; and the introduction of more modern aircraft by one company on such a route has been followed by a scramble on the part of competitors to introduce with the greatest possible speed comparable or more advanced types . . . It is again significant that the smaller carriers which have trailed in the acquisition of new property have promptly developed equipment programs when changes in route structures have placed them in competitive situations with carriers utilizing more modern equipment . . . What might be termed 'luxury' equipment has been introduced at times and under conditions that virtually precluded a conclusion that economic considerations other than competitive ones warranted or prompted the action." *Monopoly Problems in Regulated Industries — Airlines*, II, 788–89.

let alone demand for a particular carrier. In the face of uncertainty, airline executives even then looked on the bright side. In the late 1940s, overoptimistic ordering of equipment at the end of the war was blamed for the carriers' sagging profit rates. (The more common interpretation, of course, was the usual "excessive competition.") One writer made calculations which suggest that in 1946 the airlines owned or had on order equipment that would have carried double the current volume of traffic at a normal load factor.[33] The traffic recession of 1947–48 caused the cancellation of about half of these orders. The Korean War and the prosperous years succeeding it erased the threat of an overhang of excess capacity, but load-factor figures suggest that short-run excess production at prevailing fares was one of the many sources of disappointment in profits in the late 1940s.[34] With the rapidly rising load factors and steady or declining unit costs of 1950 and 1951, optimism returned to the industry. Many carriers then, as always, were prone to interpret current traffic trends as permanent phenomena. This, coupled with improved borrowing ability, encouraged another fairly substantial round of equipment orders involving the turbo-compound DC-7 and comparable Lockheed Constellation models, rather high-cost airplanes which could fly coast-to-coast nonstop.[35]

Individual carriers have often admitted to gross misjudgment in the size of their initial orders for some new types of equipment. United Air Lines had assumed that the end of the Korean War would cause traffic to "reproduce the pattern that followed World War II — namely, a cessation of the usual war-time demand and a reversion in traffic growth to something approaching pre-war experience." A second major order had to be placed for DC-7s as

[33] M. George Goodrick, "Air Mail Subsidy of Commercial Aviation," *Journal of Air Law and Commerce,* XVI (Summer 1949), 272.

[34] Board Chairman J. J. O'Connell declared: "This new equipment has created what appear to be temporary dislocations in the relation between capacity and traffic. It has also created serious competitive conflicts between those carriers which have and those which do not have the new equipment. The capacity problem has arisen in part because new equipment was over-ordered due to too optimistic estimates of traffic and in part due to a failure to retire promptly the older equipment." See *Air-line Industry Investigation,* hearings pursuant to S. Res. 50, U.S. Senate, Committee on Interstate and Foreign Commerce, 81st Cong., 1st sess. (Washington, 1949), pp. 97–98.

[35] Paul W. Cherington, "Objectives and Strategies for Airline Pricing," *Journal of Air Law and Commerce,* XVIII (Summer 1951), 259.

a result.[36] It often seems that there are no precise calculations about how new aircraft on order will be allocated over a carrier's routes. For instance, a National Airlines witness testified in *General Passenger Fare Investigation* that the airline ordered six DC-8s and twenty-three Electras without any exact plans for where they would be used. The DC-8 order was identified with the minimum fleet of a single airplane type that could be efficiently maintained. No basis was given for the size of the Electra order.[37] C. A. Rheinstrom, executive vice-president of sales of American Airlines, writes:

In this business, you have to take some risks. If, several years ago, [President] C. R. Smith had insisted that his staff tell him exactly where American was going to get traffic to fill the new planes he was thinking of ordering, he would never have bought them.[38]

And Paul Cherington, in an official report, notes that a survey of the carriers revealed "only a small minority" with "well-developed plans for the development of specific markets." [39]

The more usual situation, however, probably represents a certain amount of calculation of the market shares a carrier hopes to achieve in particular city-pairs. For instance, a Northeast Airlines executive indicated that an order for Bristol Britannia turboprops (later canceled) was based on the objective of gaining up to 25 percent of the New York–Florida market by 1962.[40] Finally, carriers sometimes appear to order equipment on the basis of hopes for route awards in cases currently before the Board. Western Air Lines recently made an order on the chance of receiving a West Coast-Hawaii award. A further tactical difficulty enters because, though the Board does not usually make ownership of suitable equipment a test of fitness in giving a

[36] United Air Lines, Inc., "Testimony of A. M. de Vourney," Exhibit No. U-D, New York–San Francisco Nonstop Investigation, Docket No. 9214, pp. 11–12, 14–15.

[37] Transcript of Hearings before Examiner, General Passenger Fare Investigation, pp. 6253–6255.

[38] *American Aviation*, XXII (Jan. 26, 1959), 35.

[39] Paul W. Cherington, *The Status and Significance of the Airline Equipment Investment Program, a Report Prepared for the President's Special Assistant for Aviation* (Washington, 1958), pp. 36–37.

[40] Transcript of Hearings before Examiner, General Passenger Fare Investigation, p. 6155.

carrier a new route, its decision might be influenced by knowledge that a marginal carrier was successfully preparing to qualify for the award. Eastern charged that Capital informed the Board on an *ex parte* basis of a new order for Convair 880 jets that improved its qualifications for a Buffalo–Florida route. In ruling on the complaint, the Board agreed that the communication had been made but denied that the favorable decision had been influenced by it.[41] If there is any tendency for success to breed success in this fashion, then some hard strategic problems face the carriers in fixing their equipment orders. One final reflection on the indeterminacy of the factors behind carriers' equipment orders is an organizational one. In the past the decision on the amount of equipment to order has rested with top management, usually men who are prone to operate on an intuitive basis. The story is told of an airline president who, when asked why the line had ordered seven planes of a certain type, thundered, "I knew we needed seven. That's why I'm president."

No matter how loosely aircraft orders are keyed to market-share calculations or aspirations, it is useful to investigate what sort of pattern of competition the orders seem to reflect. Do certain carriers order in quantities that suggest plans to strike out for a larger market share? Or is there tacit agreement to aim at maintaining existing shares? Such questions can be reasonably put only to the decisions behind recent rounds of jet re-equipment. In the past, the presence of subsidy and the near absence of competition for some carriers meant that there was no pressure on some lines to keep up with the leaders. Furthermore, a carrier could be ordering a relatively small amount of equipment and still be planning to increase the share of its competitive markets. Now, however, the situation is much different. All carriers earn most of their revenues and fly most of their plane-miles in competitive markets. Furthermore, the current round of re-equipment is so pervasive that nearly all aircraft existing a few years ago will be retired shortly from competitive domestic routes. Thus the overall size of carriers' equipment orders will be a fairly good indi-

[41] Great Lakes-Southeast Service Case — Opinion and Order Granting and Denying Stay of Effective Date of Certificates, Docket No. 2396 et al., decided Nov. 28, 1958, CCH Av. Law Rep. §22,224.03.

cation of the shares of the market at which each aims in the 1960s.

A calculation of this sort requires many different applications of judgment, and these will not be explained in detail. My chosen measure of output in the air-transport industry is available seat-miles, and so the problem is one of translating carriers' orders for new equipment into estimates of the available seat-miles these fleets will produce when delivered by the mid-1960s. For any given aircraft order (*one* airline's order for *one* plane type), this is done by multiplying the number of planes ordered, by the number of seats per plane, by the average hours per day that the plane will be used, by its average airport-to-airport speed (miles per hour). The result is the prospective daily seat-mile productivity of that portion of the carrier's fleet. The number of planes on order as of May 1960 was taken from a trade publication.[42] The number of seats planned per aircraft by each airline was taken from a Civil Aeronautics Board source.[43] Information on the average speed could be derived from the experience of carriers already operating some of the new types of aircraft. Figures for these average speeds are regularly collected and published by a trade magazine. These reflect not only the normal cruising speed of the aircraft but also the average distance it flies on a particular carrier's routes (because of the time consumed in taxiing, take-off, and landing). Thus, the average speed figures already experienced were adjusted for the route patterns each aircraft would probably be flying for each airline. Setting a proper assumption for hours of utilization per day was particularly difficult because philosophies differ in the industry. Some carriers favor high utilization (as much as twelve hours a day) with the resulting higher maintenance costs; others seem to minimize maintenance costs at the expense of lower utilization per day. Since it is not yet at all clear what utilization figures will actually be turned in when jet equipment is fully integrated, standard figures for each plane were set for all carriers on the basis of those used in a forth-

[42] *Airlift,* XXIII (May 1960), 61, 83. They appear frequently in print and have been checked against other sources.

[43] CAB, *General Characteristics of Turbine-Powered Aircraft,* "Air Transport Economics in the Jet Age," Feb. 1960, table 4.

coming Civil Aeronautics Board report. Certain variations between carriers were allowed, however, because in short-haul use an airplane can necessarily be kept in use less of the time than on long-haul routes.[44]

Still other doubts had to be resolved. What portion of the equipment ordered would be used on international routes? My assumption was generally that a carrier would use the same proportion of its turbine equipment on international routes as the revenue passenger-miles it flew in international service in 1958 bore to its total revenue passenger-miles that year. However, the stub-end routes in Canada and Mexico were not singled out as international. How many aircraft should be counted as fully competitive new equipment? Clearly all the jets and probably the Electra belong; but what of the Vickers Viscount, which will certainly succumb to short-range jets on many routes? Calculations were made both including and excluding the Viscount. What of the possibility that some carriers may plan to continue using significant portions of their piston fleet while others may not? This inquiry deals with the relation of investment to market-control motives; and since the evidence now is clearly that the older aircraft will not be competitive without price differentials, they are excluded entirely. What of equipment orders that were made and then canceled for lack of funds? This is important for the smaller carriers, since several had to cut back for lack of financing. Calculations were made both including and excluding these retrenchments.

A final difficulty is what to do about orders for short-haul turbojets. As of the beginning of 1961, there are only a few orders for such planes from the domestic trunks, specifically United's and Eastern's orders for the Caravelle and Boeing 727. It is fairly clear that these begin another round of equipment orders of yet unknown magnitude; other planes may well become involved.[45] If the large Eastern and United orders are included in the calculations of implied market shares, then the expected share of the Big Four would increase significantly. But the smaller carriers are

[44] For interesting illustrative figures, see George Gardner, "Some Aspects of Future Air Transport Possibilities," *Canadian Aeronautical Journal*, V (Oct. 1959), 326.

[45] *American Aviation Daily*, May 9, 1960, p. 47.

now ordering short-haul jets. Indeed, one could argue that because the "regional" carriers have on the average more short-haul routes than the Big Four they might order these planes in relatively larger proportions. Because of this uncertainty, computations were made both including and excluding the orders for short-haul jet equipment placed so far.[46]

Calculations of relative shares of "competitive" capacity in modern planes have been governed by several sets of assumptions, made by combining the various choices listed above. To display the results in Table 26, I grouped these assumptions to yield

Table 26. Relative capacity of Big Four airlines and smaller trunks in fully competitive turbine aircraft, and relative traffic volumes in 1958

| Carrier group | Shares of competitive equipment | | Share of 1958 revenue passenger-miles |
	Highest likely Big Four share	Lowest likely Big Four share	
Big Four	80.5	72.2	70.3
Other trunks[a]	19.5	27.8	29.7
	100.0	100.0	100.0

[a] Including those now involved in merger agreements with Big Four carriers.
Source: CAB, Office of Carrier Accounts and Statistics, *Monthly Summary of Air Carrier Traffic Statistics*, December 1958 for 1958 data; for prospective capacity shares, see text.

the maximum and minimum probable shares for the Big Four, excluding the influence of the United-Capital marger. Results for the largely prejet year 1958 are included for comparison. Obviously, whichever set of assumptions is correct, the current round of re-equipment augurs a larger share for the Big Four carriers. If the optimistic assumptions for the smaller carriers are more nearly correct, the increase (from 70.3 to 72.2 percent) is probably not significant. If the pessimistic set is correct, the significance of the gap between 70.3 and 80.5 is hardly in doubt.

[46] It might seem that including the short-haul orders would seriously overstate the maximum Big Four share, but on closer examination this is not the case. The Eastern order for the 727 is very large, and without it Eastern's implied share is sharply understated; also American and TWA will probably place significant orders for such aircraft.

These figures are so important to the workability of competition in the industry that it is well to look further into them. Does the prospective resurgence of the market share of the large carriers reflect aggressive expansion by all of them? The rate of expansion of passenger capacity due to equipment ordered so far by the various airlines — large and small — is quite variable. Counting the short-haul jets, among the Big Four, American and United show strikingly large expansions, Eastern a somewhat small one. Two of the smaller carriers also show vigorous expansions — Delta and Continental are both equipping for an expanded route network. The pattern is not one of a "conspiracy" of the big against the small. Another vital question about these figures on comparative shares is whether they represent the carriers' market-share aspirations, pure and simple, or whether they represent these aspirations filtered through the rationing mechanism of the capital market. Certainly several reductions of orders by the smaller carriers that are reflected in the maximum estimate for the share of the Big Four were due to the inability to borrow funds, and it is equally certain that most of the smaller carriers would have liked to order more equipment had funds been available. This fact is so obvious from the problems of Northeast and Capital that it warrants no lengthy documentation. What pattern of equipment orders would have emerged if all carriers had been able to borrow unlimited funds at a "going" rate of interest? This is a question of managerial motives and can receive only a vague answer. During most of the past decade, the market share of the smaller carriers as a group (and in most cases, individually) has been increasing through their success in route cases before the Civil Aeronautics Board and, to a lesser degree, their own efforts at market penetration. Had it been possible, there seems to be no doubt that the managements of the smaller carriers would have sought the equipment necessary to establish significant shares in their expanded route networks. In sum, the structural traits of the capital market, combined with the Civil Aeronautics Board's failure to come very close to equalizing the relative profitability of the large and small trunk carriers, appear as critical elements in determining an increase of seller concentration in the airlines and possibly a decrease in the workability of competition.

As a postscript to this discussion of equipment decisions, it is interesting to see what the carriers themselves have had to say about the matter. When the carriers were placing their first orders for jet aircraft, and heady comparisons of the seat-mile productivity of jets and piston-engine planes filled the air, the airlines were often accused of ordering more equipment than they needed.[47] There was a congressional demand for an investigation.[48] A prominent article in *Fortune* titled "The Airlines' Flight from Reality" received much attention and was answered by C. R. Smith, the president of American Airlines. Publicly at least, the airlines during this time seemed to adopt the line that they were ordering equipment to maintain their existing market shares of a reasonable estimate of the 1960s market.[49] In *General Passenger Fare Investigation* the following exchange took place between the Board's counsel and a United Air Lines witness:

Q. At your planning time, wasn't the thought that the acquisitions would tend to put United ahead of its competition?
A. I think the figures will show, and the exhibits which Mr. Bowers will sponsor, that our plan is to maintain our participation in the market.
Q. By maintain do you mean the same level?
A. At the same relative percentage of the total market.[50]

From these bits of testimony alone, one might tend to read circumstantial evidence of tacit collusion to maintain existing market shares. But the underlying facts do not support the testimony. Market-share aspirations are highly rivalrous, and this would be even more apparent if the availability of finance did not restrain the smaller carriers so significantly. As this volume goes to press,

[47] At first glance, this might seem to be a way of estimating the degree of competitive rivalry (or monopolistic collusion) in equipment orders: checking to see whether the aggregate capacity of the fleets ordered comes to more or less than enough for the anticipated demand at going fare levels. Unfortunately, it will not work because of the uncertainty about the rate of retirement of piston aircraft, itself an economic decision related to competitive motives and market conditions. Because of this weakness, the method summarized in the text and in Table 26 was used.

[48] "Smathers Asks Probe of Jet Investments," *Aviation Week*, LXIX (Nov. 24, 1958), 37.

[49] See, for example, Transcript of Hearings before Examiner, General Passenger Fare Investigation, pp. 6432–6435 (Northwest Airlines) and 6487–6490 (TWA).

[50] *Ibid.*, p. 6580.

the impression grows that the trunks' orders for jet aircraft have totaled more than enough to supply the probable demand, indicating a weak recognition of oligopolistic interdependence in planning aircraft investment.

OTHER PHASES OF INVESTMENT AND EXPANSION

The purchase of new aircraft is not the only dimension of air-carrier investment and growth, despite its commanding importance. The dividing line between investment and sales promotion in airline expenses is a very shaky one. Certainly the carriers view the locating of luxury ticket offices in high-rent downtown locations no differently from purveying meals created by famous chefs. Both are bait for potential customers. This kind of promotion expenditure, involving durable goods only in passing, will be left to Chapter 14. There is, however, another area of airline conduct with great potential importance for market performance — the decision to seek permission from the Civil Aeronautics Board to expand into new city-pair markets or, conversely, to abandon service now offered. One can imagine a wide range of behavioral patterns that might control such decisions. In a highly collusive situation, carriers might avoid filing any new route applications that would trespass on other carriers' prize markets. In a more rivalrous market, they might file applications for competing routes whenever such a move seemed profitable. In a highly rivalrous situation, applications to offer competitive service might be filed with abandon, ignoring some or all of the possible countermeasures.

In the 1940s the actions of the smaller carriers in seeking route extensions looked somewhat like the second of the three patterns just suggested. One instance is documented in the 1947 decision in which the Board permitted Western Air Lines to sell its Route 68 (Los Angeles–Denver) to United Air Lines. Western, a fairly small regional carrier, wanted to eliminate Route 68 because it required special equipment. Western could not profitably integrate this route and the required equipment into its system. As one way out of the dilemma, Western considered trying to have the Denver route extended to Chicago. But it felt that, if the Board gave it the Chicago–Denver extension, United (which had formerly routed its Los Angeles passengers via

Western) would seek and get an extension to Los Angeles. "Western would be a poor fourth in a competition with American, TWA, and United," and it decided that the game was not worth that risk.[51]

During the earlier years (until the late 1940s), the smaller carriers seem on balance to have been slightly more aggressive than the large trunklines in seeking new routes. No doubt this was due to generous treatment by the Board. Indeed, some of the major trunks, notably United, had almost given up trying. However, the aggressiveness of the smaller carriers then was modest by comparison to more recent years. In the large area cases of the 1950s, the smaller trunks sought new route extensions that often lay far beyond their current abilities and plans. The consolidation of the area cases was partly the result, partly the cause, of a pattern of offensive and defensive applications that developed. If Northwest applied for a route from Chicago to Miami in competition with Eastern Air Lines, then Eastern applied for trackage rights from the center of the United States to the Pacific northwest in competition with Northwest. It was this sort of tangle of highly rivalrous and retaliatory route applications upon which the Board has had to pass in the major route cases of the past decade. One inconspicuous device in the Board's own procedures probably encouraged this free-for-all approach. For some time the carriers have included in their applications in major route cases a "catch-all clause," expressing a willingness to accept any route awards the Board might hand out to them in the case, whether explicitly applied for or not. Several times the Board has seized upon these clauses to give major routes to a small carrier.[52] Thus, even if a small carrier feared disastrous retaliation if it applied explicitly for a major extension, it could toss in an innocuous application with a catch-all clause and hope for aid from on high. Indeed, the Board has even claimed that it could require at least minor extensions against the wishes of a carrier. This claim has

---

[51] United Air Lines, Inc.-Western Air Lines, Inc., Acquisition of Air Carrier Property, Docket No. 2839, 8 CAB 298, p. 302 (1947).

[52] See, for example, Denver Service Case — Supplemental Opinion and Order on Reconsideration, Docket No. 1841 et al., decided Dec. 30, 1955, CCH Av. Law Rep. §21,917.01. The practice was upheld by the Supreme Court in Civil Aeronautics Board v. State Airlines, Inc., 338 U.S. 572 (1950), reversing 174 F.2d 510 (1949).

never been pushed very far, however.[53] Collusive holding back of new route applications or intimidation of carriers considering such applications thus seems to be entirely out of the question.[54]

The kind of route expansions which the carriers have sought over time reveals more about the absence of recognized mutual dependence among the carriers in their efforts to penetrate new markets. First of all, there is the obvious point that the main effort at gaining entry to new city-pair markets has always been directed toward the larger routes in terms of passenger-miles. For instance, the majority of the trunklines sought part or all of the southern transcontinental route, probably the last major new route to be awarded in the foreseeable future. Though this has not been true in the past, there is now little to be gained in economies of scale from such route expansions.[55] This drive to enter large markets is another piece of evidence for the hypothesis that the fare structure has historically rendered the dense and long-haul markets significantly more profitable than the thin and short-haul ones. Certain other constants have been present as well. Frequently an airline will seek a new route to help iron out its seasonal traffic pattern. This is part of the explanation why the carriers operating east-west in the northern part of the United States have pushed so hard for Florida routes. Similarly, a carrier with heavy tourist and vacation traffic will seek entry into primarily business-travel markets to iron out its weekly peak-load pattern.[56] Still another type of award which the carriers regularly

[53] See Braniff Airways, Inc., Service to Fairmont and Fort Dodge, Docket No. 4052 et al., 20 CAB 720 (1955); Route No. 106 Renewal Case and Ozark Certificate Renewal Case, Docket Nos. 6050, 5988 et al., 21 CAB 86, pp. 96–103 (1955) — J. P. Adams' dissent. The precedent case on such route extensions is Panagra Terminal Investigation, Docket No. 779, 4 CAB 670, p. 673 (1944).

[54] There is one minor qualification to this argument. Airline spokesmen have often blamed the Board for granting so many requests for competitive route extensions in the mid-1950s. Naturally a carrier's management will consider all the route extensions it desires to be in line with the public interest, all competitive extensions sought by potential rivals to be hostile to the public welfare. Still, it may be that some or indeed many of the 1950s route awards were beyond the expectations of the airlines and that, if the Board's generosity had been foreseen, less generous gifts would have been sought.

[55] See Chapter 3.

[56] Note that gains from evening out its traffic pattern might make route expansion profitable for a carrier even if substantial retaliation of one kind or another resulted. This is another possible explanation for the lack of oligopolistic rationality in the search for route extensions.

seek is the extension of a stub-end route into a strong terminal. A route running from a large traffic-generating center toward a minor one tends to create problems of high load factors and inadequate capacity on segments near the strong terminal, but it also involves light loads near the weak end and poor load factors in general. Extending to a strong terminal tends to eliminate this problem and improve load factors and profitability, even if total passenger-miles sold do not increase.

One major change has come about in the past decade in the route seeking that tells something about the regulatory process. Until the early 1950s, when they received mail pay containing a subsidy based on their need for profits, the trunks often sought to take on routes which by themselves would be unprofitable. There were several cases in which both trunks and local-service carriers were applicants for the same essentially local routes.[57] Indeed, when the first round of certificate-renewal cases for the local-service carriers came in 1950, several trunks applied to take over the whole route systems of existing local-service carriers. Western Air Lines, the most active trunk in seeking to add local-service operations (and the most fearful of ultimate direct competition from the locals), applied for its subsidiary to operate the existing routes of Southwest and West Coast,[58] and both Eastern and Delta had applied to operate the routes of Piedmont Aviation.[59] The timing is interesting in the *Piedmont Renewal* case. Eastern's and Delta's applications had been made before the July 31, 1951, deadline for filing exhibits in the case. By this time it was apparent to the trunks that the days of subsidy payment according to need were almost over. Thus, after mid-1951 neither Eastern nor Delta filed direct exhibits supporting its application, and neither supported its application at the hearings or opposed Piedmont's recertification. In the same way, until they went off subsidy, the trunklines generally fought to hold on to

[57] Additional California–Nevada Service Case, Los Angeles–San Diego–Phoenix — Supplemental Opinion, Docket No. 2019 et al., 11 CAB 39 (1949); Reopened Additional California–Nevada Service Case, Docket No. 2019 et al., 15 CAB 11 (1952); Klamath Falls–Medford Service Case, Docket No. 4191 et al., 17 CAB 713 (1953).

[58] Southwest Renewal — United Suspension Case, Docket No. 3718 et al., 15 CAB 61, p. 63 (1952).

[59] Piedmont Certificate Renewal Case, Docket No. 4762 et al., 15 CAB 737, p. 753 (1952).

unprofitable cities or route segments, except where some serious operational inconvenience was involved.[60] Assuming the subsidy process actually awarded the rate of return it aimed at, a trunk taking over unprofitable local-service routes could expect a higher absolute profit level on the larger capital base that would be required. In the process, it might stunt the growth of local-service airlines operating in its territory, thereby reducing a threat of possible future competition.[61]

From 1951 on, as more and more trunklines went off subsidy, their behavior in seeking route extensions was confined to entry into currently and potentially profitable markets of dense traffic or long hauls. At the same time, they began an elaborate process of sloughing off money-losing cities and segments.[62] By one count,[63] trunk service has been replaced by local-service airlines in ninety-four cities. Seventeen points got such service transfers in the gigantic *Seven States Area* case alone, generally without objection from the deposed trunk carriers. These eliminations of unprofitable operations have come about in two ways. One is by direct application, especially in cases where the Board was already contemplating the expansion of local-service operations. Another has been to neglect service to unprofitable cities to the point where the cities themselves petition the Board to give them the more frequent and better-timed flights of a local-service carrier.[64] There are some exceptions to the rush of the trunks to

[60] For example, Frontier Certificate Renewal Case, Docket No. 4340 et al., 14 CAB 519, p. 522 (1951); North Central Route Investigation Case, Docket No. 4603 et al., 14 CAB 1027, p. 1052 (1951).

[61] This behavioral pattern is reminiscent of one found in such capital-intensive regulated utilities as electric-power producers. These firms are often reluctant to take on business that increases their gross revenue and variable costs but not their investment base, such as retailing publicly produced power. Conversely, they will take on highly capital-intensive projects of questionable intrinsic profitability and generally tend to bias their methods of production toward the capital-intensive.

[62] Two early cases that mark this turn toward disposing of unprofitable activities are Frontier Route No. 93 Renewal Case, Docket No. 4522 et al., 16 CAB 948, pp. 950, 971–974 (1953); and Spearfish Suspension Case, Docket No. 6200, 18 CAB 657 (1954).

[63] Leslie O. Barnes, "Airline Subsidies — Purpose, Cause and Control," *Journal of Air Law and Commerce*, XXVI (Autumn 1959), 319.

[64] "Adequacy of Domestic Airline Service: The Community's Role in a Changing Industry," *Yale Law Journal*, LXVIII (May 1959), 1199–1244. This article is based on a questionnaire sent to the chambers of commerce of seventy cities. It disclosed widespread resentment in smaller cities of service deterioration and reduction by the trunks (see note 65, pp. 1211–1212).

abandon relatively thin markets, notably Eastern Air Lines' declared intention of retaining the weak segments that it has undertaken a public obligation to serve. It has been noted, though, that
figures on station costs submitted by the carriers to the Board
show that Eastern is much more efficient at serving small stations
than the other large airlines are.

CONCLUSION

Consider what the conduct patterns of the airlines in purchasing new equipment tell us of the relative importance of
various features of the industry's market structure and the Civil
Aeronautics Board's policies. It would seem that air travel is not
a highly differentiable product. But the airlines do not all have
comparable access to all types of equipment because of the imperfect nature of the equipment market itself and because of
the way suppliers of funds pass upon applications for credit.
The larger airlines have bargaining power to secure favorable
delivery dates and design modifications from the aircraft producers. They have the past record of profitability needed to pry
loose loanable funds, even where a smaller carrier with no such
past success could probably earn equally large profits on the same
investment. Also important are the Board's policies that have
encouraged equipment competition. By allowing rapid depreciation, it has helped carriers once endowed with large fleets to
buy more and newer models. By permitting surcharges on new
equipment and by refusing to allow price differentials for equipment with inferior appeal to air travelers, it has forced airlines
either to join the race for new equipment or to suffer drastic
penalties in lost market shares.[65] Finally, the Board failed to see
the consequences for the industry's conduct of the ending of subsidy to the trunks early in the 1950s. When all carriers were
promised a subsidy providing a normal rate of return, and when
the smaller carriers faced less pressure from point-to-point competition, unequal profitability of the various route systems made
little difference. Changing *one* of these features (let alone changing *both*) created a great need for equalizing the relative profitability of different carriers.

[65] Note the distribution of profits between jet operators and others in 1959;
see L. L. Doty, "Profit Growth Lags Behind Revenue Rise," *Aviation Week,*
LXXI (Dec. 14, 1959), 39.

The Board did try in the mid-1950s to level the profitability of the carriers' different route systems by awarding new routes to the weaker lines. But it did not take the basic step of adjusting the fare structure so that, as nearly as possible, service in thin short-haul markets would be as profitable as service in dense long-haul markets. The carriers themselves have been eliminating services causing them out-of-pocket losses, but such losses are one thing and returns which cover variable but not fully allocated costs are another. The Board might have solved this problem through route awards, but it assumed that the expanding smaller carriers had the capital to secure the necessary equipment and finance promotional expenditures. Yet this is just the problem which unequal size and profitability makes most acute. It was not necessary that the Board's efforts at encouraging the development and purchase of new aircraft should conflict with its concern with sustaining the smaller members of the industry, but the particular policies chosen clearly have had this result.

Looking forward toward the evaluation of market performance, we can see some problems indicated in these patterns of investment conduct. Is the rate of aircraft development and commercial introduction for which the Civil Aeronautics Board strives an optimum as well as a maximum? Does the competitive pressure for aircraft innovation lead to inefficient investment patterns? Does the dominance of long-haul carriers in the equipment market lead to production of aircraft designs that are not efficient for the industry as a whole? Do the existing structural incentives for investment in new aircraft tend to breed undesirable increases in seller concentration? These involved questions of welfare economics will be considered in Part Four.

14 Product Policy and Carrier Competition

A long book, and a diverting one, could be written about product adjustments and strategies in the air-transport industry. Possibly one could date the airlines' pervasive concern with product competition from a fateful day in 1930 when S. A. Stimpson, an agent for one of United Air Lines' corporate ancestors, penned a memo proposing the use of airline stewardesses. "Imagine," he wrote, "the psychology of having young women as regular members of the air crew, the tremendous effect it would have on the traveling public." [1] Ever since that time, competitive strategies have occupied much of the attention of carrier managements and have borne great weight in determining the quality of the industry's market performance. Identifiable areas of product rivalry and strategy are extremely numerous. This chapter concentrates on a few phases of product rivalry that will permit a satisfactory interpretation of both the processes by which airlines set their strategies and the processes by which these strategies are adjusted and reconciled as they meet in the market place.

Some dimensions of the "product" are subject to open and continuous rivalry and adjustment. Others are collusively set within the industry. Still others are constrained by the Civil Aeronautics Board. Finally, some are simply passive and not subject to much management consideration. The first section that follows will discuss certain of those areas in which product competition is both open and significant. Following that, we shall turn to those areas which are subject to regulation or collusion.

OPEN PRODUCT RIVALRY

Some of the major strategies of product competition are too well-known to need elaborate documentation.[2] On their most

---

[1] *Los Angeles Examiner,* Aug. 26, 1960, part 2, p. 1.

[2] A considerable amount of information on product competition appears in Frederick W. Gill and Gilbert L. Bates, *Airline Competition* (Boston, 1949), and there have been no important changes in the sorts of patterns which these scholars found. Though I shall have to quarrel subsequently with their assessment of the welfare significance of product competition in the industry, this book remains an excellent source of information.

competitive routes or on routes where their greatest market-share aspirations lie, airlines invariably use the equipment with the greatest passenger appeal. The Civil Aeronautics Board has declared in an official report:

new equipment has traditionally been placed in operation first on the most competitive segments, and the introduction of more modern aircraft by one company on such a route has been followed by a scramble on the part of competitors to introduce with the greatest possible speed comparable or more advanced types.[3]

Sometimes extremely vigorous efforts are made to put modern equipment into markets where competitive pressures seem to require it. An excellent example is the action taken by National and Northeast Airlines to offer turbojet service in the New York–Miami market. During 1959, the airlines owning Boeing 707s reported maintenance and depreciation costs per revenue-mile ranging from $0.797 to $1.328. National, renting these planes from Pan American, and Northeast, renting them from TWA, paid charges in lieu of maintenance and depreciation that came to $1.718 and $3.00, respectively.[4]

Another well-known area of product rivalry lies in scheduling flights in particular city-pair markets. The "product" a carrier offers the public can be improved by increasing the frequency of flights (and thereby the capacity offered in the market), by improving the comfort of the aircraft used, and sometimes by raising the volume of tourist-class service. We shall consider first how carriers calculate their product strategies and then turn to evidence on how these strategies interact in particular markets.

The recent general passenger-fare investigation has provided much information on scheduling practices and their impact on carrier costs. The Board and its staff had suspected for some time that the carriers were offering more flights in major markets than demand conditions warranted, and such a charge was voiced in two Board decisions.[5] Actually, few representatives of the carriers answered the Board's charges squarely. In response to the charge that frequencies of flights undercut short-run profit maximization,

---

[3] CAB, *The Role of Competition in Commercial Air Transportation,* report . . . to the Subcommittee on Monopoly of the Select Committee on Small Business, U.S. Senate, 82nd Cong., 2nd sess. (Washington, 1952), p. 13.

[4] *Airlift,* XXIII (May 1960), 54.

[5] See above, Chapter 10.

the airlines answered by restating the procedure for scheduling to maximize profits individually, and then asserted that this was what they did. However, the discussion still provides many useful bits of information.

The carriers seem to make the calculations that set their patterns of schedules in two phases. Where competitive considerations are not a strong element, patterns for a carrier's available fleet of aircraft are adjusted marginally to maximize current profits, subject to certain restrictions for providing minimum service on thin routes. Where competition is a major factor, schedules are set wherever possible to protect or increase market shares, with a rather long period allowed for the anticipated profits. A high-level managerial group frequently reconsiders an airline's schedule pattern. Specific estimates of the extra cost and extra revenue stemming from possible changes are secured. The airlines figure, rather crudely, the variation of indirect costs (all costs not directly related to flying the planes) resulting when schedule patterns are changed. Rules of thumb are common in the industry; sometimes indirect costs are assumed to be unaffected by small changes in direct costs. Some carriers clearly do include specific estimates of indirect-cost changes in calculating the impact of schedule adjustments on total costs.[6] The way in which the carriers calculate revenue changes that result from schedule changes is harder to determine. Certainly there is no tendency to assume that total traffic between particular city-pairs is independent of the number of flights offered. If anything, the carriers seem to go to the opposite extreme and assume that the passenger-miles flown in markets where competition is at all significant will be proportional to the available seat-miles offered. In any case, at the hearings the carriers consistently denied that scheduling was keyed to adding schedules where load factors were high and removing them where load factors were low.[7] The following exchange between Bureau counsel and an American Airlines witness is typical:

Q. Does American add capacity on a priority basis to those segments with the highest load factors?

---

[6] Transcript of Hearings before Examiner, General Passenger Fare Investigation, Docket No. 8008, pp. 5596–5601, 7545–7548, 7623.

[7] *Ibid.*, pp. 7626–7627, 7711–7716.

A. Certainly other things being equal, we would try to do so. I cannot answer that in general terms because . . . each case has to be considered separately.[8]

Decisions on scheduling patterns are not closely tied to decisions either to purchase or abandon aircraft. Changes in the size of a carrier's fleet cannot be made within a few months, for there is a long delay between equipment orders and deliveries and it is usually costly to keep airplanes idle. And then there are the high market risks associated with selling them prematurely.[9] True, in the current conversion to turbine-powered aircraft, the phasing out of reciprocating-engine planes seems to have been done on a gradual basis, consistent with adjustment of schedules and profit maximization by use of marginal analysis. American Airlines testified to such a program,[10] and Eastern's pattern for removing the older Constellation aircraft from service suggests this sort of process. Nonetheless, in describing their scheduling processes, the carriers showed some tendency to think of the utilization of their fleets as a technological constraint. As long as a plane remains competitive or can be used profitably on noncompetitive routes, it is utilized up to some technological maximum portion of the time (established by maintenance requirements and the particular route pattern on which it is used). This is discernible in the figures for the utilization of various types of aircraft in the 1950s, as shown in Table 27. Imagine an airline using its fleet for some feasible maximum number of hours per day.[11] One would expect a newly introduced aircraft type at first to show a rising rate of utilization as it is phased into the company's fleet, followed by a slowly declining rate as other types of planes are added and this one downgraded to shorter hauls and thinner routes where less utilization is possible. Every aircraft listed in Table 27 shows this pattern except the two-engine Convairs (CV-240, CV-340) and Martins (M-404), which were initially designed for short-haul routes. There is only the slimmest evidence of variance between the rate of utilization and the general business cycle and thereby the rate of traffic

[8] *Ibid.*, p. 7586; also pp. 6266–6273 and 7587–7588.

[9] *Ibid.*, pp. 5515–5520, 7812–7816.

[10] *Ibid.*, pp. 7603–7604, 7613–7614.

[11] More precisely, achieving an optimum utilization that minimizes unit costs of flying and maintenance.

Table 27. Average daily utilization of selected piston aircraft, weighted average of reported experience of five trunk carriers, 1951–1959[a]

Aircraft[b]	1951	1952	1953	1954	1955	1956	1957	1958	1959
DC-6	8.9	9.0	9.4	8.7	9.1	9.2	9.0	8.3	7.8
DC-6B	8.8	9.3	9.5	8.9	9.3	9.3	8.5	8.2	7.5
DC-7	—	—	5.7	7.1	8.8	9.8	9.6	9.0	8.6
DC-7B	—	—	—	—	7.7	9.9	10.0	8.7	8.6
L-049	7.5	7.8	8.7	9.1	9.0	8.9	8.8	7.6	6.6
L-749	8.8	8.9	9.6	9.1	9.2	8.7	7.8	6.8	6.0
L-1049	9.5	8.6	8.9	9.7	9.7	9.9	9.9	8.5	7.9
L-1049C	—	—	5.9	9.9	11.2	11.8	11.2	8.7	8.2
L-1049G	—	—	—	—	7.2	8.9	10.0	9.7	8.3
CV-240	5.7	6.3	6.9	6.0	6.6	7.0	7.1	6.9	6.4
CV-340	—	2.0	4.6	5.7	5.6	6.0	5.9	5.0	4.8
M-404	5.3	6.0	7.1	7.0	7.4	7.8	7.8	6.9	6.5

[a] American, Capital, Eastern, TWA, United.
[b] For an explanation of these aircraft types, see text, p. 69.
Source: Information provided by Office of Carrier Accounts and Statistics, CAB.

growth. The effects of the 1958 recession, a relatively severe one for the industry, cannot be seen in any of the series, although all types listed in the table show a steady fall in utilization from 1957 on owing to the introduction of turbine-powered equipment.

As a historical fact, this pattern of utilization could mean either of two things. The airlines may overestimate the portion of their costs that are fixed and fly their planes up to some maximum time constraint, estimating that most of the extra gross revenue is also net. Or, more probably, over the past decade (and more) the airlines have had uses for all "competitive" aircraft for developing new markets and so have escaped the problem of lack of obvious profitable uses for new aircraft.[12] This latter view would reconcile the relatively minor role of fixed costs in air operations[13] with the airlines' apparent incremental-net-revenue approach to scheduling.

[12] An American Airlines executive testified in the general investigation that most of the carriers felt themselves to be short of equipment in the period 1953–1956. See Transcript of Hearings before Examiner, General Passenger Fare Investigation, pp. 7525–7526. This view was shared by a number of cities that complained about the quality of their air service, in answer to a questionnaire. See "Adequacy of Domestic Airline Service: The Community's Role in a Changing Industry," pp. 1211–1212, note 65.

[13] See above, Chapter 3.

This last suggestion turns our attention to another phase of the carriers' own scheduling consideration — market promotion in competitive markets. Planning under heavy competitive pressures involves decisions about short-term losses taken for the sake of long-term market shares, and consequently it does not fit the pattern of marginal adjustments just described. A witness for Braniff Airways made this clear in the *General Passenger Fare* case. The discussion had concerned Braniff's addition of nonstop service with DC-7Cs in the competitive New York/Washington–Dallas market when load factors were at a subnormal 40 to 50 percent. The witness explained repeatedly that "this is a developmental market." [14]

> First, you must have a schedule pattern, and develop it, so in the long run you can effectively penetrate the market and raise your overall load factor. That is our objective. That we will achieve in time. But this short-range period of time, I don't think the Board told us when they gave us the mandate to provide competitive service that we should do that only at the price of a load factor which exceeds our domestic system. [15]

The carrier testified that it had a seven-year planning horizon on market penetration in its new Texas–New York markets. [16] Various pieces of evidence suggest equally long time horizons for other carriers entering competitive markets or defending a share of such markets. Also, it is now common for airlines operating in competitive markets with a strong seasonal pattern to maintain most of their flights in the off-season to avoid "losing identification" with particular markets or types of service. [17] With competitive markets accounting for much of the business of most trunklines, the marginal process of schedule adjustment does not tell very much about the over-all scheduling decision as a tool of product competition. It is necessary to turn to actual patterns of interaction among the carriers, a subject studied intensively in 1949 by Gill and Bates. [18]

A common pattern is found in the reaction of a carrier whose

[14] Transcript of Hearings before Examiner, General Passenger Fare Investigation, pp. 7668–7671.

[15] *Ibid.*, p. 7683.

[16] *Ibid.*, pp. 7687–7690.

[17] *Ibid.*, pp. 8318–8319.

[18] *Airline Competition.* Cherington's *Airline Price Policy,* published a decade later, merely mentioned that the same patterns still existed (p. 11).

rival's equipment has decisively greater appeal to passengers. There is typically a gradual and experimental withdrawal from the market in question: the less-admired equipment is retired or transferred to segments lacking this competitive pressure. American Airlines faced this problem in several eastern markets with the introduction by its competitors of the Vickers Viscount aircraft. As Viscount flights were introduced by Capital Airlines and Trans-Canada Air Lines, American gradually reduced its schedules in several markets to token service.[19] A particularly interesting case was United Air Lines' scheduling in the east-west transcontinental markets when its competitors, American and TWA, had Boeing 707 turbojets but United's DC-8s were as yet undelivered. Table 28 summarizes schedules between New York and San Francisco or Los Angeles for American, TWA, and United between December 1958, just prior to introduction of turbojets, and October 1959, when American and TWA had more or less stabilized their jet schedules in these markets. It shows how United's schedules were gradually reduced and the nonstop flights demoted in order to increase service to intermediate points where jet competition had not appeared. Another phase of this process, not shown in the table, was the conversion of United's schedules from first-class to coach. For most of this period United offered no nonstop first-class flights at all. For ease of comprehension the table covers only flights making two stops or less between the terminals. Including flights making more stops and other markets in which the same planes could be used would make the process clearer still. The schedules of TWA's and American's piston-engine aircraft indeed show similar patterns.[20] This behavior in response to serious equipment inferiority is clear-cut but not too useful for unraveling the industry's conduct patterns. What of the carrier under competitive pressure from rivals with equipment not decisively superior to its own?

In markets where the number of carriers and the types of equipment in use remain stable, not much active rivalry in scheduling seems to appear. There may be tactical rearrangements of departure times or classes of service, but as long as the total

[19] Transcript of Hearings before Examiner, General Passenger Fare Investigation, pp. 7502–7504, 8366–8367.
[20] See Selig Altschul, "Breakthrough in Revenue and Earnings," *Airlift*, XXIII (Sept. 1959), 27.

Table 28. Adjustments of daily schedules in Los Angeles–New York and New York–San Francisco markets after introduction of jet aircraft[a]

Date	Carrier	Los Angeles to New York Jet	Piston	New York to Los Angeles Jet	Piston	San Francisco to New York Jet	Piston	New York to San Francisco Jet	Piston
Dec. 1958	AA[b]		4–0		5–0		—		—
			2–1		2–1		1–1		2–1
			1–2		1–2		1–2		1–2
	TWA		3–0		3–0		3–0		2–0
			2–1		1–1		—		1–1
			3–2		4–2		1–2		1–2
	UAL		3–0		3–0		3–0		3–0
			1–1		1–1		2–1		2–1
			—		—		1–2		1–2
Feb. 1959	AA	2–0	3–0	2–0	3–0		—		—
			1–1		2–1		1–1		2–1
			1–2		1–2		1–2		1–2
	TWA		3–0		3–0		2–0		2–0
			—		—		—		1–1
			5–2		3–2		1–2		—
	UAL		3–0		3–0		3–0		3–0
			—		1–1		1–1		1–1
			2–2		—		2–2		1–2
Apr. 1959	AA	3–0	1–0	3–0	1–0		—		—
			2–1		3–1	1–1	1–1	1–1	1–1
			1–2		1–2		1–2		1–2
	TWA		2–0		2–0	1–0	1–0	1–0	1–0
			—		—		—		1–1
			3–2		5–2		1–2		—
	UAL		3–0		3–0		3–0		3–0
			1–1		—		1–1		1–1
			—		2–2		2–2		1–2
June 1959	AA	4–0	1–0	4–0	1–0		—		—
			1–1		1–1	1–1	—	1–1	1–1
			1–2		1–2		—		1–2
	TWA	2–0	1–0	2–0	—	2–0	—	2–0	—
			1–1		3–1		—		—
			4–2		3–2		2–2		2–2
	UAL		2–0		2–0		3–0		2–0
			—		1–1		1–1		1–1
			2–2		3–2		1–2		3–2

Table 28 (continued)

Date	Carrier	Los Angeles to New York		New York to Los Angeles		San Francisco to New York		New York to San Francisco	
		Jet	Piston	Jet	Piston	Jet	Piston	Jet	Piston
Aug.	AA	4–0	1–0	4–0	1–0	—		—	
1959			1–1	—	2–1	1–1		1–1	—
			1–2	—	1–2	—			1–2
	TWA	3–0	—	3–0	—	3–0	—	3–0	—
			1–1		2–1		—		1–1
			3–2		4–2		2–2		2–2
	UAL		1–0		1–0		2–0		2–0
			—		—		1–1		—
			3–2		3–2		1–2		1–2

ᵃ In each hyphenated pair of numbers in the table, the first indicates the number of flights, the second the number of stops. Thus the entry "4–0" at the left of the top line indicates that in December 1958 American Airlines offered four nonstop piston-engine flights from Los Angeles to New York daily.

ᵇ Throughout the period covered by this table, American Airlines was not permitted by the terms of its certificate to offer nonstop service in the New York–San Francisco market.

Source: American Aviation Publishers, Inc., *Official Airline Guide, Quick Reference Edition* (various months).

capacity provided in the market remains unchanged these have no very serious consequences.[21] Once in a while, a flurry of scheduling rivalry will break out among the existing occupants of a market, probably reflecting one carrier's coveting a larger market share and its rivals' efforts to combat it. An excellent example stems from developments in 1959 in the New York–Miami market, a scene of periodic warfare between National Airlines and Eastern Air Lines. This market is highly seasonal, and National's monthly traffic for the year ending October 1958 was 150 percent of the average month's level in March, 84 percent in August. In earlier years the seasonality had been even more marked.[22] One would expect the volume of flights to fluctuate in somewhat the

[21] Writers on the industry have often raised the question of whether or not oligopolistic scheduling rivalry leads to a socially optimal distribution of departure times. This question concerning performance will be discussed in Chapter 17.

[22] Pan American World Airways, Inc., Exhibit No. PA-26, Pan American–National Agreements Investigation, Docket No. 9921.

same way, and National's indeed did. It scheduled twenty-one nonstop and one-stop flights in September 1958, thirty-two in March 1959, twenty-three in August 1959, and twenty-eight in March 1960. Eastern scheduled twenty-nine in August 1958, thirty-nine in March 1959, *forty-two* in August 1959, and thirty-four in March 1960.[23] Persons in the industry have ventured the guess that during the off-season months of 1959 Eastern sought to discipline National for several pricing innovations and for introducing jet service to the market by using leased equipment from Pan American.

This kind of outburst is not very common among established carriers in a market. The interesting developments usually come with the entry of a new carrier or one previously inactive. Invariably, the first reaction of the old occupants is to increase their own volume of service or, at worst, to leave it unchanged. There follows a period of time, often several years, of greatly increased capacity. Usually there is also an improvement in the average quality of aircraft used. Eventually, some carrier gives way and reduces its capacity, and some normal pattern of market shares emerges that is likely to be stable until one of the airlines in question installs a new type of aircraft. The new equilibrium is likely to involve greater capacity relative to the volume of traffic than existed before (that is, a lower load factor), especially if there had been only one carrier in the market.[24] Let us look at a few typical patterns. Table 29 shows the number of flights per day, nonstop and one- or two-stop, in the Chicago–Los Angeles market during each July over a six-year period. It is an example of an active struggle waged by a new rival (Continental) which successfully takes a large market share. The table does not reflect many other things that were occurring — increases in the amount of space available on coach flights, improvements in the quality

---

[23] See American Aviation Publications, *Official Airline Guide,* for the months in question.

[24] These generalizations are based on the Gill-Bates study and a great volume of material submitted by the carriers to the Board in connection with General Passenger Fare Investigation, New York–San Francisco Nonstop Case, and other proceedings. Also, a nonrandom sampling of major markets was taken and scheduling patterns were studied over the period 1955–1960. The following tables in the text give drastically summarized accounts of typical patterns found in this sample.

Table 29.   Number of flights per day offered in Chicago–Los Angeles market, July 1955–1960, by carrier

Year	Type of flight	American	TWA	United	Continental
1955	Nonstop	22	13	14	0
	Other[a]	4	7	1	0
1956	Nonstop	16	9	16	0
	Other	4	9	2	0
1957	Nonstop	18	13	16	0
	Other	4	10	6	6
1958	Nonstop	18	9	14	2
	Other	2	9	9	10
1959	Nonstop	10	9	8	6
	Other	3	10	8	7
1960	Nonstop	9	6	8	9
	Other	3	10	11	6

[a] One-stop and two-stop.
Source: *Official Airline Guide* (various issues).

of aircraft used, and the like.[25] The Chicago–New York market, shown in Table 30, is by contrast a case in which one invader, Capital Airlines, was unable to sustain its position after 1958 because it could not field competitive equipment. The other entrant, Northwest, also had this problem but hung on by offering relatively large quantities of coach service. Among the three historic occupants of the market, United kept its previous capacity as Capital's penetration reached its peak; American and TWA withdrew some of their less-effective equipment until they could place turbine-powered planes in the market. In 1960 the Big Three carriers had somewhat the same relative shares as in 1955, but they had collectively "moved over" to provide smaller market shares for Capital and Northwest. A final example is nonstop service in the Boston–Washington market, shown in Table 31.

[25] See *American Aviation Daily*, Jan. 6, 1960, p. 19. No inferences can be made from changes in the *total* number of flights from year to year because in this and the following cases the types of aircraft used were changing fast, generally toward larger capacities. The emphasis should be on the changes in shares of capacity; although the numbers could be deceptive on that score for the same reasons, care has been exercised here to avoid deceptive cases.

Table 30.   Number of flights per day offered in Chicago–New York market, July 1955–1960, by carrier

Year	Type of flight	American	Capital	Northwest	TWA	United
1955	Nonstop	39	0	0	22	30
	Other[a]	10	7	0	13	17
1956	Nonstop	35	0	8	12	24
	Other	7	15	2	26	24
1957	Nonstop	44	18	6	19	29
	Other	10	20	0	16	24
1958	Nonstop	35	28	8	16	30
	Other	12	15	0	10	16
1959	Nonstop	30	12	7	11	22
	Other	13	13	0	9	17
1960	Nonstop	33	11	7	12	21
	Other	12	21	0	6	17

[a] One-stop and two-stop.
Source: *Official Airline Guide* (various issues).

This is quite different from the two previous examples because, for all the carriers in question, Boston–Washington is imbedded in a larger set of markets involving points between Boston and Washington and points beyond Washington. Thus the large changes actually appearing in the table are to be expected. Northeast's strong rise in the market, reflecting the purchase of new equipment, drove out much of the competition, though American

Table 31.   Number of nonstop flights per day offered in Boston–Washington market, July 1955–1960, by carrier

Year	American	Eastern	National	Northeast
1955	4	1	0	0
1956	4	1	0	0
1957	7	2	1	1
1958	7	5	1	1
1959	2	4	2	12
1960	6	2	2	12

Source: *Official Airline Guide* (various issues).

returned when its own new turboprop equipment was fully delivered.

These examples are interesting for the size of the changes in market shares that appear and the time horizons that seem to be in operation, but they do not tell much in general about the impact of the competitive adjustment of airline schedules. In the abstract, what might a carrier do when faced with the entry of a determined rival into one of its major markets, assuming (for simplicity) that it cannot or will not sell its planes? At one extreme, it can maintain or increase its existing schedules in the face of the rival's entry until the resulting reduction in joint profits forces an adjustment by one or the other. At the other extreme, it could "make room" for its rival by a reshuffling of market shares, reducing the utilization of its aircraft or transferring them to other routes. Each behavioral pattern would have certain easily observed operational symptoms. The first pattern, "slugging it out" with the rival(s), would in an oligopoly situation tend to yield profits no higher than normal, and firms would tend to disappear occasionally by merger or bankruptcy. Airlines would serve all markets for which they are authorized. They would concentrate their best equipment in the markets with the greatest *potential* monopoly profits and accept relatively low load factors there. The second pattern, "peaceful coexistence," would imply relatively higher profits and greater stability in profit levels (except as influenced by general business conditions) and in the number of firms. There would be markets where carriers are authorized to offer service but do not do so. The markets with the greatest potential monopoly profits would show average or higher load factors.[26] It is highly tempting to try to decide which of these models best describes the reigning behavioral pattern by performing the obvious statistical tests. Unfortunately, nothing can be proved in that way. There is no satisfactory way of cal-

---

[26] Because of discontinuities of aircraft size and because all city-pair markets served receive at least one round-trip daily, it follows *ceteris paribus* that the larger a market in terms of total passengers, the higher will be the load factor. Eventually, of course, a market may become large enough to make indivisibilities insignificant. See Chapter 3, and also David W. Bluestone, "The Problem of Competition Among Domestic Trunk Airlines," *Journal of Air Law and Commerce*, XX (Autumn 1953), 384–387.

culating load factors by city-pair market.[27] Market nonparticipation can come about for many reasons, an important one being
long-haul restrictions whereby a carrier's certificate allows it to
serve a city-pair only on flights originating or terminating at
some distant point. We shall have to make do with a combination
of *a priori* and impressionistic empirical analysis.

First, though, it is worth digressing to establish the importance
of making a choice between these two models of scheduling and
market-participation behavior. An excellent report issued by
United Research implicitly considered these models and chose
peaceful coexistence on the basis of a number of instances in
which carriers do not offer service to city-pairs authorized in
their certificates of public convenience and necessity.[28] The report
concluded that it was not particularly desirable for the Board to
spend much of its time deciding whether, for example, four or
five carriers should be authorized to serve a particular large market. If, however, it can be shown that the slugging-it-out scheduling pattern is common, it would follow that the Board's concern
with keeping the "right" number of carriers in each market *is*
appropriate in view of its concern with keeping comparable levels
of service among a great many interrelated city-pair markets.

The position I shall argue runs as follows. Only evidence for
the last five years or so is relevant; before that, rapid growth of
the market and equipment shortages felt by the carriers cloud the
picture, and market nonparticipation resulted almost exclusively
from serious equipment inferiority. In recent years it has appeared that each pattern persists in part of the domestic trunk
industry. In the east-west transcontinental and western markets
served by the east-west Big Three (American, TWA, United),
peaceful coexistence tends to prevail.[29] In the eastern portion of

[27] With considerable work, one can get them for four weeks out of the year,
the periods in March and September when the airline traffic surveys have been
taken in the past. Many city-pair markets are highly seasonal, however, and
the survey periods cannot give information about average patterns in some of
the most interesting city-pair markets involving the winter-vacation cities.

[28] United Research, *Federal Regulation of the Domestic Air Transport Industry* (Cambridge, Mass., 1959), pp. 16–17, 29–30, and *passim*. The primary
purpose of the report in using this information was to argue that cases of
nonparticipation sometimes show the minimum number of carriers that can
efficiently serve a market to be less than the Board authorizes.

[29] An extreme recent exception is Chicago–Los Angeles, because of the presence
of Continental Air Lines.

the United States, especially the north-south markets served by Eastern Air Lines in competition with various smaller carriers, the pattern of slugging-it-out dominates. First of all, consider Table 32, showing the trends in the *over-all* load factors for the

Table 32. Load factors of domestic trunklines, calendar years 1955–1959 (percentages)[a]

Carrier	1955	1956	1957	1958	1959
American	68.0	68.4	64.9	66.0	70.4
Capital	59.0	60.2	58.9	57.9	58.4
Continental	53.5	54.3	53.9	51.2	54.1
Northwest	59.7	61.2	57.2	55.1	55.6
TWA	64.6	64.4	62.8	64.5	70.5
United	67.1	66.9	64.3	64.4	66.4
Western	59.1	61.9	60.0	54.4	60.2
Braniff	61.6	60.8	58.7	59.0	58.1
Delta	63.9	60.2	59.3	58.5	57.1
Eastern	61.0	60.6	59.5	52.8	50.7
National	64.1	65.9	59.7	56.1	55.3
Northeast	59.2	58.5	47.4	47.3	50.3

[a] A carrier's load factor is computed by dividing its volume of passenger-miles sold during a period by the volume of seat-miles produced.

Source: CAB, Office of Carrier Accounts and Statistics, *Monthly Report of Air Carrier Traffic Statistics* (various issues).

trunks from 1955 to 1959. The industry's load factor tends to fluctuate with the business cycle, and one would expect load factors to be high in 1955 and 1956, to sink through 1957 and 1958, and to rise again in 1959. The airlines have been grouped in the table according to the geographic division just suggested. The first group, the transcontinental and western carriers, shows the sort of load-factor pattern indicated by the general business cycle, with a significant recovery in 1959 and a fairly modest slippage from 1955–56 to 1957–58. The second group, the eastern north-south carriers, shows no improvement in load factors for 1959 and a more significant drop from 1955–56 to 1957–58. It is useful to note that the two carriers whose route structures make them hardest to classify, Capital and Northwest, are the two that show patterns of load-factor changes intermediate between the two groups.

Another test of my thesis about the difference between competitive scheduling patterns in the two segments of the trunk industry can be made by looking for cases in which carriers do not serve markets authorized by their certificates of convenience and necessity. There are many reasons why a carrier may not serve an authorized market. The certificate may contain a long-haul or other restriction which makes it unprofitable to compete with an unrestricted rival. A carrier may not have competitive equipment or may not have enough competitive equipment to stay in all of its markets. The volume of traffic in a market may be too small to allow profitable nonstop service. Finally, a carrier may not participate because of tacit agreement with its rivals. The first two of these four conditions are easy to observe; the third and fourth are not. When the cases of nonparticipation in the largest city-pair markets in terms of passenger-miles are classified, the Big Three transcontinental carriers are plainly responsible for most of those which can be explained only by tacit collusion or by a small total number of passengers.[30] In the eastern part of the United States, especially in the north-south markets, nonparticipation is nearly always due to other causes. There is a hint of confirmation for the hypothesis of greater competitiveness of the eastern carriers, but it is a faint one. First of all, American, TWA, and United operate in many transcontinental markets that are large in passenger-miles but quite small in daily passengers. Traffic sufficient to support very few daily nonstop flights certainly explains some nonparticipation, but not all. Second, the pattern of nonparticipation by the Big Three is not stable over time. For instance, during the months when the delivery of turbojet aircraft was freeing DC-7s and late-model Constellations from the prime transcontinental runs, some of these planes were transferred to provide new nonstop service between the weaker transcontinental city-pairs.

The eastern markets offer a good deal of evidence on the relative prevalence of the two scheduling patterns. A major factor is the operating habits of Eastern Air Lines — its long-standing bitter rivalry with National Airlines and its reluctance to sacrifice its market shares to the considerable number of new competitors

---

[30] For data assisting in these tabulations, see United Research, *Federal Regulation,* table B-12.

resulting from the Board's decisions in the *Southwest–Northeast, New York–Florida, Great Lakes–Southeast,* and *St. Louis–Southeast* cases. The decline of Eastern's load factor shown in Table 32 illustrates this fact. The Board complained in a 1957 case of Eastern's "overscheduling" on its Route 5 (New York–Washington–Atlanta–New Orleans–Texas), where in the last quarter of 1956 south-bound seat-miles increased by 22.4 percent while passenger-miles were falling by 3 percent. From the evidence before it, the Board declared that Eastern's low profits seemed to stem from "an attempt to make ineffective the new competition offered by Delta and Capital between the Northeast, Atlanta, New Orleans, and Texas by flooding the market with schedules." [31]

Developments in the New York–Miami market have been the most spectacular. Northeast Airlines, trying to enter the market, noted that in March 1956 Eastern offered 1968 south-bound seats, then stepped the number up to 2690 by March 1958.[32] National has called for the Board to cancel Northeast's unusual temporary certificate to serve the market, as a measure of relief. Both National and Northeast have made elaborate efforts to offset Eastern's potent scheduling practices, entering into expensive aircraft-leasing arrangements, trying price competition through the proliferation of service classes, and experimenting with a variety of other promotional plans. Other markets affected by Eastern's activities show the same sort of developments. For instance, according to complaints by Eastern, Delta Air Lines had been substituting entirely first-class aircraft for dual configuration equipment on the New York–Houston run. And Delta's policies have figured in the tendency for the surcharge on tickets for jet travel to disappear in certain markets.[33]

Which of these patterns is more important in the aggregate — vigorous rivalry or relatively passive market sharing? No very precise test can be devised, but it is worth recalling the patterns of aircraft utilization noted in Table 27. There the rate of utilization appeared to be related to a technological maximum. It did

[31] Suspended Passenger Fare Increase Case, Docket No. 8613, decided Sept. 25, 1957, CCH Av. Law Rep. §22,077.03.

[32] *Aviation Week,* LXIX (Dec. 8, 1958), 43.

[33] *American Aviation Daily,* April 26, 1960, p. 365; *Aviation Week,* LXXII (Jan. 4, 1960), 34.

not show the variation relative to fluctuations in demand that one would expect if output were being manipulated to yield monopoly profits. It is not possible to say just how much the utilization figures prove, but they are consistent with the statement that in the past decade, at least, active rivalry over market shares has been the prevailing behavioral pattern in the industry. One must emphasize the uncertainty and the danger of accepting this conclusion uncritically. I have argued that there is a structural explanation for the more competitive patterns in the eastern city-pair markets. But very few firms are involved, and it is also possible that nothing more than personal animosities among key executives of different airlines explain the situation. In 1960 there were some signs of a slackening of the bitter rivalries in some eastern markets. Following the United-Capital merger, the east-west transcontinental pattern of less active rivalry may spread to the eastern north-south markets as well.

Active rivalry among the carriers appears in many lesser forms as well. One of these is the inflation of service for a given class of travel at little or no increase in price. A major example is the inaugurating of varieties of coach service approaching first-class quality at only a slight surcharge over regular coach accommodations. Northwest Airlines introduced such a "Coronation" coach service with free meals and the like in its efforts to penetrate the Great Lakes–southeast markets, and Eastern Air Lines immediately followed with a similar plan.[34] Starting in 1955 there was an important round of such rivalry among the transcontinental Big Three. TWA, having planes with slightly less passenger appeal and speed than its two rivals, started using its best Constellation aircraft in combined tourist and first-class service rather than only in first-class. (It was pointed out that the coach passengers, riding in the front of the plane, actually got there first.) After a few months American and United countered by starting coach service in the DC-7, hitherto used only in first-class. All three inflated the quality of this coach service further with free meals and so on.[35] TWA later attempted to lead another round of

[34] *American Aviation Daily*, March 6, 1959, p. 48; March 10, 1959, p. 71. For another example, see *American Aviation*, XX (May 20, 1957), 76.

[35] William V. Henzey, "TWA Triggers Big Drive for Coach Market," *American Aviation*, XIX (Oct. 10, 1955), 77–78; Henzey, "Airlines' Future Hinges on Federal Policies," *American Aviation*, XIX (April 23, 1956), 27.

service inflation with its "Siesta Seat" plan for selling deluxe sleeper seats at regular first-class fares. American filed at the same time for a coach tariff on first-class aircraft flown in off-peak hours.[36] In the industry's earlier days, competition through offering lower seating densities was also important. When only the east-west Big Three were involved in extensive point-to-point competition, they generally offered much lower seating densities than did Eastern.[37]

Against the ample evidence that product rivalry does tend to inflate the quality of given service classes and create new ones, it is well for the sake of perspective to compare the situation in international air transport. Because of cartelized pricing practices, the international carriers enjoy a much greater profit margin on sales and have a greater incentive to indulge in product competition. Both the proliferation of service classes and the tendency to inflate given classes has gone far, despite efforts at containment by the cartel. The service inflation of the "Battle of the Sandwiches" a few years back gained widespread fame. The domestic airlines have seen no such debacle.

Of the many minor forms of product rivalry, a few examples will suffice. When it inaugurates a new route or a new plane, an airline often stages a lavish "press flight" on which assorted journalists and celebrities are generously treated.[38] There has been a "speed race" on transcontinental schedules between Los Angeles and New York. TWA shifted its intercontinental model of the Boeing 707 (the 707–331) to this route, flying it at a higher speed than that prevailing for the transcontinental jets and allowing it to advertise a fifteen- to twenty-minute time saving. The jets flown by United and American could match this speed, but only with substantially increased fuel costs.[39] TWA's move broke

[36] *Aviation Week,* LXIX (Dec. 1, 1958), 37–38; *Traffic World,* CII (Nov. 29, 1958), 120. The Board tried to keep strict control over seating densities in the early 1950s but has generally relaxed its grip since then.

[37] Gill and Bates, p. 151.

[38] For example, W. W. Parrish, "United's DC-7 Press Flight a Classic," *American Aviation,* XVIII (June 21, 1954), 38.

[39] For the Douglas DC-8 jet, a 10 percent increase of speed from Mach 0.8 to Mach 0.88 raises fuel consumption by 50 percent. Over a 2500 mile flight stage, a 3 percent increase in the sustained cruising speed cuts the block time of the flight by 2.4 percent and raises total operating costs by 7 percent. See C. H. Glenn, "Will We Be Able to Operate a Turbojet Transport Economically?" *Canadian Aeronautical Journal,* V (Jan. 1959), 24–25.

a previous tacit collusion among the three carriers not to use "fastest" jet speed as an advertising or a competitive tool. This case is an interesting one: TWA's rivals ultimately decided not to take the expensive action required to meet this move and pinned their hopes on longer-run modifications of their own aircraft that would give comparable speeds at no cost disadvantage.[40]

SUPPRESSED OR INACTIVE PRODUCT RIVALRY

Some areas of product competition in air transportation are controlled by collusion within the industry. Most of these are not particularly important. As far as available evidence indicates, most collusive controls on product competition are maintained through the Air Transport Association and its branch agencies. Fairly elaborate controls seem to exist over the advertising practices of the carriers. For instance, there has been an agreement not to purchase display advertising in telephone directories.[41] There was a dispute among the parties to the advertising restrictions (handled through the enforcement office of the Air Traffic Conference of the ATA) over terminology in advertising copy for turboprop airplanes. Western and Braniff were fined by the enforcement office for advertising the turboprop Lockheed Electra as an "electra/JET" and using illustrations in which the propellers did not show. In this case, however, the carriers threatened to withdraw from the ATC resolution covering advertising unless they were granted exemptions, and their requests were heeded.[42] At the same time, Trans-Texas Airways, a local-service carrier, was fined for honoring American Express credit cards. The basis for this was that American Express is a travel agent; ATC agreements collusively set the commission to be allowed travel agents and include no allowance for the extra percentage on credit-card

---

[40] David H. Hoffman, "TWA May Spark 707, DC-8 Jet Race," *Aviation Week,* LXXII (Feb. 29, 1960), 45. For an earlier case, see *Aviation Week,* LIX (Dec. 28, 1953), 22.

[41] Edward J. Taaffe, *The Air Passenger Hinterland of Chicago* (Chicago, 1952), p. 72.

[42] *American Aviation Daily,* May 3, 1960, p. 11; *Airlift,* XXIV (July 1960), 16. Probably the reason for this enforcement difficulty was that the accused carriers faced competition from airlines that were not members of the Air Transport Association or the agreement — international and intrastate carriers.

sales. Again, it is of interest that no enforcement action seems to have been taken against other airlines that have agreed to honor credit cards other than American Express'.

The airlines have undoubtedly tried to reach agreement on many other features of product competition through the Air Traffic Conference. One of these is the "no-show" problem — passengers holding tickets or reservations for flights who fail to use them. Obviously, liberal provisions in these matters could be used as a competitive tool. Passengers would prefer to make reservations by phone and pay for tickets only at the time of departure, rather than having to pay when reservations are made and getting no refund in case they fail to make the flight. The airlines have settled on various solutions at various times, but there has been trouble in getting general agreement to any "stiff" policy on no-show penalties.[43]

Other agreements on product competition are heard of from time to time. For instance, at one time six trunklines agreed to restrict the amount of hard liquor per customer dispensed on flights and not to advertise the fact that liquor was served.[44] The trade press has mentioned other agreements. It is not possible for an outsider to guess how numerous and important such agreements are, but their over-all significance for the industry is probably slight. What determines the particular features of product competition on which the airlines try to reach collective agreement? Firms maximizing joint profits would presumably try to control those features of product competition resulting in the greatest increase to joint net revenue. This is not perceptibly the case in the airlines. The product dimensions that get the most collective concern seem, if anything, to be those with the greatest "public relations" significance — those in which open intercarrier rivalry could result in embarrassment to the industry. Open competition in the amount of liquor served air travelers could hardly work much of an increase in costs per passenger-mile. It could,

---

[43] There are many examples of the airlines trying but failing to agree on essentially collusive measures to control product rivalry. See, for example, *Aviation Week*, LVII (July 7, 1952), 18. Since the paragraph above was written, the CAB has taken the initiative to get the carriers to agree on stiff no-show penalties.

[44] *American Aviation*, XX (July 16, 1956), 83.

however, bring troublesome pressure from those nostalgic for the Eighteenth Amendment.[45]

A few areas of potential product competition in air transport are subject neither to open rivalry nor to collusive restriction. They are simply product dimensions that receive little use. The most important of these ignored areas — call it either a feature of product variety or of price competition — is the absence of lower classes of inexpensive service in "obsolete" aircraft. In an industry of atomistic competition, older aircraft would tend to move into new lower classes of air service, assuming that their operating costs in fully depreciated condition compared favorably with the average total unit costs of their replacements. The equilibrium differential between fares would reflect this difference. There has been little tendency for this to happen in air transport. First, the Civil Aeronautics Board has shown itself hostile to such developments on several occasions.[46] Second, some of the obsolescent aircraft of the postwar period, notably the DC-3s, appear to have had fully depreciated costs that compared unfavorably with the full costs of their replacements; the same may be true of some of the current turbojets and the last round of piston-engined craft. Third, through much of the postwar era, the price of used transport aircraft on the world market has made it more profitable to dispose of secondhand planes abroad than to use them at home on lower classes of traffic. These three factors explain much of the absence of any trend toward use of older planes for "coach" services, but probably not all of it. In their public statements the carriers have always been highly fearful that increasing the supply of less luxurious service would undermine their going price- and product-discrimination practices and cut into joint profits. The great reluctance of certain carriers to start coach service a decade ago should convince anyone that a combination of managerial attitudes and recognized interdependence works hard against such competitive strategies involving older aircraft.

There are several other potential dimensions of product com-

---

[45] Still another way of emphasizing the relative unimportance of collective controls on product competition in the domestic industry is to compare it to the International Air Transport Association. For an interesting description of the IATA agreements, see Robert Burkhardt, "How IATA Curbs the Maverick Lines," *American Aviation*, XXII (Sept. 8, 1958), 57–59.

[46] See Chapter 10.

petition that have never played a major role in the industry. Variation of seating densities has played a less active role than one might expect. In a sense, the reluctance of many trunks to install or expand coach service reflects an unwillingness to vary seating densities.[47] Eastern Air Lines, no stranger to the ways of product competition, has continued to maintain higher seating densities than its rivals in some of its aircraft. Other "product" dimensions of which the carriers have not chosen to vary competitively turn on ground passenger-handling practices. Cancellation penalties, the ability to make reservations by phone, no-reservation services, and in-flight ticketing have been subject to relatively little competitive adjustment.[48] But changes of these features have become somewhat more common lately. Continental Air Lines introduced in-flight ticketing, forcing its competitors to follow, and Allegheny Airlines' introduction of no-reservaton flights has stirred Eastern to adopt this device.[49]

CONCLUSION

Of the areas of active product rivalry, aircraft scheduling and schedule density stand out as critically important. Rivalry in furnishing the best equipment is simply the application to particular city-pair markets of the rivalry in the equipment market described in the last chapter. Rivalry in scheduling, apart from injecting new types of aircraft, amounts to raising the volume of seats and/or departures in a market above the level that would maximize the participants' joint profits. Carriers usually seem to compete in scheduling without heed to the threat of retaliation. Certainly there are cases of severe retaliation,[50] and carriers have publicly declared that their failure to innovate stemmed from a

[47] *Aviation Week,* LVII (Oct. 27, 1952), 17.

[48] One proof of this assertion is that airlines engaged in otherwise vigorous point-to-point competition can have "quality differences" in these dimensions of their "product" that persist for long periods. See F. Lee Moore, "CAB-Airline Clash Brews on Coach Fares," *Aviation Week,* LVI (Jan. 21, 1952), 63.

[49] L. L. Doty, "Allegheny Drafts Commuter Service Plan," *Aviation Week,* LXX (April 6, 1959), 38; Doty, "Continental Streamlines Jet Ticket Plan," *Aviation Week,* LXX (June 15, 1959), 38–39; *Aviation Week,* LXXIII (Sept. 19, 1960), 47; LXXIII (Oct. 10, 1960), 52.

[50] For example, Capital Airlines was forced out of the Atlanta–New York market by Eastern after Capital had attempted to introduce better equipment. See *Aviation Week,* LVII (Aug. 25, 1952), 56.

fear of crushing retaliation.[51] But, on balance, scheduling strategies in the past have developed as if the carriers sought only to maximize their separate profits. This need not imply that the carriers take a naive view of their rivals' proclivity to react. The true explanation for the apparent motivation is probably a long-run profit horizon, which has made at least some carriers willing to undertake fairly prolonged struggles in the hope of ultimately strengthening market position and profitability.

Competition in equipment quality and flight scheduling is far more active than price competition and other possible forms of product competition. And these particular forms of rivalry are becoming, if anything, more pronounced. Consider the effect of the trends in aircraft technology. Travelers on a journey that takes twenty-four hours will probably be fairly indifferent about departure times. Travelers on one-hour journeys will probably have sharply preferred departure times, keyed to the bounds of the business day and hours of eating and sleeping. In the short run, the larger airline has a potential competitive advantage in a market for relatively brief journeys through its ability to offer schedules at all popular departure times and sufficient capacity for the peaks.[52] As the development of faster planes moves more markets toward this latter model, patterns of scheduling rivalry and the advantages they lend the larger carriers become more and more important. The carriers' own reported calculations of optimal schedules with jet aircraft are demonstrating this.[53]

This trend is more than a little ominous for workable competition in the industry, especially when taken in conjunction with the conclusions of the previous and following chapters. Scheduling as a key dimension of product competition throws the advantage

[51] For instance, Northwest's failure to introduce trans-Pacific coach service was allegedly because of the fear of retaliation by Pan American. See *Aviation Week,* LVII (Nov. 10, 1952), 90.

[52] This sentence in the text is loose for the sake of brevity. A small carrier might be able to pile up enough equipment in a single city-pair market to discourage a larger competitor who operates in many other markets. The point is, however, that the certified carriers, large and small, have legal responsibilities in a number of markets. The large carrier's fleet will tend to permit heavy scheduling in any one of its markets relative to what a small firm can muster, and by the "principle of pooled reserves" the latter will necessarily have either less flexibility in switching equipment from one market to another or higher costs due to relatively more spare equipment.

[53] John H. Lewis & Co., *Aviation Bulletin,* January 15, 1960, p. 2.

toward the well-equipped carrier, and patterns of equipment purchase tend to make it relatively easier for a large carrier to be well equipped. Furthermore, price competition and the rise of fare differentials are not likely to save the day, because of the Civil Aeronautics Board's traditional hostility to price cutting, the relatively slight differentiability of the industry's product, and finally the general reluctance of carrier managements to tamper with fares. In sum, the race tends to go to the swift, and the swift tend to be the large.

15 Airline Pricing and Price Policy

A discussion of the airlines' price policy rightly belongs at the end of a survey of conduct patterns. From the founding of the Civil Aeronautics Board until 1961, there were no more than a dozen changes in terms or classes of service that could be called general adjustments of the fare level. More instances of fare changes in particular city-pair markets are recorded, but even here the total number of variations is quite small, and few of these have much bearing on intercarrier rivalry. A look at the organization chart of the typical airline confirms this: there is no continuous and general attention centered on the problem of appropriate pricing. The analysis of costs that does take place for the guidance of marketing policies mainly seems to be costing of incremental changes in the pattern of flights. Part of the explanation for this is historical: until the trunklines went off subsidy in the 1950s there was little reason to worry about the problems of price policy. Another part lies in the industry's market structure: in almost no industry in which so few sellers produce such a homogeneous product is there much open price competition.

Nevertheless, a close analysis of pricing decisions in the industry is necessary. The way in which they are made and the constraints on price adjustment weigh heavily in determining whether or not competition would be workable in the industry without control by the Civil Aeronautics Board. I shall review very briefly the development of the airlines' fare level and structure after the 1930s, and then try to characterize the conduct patterns that seem to be at work.[1]

DEVELOPMENT OF AIRLINE PRICING

Early air fares were to all appearances set on a casual market-by-market basis. The existence of substantial subsidy caused fares to be unrelated to costs, and the only clear-cut determinant seems

[1] Fortunately, a very competent study of airline pricing exists in Cherington's *Airline Price Policy*. This chapter owes far more to this publication than specific references can indicate.

to have been the level of first-class rail fares, since air fares were set to permit what the airline managements felt was successful competition with rail service. During World War II the carriers moved away from these unsystematic fare schedules to a uniform fare rate per mile in setting total fares. By the end of the war the Big Four and some other carriers were using a base fare of 4.6 cents per mile. The first-class rail fare, allowing for Pullman accommodations, was about 4.0 cents per mile; and between many cities the two services worked out to yield roughly the same fare because the rail distance was greater than the shortest distance between two points.[2] The adversities of the postwar period brought a series of three increases of 10 percent each in the general fare level — two of these in 1947 and one in 1948. The third was in large part offset, however, by the introduction of round-trip and family-plan discounts and the removal of surcharges previously in force on postwar four-engine airplanes. The years 1945–1949 also saw a change in the relation of the average fares per passenger-mile charged by different carriers. Before World War II the only carriers in substantial competition with one another, the transcontinental Big Three, had had the highest fare levels in the industry. The smaller and entirely noncompetitive carriers had generally quoted significantly lower fares. This situation was reversed in the postwar period, largely as a result of the Board's urging of the larger carriers to lower their rates in 1943 and 1945. Throughout the changes of the late 1940s, the Big Four (plus Delta Air Lines) held to a fare structure calculated on a uniform per-mile base; the smaller carriers generally moved to the fares charged by the larger carriers on competitive segments, but they set higher fares per mile on noncompetitive runs. The development of this pattern had little to do with carrier point-to-point competition, which increased a good deal due to Board route awards. A tabulation by Gill and Bates of the impact of new competition on city-pair fares during 1947 and 1948 showed that the only significant changes in prices were due to the added carrier's use of a shorter mileage base from which to calculate its fare, the result of its being certified for fewer intermediate points.[3]

During the 1950s the pattern did not change significantly. As

---

[2] F. W. Gill and G. L. Bates, *Airline Competition,* pp. 421–433.
[3] *Ibid.,* p. 465 and chap. 15.

Chapter 7 indicated, there have been four relatively significant changes in general fare levels. In April 1952 a flat charge of one dollar per ticket was added, contributing an element of taper to the fare structure for the first time. February 1958 brought another one dollar increase per ticket plus a general 4 percent rise, the total increase coming to 6.6 percent. In October of the same year a number of discounts were eliminated, the effect being about equal to a 3.5 percent increase. Finally, in mid-1960, following the decision in the *General Passenger Fare* case, the Board permitted a third dollar-per-ticket rise plus 2.5 percent. There have also been changes in the fares for coach service and some changes for particular carriers and particular city-pairs. The majority of the trunks, and all the larger ones, use something approaching a flat rate per mile in addition to the flat charges per ticket authorized by the Board. Some of the smaller carriers have increased their noncompetitive fares from time to time, however, and thus have higher mileage rates on noncompetitive routes.[4] The many competitive route authorizations of the mid-1950s produced no more price competition between particular city-pairs than that seen in the 1940s, except in the indirect form of causing more low-priced coach service to be offered. Generally the new carrier has announced the same fare as the existing carriers, though there have been a few cases where the new carrier's certified route covered a shorter fare-basing mileage between the cities in question.[5] Members of the Board's staff complain that there has been relatively little tendency to reduce the fare-basing mileage on important long hauls by subtracting the mileage required to serve certified intermediate points when most flights in fact are nonstop.

MAKING AND REACTING TO FARE CHANGES

Against this sketch of the historical background of fare adjustments, we may consider the pattern of conduct whereby the airlines initiate fare changes and react to changes initiated by their rivals. What provokes price changes in the first place? Is there

---

[4] Cherington, pp. 143–146, and Bureau Counsel Exhibit No. BC-707, General Passenger Fare Investigation, Docket No. 8008.
[5] *Monopoly Problems in Regulated Industries — Airlines,* U.S. House of Representatives, II, 791.

price leadership or collusion in price determination? Is the leader always followed in fare adjustments? Do carrier managements' attitudes tend toward a common cause or are differences in outlook significant? Before taking up these questions it will be useful to clear away one point: the question of the freedom of fares in individual city-pair markets to vary independently. Air fares constitute a network of prices for a large number of geographically distinct services which may substitute for, complement, or stand independent of one another. If the industry were atomistic, and firms did not possess significant indivisibilities, then the relations among city-pair fares would be like those existing in any set of competitive markets. However, such is not the case in the airlines or in most transportation industries. Individual carriers operate in many different city-pair markets and are usually large in any one of them. Joint and through fares are subject to complicated sets of rules and agreements. Restrictions against discrimination as defined by law, such as the traditional long-haul/short-haul restraint, place complicated constraints on the price relations between different markets. Policies adopted by individual carriers for uniform treatment of various markets introduce still other constraints. In short, changing a fare in one major city-pair market typically touches off ripples of adjustment in many other markets. In an industry where many price changes are the result of negotiations among the carriers or between the carriers and the Board, it becomes very hard to get agreement on local fare adjustments that have these side effects throughout the industry. Carriers time and again have demonstrated a willingness to sacrifice profits rather than meddle with certain features of the fare structure. Most price changes in the industry come in the form of simple across-the-board adjustments or as disguised changes (such as when a carrier provides a new class of service). As a result, pricing moves tend to be large-scale adjustments affecting much of the industry. Small-scale moves aimed at affecting net revenues from particular city-pair markets are usually adjustments in product quality, and they hold price constant.

What, then, turns an airline to thoughts of price variation? The closest thing to a price-calculation principle detectable in the industry is the relation of fare increases to a significant reduction of the quarterly profit rates of the larger carriers. Through the

1950s, downturns in the profit rates for most airlines were followed shortly by petitions to the Board for fare increases.[6] There are no cases of general downward adjustments in airline fares other than those initiated by the Board. However, the outright or disguised reductions that an airline will itself occasionally make in a particular city-pair market, or set of markets, seem generally to have no relation to current or past price-cost relations. Since the pleas for general increases normally assume a fare increase for the industry as a whole whether or not the carriers are of one mind on the *amount* of the increase, this price-calculation principle must be described as one of joint profit maximization subject to severe constraints. These constraints lie in the carrier's knowledge that the Board is unlikely to allow fares that will yield profits much above a normal level, in the realization of the crudeness of the airlines' knowledge of the industry's cost and demand conditions and the resulting impossibility of accurately hitting the profit-maximizing fare, and finally in the fact that to change the general level of air fares is so complex a job that the industry is likely to avoid undertaking it more often than twice a year.

If the price-calculating process an airline uses to derive a desired change for the general fare level is one of joint maximization for the industry, the process for a single city-pair market more closely resembles independent profit maximization, even though competitive price reductions will surely be matched by rivals without interference by the Board. The best evidence in support of this assertion is this: while the carriers rarely move to lower the general level of fares, they often attempt cuts but seldom propose increases in particular markets. The obvious goal of a fare cut in a particular city-pair market is usually to raise the initiating carrier's market share. Even where rivals are expected to meet the cut, a carrier may hope for "identification" in travelers' minds as a low-price or service-minded airline. Price increases (or service deteriorations) in particular competitive markets are too rare to permit generalization from known cases as to what sort of price-calculation principle may be at work. However, there are many examples of price adjustments in non-competitive markets by both trunklines and local-service carriers. The subsidized local-service carriers are supposed to calculate

⁶ See Cherington, chap. 3.

their prices to maximize profits, with the Board's blessing.[7] When a general fare adjustment occurs in the industry, the local-service airlines frequently follow it only on routes which compete with trunklines, adjusting the prices in their monopolistic markets either not at all or in individualistic fashion.[8] They clearly show a consciousness that the optimal price can be too high as well as too low. They often seem inclined to view long-run demand elasticity as significantly greater than the short run; or they alternately feel that travelers once accustomed to going by air are unlikely to return to surface means, so that today's modest price decrease may shift tomorrow's demand curve. It was pointed out in Part Two that carriers receiving subsidy according to their need for profits have a systematic incentive to price below the monopoly level. Members of the Board's staff and others feel that this is indeed done by the local airlines.[9] Profit maximization is more easily seen in pricing by the trunk carriers on noncompetitive segments. The less profitable smaller carriers especially have often appeared to pursue maximization through custom pricing on their monopoly routes. An example would be Northeast Airlines' traditionally higher fares on its thin noncompetitive routes north of Boston. In the same vein, a carrier with uniquely superior equipment may set temporarily high fares even in competitive markets. National Airlines, the first domestic carrier to provide turbojet service, charged regular first-class fares for coach seats and a surcharge for regular first-class seats.[10]

The pricing conduct of any industry also depends on how firms react to each other's pricing moves. In the regulated airline industry the matter gets more complicated still, for it is the Board that has final say over price adjustments; so the carriers make their moves knowing that the Board will act to avert certain

[7] See *Independent Offices Appropriations for 1960,* hearings, U.S. House of Representatives, Committee on Appropriations, Subcommittee on Independent Offices, 86th Cong., 1st sess. (Washington, 1959), part 2, p. 11.

[8] *Monopoly Problems in Regulated Industries — Airlines,* II, 983; *Airlift,* XXIV (July 1960), 15.

[9] See United Research, *Federal Regulation of the Domestic Air Transport Industry,* p. 66, note 42. Wisconsin Central, for example, once applied for a substantial reduction in its basic fare per mile; see *Aviation Week,* L (April 18, 1949), 53.

[10] R. H. Cook, "Fare Case Unaffected by Jet Surcharge," *Aviation Week,* LXX (Feb. 2, 1959), 43.

results. Furthermore, there are ways in which the carriers, jointly or separately, can persuade the Board to move in a particular way.

The most obvious pattern of interseller price coordination to look for is overt collusion. It is often suggested that regulation aids and abets this type of collusion, since the agency finds it easier to deal with the regulated firms as a group. In air transport, the requirements for an integrated general fare pattern made up of particular city-pair fares enforces coordination somewhere along the line because of the great number of joint and through fares. There are many channels within the industry through which such coordination could take place — the continuing contact through proceedings before the Board and the extensive operations of the Air Transport Association and its standing committees. There is, however, very little evidence of this sort of collusion, and the pattern of the last few years has been to move away from direct collusion in the setting of the general fare level. In the industry's difficult years during the late 1940s, general fare increases were often worked out in industry-wide meetings at the behest of the Board. From these a common suggestion for a price increase was developed, despite difficulty in getting agreement among the carriers. Similarly, in the 1950s there were some industry-wide meetings to discuss fare increases and the industry sometimes presented a united front before the Board in its fare proposals. The Air Transport Association seemed to be trying to fill the vacuum left as the Board turned away from the open encouragement of collusive pricing. Its officers on occasion presented the case for fare increases to the Board. Since 1957 a rather different pattern seems to have prevailed. When industry profit levels are slipping and the Board seems receptive to a move to raise prices, some or all carriers simply file for whatever price increases they deem appropriate. There is no conspicuous effort to present a consensus before the Board, and the proposed changes often differ considerably from carrier to carrier. The Board then suspends these and announces what increase (if any) it will accept, and the carriers promptly file for the indicated amount. This pattern gives the decision on the size of fare changes to the Board, though the carriers still normally set in motion the machinery for a fare change. Probably no great emphasis should be placed on these changes in the form of intercarrier conduct and negotiation on fare adjustments: at all times there has been a good deal of contact among airlines, generally informal and fairly continuous, on matters relating to fares. On the basis of long acquaintance with the industry, Cherington says:

there appears to be a great deal of informal discussion within the industry — but not formal consultation — on the question of fares and rates. Much of this discussion is in the nature of a more or less casual passing of the time of day on the general question of "how's business?" . . . at the first sign of a possible cost-price squeeze, the carriers begin to give consideration to the possibility of fare increases of one kind or another. Because of the multiplicity of ways in which prices can be altered so as to yield increased revenues and because of the wide range of interests in various types and classes of traffic that the carriers have, it is not surprising that informal sparring and testing of various ideas are an important part of the decision-making process on price increases.[11]

The important thing to know for evaluating the industry's conduct pattern, then, is not so much the various patterns of contact and collusion that have appeared in the past, but the sources of trouble the carriers face in coming to agreement on price increases.

The limited information available on the haggling over fare changes within the industry suggests that getting agreement among the trunks is seldom easy, because of differences in the situations of different carriers, in management conjectures on the elasticity of demand, and possibly in managerial time horizons. Consider the circumstances surrounding the September 1948 fare increase of 10 percent. In July of that year the Board, while granting petitions for increased air-mail pay, urged the carriers to raise fares to match their rising costs. At about this time United Air Lines filed for a 10 percent increase, but several smaller carriers with many short-haul routes, such as Chicago and Southern Airlines, were doubtful that another fare boost would raise net revenues.[12] At an industry-wide meeting on August 19, the carriers were widely split, seven wanting no increase, one a small increase, six a general 10 percent increase, and one remaining undecided.[13] When the 10 percent increase went into effect, it was immediately obscured by a wave of discounts promoted by

[11] Cherington, pp. 133, 413.
[12] *Aviation Week*, XLIX (July 19, 1948), 47.
[13] American Airlines, Inc., Exhibit No. AA-1205, General Passenger Fare Investigation, p. 1.

various carriers. American Airlines used the opportunity to make
two major innovations in pricing that threw the industry into
some confusion — a family-fare plan allowing substantial discounts to families traveling on the off-peak days of the week and
removal of the surcharges on DC-6 aircraft. American and other
carriers also instituted a 5 percent discount on round-trip tickets.
These discounts produced a motley pattern of reactions. Eastern
Air Lines postponed the 10 percent increase. TWA announced a
group discount and Mid-Continent a substantial commuter-fare
benefit for regular travelers.[14] Gradually the other carriers fell
in line to follow American's family-fare plan. TWA, which still
had a surcharge on its best Constellation aircraft, adopted the
family plan and offered a large discount on round trips completed within thirty days on certain routes. Eastern finally went
ahead with the 10 percent increase, as did its competitor Delta.[15]
Finally, in November 1948, TWA gave up the Constellation surcharge under competitive pressure, at the same time removing
some of the special fares it had filed with the Board. This left
only Eastern and its competitors with surcharges on Constellations and DC-6s. However, this group of carriers was embroiled
over National's having filed a family-fare plan when it had still
not taken the general 10 percent increase; the Board stepped
in to block this move.[16] At the same time, the major airlines were
pondering strategy for dealing with still another pricing threat
— Capital's innovation of domestic night-coach fares. The total
picture is one of considerable disunity and uncoordinated experimentation.

In the 1950s, with no guaranteed subsidy, the carriers still had
trouble in reaching agreement on proposed fare changes. The increase of one dollar per ticket in 1952 apparently had the support
of all carriers, but they wanted it for diverse reasons. Some
favored higher prices in any form. Others wanted the higher fare
per mile on short hauls which would stem from a flat increase per
ticket.[17] While the airlines were talking of a fare increase to offset
the impact on profits of the 1953–54 recession, Eastern undercut

[14] *Aviation Week,* XLIX (Sept. 27, 1948), 41; LII (May 15, 1950), 62.
[15] *Aviation Week,* XLIX (Oct. 4, 1948), 36; XLIX (Oct. 18, 1948), 46;
XLIX (Nov. 1, 1948), 34.
[16] *Aviation Week,* XLIX (Nov. 15, 1948), 48; XLIX (Nov. 22, 1948), 37.
[17] *Monopoly Problems in Regulated Industries — Airlines,* II, 956.

them by vigorously publicizing a low-fare coach service,[18] and the other carriers disagreed over various proposals to raise both coach and first-class fares, reduce the spread between them, and eliminate various discounts.[19] True, as of the late 1950s, there seems to be less dissension. The carriers have tended to follow common tactics in their representations to the Board, especially in the general passenger-fare investigation and in the requests for special relief that punctuated its five-year course. The Air Transport Association, which took a very active part in the case, probably was partly responsible for this. Much more ominous is another practice with which the Board charged the carriers during the fare investigation: letting cost levels drift upward as insurance against the statistical appearance of a trend toward rising profits. Probably tacit collusion underlies this practice, which involves such things as overscheduling, setting abnormally large reserves for the overhaul of new jet engines, charging to current expense generous amounts of shake-down expenses on new equipment,[20] and keeping employment levels higher than past trends would suggest.[21] The only carrier that seems not to have been engaging in this activity is Continental Air Lines, which has had the same problems as the other carriers of integrating new equipment and penetrating new routes without the parallel increases in cost levels. This apparent trend toward collusive cost variation is particularly dangerous for effective regulation, since the Board lacks accounting control and must let its price regulation rest on the shifting sands of the carriers' reported cost levels and trends.

The coordination of pricing decisions in the industry is not at the point where the method could be described as a primarily collusive one. Still, difficulties are straightened out somehow when managerial pricing preferences differ, and so it is desirable to check for appearances of another common pattern of price co-

---

[18] *Aviation Week,* LX (May 10, 1954), 102.

[19] *American Aviation,* XVIII (June 21, 1954), 28–30.

[20] John H. Lewis & Co., *Aviation Bulletin,* Jan. 15, 1960, p. 4.

[21] Total domestic airline personnel per million revenue passenger-miles fell from 6.36 in 1952 to 4.62 in 1956, then rose to 4.74 in 1958. The withering away of the trend in productivity growth appears for almost all classes of employees, suggesting that a significant part of the deteriorating cost trend is really the same thing as the falling load factors discussed in Chapter 14. For statistics, see Federal Aviation Agency, *Statistical Handbook of Aviation,* 1960 (Washington, 1960), pp. 76, 79.

ordination among sellers — price leadership. There is no possibility here of the existence of competitive "barometric" price leadership. A necessary condition for such a pattern would be a general price level in the industry that rises in times of heavy demand and falls when excess capacity dominates. Instead, the general fare level in the airline industry moves, if at all, inversely with the business cycle. But does any form of dominant-firm leadership exist? Do certain firms carry the fight for higher fares before the Board? Do other firms habitually press for cuts on major routes? To get a general impression of these matters, let us consider leadership in general fare changes and in changes in major city-pair markets. Table 33 collects the instances of price leadership that have turned up in the course of this study, but certain qualifications should be kept in mind. First of all, the instances are collected from miscellaneous sources and there is no assurance that important cases of changes or attempted changes in major markets have not been missed. Second, given the regulated setting of airline pricing, it becomes likely that the appearance of leadership in price increases is spurious. There is always the alternative explanation that an arbitrarily chosen carrier is the first to announce an increase agreed to by all on a covert basis. Third, important attempts to initiate price changes have probably been suppressed within the industry. The reason for suspecting this is that all fare changes are filed with the Air Transport Association two weeks before they are filed with the Board. Probably many important changes have been withdrawn before the official filing because of pressure within the industry; it has not been possible to get information on this matter. As a final caution in using the table, the dates are approximate and in some cases may represent the date of some action by the Board rather than the actual date of filing.

Even with these qualifications, a few clear conclusions emerge from Table 33. Almost all of the efforts at increasing or maintaining the industry's fare level come from two of the transcontinental Big Three — American and United. United particularly has been a continuous and vocal advocate of higher fares for the industry. Of the other two of the Big Four, TWA has been if anything a price cutter because of its chronic problems of having

Table 33. Price leadership in major fare changes or attempted changes, 1948–1960

Carrier	Approximate date	Increase or decrease	Nature of proposed change
National	Apr. 1948	Decrease	Summer discount New York–Miami
United	July 1948	Increase	General 10% increase
American	Sept. 1948	Decrease	Generous family-plan fare
Eastern	Jan. 1949	Increase	Sought general dollar-per-ticket increase
Northwest	March 1949	Decrease	System-wide excursion fares
American	Feb. 1952	Increase	Eliminated New York–Washington coach fares
American[a]	March 1952	Increase	General dollar-per-ticket increase
American	March 1952	Increase	Elimination of round-trip discount
United	May 1952	Increase	Sought family-plan fare increase
TWA	Aug. 1955	Decrease	Cut in transcontinental coach fare
Northwest	Nov. 1955	Decrease	Coach fare cut on routes
United	March 1957	Increase	General 6% increase
Continental	Jan. 1958	Increase	Sought general 15% increase
Continental	Oct. 1958	Decrease(?)	Sought to create new low-fare service but raise fares for other classes
American	Jan. 1959	Increase	Application for jet surcharge
National	Feb. 1959	Decrease	Cut in night-coach fares
Delta	Jan. 1960	Decrease	Elimination of jet surcharge on night flights
United	May 1960	Increase	Increase of transcontinental coach fare

[a] Cherington, *Airline Price Policy*, credits Eastern Air Lines as the dominant force behind this increase.

Source: *Aviation Week*, XLIX (July 5, 1948), 41; XLIX (July 19, 1948), 47; XLIX (Sept. 27, 1948), 41; L (March 14, 1949), 43; LVI (March 10, 1952), 64–65; LVI (March 24, 1952), 18, LVI (May 5, 1952), 71; LXIII (Sept. 5, 1955), 98; LVIII (Jan. 20, 1958), 47; LXXII (Jan. 4, 1960), 34; *American Aviation*, XIX (Aug. 29, 1955), 65; XIX (Nov. 21, 1955), 105; *American Aviation Daily*, Jan. 20, 1959, p. 111; March 19, 1959, p. 140; May 9, 1960, p. 48; *Traffic World*, CII (Oct. 4, 1958), 108; Cherington, pp. 101, 420; Suspended Passenger Fare Increase Case, Docket No. 8613, decided Sept. 25, 1957, CCH Av. Law Rep. § 22,077.04.

inferior airplanes. Its competitive efforts have taken the form of providing large quantities of coach service, however, rather than pushing aggressively for lower fares, an obvious strategy because of the regularity with which price reductions are met. In the industry's earlier years, Eastern maintained a very high fare level and has often shown a pricing outlook akin to United's and American's. Its price-leadership efforts, however, have been dampened by its extensive competition with the industry's most persistent price cutter — National Airlines.[22]

The cycle of pricing decisions involved when the certified carriers started offering coach service a decade ago neatly confirms these impressions about the process of accommodation to pricing decisions. The innovators of coach service on domestic routes, following Capital Airlines' lead, were all smaller carriers with the exception of TWA. Continental filed for a Denver–Kansas City coach service, Mid-Continent for Kansas City–Minneapolis, and TWA established a Los Angeles–Kansas City coach within months of the original filing by Capital.[23] Capital expanded its coach service into the New York–Minneapolis and Chicago–Washington markets, the former decision inducing its competitor Northwest to introduce coach service on its transcontinental route. National, seeking a way of penetrating the price-conscious Florida market for vacation travel, had filed a New York–Miami coach plan in late 1948. Eastern met this and introduced the same service in the Chicago–Miami market, forcing its competitor Delta to follow suit.

TWA first tried to establish a transcontinental coach service by connecting its Kansas City–Los Angeles service with its New York–Chicago coach. This was rejected by the Board, and so the first transcontinental coach service was actually offered in late 1949 by American (followed immediately by TWA). The interesting thing about American's move into the coach field was that it set a fare of 4.5 cents a mile, one-half cent higher than previous coach fares but not restricted to off peak times of day. Several months later, American switched its equipment for coach flights from DC-4s to DC-6s, the most modern available equipment. TWA followed with its best Lockheed Constellations. At this same time there was some downward price adjustment in

[22] These conclusions about price leadership among the Big Four match rather closely those of Paul W. Cherington, whose broad experience in the industry gives considerable weight to his opinions. He stresses American's key role in all price changes, both increases and decreases, because of managerial philosophy and the strategic nature of its routes. "United and Eastern are not usually found among the dissenters to fare increases" (pp. 412–413).

[23] *Aviation Week,* L (Jan. 17, 1949), 61; L (March 21, 1949), 68–70; LI (Aug. 22, 1949), 39. See Cherington, chap. 6.

the Chicago–New Orleans market.[24] When United Air Lines, the most adamant holdout against coach service, finally entered the picture in 1950, it was in order to meet competition in its transcontinental markets and in the Los Angeles–San Francisco market. United tried to lead an increase in coach fares to 5 cents a mile, but the Board rejected it. United and the others of the Big Three settled on 4.5 cents a mile, and Northwest, competing principally with United, raised its coach fares to this level.[25]

Thus, we may reasonably conclude that price cutting has been the task of small or disadvantaged carriers trying for a larger share of major markets, and it has been more apparent among the eastern regional carriers than the western ones. This thesis is in accord with that reached on product competition in the last chapter. Competitive innovations in the air-transport industry have always come from the areas where rivals are of unequal size and where the routes of numerous carriers intermingle.

FARE STRUCTURE AND MARKET CONDUCT

It appeared in Chapter 3 that short-haul and thin routes are more expensive to operate per seat-mile than are long-haul and heavily traveled routes. And one needs only a slight knowledge of the industry to discover that the latter have always been the more profitable. Up to the early 1950s and the end of direct subsidy for the trunks, the airlines often acknowledged a duty to serve unprofitable markets at a loss. In the 1950s and 1960s there has been much abandonment of unprofitable activities and equalization of the relative profitability of service on various kinds of routes. The first general adjustment of the fare structure came with the increase of one dollar per ticket in 1952,[26] and the process has still not run its full course. At any given time there are some airline routes that will yield profits at a wide range of prices. Others are marginal in the sense of yielding normal profits only for a carefully selected small range of rates. Still others are unprofitable at the monopoly optimum fare. The relative profit-

[24] *Aviation Week,* LI (Oct. 31, 1949), 13–14; LI (Nov. 7, 1949), 12, 14; LI (Nov. 14, 1949), 59; LII (April 3, 1950), 52; LII (April 17, 1950), 54.

[25] *Aviation Week,* LII (Jan. 2, 1950), 36; LII (Jan. 23, 1950), 50; LIII (Aug. 7, 1950), 47.

[26] F. Lee Moore, "Switch to Coach May Alter Plane Design," *Aviation Week,* LVII (Nov. 10, 1952), 88.

ability of various routes has strongly influenced the economic position of the various airlines. Therefore, the industry's conduct in adjusting the fare *structure* demands attention separately from matters of fare *level*. The Board's influence on the industry's fare structure has been casual and random; the structure is within the purview of the industry.

There are two ways in which the airlines' fare structure might get adjusted toward the competitive standard of normal rates of return in all city-pair markets. One would be through the direct working of competitive forces; the other would be through fiat action by the oligopolistic firms. The presence or absence of the fiat move is the main concern here, but the occasional working of competitive adjustments is worth note. Competitive price adjustments in city-pair markets have been common only with carriers that are outside the select club of holders of certificates of public convenience and necessity. At the height of the influence of the irregular carriers around 1950, their rivalry was responsible for a fair amount of price competition in certain large city-pair markets. For example, in the third quarter of 1949, the irregulars charged $79 for a one-way Chicago–Los Angeles ticket when the standard fare was $114. In the last quarter of that year, the certified carriers introduced a coach service at $85. Later, in 1951, the irregular fare dropped to $75. In the Chicago–Miami market in the late 1940s, the standard fare had been $72 and later $79 while the nonskeds were charging $42. In the fourth quarter of 1949, a standard coach service was introduced at $47, and the irregular fare fell to $39. Later, in 1950, the standard coach fare rose to $55, and in 1951 the irregular coach fare rose to $44 and $48. More examples could be supplied from other markets in which the nonskeds operated.[27] Similarly, in the New York–San Juan market the certified coach operator Trans-Caribbean got Board approval for a $45 thrift-class fare. Shortly after, Eastern and Pan American sought Board permission to raise their first- and second-class fares. Within a month after this was

[27] *Future of Irregular Airlines in United States Air Transportation Industry,* hearings before a subcommittee, U.S. Senate, Select Committee on Small Business, 83rd Cong., 1st sess. (Washington, 1953), pp. 273–274. This information comes from a document prepared by Robert R. Nathan Associates. See also F. Lee Moore, "CAB-Airline Clash Brews on Coach Fares," *Aviation Week,* LVI (Jan. 21, 1952), 63, which details the tendency of these cuts to erode fares to intermediate points.

granted, they cut their thrift-class fares from $52.50 to $45 to meet Trans-Caribbean's rate.[28]

The best continuing example of competitive pricing is in the Los Angeles–San Francisco market, by far the largest city-pair lying within one state and thus effectively out of the reach of the Board. In August 1949, Western Air Lines introduced coach service on this route in high-density DC-4s at a $9.95 one-way fare to meet the competition of intrastate carriers; Western's first-class fare at the time was $20. When United Air Lines finally abandoned its holdout position against coach service seven months later, its first coach flights were in this market. These moves thinned the ranks of the intrastate carriers, and with the cost increases of the early months of the Korean War the strongest intrastate carrier, California Central, led an increase of coach fares to $11.70. The coach business, and with it California Central, flourished during the war. However, to meet the inroads of coach service offered by its certified rivals, in early 1952 California Central procured postwar aircraft, Martin 2-0-2s, and started a more luxurious service. This change along with generally rising cost levels cut into its profits, and California Central raised its fare to $13.50. Possibly hoping to eliminate the intrastate carrier, United and Western did not follow this increase, even though they had just taken a dollar-per-ticket general increase on all of their other routes. Finally, under pressure from the Board, Western and then United and TWA followed California Central's increase. But by this time more intrastate rivalry had emerged, and California Central complained to the California Public Utilities Commission about competition from Pacific Southwest Airlines, still charging the old $11.70 fare. California Central tried to meet this by charging $11.70 for DC-3 service while keeping the higher price for trips in its Martin aircraft, but the carrier lost money in both 1952 and 1953. It soon disappeared, and Pacific Southwest took over its role as the dominant intrastate carrier.[29] More recently, Pacific Southwest has played a passive role in pricing in the market, and competition has turned

[28] *Aviation Week,* LXX (June 8, 1959), 45.

[29] *Aviation Week,* LI (Aug. 22, 1949), 39; LII (March 20, 1950), 14; LVI (Feb. 11, 1952), 44–46; LVII (July 28, 1952), 52–53; LVII (Dec. 22, 1952), 67; LVIII (April 27, 1953), 95; LIX (Sept. 7, 1953), 84; LIX (Nov. 23, 1953), 20.

on the same service features as those in interstate markets. By 1960, the Los Angeles–San Francisco coach fare for the interstate carriers had moved up to $15.05 one-way; Pacific Southwest's fare remained at $11.81 and its market share was estimated at 25 to 30 percent. Before the Board's decision in *General Passenger Fare Investigation,* Pacific Southwest had applied to the California Public Utilities Commission for an increase to $12.71. Presumably this was done in part because the airline's new Lockheed Electras were reasonably competitive with other aircraft serving the market. When the Board granted an increase to the interstate carriers to $16.45, Pacific Southwest amended its application to the commission and took an increase to $13.50.[30]

Very few examples of this kind of periodic price adjustment turn up in the domestic air industry when nonsked or intrastate competition is absent. When adjustments of the fare structure do appear, they usually take the form of juggling the classes of service offered rather than changing fares directly, and they generally stem from the efforts of a disadvantaged carrier to protect or advance its market share, as described above. One example would be Continental Air Lines' 1958 proposal to increase its Chicago–Los Angeles fares for first-class and regular tourist-class service while creating a lower class of service priced to compete with bus and auto travel. This move, rejected by the Board, came at a time when Continental was new to the Chicago–Los Angeles market and was trying to create a place for itself. Other examples have been National's various moves in the New York–Miami market (daylight coach service, lower night-coach fares, low off-season fares), Northwest's introduction in 1955 of lower fares on DC-4 coaches, and Delta's recent removal of the surcharge for jet coach flights at night. The price adjustments in the bitterly competitive Miami–New York market are interesting because they tend to spread to other markets, especially Chicago–Miami.[31] The reason for this, however, is merely Eastern's policy of treating the two markets similarly. There are no very general structural reasons why competitive price adjustments in one market should spread to others. However, the complex

---

[30] California, Public Utilities Commission, Decision No. 61120, Application No. 42253, November 23, 1960.
[31] *American Aviation Daily,* April 7, 1959.

technical interrelation among fares in different city-pair markets means that some spreading will often take place.[32]

Competitive pricing adjustments have been rare, but general moves by the carriers to adjust the fare structure have been rarer still. A glance at the history of such efforts will lead to some conclusions about the great constraints that bind them. The first industry-wide move for a change in the fare structure came in 1948 and 1949 when Eastern Air Lines proposed a price increase in the form of a flat "terminal charge" of one dollar per ticket. This was designed to align the industry's fare and cost structures. By 1948 most carriers believed that their average fixed costs of handling a passenger independent of the distance he traveled were at least one dollar. Cherington has shown that American Airlines was considering a similar proposal.[33] All of the Big Four plus National Airlines supported the increase, but a number of short-haul carriers, mainly Capital, Northeast, and Northwest, opposed it. They feared that the large percentage increase in the price of short-haul tickets would "dry up traffic," presumably meaning that the price would be pushed beyond the monopoly optimum. Civil Aeronautics Board Chairman J. J. O'Connell was persuaded to approach the holdouts, but to no avail. The suggestion for a terminal charge came up again at the beginning of 1952, as the carriers' profits dropped off slightly from inflated Korean War levels. Again some small carriers were fearful of the effect on their revenues, but their objections were overcome in discussions within the industry, and the carriers collectively sought an addition of one dollar to the price of each ticket along with elimination of the round-trip discount. But this change was a fortuitous compromise rather than a fare-structure reform demanded by all; some carriers wanted a higher fare level in any form, while others specifically favored an adjustment of the fare structure.[34] The Board granted the increase of a dollar per ticket, though it turned down the removal of the round-trip discount. Since 1952 there have been two more fare increases that were partly in the form

[32] CAB, *Materials Relative to Competition in the Regulated Civil Aviation Industry, 1956,* transmitted . . . to the Select Committee on Small Business, 84th Cong., 2nd sess. (Washington, 1956), p. 9.

[33] Cherington, pp. 392, 420–424.

[34] *Monopoly Problems in Regulated Industries — Airlines,* II, 956.

of an increase of a dollar per ticket. These came in 1958 and 1960, and in both situations the Board announced what fare increase it would accept and the carriers promptly made the appropriate filing. Thus, the responsibility for these two increases lay primarily in the Board and its staff, which had become seriously concerned about the fact that profits of the Big Four carriers, which had relatively long passenger hauls, were chronically higher than those of the other trunks. In 1958 most of the trial filings by the carriers themselves included an extra dollar per ticket, but even then much more of the responsibility for the result rested with the Board.

Though the carriers seemed to be aware of the problem of the fare structure because of its impact on their relative profitability, they were unable or unwilling to do anything about it collectively. The fact of awareness is easy to document. The foremost argument used against admission of the large irregular carriers to certified status in the late 1940s and early 1950s was that the substantial profits on dense long-haul routes were needed to subsidize other services. This was repeated in all of the later hearings on the issue, even by carriers with mainly short-haul route systems, and precise figures on the relative unprofitability of short-haul and thin routes were periodically proffered.[35] But this evidence was never used to support a serious effort at overhauling the fare structure, and all indications are that the carriers never thought of using it in this way. For instance, it is apparent that the Board could have pursued its objective of equalizing the intrinsic profitability of the route systems of the different carriers in two different ways — by granting entry to lucrative routes to airlines with weak structures or by adjusting the fare pattern to boost the financial strength of the weaker systems. During the 1950s the Board and the smaller carriers both pursued the latter course, and neither seemed to see the two policies as alternatives. Consider this exchange with an Eastern Air Lines witness in the *General Passenger Fare* case:

Q. Would your personal preference be to even up this matter of rate of return to the airlines to juggle fares according to routes or to juggle routes?

[35] *Revision of the Civil Aeronautics Act,* hearings on S. 2647, U.S. Senate, Committee on Interstate and Foreign Commerce, 83rd Cong., 2nd sess. (Washington, D.C., 1954), pp. 935–940.

A. I am sorry, but I haven't even thought of that, and I just don't have any personal preference.[36]

Whether or not one gives much emphasis to the "blind spot" this quotation suggests, it is clear that almost no structural adjustment is likely to enjoy unanimous support from the carriers. The fears of a high demand elasticity felt by the smaller carriers have already been mentioned. There are many other examples. For instance, United Air Lines resisted elimination of the common fare from the east coast to major west-coast cities, even though this meant free transportation between Los Angeles and San Francisco for many passengers at the beginning or end of their transcontinental journeys. United apparently felt that the advantage it gained in competing for traffic between Los Angeles and points east was worth this cost.[37]

With this extreme difficulty in getting carrier unanimity on changes in fare structure, the Board and its staff have never pressed the matter. Fare structure was supposed to have been an issue in the first *General Passenger Fare* case, but that investigation was dropped. It was explicitly excluded from the second investigation, completed in 1960. The Board is theoretically committed to a separate general investigation of the fare structure, but there has been no evidence that it will go ahead. The staff feels that the only feasible changes of the fare structure are those which all carriers will agree to: for the carriers' procedural rights allow dissenters to force a full hearing on the reasonableness of the fare for every class of service in every city-pair market, and the issues in any fare-structure investigation are almost sure to become unmanageable at the start. Even if it were not so pessimistic over the legal tangles ahead, the Board's staff has by and large accepted the view that the carriers' earnings opportunities should be equalized through route extensions, not through adjustments of the fare structure. The staff's complaints about the structure tend to run in terms of technicalities — such points as the highly circuitous mileages that still serve as bases for some important fares. Finally, the one other possible source of pressure for reforming the fare structure, the Air Transport Association, has

[36] Transcript of Hearings before Examiner, General Passenger Fare Investigation, p. 8579.

[37] Cherington, pp. 353–354.

remained passive, even though it serves as the industry's agent in filing tariff changes with the Board.[38] Only on rare occasions have the carriers individually asked for any significant reforms.[39]

CONCLUSION

The material discussed above shows both the nature of price adjustment in the airline industry and the relation of price policy to other features of market conduct. Price policy is a subordinate element of the carriers' conduct for many reasons. There are the reasons that would pertain to any oligopolistic industry selling a relatively undifferentiable product. There is also the fact that until the early 1950s the presence of a subsidy designed to fill the gap between commercial·revenues and costs removed most of the pressure on carrier managements to consider alternative pricing strategies. There are the complexities of making price adjustments when "price" is really a network of thousands of interrelated prices. The Civil Aeronautics Board's historic near-indifference to any definite standard for pricing was an additional reason (or at least an excuse) for carrier indifference in the same area. Finally, the differences in size and profit opportunities of the trunk airlines and the conflicts in their market objectives have often spelled difficulty for reaching agreement on general price adjustments; yet the certainty that a city-pair market price cut would be met and the frequent uncertainty that a rise would be followed have discouraged fare adjustments in particular markets.

The process of adjusting the general fare level has been an offspring of the industry's regulated status. Even though the Board was notably slow about establishing a normal rate of return for the industry, the pattern has been firmly set by which the industry seeks price increases on the basis of fairly short-run decreases in the rate of return. The leadership in pressing for these increases falls to American, Eastern, and, especially, United. Because of their size in the industry and their strategic route systems, any one of the three, given enough determination, can play a dominant

---

[38] *Monopoly Problems in Regulated Industries — Airlines*, III, 1745.

[39] One instance was TWA's request in early 1958 for action by the Board to eliminate differences in the base fare per passenger-mile on different routes (apart from the 1952 one-dollar terminal charge). See L. L. Doty, "Airlines Prod Board for Higher Fares," *Aviation Week*, LXVIII (Jan. 27, 1958), 38–39.

role in setting fares. No one of the three, however, takes a regular role of leadership, and open disagreements on the structure of discounts in the industry and other basic policies outside the fare field are common.

The pattern of price adjustments in particular city-pair markets and sometimes for particular classes of service is quite different from the pattern for the general fare level. These structural changes go in the direction that competitive theory would indicate, as general fare changes do not. Price reductions in particular city-pair markets almost always come from disadvantaged carriers — airlines whose market positions fall short of their objectives and usually airlines suffering from inferior equipment, lack of public familiarity, or some other drawback often associated with small size. Once again, one can note the conspicuous differences between the amount of pricing innovation in the eastern United States markets, where the size distribution of firms contributes to active competitive behavior, and most of the east-west transcontinental markets, where recognized interdependence and the absence of competitive tactics is the rule.

It is a matter of great interest that several industry observers have predicted that the scurry to integrate and sell jet travel would produce enough competitive price reductions (or the equivalent in low-fare service classes) to pull down the general fare level.[40] Nothing like this has happened before. Even when product rivalry has created excess capacity in particular city-pair markets, fare reductions have been uncommon. If they should emerge now in reaction to the jet age, it would be the first time that the highly rivalrous pattern of product competition in the industry had overcome the complex and somewhat collusive pattern of interseller price coordination.

[40] "Cherington Foresees Airline Fare Cuts," *Aviation Week*, LXX (April 20, 1959), 40.

16 Conduct and Its Determinants

The general evidence on industrial organization in the American economy does not lend much hope to any attempt to summarize the relation of an industry's conduct to its structure. A given pattern of market structure seems to go hand in hand with a broad range of patterns of market conduct, even though many of these behavioral patterns often yield approximately the same level of social performance. However, some features of conduct may still be completely explainable in terms of structural features. And it is desirable to sort out the influence of the Civil Aeronautics Board from that of the industry's purely economic structure. The first of the two sections that follow attempts a brief summary of the association between the market-conduct patterns discussed above and the elements of the industry's economic and regulatory environment. The second section deals with the view, promoted by the certified carriers and accepted by the Board, that without regulatory restraints on competitive conduct the industry would fall into a maelstrom of cutthroat competition.

CONDUCT, STRUCTURE, AND REGULATION

At the start, we must distinguish two levels of the Board's influence. The first level is simply the direct impact of the Board's decisions or policies on an industry whose structure is partly determined by its own past decisions. The second level of the Board's influence lies in this deflection of the industry's market structure way from what purely economic forces would probably produce if left to work alone. The net impact of the Board on the industry's market structure is a good deal easier to understand now that market conduct has been described. The most important difference resulting is the decrease of the total number of carriers in the industry. This does not mean too few carriers in the typical city-pair market — at least not at the present time — for the Board usually admits as many carriers as seem able to achieve a marketing operation of minimum efficient scale.[1] But without the Board's limits on entry, many large city-pair markets would undoubtedly resemble the Los Angeles–San Francisco market. They would tend to have one or more "specialist" carriers offering a compact turnabout service in aircraft best suited to such a market; these specialists seem to avoid most of the disadvantages of small conventional trunks. They would also have one or more carriers providing through service, and the specialist carriers would set a fare slightly lower than the through carriers would.[2] Another major result of the public certification and regulation to which the airlines are subject is the historic problem of unequal size and profitability of the carriers. This uneven distribution was a result of the historical pattern of mail-route certification and subsidy and has never been fully eliminated by the Board. Until recently this has meant significant differences in unit costs among the trunks, and it still means differences in intrinsic profitability, in access to capital and to aircraft, and in managerial aspirations and strategies.

Now, what of the determinants of market conduct? The dominant role played by equipment competition is made possible by economic elements of market structure, but regulatory policies strongly support them. The controlling elements of market structure are the paucity of sellers in the individual city-pair market and the trait of product demand whereby travelers flock to the most "modern" aircraft. The Civil Aeronautics Board intervenes, through the complex of policies discussed in Chapter 13, to reinforce the prominence of equipment competition by shutting off most other outlets for market rivalry. Also important

[1] My conclusion has been that a minimum efficient scale of operations exists for a city-pair market with regard solely to the average cost of producing seat-miles, but that it is impossible to measure under any general assumptions and, in any case, that it is much less significant than the minimum scale imposed by considerations of selling the service to passengers.

[2] The reader may wonder why through carriers could prosper under conditions of unrestricted entry, let alone command a differential in fares. A moment's reflection on the history of rail transport or on the segment of the trucking industry specializing in moving household goods shows that, when a substantial amount of business moves between far-flung points that would not support specialist firms, a strong market opportunity arises for an integrated firm. Such a firm is also likely to gain slight advantages in sales promotion from its widespread operations. The more traffic in a particular market originates or terminates beyond the terminals, the greater is the relative opportunity for the "through" operation.

is a historical feature of the industry: its top leadership in the past has been drawn from operating pilots who found a special fascination in new aircraft.

The pattern of product competition chosen in the individual city-pair market is subject to many degrees of freedom: neither market structure nor regulatory pattern explains just which features of the product should be objects of competitive adjustment. Again, the fewness of firms and various characteristics of demand largely control the amount of product rivalry and the airlines' choice of product over price rivalry. Collusion, tolerated by the Board, banishes some forms of rivalry. The Board directly suppresses others, such as the competitive creation of new classes of service or the inflation of old ones. Despite these restraints, there is not much parallel action in setting product strategies, or at least not so much as in setting fares at the national level.

Some features of market structure tend to discourage parallel action. One is the rapid growth of demand for the industry's product and the resulting long-run payoff to the carrier that successfully raises its market share. Another is the demand characteristics that make a large share of a city-pair market easier to defend than a small one. But the secondary level of the Board's influence is also very important. By creating and maintaining the inequalities in size and profitability, the Board fosters a strong incentive for product rivalry among have-not carriers with little to lose. The presence of subsidy for the trunks in earlier years strongly encouraged this habit. Furthermore, though the Board has never let new carriers into the industry, it has admitted new tenants to individual city-pair markets. By granting entry on the basis of the size of city-pair markets and the performance of carriers already operating there, the Board has not changed the effective threat of entry to the city-pair market so very much from what it would be in the absence of certification requirements. Thus, carriers might have some ground for going ahead with product strategies only to help ward off new rivals.[3] Finally, there is a "first-level" reason why the Board's

---

[3] This factor is weakened somewhat now that fewer markets can support efficient marketing operations by additional carriers. Barriers to the entry of newcomers to such city-pair markets are effectively raised.

regulations should cut the incentive for parallel action in product strategies: the Board normally halts product competition that would seriously threaten the industry's profit level. A carrier planning a strategy that might provoke furious retaliation from a rival may be comforted by knowing that the Board is likely to step in to prevent any financial violence. In summary, the airline industry without regulation would probably have enough firms, enough diversity of firms, enough turnover of firms, and sufficiently little product differentiation to guarantee that product strategies would run their course without extensive collusion. The Civil Aeronautics Board gets much of the credit or blame for the limited amount of effective price rivalry in the air-transport industry, but the economic structural elements of the industry do not add up to the conditions for extreme oligopolistic price rigidity. This usually seems to require fairly strict absence of product differentiability; a substantial problem of "overhead costs" resulting from a cyclically sensitive demand curve and high capital-output ratio; and fairly substantial barriers to entry to the national market and submarkets. The Board has usually opposed downward price adjustments, either direct or when disguised as low-fare classes of service, discounts and promotional fares that resemble price cuts, and the like. However, it has allowed some upward adjustments, such as the taking of monopoly profits on new equipment. The Board is chronically nervous about price competition in marginal phases of the industry, such as military-charter activity and air freight. The complex of Board policies which aims at maximizing the rate of development of new aircraft is hostile to price competition, in that it involves protecting the margin of price over variable cost to permit rapid amortization. The Board has discouraged price rivalry by restricting the entry of specialist carriers, such as the air-coach operators, and by promoting a system of internal subsidy so that the profits of lucrative routes have to be protected to insure the providing of unprofitable service elsewhere.

Thus, without the Board's influence, the air-transport industry over the past two decades would have presented a reasonably flexible pattern of oligopolistic conduct, conditioned by easy entry to the individual city-pair market and reasonably easy entry to the industry as a whole. Competitive conduct would have involved a moderate amount of price competition, though perhaps with much of it in disguised forms. More diversity in patterns of product competition would also have been likely, with considerably less emphasis on superior aircraft. Whether there would have been more, or less, product rivalry without the Board's pattern of regulation is impossible to say; but the particular devices used certainly would have been different.

The previous chapters seem to confirm the hypotheses developed in Chapter 11 about the influence of direct subsidy on market conduct. Public subsidy placed the trunk carriers on a cost-plus basis until the early 1950s. Among the costs covered by mail pay, except when the Board disallowed them, were those growing out of product competition and investment in market penetration. Apart from losses planned by carriers invading new city-pair markets, short-run maximization of profits now seems to be the rule in the carrier's adjustments of the air service they offer. One cannot show that the patterns of competition have measurably changed from the 1940s to the 1950s because of the withdrawal of direct subsidy; too much else has happened. But there have been many other changes in the carriers' behavior that are explainable this way (such as the dropping of unprofitable services). These, plus scraps of direct evidence, seem to establish the point. As the industry's conduct patterns have been readjusted to the absence of subsidy, the net impact of the Board's policies on product competition has grown clearly restrictive; no indirect encouragement through subsidy offsets the direct discouragement created by the Board's hostility to competitive moves.

DESTRUCTIVE COMPETITION AND HISTORY

This section must be included because of prevailing myths which hold that, without the Board's restraining hand, the airlines would collapse in a Hobbesian war of destructive competition and that something like this actually occurred before the passage of the Civil Aeronautics Act in 1938. Consider, for example, the following vision conjured up by two spokesmen for the industry:

On the day [when entry controls were eliminated], every airline would tear up its time tables, disregard its certificates, forget that it has franchise responsibilities, and do what business it pleased in the interest of greater profits and not public convenience . . . The industry, in such a chaotic struggle for survival, would then have to abandon service to roughly some 500 of the cities to which it is now certificated, and operate only between the 50 most profitable pairs of cities.[4]

The quotation is basically correct in its suggestion that the present pattern of certification and regulation maintains service to some points that would not receive it otherwise. It also shows, however, a common impression that stems from the Board's years of blocking the entry of carriers to the largest city-pair markets — that without entry control all present airlines, and untold new ones, would set up a chaotic struggle over a few major markets. Nothing in the industry's structure supports this concern. Apart from the fact that some aircraft are more efficient for any given market than others, they are freely transferable from one market to another. In the short run, this stock of aircraft will produce only so many seat-miles of service,[5] and there is just no reason to expect that market forces would allocate them in such a way as to produce a great volume of unprofitable service in a few large markets and a small volume of very profitable service in others. In the long run, it is impossible to see why funds would be used to buy new aircraft that would raise the output of the industry to a level that could not earn depreciation plus a normal rate of return. The same can be said for the possibility of a retarded rate of scrapping of older aircraft; in the present-day air-transport industry this decision is clearly subject to the appropriate short-run marginal principles.

What of the period before the Civil Aeronautics Board received its regulatory powers in 1938? The industry did suffer substantial losses before that time, particularly in the years 1934–1938. On the surface, it might seem desirable to compare the industry's conduct before and after the Civil Aeronautics Act. In fact, this comparison turns out not to be very fruitful. The airlines were never without some protective regulation in the form of entry control and subsidy. The losses of those days are easily explained and have nothing to do with competitive market conduct.

[4] S. G. Tipton and S. Gewirtz, "The Effect of Regulated Competition on the Air Transport Industry," *Journal of Air Law and Commerce*, XXII (Spring 1955), 190.

[5] It was argued above that statistics on aircraft utilization suggest that airlines normally seem to use their fleets up to some technological maximum. This is not literally true, but the present fleet of the industry could not produce any enormously increased number of seat-miles.

Essential background here is the Air Mail Act of 1934 and its political origins.[6] Before 1934, all air-mail service and nearly all commercial aviation lay in the hands of three complex and interrelated groups. These contained recognizable ancestors of most of today's trunk carriers, but all were essentially controlled by a few persons through holding companies, stock interests, and dozens of interlocking directorships. In 1930, following the passage of the McNary-Watres Act, agents of these groups, at the instruction of the Postmaster General, had carved up the available air routes among themselves in a closed spoils session. From 1932 on, investigation after investigation began to delve into this episode; and because of it the Postmaster General under the Roosevelt administration, James A. Farley, canceled all existing mail contracts in 1934. The Air Mail Act of 1934 was basically a particularized antitrust bill applied to the air industry. It forced vertical and horizontal disintegration of the holding companies and established competitive bidding as the only way for the carriers to get back into business. Because this was the only choice for the existing carriers, and because there was a prospect of later renegotiation of the rate of pay under a successful bid, the bids submitted under the 1934 act were extremely low. And this was largely responsible for the low profits of the industry in the years preceding the Civil Aeronautics Act. Thus, the Post Office's payments to the industry dropped from $19,400,000 in 1933 to $12,130,000 in 1934 and $8,835,000 in 1935. By 1938 payments were still under $15 million, though the volume of mail had tripled over the 1934 level. In hearings leading to the passage of the Civil Aeronautics Act, the carriers' spokesmen admitted that "enormous operating losses" had resulted from the post-1934 bids for mail routes.[7] Another important factor, unrelated to competition, was that during 1934–1938 many airlines were writing off substantial losses from other phases of aeronautics,[8] and it

[6] Many sources discuss the successive acts dealing with air transport in the 1920s and 1930s, but the only scholarly source that relates them to the conduct of the industry is J. Howard Hamstra, "Two Decades — Federal Aero-Regulation in Perspective," *Journal of Air Law and Commerce,* XII (April 1941), 105–147.

[7] *Regulation of Transportation of Passengers and Property by Aircraft,* hearings on S. 3027, U.S. Senate, Committee on Interstate and Foreign Commerce, Subcommittee, 74th Cong., 1st sess. (Washington, 1935), p. 92.

[8] *Ibid.,* p. 82.

seems quite likely that, owing to the previous holding companies, some water was being squeezed out of their capitalization.

There was little significant point-to-point competition in the industry before World War II. The prevailing mail routes resulted in competition for only a few city-pairs; New York–Los Angeles, New York–Chicago, Chicago–Dallas, and Detroit–Washington were the main ones.[9] Though fares had fallen from an average of 11.0 cents a mile in 1928 to 8.3 cents in 1930 and 5.3 cents in 1940, the main cause of the reduction was not airline competition but a growing interest in passenger service and hence growing efforts to price competitively with first-class rail service.[10] The Air Mail Act of 1934 did not prohibit competitive operations by air-mail carriers in noncontractual routes, though the Interstate Commerce Commission could find offline service to be unfair competition. This situation was responsible for a certain amount of extra direct competition. Pennsylvania Airlines and Transport Co., losing its former Detroit–Washington route to Central Airlines in 1934, decided to offer service there anyway, supporting itself in part by a Detroit–Milwaukee mail contract. The struggle between Pennsylvania and Central, incidentally, produced the only known case of price rivalry from this period.[11] In 1935 Congress stepped in to halt it by banning competitive offline service by air-mail carriers. It excepted service started before July 1, 1935, as a favor to Pennsylvania Airlines, but that carrier merged with Central in the following year to form the predecessor of Capital Airlines.[12] There was no significant competition from nonmail carriers during the years prior to the Civil Aeronautics Act. Many would-be operators sought mail contracts over the most lucrative routes, but the Post Office resisted them entirely.[13] Some carriers operated without mail contracts, but they had short lives and for some reason chose to operate in relatively thin, non-competitive routes. Their number had been declining on the

[9] *Aircraft Year Book,* 1934–1939.

[10] Emory R. Johnson, *Transportation Facilities, Service and Policies* (New York, 1947), p. 370.

[11] Hearings on S. 3027, pp. 33–34, 119. A table on p. 126 also indicates that American was flying some off-line mileage in 1935.

[12] See *Regulation of Transportation of Passengers and Property by Aircraft,* Hearings on S. 2 and S. 1760, U.S. Senate, Committee on Interstate and Foreign Commerce, Subcommittee, 75th Cong., 1st sess. (Washington, 1937), p. 148.

[13] Hearings on S. 3027, p. 111.

average through the 1930s up to the passage of the act; there were about forty passenger-carrying airlines in the United States in 1930, but only twenty to twenty-five in the years just before 1938.[14] It is fair to say that their activities had no effect on the profitability of the mail-carrying trunks.

It is true that a re-equipment cycle took place in the 1934–1938 period which bore some relation to the rivalry on the three east-west transcontinental routes. American, TWA, and United were the first to acquire the new DC-3 to replace the DC-2 and an early Boeing plane previously used on the transcontinental route. Some smaller noncompetitive carriers bought early Lockheed and Boeing aircraft at the same time.[15] Competitive considerations had far less to do with these equipment purchases than they did in later years. The DC-3 was an enormous advance over the transport aircraft in use before it. Except for the shakedown costs of putting new planes into service, re-equipment could hardly have been a significant source of excessive competition or subnormal profits before the passage of the Civil Aeronautics Act.

Market conduct and patterns of competition were mentioned often in the various congressional hearings on aviation in the years 1935–1938. The main features of the Civil Aeronautics Act were supported by the carriers, which were, indeed, the principal interest seeking the legislation. Their representatives' statements about competition largely took the form of pleas for public control of price, product, and entry. The main demand was for permanent certificates of public convenience and necessity to replace the theoretical uncertainty of competitive bidding for air-mail routes, not to mention a legion of undesirable features that had arisen under the Air Mail Act of 1934. This was the principal substantive change which the 1938 legislation made.

In short, conduct patterns in the air-transport industry under the Air Mail Act of 1934 showed no significant "destructive competition," and the low profits prevailing were due to a number of

[14] Stuart Daggett, *Principles of Inland Transportation* (New York, 1941), p. 107. See also Interstate Commerce Commission, *Regulation of Transportation Agencies,* Senate Doc. 152, 73rd Cong., 2nd sess. (Washington, 1934), p. 51.

[15] *Aviation,* XXXV (April 1936), 68; XXXVI (April, 1937), 77. This periodical was the predecessor of *Aviation Week.*

other factors. Behavioral patterns before the 1938 legislation were, as one would expect, the result of the pattern of regulation then prevailing and the structural conditions of the young industry at that time. They tell little or nothing about what the industry's behavior would be in a "state of nature."

PART IV

MARKET PERFORMANCE

17 Measurements of Market Performance

How well has the performance of the domestic air-transport industry satisfied the public interest? To what extent is its performance determined by its economic environment and by the law which the Civil Aeronautics Board administers? Finally, how might this performance be improved by changing the industry's structure or by changing the regulatory framework? The last chapter of this study deals with such questions as these. Before reaching that stage, several measurements or evaluations of specific features of the airlines' market performance are needed. The following sections deal with various features of resource allocation in the industry, the quality and variety of the product it offers, and its innovative and developmental efforts.

THE RATE OF RETURN

Table 34 shows the profit record of the trunkline industry since 1939 and the local-service carriers since their beginning in 1946. As with any industry, one could devote many pages to pondering adjustments of the data to make accounting profits more nearly resemble "true" economic profits. Few of these, however, seem to help much in the case of the airlines, excepting the adjustment for capital gains. Public control since 1938 has largely prevented write-ups that would increase the investment base, and this common source of distortion does not appear.

The average annual profit rate for the trunk carriers over the twenty-year period was 8.9 percent; if the war years 1942–1945 are excluded, the figure drops to 7.3 percent. The local-service carriers in the years 1946–1959 earned only 0.4 percent on their total investment. Even this rate is overstated, since it appears to exclude some carriers that have disappeared. Simple averages were computed of the rates of return for the four largest trunks and for the smaller trunks; the former earned 9.5 percent on the average over 1939–1959, the latter 7.0 percent. If the war years are excluded, these figures drop to 7.9 and 5.8 percent, respec-

Table 34. Rate of return, after taxes but before interest, on average total investment, trunks and local-service carriers, 1939–1959 (percent)

Year	All domestic trunks[a]	Big Four[b]	Regional trunks[b,c]	Local-service carriers[a]
1939[d]	2.3	5.8	4.4	—
1940[d]	13.2	15.5	8.1	—
1941[d]	4.5	4.6	−0.8	—
1942	20.3	20.1	17.9	—
1943	17.1	18.2	11.2	—
1944	17.5	18.3	7.3	—
1945	9.4	8.0	12.1	—
1946	−1.9	−1.5	−3.0	4.5
1947	−4.6	−3.2	−12.0	−3.9
1948	1.7	3.0	6.5	−22.2
1949	5.8	6.2	9.5	−0.1
1950	12.3	13.0	13.0	−9.9
1951	13.1	12.9	12.4	11.2
1952	15.3	15.0	12.6	−3.2
1953	11.4	10.8	13.6	5.9
1954	11.0	11.5	8.9	8.5
1955	11.6	10.9	9.6	8.6
1956	9.4	8.9	8.2	−1.9
1957	4.7	5.3	1.1	−1.2
1958	6.3	6.6	3.7	4.2
1959	7.2	8.9	3.0	4.5

[a] Weighted average: sum of profits divided by sum of average investments.

[b] Simple average. Simple averages for the two subgroups of trunks need not lie on opposite sides of the weighted average for the group.

[c] Number of carriers varies. Figures for Colonial Airlines are not available for 1939 and 1940, and Colonial, Chicago and Southern, Inland, and Mid-Continent were dropped as of the year in which they merged with other carriers.

[d] Fiscal year.

Source: unpublished material provided by Office of Carrier Accounts and Statistics, CAB.

tively.[1] The usual test for the reasonableness of an industry's rate of return is to compare it to the long-term rate of interest. Economic theory suggests that the rate of return on the total capital of a competitive industry, taking the firms that fail as well as the firms that succeed, should approach the percentage

[1] Simple averages had to be used in securing average figures for the large and small trunks because the parent figures on total investment from which the data were calculated were not readily available. The distortion from a weighted average is not serious for the large trunks, but there is a significant downward bias in the figures for the smaller group, since the smallest members chronically had the lowest profits.

that loanable funds can earn elsewhere in the economy. The exact value of *the* long-term rate of interest is too uncertain to give any exact value for the amount of excess profits in the airline industry. An average figure of 5 percent for the 1939–1959 period would probably be appropriate, allowing for some capital rationing to the industry. The 7.3 percent the trunks have earned on the average in peacetime years thus contains a relatively modest amount of excess profit, not much over two percentage points. One tabulation has shown that in the years 1951–1956 capital gains (net of capital-gains taxation) accounted for 15.2 percent of the profits of the trunk carriers.[2] These years probably brought the largest capital gains in the industry's history. Consequently, if we assume that 15.2 percent of profits for 1939–1941 and 1946–1959 were unanticipated capital gains, the remaining earned and anticipated profit rate would be about 6 percent. Finally, the last two decades have brought rising prices in general and for the inputs of the air industry in particular. This normally means an unmeasurable upward bias to reported figures on profits.

Another crude test of the reported profits of the air transport industry is by comparison with the profit rates reported for the same period by all active United States corporations. These figures are shown in Table 35 for the period 1939–1958, excluding 1942–1945. A simple average of the profits before interest on total investment over these years gives a figure of 7.6 percent for all corporations. This rate includes true costs of debt and equity capital, an unknown amount of windfalls that may or may not cancel out, and finally a certain amount of monopoly profits. Economists studying these figures in the past have concluded that they probably contain 2 or 3 percent of monopoly profits on shareholders' equity.[3] Besides this figure of 7.6 percent for all corporations, we can place the rate of 7.3 percent for the trunk airlines. The meaning of these figures for airline profits remains the same: profits in air transport have been at least normal but not significantly in excess of normal.

With this apparent normality of profits, it is a bit surprising

[2] American Airlines, Inc., Exhibit No. AA–918–A, General Passenger Fare Investigation, Docket No. 8008.

[3] For example, Joe S. Bain, *Industrial Organization* (New York, 1959), pp. 382–384.

Table 35.   Rate of return, all active United States corporations, 1939–1941
and 1946–1958 (percent)

Year	Net profits before interest, after taxes, on total investment	Net profits on net worth
1939	4.5	4.1
1940	5.1	5.0
1941	6.1	6.7
1946	8.8	9.9
1947	9.9	11.3
1948	9.9	11.4
1949	7.9	8.9
1950	9.9	11.3
1951	8.1	9.0
1952	7.1	8.0
1953	7.3	7.5
1954	7.0	7.1
1955	8.2	8.5
1956	7.8	7.9
1957	7.4	7.1
1958	6.3	5.5

Source: U.S. Treasury, Internal Revenue Service, *Statistics of Income* (various years).

that the Civil Aeronautics Board recently heeded the pleas of the carriers that their return should be at least 3 percent higher. The decision in *General Passenger Fare Investigation* set a rate of return of 10.5 percent on total capital as a standard.[4] This was based on a cost-of-capital approach. The rate was a compound of separate rates on debt and equity for the larger four and smaller eight trunks, respectively. The two rates on debt capital were uncontroversial values of 4.5 and 5.5 percent, respectively. A reasonable return on equity was found by the Board to be 16 and 18 percent, respectively, for the large and small carriers. These spectacular rates, which at first glance seem to contain about 10 percent excess profits on equity, were reached in the following way. First, the trunks' actual earnings-price ratios for recent years were calculated. These numbers struck the Board as unsatisfactory because they had been rather unstable. Consequently, the apparent supply price of equity funds was boosted by several

[4] Order Serial No. E–16068, Nov. 25, 1960, General Passenger Fare Investigation, pp. 12ff.

percentage points. A number of alleged reasons were given for this, most of them drawn from arguments which the carriers had pressed upon the Board. The airlines should earn more than normal profits because their rate of return has historically varied so much from year to year, imposing some sort of risk on their investors. They have a low capital-output ratio by comparison to other regulated industries, and so should earn a high rate of return because of the risk created by the resulting low rate of gross profit on sales. Finally, the regulatory standard is being set for the industry as a whole, and, since it conveys no specific guarantee to individual firms, an additional risk is created.[5] A proceeding on the rate of return for local-service carriers, completed at about the same time, built upon the *General Passenger Fare* decision and set a maximum rate of return on total capital of 12.75 percent for the local airlines, based on a 21.35 percent rate of return on equity.[6] Is there any sense to the reasons for promising the airlines apparently huge excess profits? I shall argue, first, that the earnings-price ratios used in the decision are probably somewhat high and, second, that the reasons for adjusting them upward still more are uniformly fallacious.

Table 36 shows the price-earnings ratios for trunkline securities and other major price-earnings series. The years covered are 1950–1956, the span surveyed in certain important documents before the Board in the general fare investigation and the only ones yielding remotely normal results for the industry. The results are not surprising. The airlines do not enjoy the high ratios of blue-ribbon banks and insurance companies or public utilities with protected monopoly positions, but they are not conspicuously out of line with the ratios for industrials and general common stocks. In recent years the airlines have had somewhat less favorable price-earnings ratios than industrial stocks, although theory might suggest that in the long run the airlines' ratios ought to lie somewhere between those for public utilities and those for industrials because of the guarantee which public regulation offers against continued low earnings. The comparison is probably a little more unfavorable than the table suggests: during the years in question

[5] *Ibid.*, pp. 22–26.
[6] Order Serial No. E–15696, Aug. 26, 1960, Local Service Carriers Rate of Return Investigation, Docket No. 8404, pp. 2–3.

Table 36.   Price-earnings ratios of trunkline securities and other major groups
of common stocks, 1950–1956

Year	12 trunk airlines	200 common stocks	125 industrials	25 railroads	24 public utilities	15 banks	10 insurance companies
1950	7.76	7.33	6.84	4.57	11.92	14.74	12.52
1951	8.11	9.85	9.60	6.11	13.34	14.31	13.95
1952	7.99	10.55	10.53	6.03	13.54	13.10	11.98
1953	7.06	10.04	9.86	5.88	13.60	12.90	12.98
1954	7.32	11.81	11.43	8.51	15.07	13.35	21.08
1955	11.39	12.50	12.43	8.25	15.34	14.93	19.12
1956	11.76	14.11	14.44	8.59	14.81	13.13	23.39

Source: Airline ratios from Order Serial No. E-16068, General Passenger Fare Investigation, Docket No. 8008, p. 20; other indexes from *Moody's Industrial Manual, American and Foreign* (New York, 1960), p. a26.

the airlines were not issuing any new common stock, whereas some of the firms represented in the Moody's indexes were.

There is a reason for the airlines' common stocks to have this unfavorable price-earnings relation, however. On a year-to-year basis, both the earnings and dividends of a common stock affect its attractiveness to the average investor. But over a longer period a stock is bought primarily for the income it yields, and its price tends to be the price of an income stream of dividends.[7] Relatively high earnings are not much comfort if they are never paid out in dividends. The air-transport industry has been extremely conservative in its payment of dividends. As Table 37 shows, during the first half of the 1950s the airlines paid out a little more than a quarter of their net earnings as dividends, whereas all United States corporations averaged a little more than half. The carriers' rate of dividend payout was probably somewhat low in the earlier years as well. More recently it has risen. Thus, there

[7] This is the conclusion of what appears to be the only satisfactory study of the matter, Edward D. Zinbarg, "Price-Earnings Ratios and Yields," *Analysts Journal*, XV (Aug. 1959), 35–42. Zinbarg developed a very long-run index of stock prices covering twenty-nine industrial groups, along with a variety of measures of dividends and earnings (lagging, leading, moving average, and so on). Nearly *all* of the various measures of dividends had higher correlations with price than *any* of the measures of earnings. The moving averages of dividends gave the highest correlations of any series, while the moving averages of earnings gave relatively low correlations. By analysis of medians, Zinbarg suggests a normal price-earnings ratio of around ten for both the 1920s and 1950s.

Table 37. Relation of dividends to net profits, domestic airlines and all U.S. corporations, 1951–1955

Year	Airlines' dividend-payout rate	All corporations' dividend-payout rate
1951	28.7	48.7
1952	23.7	55.9
1953	26.9	54.7
1954	29.1	61.9
1955	29.8	52.4

Source: *American Aviation*, XX (Sept. 10, 1956), 52.

is no knowing whether this low rate of payout will be a permanent feature of the industry, but, if it is, the apparent earnings-price ratio on which the Board bases its cost-of-capital determinations will be accordingly high.

The Board was right, then, in thinking that earnings-price ratios for airline securities in the 1950s were not a very accurate guide to the future cost of equity capital. Furthermore, it was not grossly unreasonable to add a 15 percent allowance to the observed ratios to allow for the cost of floating new security issues, as was done in the important Howell study commissioned by the Board.[8] The supply of airline equities was not expanding during the period from which the earnings-price ratios were drawn; if it had been, the ratios would have been lower still. But with the allowance made, the cost of equity capital found in the Howell study became 12.9 percent for the Big Four and 14.1 percent for the smaller trunks. These figures are higher than would be reasonable for most industrial concerns. They reinforce the suggestion that the industry's stingy dividend policy necessarily extracts a high cost of equity capital in the long run. By sanctioning this, the Board essentially promises the carriers a future choice between excess returns to equity shareholders and a built-in source of retained earnings to finance net investment.

But the Board did not accept the Howell earnings-price ratios of 13 and 14 percent; it boosted them to 16 and 18 percent. Now, the Howell ratios were surely an uncertain guide to the cost of

[8] This study is described in Paul L. Howell, "The Rate of Return in Air Transport," *Law and Contemporary Problems*, XXIV (Autumn 1959), 677–701.

equity capital; they could err on either the high or the low side. The Board saw only the latter possibility. To evaluate the reasons it gave for the upward adjustment, one must go into the arguments which the carriers advanced to the Board. One of these was that the industry deserves a high rate of return because of the great fluctuations in its rate of return.[9] This variability is supposed to be an additional source of risk to equity stockholders. One exhibit presented an interesting set of figures which purports to show that the mean annual change of an industry's profit rate is a significant determinant of its average level of profits. Insufficient information was given on the selection of industries making up the sample to decide whether it could be accepted or not. The hypothetical relation seemed worth testing, however, and so a multiple regression was calculated, using the sample's profit data as the dependent variable. One independent variable was the sample's series on mean annual change of profits; as a second independent variable, concentration ratios were drawn from those available for 1947 to match as nearly as possible the sampled industries. The results[10] cast suspicion on both the sample and the main hypothesis. The intercept term, theoretically representing the normal rate of return of an atomistic industry with a constant profit rate over time, was 13.70 percent, two to three times what one would expect over the 1933–1955 period. Furthermore, the coefficient relating the level of profits to their variability, was not significant, though its value was relatively high.

Finally, the hypothesis is largely untenable on theoretical grounds. Most economists would grant that some circumstances affecting an industry would cause its rate of return to be high owing to elements of risk. One might pose a case in which there was a highly variable demand curve for the product, coupled with a high portion of fixed costs for individual firms in the in-

[9] For example, American Airlines, Inc., "Instability of Earnings," Exhibit No. AA–925, General Passenger Fare Investigation; also Exhibits No. AA–501, AA–503. For a published description, see *American Aviation*, XXI (Dec. 16, 1957), 51.
[10] Let Y stand for the profit-rate variable, X_1 the mean annual change, X_2 the 1947 concentration ratio. The resulting regression equation is:

$$Y = 13.70 + 0.9409X_1 + 0.0247X_2$$
$$(1.810) \qquad (0.0034)$$

dustry. If profit rates for firms were normally dispersed about the industry mean, the chances of business failure and large losses to stockholders would be substantial. But the airline industry is no such case. The volume of air travel shows the imprint of the business cycle only faintly and, in comparison with durable-goods industries, its demand is relatively stable. Truly fixed costs are probably less important than for the majority of manufacturing industries. Why, then, should profits show the great annual variability which they do? One reason is the way in which the Board handled subsidy payments to the trunks in the 1940s, with large amounts paid retroactively; another is the uneven distribution of investment over time; a third is the uneven distribution of route awards over time. But the most important reasons lie in the industry's conduct pattern. In the late 1950s the very low load factors permitted by certain carriers dragged their profits down abnormally over a three-year period, and at all times the insensitivity of the volume of service to slight variations in traffic created relatively great variability of profits. Finally, many of the wounds are self-inflicted by the carriers' accounting practices, since their short depreciation periods and habit of expensing many investment-type costs[11] cause profits to seem uneven over time.

A related argument has been used, with apparent success, by the carriers to establish the especially risky nature of their operations and the resulting need for a high rate of return. It turns on the fact that the airlines as an industry are much less capital-intensive than such classic public utilities as electricity, telephone, and railroads. Therefore, their operating ratio, the percentage of their revenues that covers costs before interest, is smaller than for other public utilities. If, in two industries, "variable" costs are held constant and total revenues are reduced by the same percentage, the margin covering interest and profits will shrink by a greater percentage in the industry with the lower capital intensity and the smaller margin over costs. From this, the airlines infer that theirs is a particularly risky business which requires either a generous rate of return on capital or price and profit regulation by way of the operating ratio. The argument is

[11] *Monopoly Problems in Regulated Industries — Airlines,* U.S. House of Representatives, III, 1348–1349.

clearly fallacious insofar as it refers to the nature of business
risks. In effect it reverses the normal roles of fixed and variable
costs. A conventional theoretical analysis would hold that an industry with low capital intensity (and a small operating ratio)
is in a particularly *riskless* position. Most of its costs are avoidable, so that a catastrophic reduction of demand would be quickly
met (with or without bankruptcy of firms) by the discharge of
variable factors of production. Even if the industry's capital goods
are "specific" and long-lived, it would not be likely that they
would suffer prolonged subnormal returns. Conversely, when capital costs are a large portion of an industry's total costs, suppliers
of capital are in a more exposed position and face a greater chance
of receiving very low rewards, or rewards that are subnormal over
a long period of time.[12] In short, the theoretical prediction would
be that an industry's suppliers of capital would, in the aggregate,
demand a higher rate of return, the *greater* is the industry's
capital intensity or the *lower* its capital turnover. The high rate
might reflect either outright high costs of capital or a high ratio of
equity to debt.

Finally, the whole economic notion of risk is done much
violence in discussions within the industry. Risk, seen by a
supplier of loanable funds, adheres in a distribution of expected
returns to investment in a *particular* firm. Undoubtedly the most
important feature of this distribution (other than its expected
value) is the chances of total loss of capital through failure of
the business. Such risks, calling forth a high expected rate of return, would exist in industries with a substantial turnover of
firms or a high percentage of business failures. If capitalists are
risk avoiders, it should be the industries with a high turnover of
firms that must pay a high price for loanable funds. In cross-section, such a condition would appear as a wide dispersion of the
annual profit rates for going firms about their mean value. Now,
this is not what the discussion before the Civil Aeronautics Board
has centered on. The two arguments allegedly relating to risk,
outlined above, both refer to the variation of profits *for the
industry* over a number of years. This bears only the slightest

[12] The reader will recognize that this argument omits a number of inessentials,
such as the degree of substitutability between capital and variable factors of
production.

relation to risk to the investor. If an industry's rate of return fluctuates over time but averages at least a normal rate over a long period, and if the profits for all firms fluctuate in the same way so that none ever goes bankrupt, it is very difficult to see why suppliers of funds should extract a risk premium. This is not to deny investors the moral right to avoid such a situation; the point is rather that such avoidance would not be consistent with rational evaluation of risk.[13]

Has the air industry been a risky one in the correct sense — one that has frequently dealt subnormal returns to its suppliers of capital? No trunk has gone into actual bankruptcy, and regulation makes it unlikely that one would, except in cases of serious managerial ineptitude. There have been times when bank loans were in technical default, either through outright postponement of interest or repayment or through the violation of certain protective conditions imposed by the lenders. These have undoubtedly brought some nervous moments but no significant outright losses.

The Board accepted a third and equally invalid reason for justifying a 10.6 percent rate of return to the trunk airlines. That was the fact that the return was being set for the industry as a whole and not for individual firms. The Board's sporadic efforts to equalize the profitability of the various trunks' systems have still not succeeded, and the Board itself calculated that a 10.6 percent return to the industry would yield losses for the weakest carrier but profits as high as 13.95 percent for the strongest.[14] Actually, only one airline, Northeast, would be threatened by less-than-normal profits even if the aggregate return allowed the industry were as much as 2 percent less. On pragmatic grounds, it hardly seems sensible to allow excess profits to the rest of the industry to reduce the anticipated losses to one carrier. Generally speaking, the Board's handling of the problem of differing profitability of carriers in the two rate-of-return cases is unsatisfactory. The weaker trunks and local-service carriers have chronically disappointed their stockholders' expectations of profits, with the result that their earnings-price ratios have been high. Confronted with this evidence of its past inability (or failure) to

[13] Zinbarg's study (p. 40) finds no evidence of a relation between common-stock yields and the variability of yields.

[14] Order Serial No. E–16068, General Passenger Fare Investigation, p. 25.

rationalize the systems of the various carriers, the Board moved
to the conclusion that these weaker carriers required supranormal
rewards in the future. The weakest of all, the local-service carriers, were found to need a 21.35 percent rate of return on equity
to attract new capital. Can anyone believe that firms which
actually earned this return over a period of time would find it
only sufficient to attract new capital? This paradox seems to have
escaped the Board entirely.[15]

In summary, the arguments heard in the industry and accepted
by the Board for a high "normal" rate of return are generally
invalid. Furthermore, the Board has been led by certain inadequacies in its past policies to promise equally inappropriate
remedies in the future. There is, of course, no way of knowing
whether the airlines will now proceed to earn these higher rates of
return, even though the Board has sanctioned them; but the point
is that there is no regulatory force to stop them.

The rate of profit is only one significant measure of the market
performance of an industry. It was stressed earlier in this study
that the airlines' level of cost is anything but an absolute and
unique notion, and that costs indeed have some tendency to adjust
to yield a normal return on whatever prices are allowed (the
"product" offered being changed as necessary). Furthermore, a
normal rate of profit to the industry as a whole could mean either
full equilibrium in all city-pair markets or, instead, disequilibriums in many of these markets that just offset each other in
their impact on aggregate profits. It is important, then, to turn
to these other phases of performance.

RATE OF RETURN IN VARIOUS MARKETS

Throughout this study, it has been suggested that differences
in the profitability of air service on various routes have always
existed and that they have had an enormous impact on the industry's conduct and the Board's policies. The carriers' conduct
has been heavily oriented toward protecting shares in potentially
or actually lucrative, dense, long-haul markets. The Board has
explicitly justified its hostility to the entry of new carriers on

---

[15] The Board's difficulty here resembles certain general paradoxes that plague
the regulation of public utilities via the cost-of-capital approach. See S. L.
Margoshes, "Price Earnings Ratio in Financial Analysis," *Financial Analysts
Journal,* XVI (Nov.-Dec. 1960), 130.

grounds of perpetuating internal subsidy — allowing certified carriers enough profits on thick routes to cover their losses on thin ones.[16] The best simple description of the Board's aims is this: to maximize the number of city-pair markets receiving some air service, subject to the constraint of acceptable profits for the certified airlines and an acceptably small volume of public subsidy. Such a goal calls for exploiting profitable markets to subsidize loss operations in others. Whether this objective has social merit or not, an economist would normally choose a different one. He would prefer to see scarce resources used to provide air transportation in various city-pair markets up to the point where they earn merely a normal return in each market. If citizens of New York pay a higher price relative to cost for air transportation than citizens of Kokomo, a trade of consumable goods and services could theoretically be worked out whereby New Yorkers acquired more air service (and slightly less of other things) and Kokomoans more of other things (and slightly less air service).[17]

Postponing analysis of the choice between these two standards, the Board's and the economist's, one must at least try to measure crudely the extent to which there is internal subsidy of thin routes with the profits of richer ones. As has been shown, the extent of internal subsidy has probably changed a good deal over the past two decades. When the trunklines were still on subsidy, they not only went along with the task of serving unprofitable routes but, indeed, had an incentive to provide as much service as possible on as many routes as possible. When subsidy according to need ceased in the early 1950s, the situation abruptly changed and many of the trunks began dropping their unprofitable stations by the dozen. Furthermore, the forces of product competition have made the differences in the quality of service between weak and strong markets more and more pronounced over the past decade. Finally, coach service, which is in some ways a price reduction for the fare-sensitive segment of air travelers, has been offered extensively only on strong routes.[18] So it is clear

[16] For example, CAB, *Materials Relative to Competition in the Regulated Civil Aviation Industry, 1956,* transmitted to the Select Committee on Small Business, 84th Cong., 2nd sess. (Washington, 1956), p. 11.

[17] This paragraph abstracts from joint and common costs, which essentially place a band of uncertainty around the efficient allocation of resources.

[18] For an anticipation of its effects, see *Aviation Week,* LVII (Nov. 10, 1952), 88.

that the amount of internal subsidy has been falling continuously. It is not feasible to make tests for its presence in every year of the industry's history. Hence, the best solution seems to be to base measurements on the most recent data. If they still show significant differences in the rate of return apparently earned in different classes of city-pair markets, we know that the situation earlier was as bad or worse.

First, let us consider the way in which the airlines' fares vary with the distance between pairs of cities and the volume of traffic moving between them. There is a good deal of general information about these variations, since changes in fares have usually been made through large segments of the industry rather than in individual markets. At one time air fares were more or less constructed from a fixed base rate in cents per mile. A "taper" of fares with distance has come about through the extension of coach service in long-haul markets and the addition of three flat fare increases of one dollar per ticket. The first of these apparently did not create much of an effective taper,[19] and the third came after the statistical work for this study had been finished. However, after the second dollar increase in early 1958, an effective taper certainly existed. A taper with regard to the volume of traffic moving in the market has come about because adding competitors on dense routes has sometimes cut circuitous mileages used for calculating total fares, and because the local-service carriers and some trunks use a higher base rate in cents per passenger-mile on thin noncompetitive routes. It seemed desirable to check this *a priori* information statistically, since there is no general summary of air fares that states how widespread these changes have been. A sample of fares was taken in the following way. First a sample of a hundred fares between city-pairs was drawn from a complete alphabetical list of United States city-pair fares by taking every tenth fare from a random start. Elimination of those pairs not actually served during 1958 or having on the average less than ten passengers per month reduced this number to seventy-eight.[20] To this panel were added the top

[19] See Transcript of Hearings before Examiner, *General Passenger Fare Investigation*, p. 8105.

[20] At first glance this elimination might seem inappropriate on the grounds that relatively high fares might be the cause of the lack of or the few passengers on these routes. A check of the eliminated fares suggested, however,

fifty city-pairs in passenger-miles generated during 1958. Thus the sample consists of a complete enumeration of the largest city-pairs plus a random sample across the smaller markets.[21]

For each city-pair in the sample, the first-class fare was recorded, along with the coach fare where one existed. Previous studies of the airlines' fare structure have dealt with coach and first-class fares separately.[22] That is inappropriate here because one source of effective price cutting on dense and long-haul routes is to offer relatively more coach service. Typically, little or none is available on thin and short-haul routes. Hence I combined the coach and first-class fares on each route into a weighted average, using as weights the volume of first-class and coach traffic during 1958.[23] Traffic figures were available only for two-week survey periods in early March and late September. As is customary, traffic in these survey periods was assumed to be one thirteenth of traffic for the year.

At first the natural strategy seemed to be multiple correlation of the fares with the distance and density of the routes. However, both partial relations were known in advance to be nonlinear. Furthermore, there was no particular use for the partial-regression coefficients that would result across the total distribution; interest lay in the significance of differences from segment to segment within the distribution. Hence analysis of variance was used in-

---

that they did not differ significantly from included fares on thin routes of the same character, and that the cause of low or nonexistent traffic was either airport inadequacies or intrinsic lack of demand for travel between small towns having little community of interest. The positive reason for the exclusion was the desire to include only those fares whose market impact presumably had had some consideration by carrier managements.

[21] Fares and official distances between cities were taken from American Aviation Publications, *Official Airline Guide, Quick Reference Edition* (Chicago, 1958), May 1958 edition (for fares) and May 1960 edition (for distances). Traffic densities are taken from CAB, Office of Carrier Accounts and Statistics, *Origin-Destination Airline Passenger Survey, March 1–14, 1958* (Washington, 1959), vols. 1–3, and *September 17–30* (Washington, 1960), vols. 1–3.

[22] See "Preliminary Report on the Domestic Passenger Fare Structure Based on a Sampling of Individual Rates" by the Commercial Rates Section of the Rates Division, CAB, reprinted in *Monopoly Problems in Regulated Industries — Airlines*, I, 221–293.

[23] On some routes there are separate fares for night and day coaches. Since there are no separate traffic figures for these, a simple average was taken as "the" coach fare. The same was done in the very few cases where different airlines with significant shares of the same city-pair market quoted slightly different fares.

stead. The sampled fares were sorted into five classes with regard to both the distance and density variables, making 25 cells in all. The distance classes were over 1,200 miles, 801 to 1,200, 401 to 800, 201 to 400, and 1 to 200. Density classes were over 100,000 passengers annually, 25,001 to 100,000, 5,001 to 25,000, 1,001 to 5,000, and 1,000 and less. The number of observations naturally varied from cell to cell, so I reduced each cell to the mean of its elements and continued the analysis of the variance of these means. The class means are shown in Table 38. Table 39

Table 38. Class means of the fare-structure sample of weighted averages of first-class and coach fares on selected routes, 1958 (cents per passenger-mile)

Density of route (passengers per year)	Distance (miles)				
	Under 200	201–400	401–800	801–1,200	Over 1,200
Under 1,000	9.38	7.63	6.92	7.29	6.80
1,001–5,000	8.55	6.89	6.98	6.46	5.83
5,001–25,000	8.77	7.17	6.47	6.36	5.39
25,001–100,000	7.49	7.04	6.71	6.29	5.70
Over 100,000	7.11	6.85	6.30	5.90	5.35

Source: see text.

Table 39. Analysis of variance of fare-structure class means shown in Table 38

Source of variation	Sum of squares	Degrees of freedom	Mean square	F	$F_{.95}$	$F_{.99}$
Density of route	4.5805	4	1.1451	3.429	2.45	3.50
Distance of trip	16.5621	4	4.1405	12.400	2.45	3.50
Interaction	2.0814	16	0.1301	0.390	1.74	2.18
Error	—	104	0.3339	—	—	—

Source: see text.

shows the analysis of the variance of these cell means. The significance test shows that the variation of fares with distance of route is highly significant at both the 95 and 99 percent confidence levels. Their variation with respect to density is significant at 95 percent and nearly significant at 99 percent, and consequently will be accepted. Variation due to interaction of rows and columns is not nearly significant; that is, the cell means can be regarded as the sum of the deviations of their respective row and column means from the grand mean of the distribution. Economically, this means roughly that the way air fares vary with route density is independent of the distance class being examined, and vice versa.

This partitioning of variance was pressed further by making several orthogonal comparisons to find where the significant breaks come in the distribution with regard to distance and density. The results are shown in Table 40. Only one partitioning

Table 40. Subdivisions of sums of squares from fare-structure sample

Source of variation	Sum of squares	Degrees of freedom	Mean square	F	$F_{.95}$	$F_{.99}$
1. *Rows partitioned into markets under and over 5,000 passengers*						
Over and under 5,000	2.7614	1	2.7614	8.270	3.94	6.90
Other row variation	1.8191	3	0.6064	1.816	2.70	3.98
2. *Columns partitioned into markets under and over 1,200 miles*						
Over and under 1,200	7.0193	1	7.0193	21.022	3.94	6.90
Other column variation	9.5428	3	3.1809	9.526	2.70	3.98
3. *Columns partitioned into markets under and over 800 miles*						
Over and under 800	8.8297	1	8.8297	26.443	3.94	6.90
Other column variation	7.7324	3	2.5775	7.719	2.70	3.98
4. *Columns partitioned into markets under and over 400 miles*						
Over and under 400	8.5195	1	8.5195	25.514	3.94	6.90
Other column variation	8.0426	3	2.6809	8.029	2.70	3.98
5. *Columns partitioned into markets under and over 200 miles*						
Over and under 200	12.1494	1	12.1494	36.385	3.94	6.90
Other column variation	4.4127	3	1.4709	4.405	2.70	3.98

Source: see text.

with regard to density seemed of interest — that of routes traveled by more than and less than 5,000 passengers annually. This difference proves significant at the 99 percent confidence level, whereas other sources of variation among the rows (that is, with respect to density) are not significant at the 95 percent confidence level. This finding suggests the split in fare-structure patterns between the trunklines and the locals. Among the trunks' markets and among the locals' markets there is little significant variation of fares with density, but there is a significant difference between the two classes of carriers. The remainder of Table 40 deals with partitioning the sample with respect to distance. Each possible partitioning of columns is checked — over 1,200 versus the balance of the sample, over 800 versus the balance of the sample, and so on. Each of these partitionings proves significant at the 99 percent confidence level, and in each case other sources of variation among the columns are also significant. This suggests that the effective taper of fares with regard to distance operates throughout the range of distances covered in the sample. Because the significance of variation among the cell means of Table 38 has been generally established, these cell means will be used in what follows in the same way as regression coefficients whose significance is established in a multivariate analysis.

The next step is to construct comparable figures for the cost of providing service in markets of varying distance and density. Much of this work was already described in Chapter 3. Table 22 offered an estimate of the variation of average total costs per seat-mile according to distance. It is easy to adjust the information used to produce this table to transform these numbers to costs per passenger-mile. But no hope was given in Chapter 3 for reaching any reliable measure of the way in which costs vary with the volume of traffic on a route, yet that is also needed. It seemed at first that these might be drawn from the station expenses for various sizes of cities reported by the airlines to the Civil Aeronautics Board. Eastern Air Lines' station costs were analyzed, since Eastern serves a wider range of sizes of city than other members of the Big Four. However, a serious difficulty immediately turned up. Carriers spend much more per passenger on advertising and sales-promotion activities in cities which they serve competitively than elsewhere. Competitively served cities are large cities. Hence, the figures seemed to show diseconomies of scale in serving large cities, and there was no practical way of removing the influence of competition. So other tactics were necessary. We know the way in which *some* costs change with the volume of traffic in a market, namely, the direct flying costs. They vary because in thin markets either smaller and higher-cost aircraft must be used, or lower load factors must be accepted, or both. There are unknown economies of scale in operating larger terminals. There are also effective diseconomies of scale in the special sense that competitive pressures automatically require a higher-quality "product" in denser markets. This factor is largely unmeasurable and no doubt a good deal stronger than the sources of scale economies with increasing density just mentioned. Thus, if we estimate the way costs vary with the volume of traffic on a route *solely* because of the higher direct costs on thinner routes, this is likely to be a maximum estimate of variation due to all factors, or at least it seems likely to be nearer a maximum than a minimum estimate. So, on this basis, we proceed to Table 41,

Table 41. Estimated ratio of average costs to average revenue per passenger-mile, by distance of trip and volume of traffic, 1958

Volume of traffic (passengers per year)	Distance (miles)				
	200 and under	201–400	401–800	801–1,200	Over 1,200
Under 1,000	1.49	1.10	1.04	0.89	0.91
1,001–5,000	1.37	1.01	0.86	0.83	0.89
5,001–25,000	1.09	0.78	0.74	0.68	0.77
25,001–100,000	1.06	0.66	0.60	0.57	0.60[a]
Over 100,000	1.05	0.64	0.60	0.57	0.61[a]

[a] The higher ratio for flights over 1,200 miles than for those in the 801–1,200 mile class results from the fact that piston aircraft of transcontinental nonstop capability cost more to operate than those usable for intermediate-range nonstop flights.

Source: see text.

which gives my estimate of the ratio of average costs to average revenues. The figures on costs entering into these ratios are subject to so many uncertainties that it is vital to state just what can and cannot be concluded from the results. It seems safe to say that the taper of fares existing in 1958 seemed to be reasonably well adjusted to the variation of costs on hauls greater than 200 miles in length and about 25,000 passengers annually in volume. Air service on shorter hauls and in thinner markets, however, was yielding lower rates of return and probably suffering implied losses. Nothing precise can be said about the rate of profit from the ratios in Table 41; only their order can be defended confidently. There is probably some significance in the size of the difference between the ratios for very short and very long routes, and possibly some in the difference between the most heavily and most lightly traveled routes.

What of developments since 1958, the year on which these figures are largely based? There has been another fare increase that involved a flat dollar-per-ticket rise, creating a further taper of the fare structure with distance. However, there has also been a substantial increase in coach fares. The volume of coach service offered and used on medium and long hauls is much greater than on short hauls. This has done a good deal to offset the net effect of the last dollar increase. If the introduction of jet aircraft has not changed the taper of costs much, and if these two changes of the fare structure approximately offset each other, then the figures of Table 41 may still be of some significance. This is a sheer guess, however, and only redoing the calculations would reveal the truth.

The general conclusions from these calculations are, unhappily, rather obvious. The trunks do most of their business in markets of more than 200 miles and much in markets with more than 25,000 annual passengers. The changes during the 1950s in the fare structure, differential extensions of coach service, elimination of small stations, and adjustments of the quality of service in different markets, have greatly reduced internal subsidy for the trunks, except for some such as Northeast, Continental, and Eastern that have hung on to markets of primarily local character.[24] The local-service carriers, of course, have many routes that are both too short and too thin to be normally profitable. These airlines have recently been gaining access to some markets large enough to be profitable, with the Board's approval and encouragement. Thus they are taking up the mantle of internal subsidy cast off by the trunks during the past decade. Presumably, when the local-service systems become self-supporting and go off subsidy, they in turn will abandon their weaker points and in other ways go through the same process of equalizing the rate of return on resources in different markets. The Board during the 1950s set great store upon equalizing the opportunities and profit-

[24] *Cf.* Paul W. Cherington, *Airline Price Policy*, pp. 442, 447–448.

ability of the certified trunks through competitive route extensions. In some ways the goal has been achieved, though these extensions were only one of the many factors that brought it about. Indeed, were it not for the shake-down losses the smaller carriers have suffered on new routes in recent years, the success would be more apparent than it has been. Internal subsidy, and the Pandora's box of regulatory difficulties it brought to the Board, should not constrain public policy so much in the future.

RESOURCE ALLOCATION: THE AMOUNT OF SUBSIDY

The air-transport industry has always been extensively subsidized. All the certified passenger carriers have received direct subsidy from the government in the past, though the trunk carriers are now out of this class. Besides, there are many other types of subsidy provided in the form of services or inputs to the industry available at less than cost. Federal airways, navigation aids, and weather information are provided free of charge. Airports, mostly run by agencies of city governments, charge airlines for landing rights and hangar rentals but usually do not cover their total costs. The aircraft manufacturers' research and development expenditures on civil aircraft have been partly a by-product of military expenditures, thus subsidized in a sense. The tax-free status of interest on local-government bonds, which finance airport construction, is another effective subsidy. It is easy to see that the amount of subsidy an industry gets is not at all a simple matter. Even subsidies to the farm sector of the economy probably have some net effect on the aggregate cost or revenue of the air-transport industry. How far do we track elements of subsidy through the tangles and interstices of general equilibrium? [25] Elaborate analysis would surely do no good. The purpose of this section is to give some idea of the size of the major sources of subsidy to the air industry and make some judgment about their effect on the amount of resources employed there. There is no implication intended that the subsidy should necessarily be discarded; its welfare significance will be discussed later.

A first step is to review the record of subsidy paid directly by the United States government. Since 1951, the Civil Aero-

[25] See Carl Kaysen, "On Defining a Subsidy," *Public Policy*, IV (1953), 3–10.

nautics Board has issued a regular estimate of the amount of subsidy paid to all classes of certified carriers. Before that, for the years up to 1949 there exists an estimate based on a method developed by the Federal Coordinator of Transportation and the Board of Investigation and Research.[26] Neither the Board's official estimates nor the earlier approximations can be defended as more than a reasonable guess. Air-mail service is a joint product with passenger or air-freight service or both. For the earlier period, joint costs of mail and other services were three fourths of the industry's total costs. This large fraction must be apportioned to mail and other services on some arbitrary basis, such as relative revenue ton-miles. Where such a condition exists, the only completely logical solution is to indicate a minimum and maximum extent of subsidy, based on allocating joint costs both entirely and not at all to mail service. An estimate which makes a compromise allocation, if useful at all, must be thought of as some kind of average of such limits. Table 42 gives the pre-1949 estimates of subsidy and the official figures for 1952–1958. For comparative purposes they are related to the total revenues of the domestic carriers. (Before 1952 it has been necessary to neglect a difference between fiscal and calendar years.) Subsidy to the domestic carriers (local-service, helicopter, and territorial airlines) now amounts to 2 or 3 percent of the domestic airlines' total revenues. Before World War II, subsidy to the trunks accounted for nearly a quarter of their gross revenues.

What does the government buy with this expenditure on direct subsidy? Fortunately, there exists a careful estimate of the amount of subsidy that can be imputed to service to small points served by a single local-service carrier. The estimate by United Research[27] identifies five types of costs associated with service to a small city: (1) direct operating costs of the airport station; (2) extra general and administrative costs associated with these station costs; (3) landing and take-off costs of stopping the minimum number of flights at the station; (4) general and administrative costs associated with these extra landing and take-

    [26] *Public Aids to Domestic Transportation,* Board of Investigation and Research, H. Doc. 159, 79th Cong., 1st sess. (Washington, 1945).
    [27] *Federal Regulation of the Domestic Air Transport Industry* (Cambridge, Mass., 1959), pp. 56–63 and tables B-26, B-27, B-28. This will be described in detail, since the report has not been widely distributed.

Table 42.   Estimated size of direct subsidy to domestic air carriers[a] in dollar amounts and relative to gross revenues, 1938–1958

Year[b]	Official subsidy (millions of dollars) (1)	Estimated subsidy (millions of dollars) (2)	Subsidy as percentage of gross revenues (3)
1938	—	$ 9.7	22.7
1939	—	11.9	21.3
1940	—	14.5	18.9
1941	—	14.2	14.6
1942	—	16.8	15.5
1943	—	12.5	10.2
1944	—	13.1	8.1
1945	—	14.9	6.9
1946	—	10.3	3.3
1947	—	14.2	3.9
1948	—	30.8	7.1
1952	25.7	—	3.1
1953	32.7	—	3.5
1954	35.3	—	3.4
1955	31.3	—	2.6
1956	31.5	—	2.3
1957	38.5	—	2.5
1958	44.3	—	2.7

[a] Includes trunk, local-service, helicopter, and territorial airlines.
[b] Official subsidy and gross revenue, calendar years; estimated subsidy, 1938–1948, fiscal years.
Source: M. G. Goodrick, "Air Mail Subsidy of Commercial Aviation," *Journal of Air Law and Commerce*, XVI (Summer 1949), 259; Federal Aviation Agency, *Handbook of Aviation Statistics, 1959* (Washington: 1959), p. 84; CAB, *Quarterly Report of Air Carrier Financial Statistics* (various issues).

off costs; and (5) extra flying costs due to the average distance detoured to reach the station on through flights. The second and fourth types were estimated by cross-sectional statistical analysis of the local-service carriers' reported costs. The first was a rough median value from reported station costs. The third reflected prevailing operating costs of the DC-3, the aircraft most commonly used in such service. The fifth was estimated by experimental analysis of the routes of several local-service carriers and takes account of the possibility that elimination of enough marginal stations would allow elimination of whole routes or segments. The total annual saving from abandoning minimum service to a small city was figured to be $40,333. Actually, the saving would be somewhat greater since many small cities receive more than the minimum service, in the form of more flights per day or of more comfortable planes having higher landing and take-off costs. Also lost in abandoning a small city would be the commercial revenue from those passengers who would give up travel by air rather than go to another airport. By an iterative process, the study calculated how many cities would have to be abandoned, starting from the smallest, before the reduction in revenues to the industry from a further abandonment exceeded the reduction of cost. Of the 530 cities served in the United States at the time, it was found that this condition would be fulfilled when the bottom 250 to 280 were dropped, and that the net reduction of subsidy would be between $12.1 million and $12.6 million. Of the rest of the $33.3 million subsidy to the local-service industry, $3.5 million covered a rate of return on investment, and the remaining $17.2 to $17.7 million subsidized service to cities also served by trunks or other local airlines. Since the trunk carriers probably lose money on service at some of these cities, the total cost of subsidizing service by more than one carrier to cities of intermediate size would be $20 to $23 million. These would be the cities lying between 150 or 175 and 250 in the ranking by traffic generated of the 530 cities served.

These estimates seem to be acceptable except for a few minor features. There are some problems, however, in using the conclusions drawn from them. The report is not hostile to subsidy generally nor to the cost of serving the smaller 250 to 280 cities. But it does recommend a reshuffling of routes to eliminate duplicating service at medium-size cities, generally by deleting the trunk airline.[28] This would follow readily in certain cases, where the trunk and the local-service carrier serve a medium-size city in the same direction. Dropping the through service of the trunk then means no significant loss of revenue — only an inconvenience to some travelers of enduring a few intermediate stops before reaching their destination. But what of the case in which one carrier offers service north and south, the other east and west? Then deletion of one carrier means a loss of revenue to the industry generally, since not all travelers will accept a circuitous route involving changes of plane. More important, those travelers

[28] *Ibid.*, pp. v–vi.

who endure a roundabout routing and those who change to other means of travel both suffer some loss of "surplus," just as do those who cannot travel by air to or from a small city that has lost its sole air service. We need further information on demand and substitution elasticities before applying the United Research conclusions to particular cases.[29] In short, the calculations of the United Research report provide a valuable indication of how much transportation is supported by subsidy dollars, but they do not tell very much about where subsidy should first be cut, if the public should insist that cuts be made somewhere.

There is some possibility of measuring the effective subsidy to air transport coming from two other sources. One is the subsidized net losses of municipal airports. The authorities are in general agreement that losses are the rule, whatever the problems of securing comparable accounts for different airports. The outlook of public authorities, at least until the last few years, has been that airports were either not expected to be self-supporting or at best were asked to cover only current costs, not including interest.[30] An estimate for the prewar years 1936–1940 found that all publicly owned airports of the United States covered 62.8 percent of their expenditures for operation and maintenance.[31] A thorough study of twenty-one large airports, using data for the wartime years 1943–1945, included estimates of imputed interest and depreciation charges that allow calculation of (negative) rates of return. Five major airports, generally serving cities of over a million people, were found to earn a rate of return of −4.7 percent; eleven intermediate airports serving cities of 250,000 to 1 million earned −5.3 percent; and five limited-stop airports serving cities of 50,000 to 250,000 returned −5.7 percent.[32]

[29] One bit of *a priori* theorizing may be of some help here. Suppose one knew that a slight increase in the fare charged by a trunk carrier at a particular city would cause many travelers to switch either to a local-service carrier serving the same city or to surface transport. In such a case, eliminating the trunk completely would cause little net loss of consumer satisfaction.

[30] Kent T. Healy, *The Economics of Transportation* (New York, 1940), pp. 128–129; Emory R. Johnson, *Transport Facilities, Service and Policies* (New York, 1947), p. 354; S. E. Veale, *Airliners and Airways of Today* (London, 1947), p. 286.

[31] Richard W. Lindholm, *Public Finance of Air Transportation* (Columbus, 1948), p. 32.

[32] Calculated from L. L. Bollinger, A. Passen, and R. E. McElfresh, *Terminal Airport Financing and Management* (Boston, 1946), chap. 8.

This report also offered an estimate of investment in terminal airports, defined as those whose size is determined mainly by the requirements of transport aircraft. The figure was $775 million, which compares reasonably well with an estimate made by the Civil Aeronautics administrator two years later of $1.5 billion for *all* airports.[33] Still another estimate was given by C. J. Lowen, Civil Aeronautics administrator, before the Senate Appropriations Committee. He placed the capital stock of domestic airports at $4 billion,[34] presumably for 1955. This figure seems impossible to reconcile with the earlier estimate of one and a half billion. Between 1948 and 1955, probably half a billion was spent on airport construction involving matching funds under the Federal Airport Act of 1946.[35] It seems impossible that enough more could have been spent outside of this program to bring the total to $4 billion. Either this figure or the earlier two must be wrong. Unfortunately, the data are too scanty to tell which is the case.

Whichever estimate is taken, it is possible to make a guess about the net loss earned by airport facilities in recent years. Bollinger's work gives acceptable estimates for the relation of annual operating and maintenances expenses to investment for various sizes of airports.[36] Starting from the largest, these range from 1.5 to 2.5 percent. (Because of the extreme capital intensity of the operation and the relatively long life of airport structures, the largest negative rate of return could thus not go beyond −9 percent even with no revenue at all.) The *Municipal Year Book* has presented unadjusted figures for operating revenue and total expenditures for a number of airports,[37] indicating whether depreciation is included in expenditures. Ratios of operating reve-

[33] *Ibid.*, p. 168. Later estimate cited by B. N. Behling, *Subsidies to Transportation,* Public Affairs Bulletin No. 86, Legislative Reference Service, Library of Congress (Washington, 1950), pp. 45–46.

[34] *Department of Commerce and Related Agencies Appropriations, 1957,* hearings on H.R. 10899, U.S. Senate, Committee on Appropriations, Subcommittee, 84th Cong., 2nd sess. (Washington, 1956), p. 171.

[35] Federal funds appropriated under the program in the years 1947–1955 which were to be matched by local expenditures came to $228,721,154; presumably they were not all spent during the period in question. See Civil Aeronautics Administration, *Statistical Handbook of Aviation, 1956* (Washington, 1956), p. 10.

[36] Bollinger, p. 133.

[37] *The Municipal Year Book, 1958,* International City Managers' Association (Chicago, 1958), table 16, pp. 352–356.

nues to expenditures were calculated for those airports shown as not including depreciation among expenditures. For seventeen cities over 100,000 the ratio was 0.89; for twenty smaller cities sampled at random, it was 0.60. Now, from these ratios the following very crude procedure can be developed. Using available statistics on the number of airports of various sizes, a weighted average ratio of revenues to current expenditures can be set at 0.85. On what investment base was this loss taken, and what was the implied total rate of return? The various estimates of capital invested in airports, reviewed above, would set limits of $2–$2.5 billion on airports used by commercial aviation in the mid-1950's. Total operating costs would have been $40–$50 million, and with imputed depreciation and interest costs taken into account the aggregate negative rate of return would have been −7.5 percent or, in absolute terms, about $150 million. Only part of this can be viewed as subsidy to commercial aviation, but the total is impressive when compared either to the industry's $1 billion in gross revenues or its $30–$40 million of direct subsidy.

The federal airway system is also a measurable cost of air transportation that is not borne by the industry. The Department of Commerce has regularly sought a system of taxes on the commercial airlines to cover part of the cost of these facilities; in 1953 it issued an extensive report estimating their operating cost and suggesting various ways of splitting the joint costs among military, commercial, and private users and of extracting the calculated rightful share from the airlines.[38] It placed the total cost of the airways for fiscal 1952, including amortization and interest, at $75,692,993, and urged that the airlines should pay between $28,500,000 and $36,600,000 of this depending on whether the allocation was on a straight basis of use or whether value-of-service considerations were slipped in by taking into account the weight of aircraft. It would not be too difficult to construct roughly comparable figures for other years, but there is an excellent reason for not doing so. It is true that costs of the airway system are somewhat variable with the amount of use they get, so that the air traveler is not paying for at least this portion of the marginal cost of his journey. However, the Department of

[38] U.S. Department of Commerce, Civil Aeronautics Authority, *A Program of Charges for the Use of the Federal Airways System* (Washington, 1953).

Commerce report specifically rejects any notion of charging users directly for the airway system, for the obvious reason that it would raise the cost of safe air operations and create an economic incentive for socially undesirable, risky operations.[39] If this is the case, there is no compelling reason why civil aviation should be charged for this service at all. Even the argument that "every tub should stand on its own bottom," put forth to defend average-cost pricing against marginal-cost pricing, is not particularly relevant since the system has to be maintained for military aviation in any case.

Still, without trying to pass judgment on subsidy to air carriers, it is worth noting the size of the total of essential costs that are not borne by the carriers. Suppose that in the late 1950s the airline industry had suddenly been forced to do without direct subsidy and pay the fully allocated costs of its own airports and airways. Making some very crude calculations that assume, among other things, a demand elasticity equal to unity, when the industry had readjusted to earn normal profits, its output in ton-miles would have dropped from 15 to 20 percent and the number of cities served from over 500 to between 100 and 150. This does not take into account several obscure and incidental forms of subsidy mentioned above.

THE PRODUCT AND ITS COST

It was suggested above that the historical normality of profits in air transport could cloak other deficiencies in the industry's performance. One was an economically inappropriate distribution of service among various types (and sizes) of city-pair markets. This has been shown to be the case. Another possible deficiency lies in the fact that "costs" in an industry like air transport are highly variable, along with the quality and nature of the product. When the industry is highly concentrated and the price is "sticky" in money terms, it is possible that adjustments within the industry might yield a variety of undesirable conditions — firms operating at an inefficiently small scale, firms persisting despite conspicuous internal inefficiency, inappropriately high or low quality of product, an inappropriately expanded or constricted range of varieties of the product.

[39] *Ibid.*, pp. 62–63.

The study of cost characteristics of the airlines in Part One showed that there are no longer significant problems of firms of inefficiently small size. This was not always true, but in recent years all of the certified trunks have reached a scale of operations which suggests that most disadvantages in higher costs facing the smaller carriers are not due to size alone. A carrier operating in a limited number of city-pair markets could surely achieve minimum average costs at a much smaller total level of operations than the certified airlines could. The local-service carriers have substantially higher costs than the trunks and are much smaller. As has been shown, their disadvantages reflect mostly the types of aircraft they operate, the short distances they fly, and the short length of the average passenger's journey. Referring to Table 18 above,[40] the only category of their costs which seemed to be higher due to outright small scale was "general and administrative." This does not account for much of the difference between the trunks and the local airlines.

In managerial efficiency, the airlines do not seem to score very highly. Most observers agree that up to the late 1940s the industry had felt little pressure to pursue internal efficiency.[41] Since then the situation has improved greatly, but still airlines have survived over long periods of time with what seem to be grossly ineffective managements. TWA and its troubles with the whims and fancies of its principal stockholder, Howard Hughes, come immediately to mind. The Civil Aeronautics Board once set forth a lengthy opinion excoriating his business decisions for the carrier but was unable to do anything about them;[42] business periodicals have discussed his activities at great length.[43] Similarly, there is a good deal of evidence that the chronic difficulties of Capital Airlines were partly the fault of its management, and one trade publication which normally blames the Board for nearly everything attacked the carrier's executives for failing to get it

[40] See p. 58.
[41] See *Air-line Industry Investigation,* hearings pursuant to S. Res. 50, U.S. Senate, Committee on Interstate and Foreign Commerce, 81st Cong., 1st sess. (Washington, 1949), p. 121.
[42] Trans World Airlines, Inc., Further Control by Hughes Tool Company, Docket No. 2796, 12 CAB 192, pp. 198–214 (1950). The carrier has now brought suit against Hughes for some of these abuses.
[43] For example, Charles J. V. Murphy and T. A. Wise, "The Problem of Howard Hughes," *Fortune,* LIX (Jan. 1959), 79–82, 160–171.

off the road to bankruptcy.[44] Finally, it is not certain that the trunk industry has disposed entirely of certain kinds of inefficiency. Suboptimization seems to be common within firms, particularly in the form of minimizing maintenance costs at the expense of optimizing the firm's general position.[45] The extent of the inadequacy of the airlines' performance due to inefficiency is impossible to measure. But there is no denying that this is one way in which regulation by the Civil Aeronautics Board extracts its cost. The Board's policy of no-entry implies a policy of no-exit to the extent that the Board will act to avoid an embarrassing shrinkage in the total number of firms. The significance given to the individual firm by the certificate of public convenience and necessity and the profit umbrella held by the Board do not encourage maximum efficiency.

Other features of the regulatory pattern also raise the costs of the industry. The system of certificates of convenience and necessity slows the periodic redrawing of a carrier's system of routes implied by changes in the cost characteristics of successive aircraft. When carriers are not free to invade markets where their current equipment would be efficient, and are therefore reluctant to desert markets for which they are certified but ill equipped, they are driven to inefficient operations. These take the form of owning small numbers of many kinds of planes or of using planes on a route that are less suited than other types available.

What of the quality and variety of the product produced by the industry? The new aircraft introduced in the last two decades by the domestic carriers have represented enormous gains in terms of lower costs, greater safety, comfort, and speed. However, it is not so sure that every new type of plane introduced has been a socially desirable investment, or that the direction in which the airlines' demands have pushed the efforts of aircraft

[44] *Airlift,* XXIII (May 1960), 33, spoke of Capital's "faction-ridden top management and directorship" and found that "control of the airline's destiny has slipped away from a management too widely split to direct it in the first place." In an effort to stay the hand of fate, Capital had earlier hired Lippincott and Margulies, a firm of corporate-identity specialists. They reported that the carrier had no corporate image and advised it to spell its name with capital letters. See *Airlift,* XXIII (March 1960), 26.

[45] R. J. McWilliams, "Airline Planned Maintenance," *Canadian Aeronautical Journal,* IV (Sept. 1958), 217–223, and his "Operations Research — Some Airline Applications," *Canadian Aeronautical Journal,* V (Nov. 1959), 369–374.

manufacturers has always been the best one. The last generation of piston-engine planes, using turbo-compound engines, came into use in the mid-1950s. These planes permitted nonstop transcontinental flights and were slightly faster than their predecessors. They were also noisier and more expensive to operate. Yet, because of the dominance of the largest carriers in the transcontinental markets and a route structure which also places them in competition with other carriers in shorter-haul markets, these planes were adopted throughout the industry. It cannot be proved that this was wrong, but only that the decision was definitely influenced by elements of the oligopolistic structure of the industry.

Also, consider the sorts of new aircraft developed in recent years, especially in the United States. There have been charges that if developmental efforts on long-range turboprop planes had been pressed in recent years, they could have been produced to operate at lower cost than the pure jets and with only a little sacrifice in passenger comfort or speed.[46] Though military research has been the overwhelming determinant of civil aircraft development, some room remains for the nature of demand voiced by the airlines. Aircraft might have developed differently had not market structure and regulatory policy encouraged product rivalry and suppressed price rivalry and, for a long time, protected monopoly profits and prevented entry in long-haul markets.[47] "Price rivalry" here is distinguished from the theoretical model of the adjustment of the single price in a competitive market. If the carriers did not recognize interdependence and if the Board did not discourage price cutting, the traveler in a large city-pair market would tend to have a greater choice of services. He would not have to choose only between high-priced first-class service and air-coach service (the same, with less leg room and no martini). He would also have the option of cheaper service in any older planes that could cover their variable cost or possibly in less speedy but lower-cost new planes. There are no data to tell us what mixture of travel services would be bought in a market without restrictions on entry and on price and product

[46] Lord Douglas of Kirtleside, "The Economics of Speed," *Journal of the Institute of Transport,* XXVI (May 1957), 115–131.

[47] Peter G. Masefield, "Anyone Want the 'Economy' Transport?" *Airlift,* XXIII (July 1959), 29.

rivalry. *Possibly* the only profitable services would be the same as those now offered. Perhaps such a large portion of the public will pay more for the fastest possible air journey that no significant amount of service in last year's airplane or the "economy transport" would ever be well received. Certainly the certified industry (and the Board) is less vulnerable to these criticisms now than just after World War II, when the war of attrition was being fought with the nonskeds. Coach service has developed extensively, low-priced night service is available in some places, and there are experiments with low-cost no-reservation service. But these developments have come in spite of many features of the industry's structure and many attitudes of the Board. Furthermore, what such an industry gives it can take away as well: witness the 1960 increase in coach fares. In summary, the industry has offered the traveler an insufficient variety of services. It has possibly caused an inappropriate mix of transport aircraft to be produced. And it has probably extracted too much from the traveling public in rapid depreciation to finance at times an inefficiently rapid (or inefficiently extensive) replacement of older aircraft. Boeing, Douglas, and Lockheed, the major American aircraft manufacturers, have produced a new design as often as a profitable volume of sales seemed likely, which is appropriate. At least in the 1950s, their efforts were biased toward serving the largest single market, luxury transcontinental service. Nothing has changed to guarantee the avoidance of this bias or others in the future.

There is a widely prevalent view in the airline industry that oligopoly produces a less appropriate variety of products than pure monopoly would. This view was developed extensively in the 1949 study by Gill and Bates[48] and is periodically trotted out be-

[48] F. W. Gill and G. L. Bates, *Airline Competition,* chap. 3 and pp. 248, 260, 491. This book is a very useful compilation of patterns of competitive adjustment of price and product, but its standards of welfare evaluation are unacceptable. What it basically did was to take a large sample of competitive markets — large and small, interrelated and unrelated. In these it looked for a few arbitrarily chosen manifestations of competitive service improvement, mainly the use of better aircraft and the offering of more departure times. These it found in something less than half of the markets studied, from which it concluded that competition was somewhat less than half-desirable. It gave either no recognition or inadequate recognition to the role of competition in achieving an appropriate total volume of service, the general-equilibrium interrelation of

fore the Board.[49] To take the main example offered, carriers actively fighting for shares of a competitive market will often schedule identical departure times at the most popular hours, such as 9 A.M., noon, and 4 P.M. The argument is that these duplicating schedules, except for the extra seats offered, provide no improvement in service yet incur a higher total cost. Indeed, a good deal of energy in the air-transport literature has gone into proving that the total cost of a monopolized service would be less than the sum of the costs incurred by a set of competing airlines. These arguments are economically unacceptable. Scheduled departure times that cluster at certain hours are not inefficient unless travelers' preferred departure times are evenly distributed through the day. There is no way to prove that the distribution of flight times in an oligopolistic city-pair market will be ideal, or that it will not. The analytics of the situation would take many pages to explain, but there seems to be no likely set of assumptions under which oligopolistic firms in open rivalry would schedule a given number of flights at inappropriate hours. On the other hand, with the oligopolists' mutual interdependence fully recognized, inappropriate departure hours become quite likely, as does an economically insufficient volume of service. Thus, theory suggests that any inefficiencies of scheduling in an oligopolistic market probably result from too little rather than too much rivalry. In any case, a recent and highly competent report has suggested that inappropriate scheduling of flights is not a significant problem of performance in the competitive airline markets.[50]

The argument that the higher aggregate costs of service by a competitive industry render monopoly preferable would be beneath notice, if we were dealing with an unregulated industry producing a homogeneous product in a single market. However, when an industry's conduct involves adjustment of many dimensions of price and quantity in many markets, the logic of con-

---

markets (for instance, adding competition to a large market may rightfully deteriorate service to a small intermediate city), the impact of then-existing subsidy on the industry's conduct, and a host of other things.

[49] For example, United Air Lines, Inc., Exhibit No. U–172, New York–San Francisco Nonstop Case, Docket No. 9214, p. 18.

[50] United Research, *Federal Regulation of the Domestic Air Transport Industry*, p. 43.

strained optimums[51] tells us that we can never be certain that a slight move toward the competitive norm in one of these dimensions will produce a net gain in welfare after appropriate adjustments occur in all the related dimensions. To put it very crudely, it is logically possible that, though many sellers are preferable to one seller, one may be preferable to several. With the airlines recognizing mutual dependence and the Board maintaining a high margin of price over marginal cost in a certain market, is it a good thing to have several oligopolists flood the market with schedules and raise the quality of the service until marginal cost rises to fixed price? There is no magic word that will make such doubts disappear, and only an enormous investigation would still them entirely. But the evidence of the stimulus that rivalry gives to the improvement of service in every way leaves little doubt that a regulated airline oligopoly, subject to many disequilibriums, produces a more socially efficient performance than would a more monopolistic industry.[52]

INNOVATION, RESEARCH, AND PROMOTION

The final traits of market performance to be evaluated are the rates of innovation, research activity, and sales promotion and advertising. This is territory in which the economics profession has a bad record. There is something of a running debate between those who prefer a high concentration of sellers for its performance in innovation and research and those who prefer competition for its efficiency in resource allocation. Usually neither side is very precise about what sort of market structures it prefers in particular circumstances, or indeed what it means by the basic terms of the argument. Certainly no work has gone into trying to state some of the hypotheses at issue clearly and test them carefully and dispassionately.[53] There is almost no reputable study on the problem of evaluating in absolute terms the social efficiency of a particular industry's rate of innovation and research. For in-

---

[51] See R. G. Lipsey and K. Lancaster, "The General Theory of the Second Best," *Review of Economic Studies,* XXIV (1956–57), 11–32.

[52] This is the conclusion of United Research (p. 41) and of many individuals who have studied the industry.

[53] One of the few serious efforts, which nonetheless contains basic flaws, is A. Phillips, "Concentration, Scale, and Technological Change in Selected Manufacturing Industries 1899–1939," *Journal of Industrial Economics,* IV (June 1956), 179–193.

stance, one writer has tried to show that the cotton-textile industry had an inefficiently low rate of research and development because it did not develop any of the artificial fibers. By the same reasoning, Henry Ford becomes hopelessly backward for not inventing the airplane. To avoid similar pitfalls, the present study can do little more than try to be more careful about what it attempts to prove.

It makes little sense to think of research and development in an industry like air transport in the same way as one would of, say, the chemical industry. Much of the research that produces a better airplane ride necessarily goes on in the aircraft industry. The role of the airlines in this process seems to lie mainly in providing data on existing operations and evaluations of proposals from the manufacturers. Research and innovation within the airline industry itself relates to the combining of airplanes and other inputs to provide a more efficient transportation service. Today, some improvements of this type come through expensive and risky exploratory ventures. An example would be American Airlines' elaborate electronic reservations system, to come into use in 1962, which would link all of American's ticket offices and make canceled space on flights available for resale within seconds. The annual cost of its operation is estimated to be $5 million, and a substantial investment must have gone into its development.[54]

The restraint on many innovations in a service industry like air transport comes, however, not from the great investment cost but from unwillingness to take commercial risks. It was a local-service carrier, Allegheny, that first put into effect a low-fare service of commuter flights requiring no reservations.[55] (Eastern is currently experimenting with a similar service.) This would seem to be an innovation in just as real a sense as American's system. Both involve the firm in an activity that may yield either gains or losses. The only distinction is whether the innovation is technical or marketing.

The hypothesis I shall argue is that large carriers, historically the more profitable, contribute most of the technical innovations, while small carriers (or large ones suffering from an unsatisfac-

<hr>

[54] *Airlift,* XXIII (Dec. 1959), 23.
[55] *Aviation Week,* LXXII (Sept. 14, 1959), 48; *Airlift,* XXIII (Jan. 1960), 46.

tory market situation) generally provide the marketing innovations. The first part is the easier to document. The large trunks have always retained relatively large engineering staffs, both to work on internal problems and to cooperate with manufacturers on new aircraft. The Board mentioned in an early case that "it is not an uncommon policy of the smaller carriers to obtain from the larger companies the findings and benefits of their research results." [56] Marketing innovations, on the other hand, cannot be measured and one can only report impressions from the record of the industry's conduct over a period of years. My impression[57] is that marketing innovations come predominantly from disadvantaged airlines, often the smaller ones.[58] There is nothing mysterious about this. Small carriers — and some not so small — have always suffered disadvantages that kept their profitability below that of the industry's giants. A disadvantage in equipment or market shares has tended to be self-perpetuating, and such carriers often find themselves in a situation with little more to lose. Innovation, for better or worse, is born of desperation.[59] Marketing innovations associated with the Big Four trunks relate largely to the use of new types of aircraft in services for which they had not previously been used. This reflects the financial ability of these carriers to procure new planes rather than an outstanding willingness on their part to take commercial risks. There is no doubt that if one were to set the structure of the air industry solely with regard to maximizing the flow of technical and marketing innovations, the industry would be an "off-balance" one, consisting of a motley group of large and small airlines of varying profitability.

Another significant trait of market performance, and one equally hard for the economist to measure and evaluate, is expenditures on advertising and sales promotion. Again, the problem is a lack of objective standards. The evaluation of market performance, except in regard to the technical efficiency of firms,

[56] United Air Lines Transport Corporation — Acquisition of Western Air Express Corporation, Docket No. 270, 1 CAA 739, p. 743 (1940).

[57] See Chapter 14.

[58] The local-service industry seems to bear out this generalization. See *Permanent Certificates for Local Service Air Carriers,* hearings on S. 651, U.S. Senate, Committee on Interstate and Foreign Commerce, Subcommittee, 84th Cong., 1st sess. (Washington, 1955), p. 209.

[59] Cherington's study contains many examples; see pp. 190, 203, 211–212.

rests on the notion that the allocation of scarce resources should reflect the preferences of consumers among available goods and services. If consumers' tastes can be swayed by the blandishments of advertisers, there is no firm place to stand in evaluating market performance. By contrast, advertising which conveys objective information about the product improves the knowledge underlying consumers' choices.

There are no serious problems with the advertising and selling outlays of the domestic passenger airlines. The great bulk of advertising is in newspapers and contains objective information about schedules of flights, equipment used, classes and prices of service available, and the like.[60] Only the largest carriers do any significant amount of "institutional" advertising. Expenditures on advertising and publicity by the domestic carriers run between 3 and 6 percent of their passenger revenues. They do not vary significantly with the size of the carrier; the only important exception is that, over the years, airlines with large amounts of resort traffic seem to spend relatively more on promotion.[61] By comparison, advertising and promotion expenditures by the international carriers are much higher. However, advertising expenditures reported by all corporations in the Treasury's *Statistics of Income* run a little over 1 percent of gross receipts, and only in such industries as cigarettes is the percentage much higher than in air transport.

[60] *Ibid.*, pp. 16–18.

[61] *American Aviation*, XVIII (Aug. 2, 1954), 24; Eric Bramley, "Advertising Costs 'Big Four' Up to 70¢ per Passenger," *American Aviation*, XXI (July 15, 1957), 69.

18 Performance, Structure, and the Goals of Regulation

The record of market performance and the pattern of market structure have been presented. We may now ask how performance is determined by structural factors, both the economic elements of market structure and the controls of the Civil Aeronautics Board. Consider these particular features of performance: approximately normal profits; some maldistribution of resources among city-pair markets (serious in the past, now substantially improved); firms of efficient size (also a recent achievement); a somewhat limited range of classes of service offered; costs that are affected by such undesirable factors as the survival of inefficient firms and "uneconomic" types of product rivalry; rigid prices that sometimes change perversely; reasonable selling costs; and reasonable rates of technological and marketing innovation. On the whole, the airlines' record is not bad if compared with unregulated industries of similar seller concentration in the American economy, and it is definitely good by comparison with many consumer-goods industries.

THE IMPACT OF STRUCTURE

Seller concentration, usually a key determinant of an industry's performance, here plays a lesser role because it is an effect of other environmental factors. Demand characteristics and the condition of entry (along with the cost characteristics that underlie it) seem more important. The traits of the demand for air transport rule out product differentiation, a fecund source of barriers to entry in other industries. They also have something to do with the minimum efficient scale of operation in a given city-pair market and thereby determine the maximum number of carriers likely to be found there. The efficiencies of marketing a variety of daily flight times, plus the economies of fully utilizing a carrier's planes and spreading overhead items, create moderate barriers to the entry of new firms into city-pair markets. On the other hand, cost conditions facilitate exit from a particular city-pair.

This, plus the ease of entry by an established carrier, makes competition workable in these markets despite the necessarily high seller concentration. Now, contrary to first impressions, the Civil Aeronautics Board's absolute control of entry has not entirely upset the influence of these traits. Some city-pair markets have been exploited by monopoly carriers and by tight oligopolies now and then. But over the history of the Board, entrenched carriers have seldom been free from the fear that a route case would unleash new competition; the legal possibility of entry seems to have kept its economic ease effective. The national market for air transportation is really the sum of a great number of city-pair markets; so the implication of demand and entry conditions at the national level is much the same. Again, even with regulation that has been implacably hostile to direct forms of entry, the moderate ease of entry to the industry has been responsible in part for the existence at all times of potential entrants. In the past decade these have been the nonskeds or supplemental carriers. The local-service carriers are now taking somewhat the same role, and there is talk of a new layer of local airlines.

These features of demand and entry have some impact on the aggregate level of profit and, lately, a strong effect on the reallocation of resources to even out the rates of return earned in different city-pair markets. These facts have also influenced the relatively moderate amount of interdependence recognized in many city-pair markets and have motivated various forms of seller rivalry and marketing innovation. Though many advantages of easy entry have been preserved, the Board's absolute ban on full-fledged entry has extracted a cost. The restricted choice of classes of service and cost-increasing phenomena, such as the general decline of load factors in the first years of the general passenger-fare investigation, probably must be explained this way. The same is true, in part, of the rigidity of fares and the slowness of such changes as the extension (or contraction) of coach service that has taken the place of fare adjustments.

Another group of important structural features is that which has tended to make smaller carriers less profitable than larger ones. This situation has partly rested on pecuniary advantages of size, partly on artificial disadvantages created for the small carriers by the "grandfather" route patterns of 1938. It seems to have had two major results. The direct one, indicated above, was to increase the market rivalry in the industry and multiply the kinds of product rivalry. Indirectly, this condition has been very important through its impact on the Board's policies. In a series of cases in the 1950s, a chance to allow new carriers into the industry was sacrificed, in a sense, to the goal of improving the position of the smaller carriers by putting them into profitable routes. Furthermore, the protection of weaker carriers must be one of the mainsprings of the Board's chronic fear that some types of competitive strategies may get out of hand.

Other economic traits of market structure deserve brief mention. All the facts suggest that the rapid growth of demand for air transport has influenced conduct and performance by raising the extent of market rivalry. The carriers' long-term schedules for penetrating new city-pair markets are but one feature of the many which point to their willingness to sacrifice today's profits to tomorrow's greater market share. Since air transport is not a readily differentiable good and is bought primarily by experienced customers, its nonfunctional advertising has been held at a minimum, and crippling barriers to entry have not arisen.

As an independent force, the Board's policies have had a number of effects on market performance. The certification provisions of the Civil Aeronautics Act have certainly increased the stability and quality of service to marginally profitable city-pairs. Taking a purely economic view of performance, this has both good and bad features. Subsidized service has no attraction in the absence of proof of external economies or other indirect social worth. On the other hand, fluctuations in marginal services resulting from the ebb and flow of oligopolistic rivalry in major markets have no particular virtue. The Board's restrictions on the forms of product competition and its methods of evaluating profits have given an enormous boost to the rate of development and adoption of new aircraft. These same restrictions on product and also on price rivalry have been largely responsible for the inflexibility of the price of air transportation and for the possibly inadequate variety of services offered. The control of entry and exit, both in the national market and in city-pair markets, has raised the cost of air transportation through protecting inefficient firms and through maintaining seasonally imbalanced route structures that require firms to own many types of aircraft. Paradoxically, the Board's policies, on the whole, have probably had little effect on the rate of profit earned by the industry; but, without the Civil Aeronautics Act and the Board, these profits would have resulted from quite a different sort of operation. Supporting this view is the lack of clear evidence that the Board's actions have either increased or decreased the recognition of mutual dependence and the achievement of collusion among the carriers. On the one hand, the regulatory setting tolerates a certain amount of common cause among the regulated firms; on the other, during the period of direct subsidy to the trunks the premium was taken off collusion and the highly rivalrous behavioral patterns which resulted are slow in dying out.

How would the traits of the air-transport industry change in the absence of direct public control? Seller concentration in the typical city-pair market would not differ much from what it is now, but seller concentration at the national level would probably be much lower. Giants like the present Big Four would still exist, but they would compete against different, smaller specialist carriers in particular markets. Both large and small carriers would have more homogeneous operations. Route structures of individual carriers would be stable in the short run but nonetheless adaptable to changes in the types of airplanes used and to shifts of demand. The total number of city-pairs served would be reduced as indicated in Chapter 17, although the evolution of aircraft designs might have taken a different course and produced planes more suitable for thin markets, thereby partly offsetting the absence of subsidy. Without regulation, more flexibility and possibly more variety would exist in the range of product and price offered to the traveler.

These conclusions can be adapted to answer a variety of questions about the consequences of any partial change in the scope or substance of aeronautics regulation. For instance, a decade ago the proposal was often made that the trunk carriers merge into a few strong systems to improve their balance and self-sufficiency and to reduce the "costs of competition." [1] Assuming no other changes, this would result in an increase in profit

---

[1] H. D. Koontz, "Domestic Air Line Self-Sufficiency: A Problem of Route Structure," *American Economic Review*, XLII (March 1952), 122–123.

rates earned by the carriers, in the near elimination of effective public control over the price and product policies of the surviving firms (because of an extensive recognition of mutual interdependence), and in unchanged costs to the industry. Assuming that the firms of the rationalized industry were similar in size and profitability, marketing innovations would be reduced to those deemed profitable for the industry as a whole. Sales-promotion expenditures and efforts at product differentiation generally would probably be higher to an undesirable degree. Price flexibility would be less, if possible, than today. The picture in general is quite unattractive.

The effect of lesser changes may also be predicted. For example, relaxing controls over price and product competition without changing the controls over entry would have a variety of effects. On the one hand, effective collusion among the trunks is probably such that the general fare pattern would tend to adjust to yield somewhat higher average fares than now. On the other hand, there would be more variety in the strategies of product rivalry used and more variability of price in particular city-pair markets. The emphasis on new aircraft as a product strategy would be reduced. On balance, the industry might possibly earn a higher aggregate rate of return and also furnish a more flexible and satisfactory variety and quality of product, perhaps at no higher an average fare; it is hard to tell whether any net gain in performance would be involved. To remove restrictions on entry without changing the existing policies on price and product changes (and assuming no subsidy to entrants) would tend to guarantee normal profits in individual city-pair markets and in the industry as a whole. It would insure the ending of unprofitable service by unsubsidized carriers in thin markets. The normal profits, however, would occur at whatever level of fares happened to prevail, with average costs being driven up through excess capacity and real or spurious product differentiation or improvement. If the Board still permitted fare adjustments to yield a normal profit over current levels of cost, both price and cost would rise in successive and possibly rapid stages, depending on the elasticity of supply of aircraft. The whole situation, again, would be highly undesirable.

Throwing open the major city-pair markets to unrestricted

entry by *existing* trunks, however, would be much different. This change would improve the flexibility of the allocation of transport resources among major markets and keep the airlines' route structures in good balance with changes in the cost characteristics of new aircraft. Problems of seasonal imbalance would be substantially corrected. The rising recognition of mutual interdependence among the trunks would be set back sharply unless too many were eliminated from business in the process; this seems unlikely because, in spite of the operating disadvantages of some of the smaller carriers, all could surely survive on rationalized systems. The Board's problems with a rising cost level and the resultant price increases would be no worse than at present, and probably less troublesome for a while. Monopoly service to weak points would not be affected except in transition. The variety and flexibility of service offered in richer markets would improve, and the cost of producing it might well be reduced. Thus, a reform consisting of removing barriers to entry into major city-pair markets by existing certified trunks is the one partial loosening of the Civil Aeronautics Board's restrictions that has a number of points in its favor. To forestall an objection that the industry would immediately raise, there is no reason why it should induce cutthroat competition. At any one time, there are only so many aircraft in the hands of the trunks, and usually these are fully utilized. Such a reform would hardly reduce recognized mutual dependence enough to encourage great investment of capital in new equipment by the present trunks; and without this it is difficult to envision the proliferation of any undesirable forms of competitive conduct.

GOALS OF THE CIVIL AERONAUTICS BOARD

We have seen that the major standing policies of the Civil Aeronautics Board do not coincide with the economist's usual criteria of efficiency. The Board aims at more than a normal amount of resources in the air-transport industry, service in more city-pair markets than can sustain it commercially, and probably a faster rate of development of new aircraft than unrestricted market forces would produce. Any final conclusions about the best policies for air transport must depend on whether one concedes the worth of such objectives. The question is: can the loss of economic welfare so caused be repaid by what these policies achieve?

Let us recall those objectives, stated or implied, of the Board's regulation which lie outside of the usual norms of economic welfare. First, the airlines contribute to the military potential of the nation in a variety of ways. The Board has felt that some of them warrant subsidy and other actions to raise the output of the industry above what commercial considerations would indicate. A second objective is to maintain a regular network of air routes uniting the nation's cities and towns. On heavily traveled segments, private enterprise would do this without any public attention; if meaningful, the objective calls for service which commercial revenues would not support. A third major objective, one which this study has inferred from a great number of Board policies, is to speed the development of transport aircraft. A fourth objective, also implicit, has been to maximize the safety of air travel by maintaining economic stability in the industry. Finally, the Board has two minor aims relating to the sort of service offered by the industry. One is to keep air fares as stable as possible over time. The other, drawn directly from the Civil Aeronautics Act, is to restrict the use of certain types of price discrimination.

It is often said that the airlines' trained personnel constitute an important resource in the case of military emergency, and many of the large transport aircraft are subject to an agreement to cover their immediate transfer to military service. There is no evidence, however, that this defense potential requires more support than market forces would give. If so, this is no argument for departing from a market-determined situation. But the Board has felt at times that specific services require subsidy because of their contribution to defense. The military value of service experience accumulated by the helicopter airlines has been cited to justify their heavy subsidies,[2] and a local-service route was established in Montana and North Dakota at a subsidy cost substantially higher than usual because it served isolated military in-

[2] Chicago Area Service Case, Docket No. 6600 et al., decided June 7, 1956, CCH Av. Law Rep. §21,965.01.

stallations.[3] The Board has also said that air service desired by the military would justify *some* extra subsidy;[4] but there is no experience to tell how this worth for defense purposes is or ought to be evaluated. Thus, subsidy to particular air services has brought substantial returns in aid to the military, but these contributions come in specific cases, and they do not seem to warrant the raising of the aggregate output of the industry above a market-determined level.

The annals of economic history contain example after example of public subsidy to forms of transportation. One justification for such policies is that the gain in national unity through making first-class transportation available to small cities is worth a certain amount of subsidy. A more technical argument would be that there are always a few persons in any small city who would pay much more than the nondiscriminatory market price for air travel; subsidy of minimum service is justified by the "surplus" which accrues to them but which cannot be collected directly. This argument cannot apply to large cities, with good alternate means of transportation. Neither the economic argument nor the noneconomic one can be tested formally. One might doubt that such a case carries much weight in an advanced country like the United States, where there is no lack of national unity or no need to subsidize transportation in developing new regions. But there is no way of disposing of it entirely. Certainly, if public sentiment, expressed by Congress, supports it, there is not much ground for counterargument. The Civil Aeronautics Board has always favored the extension of air service to the largest possible number of cities. When the trunks were receiving direct subsidy, this was done by trying to force the airlines to use the profits from lucrative routes to subsidize money-losing routes. With the withdrawal of subsidy it was no longer to the carriers' interest to do this. The Board gave tacit approval to their abandoning of this arrangement and started to spread air service by extending the local-service carriers. This step, which seemed responsive to the will of Congress, shunted the burden of subsidy from the

[3] Montana Local Service Case, Docket No. 6293 et al., decided July 2, 1959, CCH Av. Law Rep. §22,290.01.

[4] The City of Portsmouth Service Investigation, Docket No. 7887 et al., decided Nov. 9, 1956, CCH Av. Law Rep. §21,997.02.

"internal subsidy" reaped by overcharging passengers on dense routes to a straightforward subsidy from the government covering the losses of the local airlines. The newer arrangement is strongly preferable, if this sort of subsidy is desired at all. First, there is no reason why impoverished grandmothers flying from New York to Los Angeles should be the ones to subsidize well-off businessmen traveling between small towns. Second, enforcing internal subsidy required the Board to use many auxiliary restrictions, such as blockading entry to rich markets, that take a heavy toll in economic efficiency.

A third objective of the Board's policies that lies outside the normal criteria of economic welfare is to speed the development of new aircraft. This is not very explicit in the Civil Aeronautics Act or in the Board's policy pronouncements, but it is strongly implied by the general drift of the Board's decisions as well as by the results of its regulations curtailing the available means of price and product competition. Now, the rate of development of civil aircraft is no doubt a matter of concern to the American public. In the late 1940s the British embarked on a massive program of subsidization of turbine-powered aircraft. With the coming of the Comet I, it was clear that the United States was behind, and numerous congressional hearings were held to consider subsidization of a turbine prototype. There was much support for such a move, even though nothing substantial resulted because the aircraft industry was of several minds and the only legislation, the Prototype Testing Act of 1950, was never implemented.[5] Again, in the last few years there has been much alarm that the British or the Russians would be the first to produce a supersonic commercial transport, to the enduring injury of American dignity. Once again, no serious action has been taken, but the existence of popular concern is undeniable. The public would prefer the rate of development of new aircraft to be, if anything, faster than at present; and the present rate is faster than an unregulated industry would generate. So the Board's policies cannot be rejected out of hand. As with service to unprofitable points, it is a case of hard-to-measure costs and intangible benefits.

[5] The President's Air Coordinating Committee, *Civil Air Policy* (Washington, 1954), pp. 62–63.

It is hard to tell how much the influence of the Board's economic policies has to do with the promotion of safety in air commerce, the fourth major special objective. The only extensive discussion of this came during the debates over treatment of the irregular carriers in the 1940s. Whether or not these carriers cut corners on safety was widely argued, but the evidence is not conclusive. Furthermore, no evidence has turned up in the course of this study which shows that those policies which reduce the turnover of firms in the industry make a substantial contribution to safety. On the one hand, one can imagine a licensing system for air carriers that would require them to meet minimum safety standards independent of any economic regulation. Indeed, the division of labor between the Civil Aeronautics Board and the Federal Aviation Agency operates on that principle now. However, it is not possible to refute the assertion that regulating turnover is a safety measure.

There remain two minor objectives more directly economic in their significance. One is the Board's preference for stable air fares. This was officially adopted with the dismissal of the first general fare investigation and has been restated at various times. Whether or not fares should be stable in a regulated industry has often been debated but never settled. If we count on changes in relative prices to allocate resources properly throughout the economy, there is an *a priori* case against the rigidity of any price. On the other hand, regulation that aims at normal profits implies a movement of prices counter to the business cycle and counter to most other prices in the economy. Meaningless shifts of relative prices would occur — shifts that might draw too many resources into the regulated industry in time of prosperity only to force the regulatory authority to raise prices to guarantee a normal reward in time of recession.[6] This is not better than rigid prices, and probably is worse. If regulation is necessary on other grounds, the best the regulatory authority can do, when it is bent on setting *some* prices subject to normal constitutional guarantees, is to maintain rigid prices or, if possible, to encourage promotional discounts only in recession. But if the achieving of rigid prices is advanced as an argument against an unregulated

[6] For discussion, see Ben W. Lewis, "State Regulation in Depression and War," *American Economic Review*, XXXVI (May 1946), 384–404.

status, then it has no economic standing. As we saw in Chapter 7, one regulatory goal of the Civil Aeronautics Act has been to restrict the amount of discrimination in the air-transport industry. However, most of the matters the Board has worried about are actually not forms of discrimination. Some price differences, such as special group fares, reflect cost differences. Only a few pricing practices of the airlines are discriminatory in the classical sense; one of these is the family fare, which the Board has regularly, if grudgingly, allowed. Would price or service discrimination be a major problem in an unregulated air industry? Certainly not in general, for discrimination is possible only when two conditions are satisfied: monopoly (or collusion achieving the same result) and the ability of the seller to distinguish among buyers and prevent resale of the product. Even in thin markets where monopoly service would be normal, distinguishing among persons and preventing resale would not usually be possible. The opportunities for discrimination among persons that were exploited by rail freight services before the Interstate Commerce Act would not be open to the airlines in the absence of regulation.

Thus, none of the Board's special objectives seems very compelling. However, not all of them can be dismissed as worthless, and so we shall consider the workability of the present administrative arrangements — the efficiency of the Board's historic pursuit of its own goals, the current effectiveness of its policies, and the possibility of improvement through minor changes.

PERFORMANCE OF THE CIVIL AERONAUTICS BOARD

According to the terms of the Civil Aeronautics Act, how efficient has been the pattern of regulatory actions imposed by the Board? It has been reasonably faithful to the broad goals set for it, and even in its detailed policies its performance compares very favorably with the other major regulatory commissions. It has largely avoided the trap of outright protectionism of the industry it regulates. It has handled well many of the problems of regulating a competitive industry, such as the need for manipulating the incentives rather than directly molding conduct and performance. Many other accomplishments have been mentioned above and should be recalled through the critique that follows.

Still, a good deal has been wrong, and the situation is not clearly improving.

The difficulties of the past seem to come from three major sources. One is the restrictions of the political environment in which the Board works. Whether one sees in them the vices of government-by-pressure-group or the virtues of continuous voicing of the popular will, they are an ingrained feature of regulation by any independent commission. The political equilibrium surrounding the Board was analyzed in Chapter 12 and will not be considered further here. A second general problem for the Board is appropriate timing for its policies. It has too often steered into the future while watching the rear-view mirror. A third problem, somewhat related to the second, is that the Board has not been able to foresee all the consequences of its decisions and has not secured the information necessary to clear its vision.

Taking the second of these problems, the Board has not only had to decide important questions of the future from a dated record of the past; it has also been particularly unlucky with accidents of timing. At about the time of the Korean War, the Board was holding back on authorizations of new point-to-point competition and declining to hold a general investigation of standards for setting fares. The prosperity of the early 1950s was an ideal time for extensions of competition. But it was only in the mid-1950s that these were actually granted, and the resulting shake-down losses from the new situation coincided with the severe 1957–58 recession and a period of heavy capital outlays for new equipment. Facing this rather accidental crisis of low profits and fast-rising capacity, the Board set out to find a general standard for fixing fares and profits. A worse time could hardly have been imagined, and the decision showed the scars of its environment.

Apart from the problem of forecasting the future, the Board has not been able to sense important changes in the conduct or structure of the industry and adjust its policies accordingly. In part this resulted from personnel conditions on the Board, which had a rapid turnover of members not fully trained to deal with the economic complexities of the industry. In part it resulted from the failure of the Board to secure from Congress appropriations that would give it a staff large enough to work beyond the press of current problems.

The best general illustration of these troubles is the Board's failure to anticipate the great changes in the industry's conduct that followed when the trunks went off direct subsidy. Under subsidy it was logical that the airlines would have little incentive to adjust fares upward with rising costs, that they would be willing to maintain good service over particular route segments on which revenues were not covering costs, and that cutthroat rivalry for shares of highly profitable markets might be a very real problem. It was also logical for the Board to be chary about admitting new firms to the industry. By the late 1940s, despite many short-run problems, the Board's policies had become rather well adjusted to this situation. With direct subsidy ended, and neither the Board nor the carriers anticipating its return, the incentives before the trunkline carriers changed completely. Unprofitable services were sloughed off or allowed to deteriorate. The carriers' interest in higher fares took a sharp upturn. The problem of excess competition, such as it was, threatened only where one carrier saw a good chance of driving a rival out of business; otherwise, there was enough, often more than enough, recognition of mutual interdependence to take care of the problem. A major rationale for restricted entry evaporated. The problem of weak and strong carriers, which could be ignored while subsidy existed, immediately became critical; of the several possible solutions to it, the Board picked the one (route extensions) most cumbersome administratively and most likely to fail in the short run. One might say that by the end of the 1950s the Board was adjusting to this new situation. From efforts in the early 1950s to keep the quality of air service down and the price up, it had gone some distance toward reversing the emphasis. Still, a lag of ten years is not very admirable.

There are many other examples of dim vision. The Board was handed an extremely inefficient network of airline routes by the "grandfather" certifications. Yet there has never been any comprehensive consideration of how these might either be rationalized or made sufficiently flexible to adapt to changing airplane technology or changing patterns of demand. There have been piecemeal efforts at correction through route extensions and mergers, but the former have been haphazard and the latter have often had undesirable side-effects. The weak record in the regulation of air fares and the doubtful general standard finally adopted have already been discussed. Lacking the confidence to force the industry to extend special services or to experiment with promotional fares, the Board has rendered important decisions in the industry's favor, announcing that it expected these reforms in return; yet it has not used any leverage to enforce its requests or obtained any impressive results. (One example is the *Transcontinental Coach-Type Service* case, which asked for prompt and extensive entry of the trunks into air-coach service; the 1958 fare-increase decision urged more experimentation with promotional fares, but few appeared before 1961.) The Board has understood some of the consequences of an increasing recognition of mutual interdependence among the carriers, such as the collusive increases of costs and reductions of load factors during the early phases of the second general fare investigation. Yet in the decision to that same case it accepted the carriers' arguments that there was *not enough* recognition of mutual dependence. The Board has not kept continuously in mind the sources of marketing innovation. Without the occasional entry of new firms, these come largely from small, aspiring, and "imbalanced" carriers. It has often seemed to accept the Air Coordinating Committee's 1954 suggestion that, with the industry reduced to a few giant carriers, "the greater strength resulting from merged operations would actually increase the keenness of competition within the industry." [7] This is refuted by all evidence of conduct within the air-transport industry, as well as by much evidence concerning unregulated industries in the American economy. And if this were not enough, the logic of the quotation implies that reducing the number of firms in an industry renders it more and more competitive until, with only two left, competition reaches its maximum effectiveness; no comment seems necessary. Thus, in the hope of securing more effective competition, the Board has attempted to equalize the size and profitability of the carriers, at the same time preventing the entry of new ones and allowing the normal attrition of existing operators — a combination of policies almost sure to defeat the objective.

[7] *Civil Air Policy,* p. 12.

A similar critique could be leveled at the Board's detailed procedures, though this seems a task better left to a scholar versed in administrative law.[8] For better or worse, the efficiency of the Board's decision making is heavily impaired by the requirements of due process. The Board operates in the same way, and with the same attention to detail, as when it started operations.[9] It has spent enormous amounts of time on route cases, especially in mulling over great mountains of irrelevant evidence on which carrier ought to perform what service, without securing the information it really needs about the cost characteristics of various route structures. Procedures are generally aimed at giving a fair hearing to all carrier parties, and the Board has not faced the fact that this often makes impossible any firm or consistent pursuit of the public interest.

The results of these substantive and procedural inadequacies appear in the weaknesses of the industry's performance mentioned above — unnecessarily high costs and restrictions on the responsiveness of the industry to expressions of consumer choice. Is the situation getting better or worse? Unfortunately, the signs seem to point to continued deterioration. Consider some current trends. The number of trunklines threatens to shrink rapidly to eight or less, partly with the Board's encouragement. The probable consequences have already been seen. With entry to the industry blockaded by the Board's standing policy, but with carriers now and then leaving by merger, the chances for tacit collusion and the resulting payoff rise sharply. The outlook is for more collusive behavior by the carriers, though it may be enlivened at times by attempts to dispatch a vulnerable rival. With blockaded entry a carrier enjoys an enormous reward from seizing any opportunity to eliminate a competitor. It has antitrust immunity plus a guarantee that the rival will not be replaced at least until another

[8] For some relevant discussion, see P. N. Pfeiffer, "Shortening the Record in C.A.B. Proceedings through Elimination of Unnecessary and Hazardous Cross-Examination," *Journal of Air Law and Commerce,* XXII (Summer 1955), 286–297; Louis J. Hector, "Problems of the C.A.B. and the Independent Regulatory Commissions," *Yale Law Journal,* LXIX (May 1960), 931–964; Earl W. Kintner, "The Current Ordeal of the Administrative Process," *Yale Law Journal,* LXIX (May 1960), 965–977; M. H. Bernstein, *Regulating Business by Independent Commission* (Princeton, 1955); E. S. Redford, *Administration of National Economic Controls* (New York, 1952).

[9] United Research, *Federal Regulation of the Domestic Air Transport Industry,* p. 4.

existing carrier can win a route award.[10] The rising barriers to entry from economic sources reinforce this situation, as do the chronic disadvantages of the relatively small carrier with low historic profitability and a structure of weak routes. The Board made a brave effort at removing the weaknesses of the smaller carriers in the route cases, but its success has been incomplete. The Board wanted to preserve the same number of trunks but to equalize their profitability; earning power will probably be equalized, but for a significantly smaller number. Sources of marketing innovation and product rivalry may be drying up because of this trend, as well as because of the shift of the carriers' top managements from ambitious and combative operating men to "business" personnel of more conventional outlook.

Another worsening problem for the Board is reflected in the adequacy-of-service cases. Some of these (Baltimore, Fort Worth) seem to reflect tacit understandings by the airlines to force travelers at the smaller of two nearby cities to use the airport of the larger. Others (Toledo, Flint–Grand Rapids) reflect the decision of a weak carrier to concentrate its limited equipment in competitive markets. Similarly, the complaints of many small cities about their trunk service reflect either this same strategy of weak carriers or the unwillingness of stronger trunks to waste resources on unprofitable or marginally profitable services. All of the cases suggest that the Board is restricting competition in strong markets without benefiting the traveling public at weaker points.

Finally, the Board still employs cumbersome proceedings to pass on particular strategies of price and product adjustment, although it has less and less control over the amount and substance of effective rivalry within the industry. This is the story of changes that have followed the ending of direct subsidy to the trunks. When subsidy was in force, the Board had powerful tools for shaping the quantity and quality of price and product to its own tastes. Its ability to enforce *any* set of tastes or preferences continues to decline, but no adjustment has been made.

[10] Conversely, where entry is easy, predatory and exclusionary conduct is not likely to be either profitable for existing firms or a serious worry for public policy. Paradoxically, the most determined antitrust attack against alleged predatory conduct of recent years was mounted against the A & P grocery chain, which operates in markets of very easy entry. See M. A. Adelman, *A & P: A Study in Price-Cost Behavior and Public Policy* (Cambridge, Mass., 1959).

IMPROVING THE REGULATION OF AIR TRANSPORT

How can the Board increase the efficiency of the pursuit of its present set of objectives? These include, beyond the usual criteria for good market performance, rapid development of new transport aircraft, subsidized service to weaker traffic-generating points, low turnover of carriers to promote safety, and price rigidity. One step is to recognize that the amount of internal subsidy in effect has been dropping sharply and that it always tends to disappear among carriers not receiving direct subsidy. Thus the best strategy, as the United Research report urged, is to continue shifting the trunks out of marginally profitable points, to continue direct subsidy to the local-service carriers, and to drop all policies toward the trunks that are used solely to protect internal subsidy. So far, this is a very helpful suggestion. The Board is already in the process of converting subsidy for the local-service carriers from payment to each of them according to need toward payment of the difference between average or normal costs and commercial revenues.[11] Of the policies affecting the trunks, restriction of entry to city-pair markets no longer protects profits significantly because the typical market has its full quota of authorized carriers. Also, the policy on fares designed to exploit the richer markets has been in large part frustrated by the extension of coach service and outright differences in the quality of first-class service from route to route. Thus it is pointless for the Board to spend much time in deciding whether four or five carriers should be authorized for a given market. Since the number of carriers that can efficiently operate in a given city-pair market is probably falling, this essentially means that there will be no more major route cases unless mergers should continue to eliminate a good deal of point-to-point competition.[12] There is no reason not to allow the carriers more freedom to experiment with changes in the fare structure, classes of service offered, and the like; happily, the Board has been doing so in 1961 and 1962.

One definite implication for the Board's policy is that it should be very cautious about allowing mergers, let alone encouraging them as it periodically does. Mergers always have some attrac-

[11] Order Serial No. E–15696, Local Service Carriers Rate of Return Investigation, Docket No. 8404, Aug. 26, 1960.

[12] For a similar position see the United Research report, p. 43.

tions. They can eliminate a carrier whose route network has never been rationalized. They can bolster a carrier weakened through misjudgments of its management or predation by large competitors. Both of these gains will usually be accompanied by a short-term increase in the quality of service offered the traveling public. However, mergers also have their costs. The Board has recognized that they can reduce point-to-point competition and threaten the rivals of the merged carrier. It is high time that it recognized another effect of mergers: by reducing the total number of trunks and (usually) reducing the imbalance among them, they encourage the slow rise of parallel action by the carriers which is aimed at frustrating the Board's regulations. For this reason, even a merger between weak carriers that will strengthen both is a mixed blessing. As long as the Board blocks entry to the industry, it should be hesitant about allowing mergers. If mergers become inevitable, it should consider expanding the activities of the local-service carriers, giving continental routes to Pan American, or other devices that directly or indirectly involve entry.

It is often suggested that some change should be made to eliminate the Board's concern with the carriers' need for revenue. The usual argument is that the period of direct subsidy to all airlines infected the Board with the need for protecting the carriers' profits and that the provisions of the Civil Aeronautics Act relating to "need" should be amputated.[13] This would be a valuable change, but the Board would show concern with protecting individual firms, even if it had never authorized a cent of subsidy. The root of the problem is the notion of a certificate of public convenience and necessity. The certificate confers an obligation to serve upon its holder. Theoretically, public authority gives nothing in exchange except permission to operate and a promise not to revoke wantonly. In air transport there is no conveying of a monopoly privilege or a guarantee of profits. Nevertheless, for the regulatory authority, especially one charged with promoting as well as regulating, there is a great difference between setting the conditions of service by all comers and setting the conditions of service by authorized firms. The public need for the services of a certified carrier is established by law. It becomes inconceivable for the Board to enforce some secondary policy that would drive

---

[13] For example, see *ibid.*, pp. 111–112 and *passim*.

a carrier out of business. From this, it is a short and easy step to granting any request that seems at all necessary to keep the holder of the certificate in good health.

Therefore, it seems that, as long as the Board keeps its present set of objectives and the certification machinery remains in effect, no major improvements are possible. It is hard to see how entry to the industry could be much less restricted than it is now. The problems of unnecessarily high costs of air service will remain. The variety of services offered to travelers can be improved somewhat if the Board allows the carriers more freedom to experiment, but the Board's ultimate fear of subnormal profits will remain. The number of carriers may continue to shrink, even if profits for the industry as a whole average better than normal, unless the Board sees the long-run danger in mergers. Maintaining a high quality of air service and steady competition for its improvement by means of point-to-point rivalry alone will probably no longer suffice. More direct controls may be necessary.

This is not a very attractive picture and not much of an improvement in the efficiency of regulation. Yet it seems to be the best that can be done if we allow the Board its traditional objectives — maximum safety, maximum incentive to develop new aircraft, continuous promotion, and extension of air service. Reasonable men, however, may surely doubt that these goals are worth the cost. If national prestige requires rapid development of transport aircraft, this could be done by subsidizing the development of prototypes directly, a practice widely used by other countries. There is no reason why adequate safety could not be assured in an otherwise unregulated industry by requiring letters of registration for all carriers from the Federal Aviation Agency, subject to stiff penalty or revocation for violation of safety requirements.[14] Internal subsidy to short-haul service in competition with good surface travel is of doubtful worth. The Board no longer gets much internal subsidy for its trouble, and so the traditional objective of extending the network of air routes could be achieved by maintaining subsidy for the local-service

---

[14] The mere fact that barriers to entry from economic sources are much higher now than after World War II means that the problem of enforcing standards of safety would be much reduced. The total number of entrants to an unregulated industry would not be large, and they would have to have relatively ample financing.

airlines and throwing the trunk routes open to market forces. This study has emphasized throughout the interrelation of different controls used by the Board. This was particularly pronounced when all carriers received subsidy, but it still exists. If entry is blockaded by public policy, regulation of maximum fares and minimum quality of service is necessary. If the setting of minimum fares is used to guarantee profits that sometimes run higher than normal for part or all of the industry, the control of entry must be used to prevent bothersome fluctuations in the number of firms in operation. This is why, today, the only promising reforms are the minor ones of permitting more experimentation in pricing and service and of trying to get a longer-range perspective on the consequences of particular decisions.

We have already seen that the air-transport industry has characteristics of market structure that would bring market performance of reasonable quality without any economic regulation. How could public policy move, without serious transitional difficulties, from the present system to one of relatively free competition? [15] The period in the 1960s when the trunks have completed their conversion to turbine equipment will offer a relatively good chance. Assuming that the general level of employment remains satisfactorily high, the carriers should be enjoying relatively high profits in a stable situation; the industry would be well able to withstand major changes in public policy. A first step would be for the Civil Aeronautics Board to sort the network of air routes into three parts. Class 1 would be the city-pair routes large enough to sustain more than one carrier with entry unrestricted. Class 2 would be those local-service cities or routes that probably could not be served without subsidy. Class 3 would be a residual of cities or city-pair markets that would be profitable for a single carrier. The critical first step would be to open the class of large city-pair markets to all certified carriers not receiving subsidy.[16] If this were done at a time when the airlines

[15] I do not distinguish between changes that would require amending the Federal Aviation Act and those that would affect only the policies of the Board.

[16] Local-service carriers could participate, too, if the method for calculating their subsidy could be set to keep the government from subsidizing their entry into open trunk markets. Including them would be desirable, since they would be well equipped for providing commuter service in dense short-haul markets.

were running normal load factors, and if the trunks still retained their obligation to provide service in Class 3 markets, the effect apart from some transitional sparring would be to encourage airlines to rearrange their market territories in order to use their current aircraft and facilities more efficiently and to reduce problems of seasonal traffic fluctuations. At this same time, possibly even earlier, the Board could use its power to set minimum and maximum fares by placing the legal limits 10 percent above or below the currently prevailing fare for any given class, and by removing restrictions on creating new classes of service. The second step would be to eliminate restrictions on entry of new carriers to city-pair markets in Class 1. This would probably bring no great influx of new airlines, but there would be a few specialists that would enter to operate relatively compact route networks. Both the maximum and minimum limits on legal air fares should be removed. The net result after these measures would probably be that some of the certified trunks will have disappeared by merger or have consolidated and rationalized their route networks. The industry would move toward the pattern suggested previously: a few large carriers with networks serving nearly all major cities, perhaps some similar but smaller regional carriers, and some carriers offering specialized services in limited numbers of markets. A final step, once the situation had again stabilized reasonably, would be to consolidate the first and third classes of markets, leaving only subsidized local-service routes subject to separate regulation. If necessary and desirable, new classes of experimentally certified air services could still be created. The remaining role of the Civil Aeronautics Board would be strictly promotional.

A nation must make a political choice about how many of its industries will be subject to intensive public regulation. The economist can provide two kinds of information useful in making this decision. One is an evaluation of the market performance that is likely to come from any particular industry with or without such regulation. Another is a ranking of industries according to the likelihood that public regulation will improve their performance. Thus, this study has found that the airlines have a market structure which makes them more workably competitive than some unregulated industries in the economy. There are certain goals that can be achieved by airline regulation, but some sacrifices are necessary to achieve them. An economist may feel that the sacrifices are hardly worth the gains, but the decision is ultimately a political one and his role is only to inform.

BIBLIOGRAPHY

INDEX

Bibliography

BOOKS AND PAMPHLETS

Adelman, M. A. *A & P: A Study in Price-Cost Behavior and Public Policy.* Cambridge, Mass.: Harvard University Press, 1959.

Annual Report. Washington: Air Transport Association of America, 1955.

―――― *The Large Irregular Service Air Carrier Industry in 1952.* Washington: Air Transport Association of America, 1953.

Aircraft Year Book. Washington: Aeronautical Chamber of Commerce of America, 1934–1959.

Aldrich, Grahame H. *Market Analysis of Air Traffic Potential.* Delivered before the Radio Technical Commission for Aeronautics, Philadelphia, April 22, 1954. Washington: Air Transport Association of America, 1954.

Altschul, Selig. *A Study and Appraisal of National Airlines.* New York: Aviation Advisory Service, 1953.

―――― *United Air Lines, Inc., A Reappraisal.* New York: Aviation Advisory Service, 1953.

American Aviation Publishers, Inc. *Official Airline Guide, Quick Reference Edition.* Chicago: 1958–60.

Bain, Joe S. *Barriers to New Competition: Their Character and Consequences in Manufacturing Industries.* Cambridge, Mass.: Harvard University Press, 1956.

―――― *Industrial Organization.* New York: John Wiley, 1959.

Beecken, Henry, and Associates. *A Comprehensive Financial Study of the Domestic Trunk Line Industry and of American Airlines, Inc., and Capital Airlines, Inc.* Washington: Henry Beecken and Associates, 1954.

Bernstein, Marver H. *Regulating Business by Independent Commission.* Princeton: Princeton University Press, 1955.

Bollinger, L. L., A. Passen, and R. E. McElfresh. *Terminal Airport Financing and Management.* Boston: Division of Research, Graduate School of Business Administration, Harvard University, 1946.

Cherington, Paul W. *Airline Price Policy: A Study of Domestic Airline Passenger Fares.* Boston: Division of Research, Graduate School of Business Administration, Harvard University, 1958.

Daggett, Stuart. *Principles of Inland Transportation.* New York: Harper, 1941.

David, Paul T. *The Economics of Air Mail Transportation.* Washington: The Brookings Institution, 1934.

Dearing, Charles L., and Wilfred Owen. *National Transportation Policy.* Washington: The Brookings Institution, 1949.

Dhekney, M. R. *Air Transport in India* (*Growth & Problems*). Bombay: Vora & Co., 1953.

Ferguson, Allen Richmond. "A Technical Synthesis of Airline Costs." Unpublished dissertation, Harvard University, 1949.

Fisher, Waldo E., and C. M. James. *Minimum Price Fixing in the Bituminous Coal Industry*. Princeton: Princeton University Press for National Bureau of Economic Research, 1955.

Frederick, John H. *Commercial Air Transportation*. 4th ed. Homewood: Richard D. Irwin, 1955.

Freudenthal, Elsbeth E. *The Aviation Business, From Kitty Hawk to Wall Street*. New York: Vanguard Press, 1940.

Gasser, Erik B. *Die staatliche Regulierung des Wettbewerbs in internationalen amerikanischen Luftverkehr*. Schweizerische Beiträge zur Verkehrswissenschaft, Heft 45. Bern: Stämpfli & Cie., 1953.

Gifford, G. L. "The Economic Aspects of National Aviation Policy." Unpublished dissertation, University of Pennsylvania, 1953.

Gill, Frederick W., and Gilbert L. Bates. *Airline Competition: A Study of the Effects of Competition on the Quality and Price of Airline Service and the Self-Sufficiency of the United States Domestic Airlines*. Boston: Division of Research, Graduate School of Business Administration, Harvard University, 1949.

Goodman, Gilbert. *Government Policy Toward Commercial Aviation: Competition and the Regulation of Rates*. New York: King's Crown Press, 1944.

Gotch and Crawford. *Promise . . . Progress . . . Performance Without Profit, A Report on the Earnings Experience of the Local Service Airlines*. Prepared for the Conference of Local Airlines. Washington: Gotch and Crawford, 1956.

Grossman, William L. *Air Passenger Traffic*. New York: Remsen Press, 1947.

Hagen, Everett E. *Handbook for Industry Studies*. Glencoe: Free Press, 1958.

Healy, Kent T. *The Economics of Transportation*. New York: Ronald Press, 1940.

Hector, Louis J. *Memorandum to the President: Problems of the CAB and the Independent Regulatory Commissions*. Washington: 1959 (mimeographed).

Heinrich, H. J. *Contribution of Production Planning and Control to Jet Operations*. Address at Annual Air Transport Association Engineering & Maintenance Conference, New Orleans, Oct. 22, 1959.

Hocking, D. M., and C. P. Haddon-Cave. *Air Transport in Australia*. Sydney: Angus and Robertson, 1951.

Huntington, Samuel P. "Clientalism: A Study in Administrative Politics." Unpublished dissertation, Harvard University, 1950.

International City Managers' Association. *The Municipal Year Book, 1958*. Chicago: 1958.

International Civil Aviation Organization. *The Economic Implications of the Introduction into Service of Long-Range Jet Aircraft.* Montreal: International Civil Aviation Organization, 1958.

Johnson, Emory R. *Transportation Facilities, Service and Policies.* New York: Appleton, 1947.

Kahn, Mark L. "Industrial Relations in the Airlines." Unpublished dissertation, Harvard University, 1950.

Keyes, Lucile S. *Federal Control of Entry into Air Transportation.* Cambridge, Mass.: Harvard University Press, 1951.

Knowlton, Hugh. *Air Transportation in the United States: Its Growth as a Business.* Chicago: University of Chicago Press, 1941.

Lindholm, Richard W. *Public Finance of Air Transportation, A Study of Taxation and Public Expenditures in Relation to a Developing Industry.* Columbus: The Ohio State University, 1948.

Lissitzyn, Oliver J. *International Air Transport and National Policy.* New York: Council on Foreign Relations, 1942.

McKie, James W. *Tin Cans and Tin Plate: A Study of Competition in Two Related Markets.* Cambridge, Mass.: Harvard University Press, 1959.

Mayer, Meyer, Austrian, and Platt. *Corporate and Legal History of United Air Lines, and Its Predecessors and Subsidiaries, 1929–1945.* Chicago: Twentieth Century Press, 1953.

Moore, Byron. *The First Five Million Miles.* New York: Harper, 1955.

Nicholson, Joseph L. *Air Transportation Management: Its Practices and Policies.* New York: John Wiley, 1951.

Planning Research Corp. *Public Benefits Provided by the Local Airline Industry.* Los Angeles and Washington: 1960.

Puffer, Claude E. *Air Transportation.* Philadelphia: Blakiston, 1941.

—— *Regulation of Air Carriers.* Scranton: International Textbook Co., 1949.

Putnam, Carleton. *High Journey: A Decade in the Pilgrimage of an Air Line Pioneer.* New York: Scribner's, 1945.

Redford, Emmette S. *Administration of National Economic Control.* New York: Macmillan, 1952.

—— *The General Passenger Fare Investigation.* University, Ala.: University of Alabama Press, 1960.

—— *National Regulatory Commissions: Need for a New Look.* College Park: Bureau of Governmental Research, University of Maryland, 1959.

Rhyne, Charles S. *The Civil Aeronautics Act Annotated, with the Congressional History which Produced It, and the Precedents upon which It Is Based.* ["Scotus Series."] Washington: National Law Book Co., 1939.

Richmond, Samuel B. *Regulation and Competition in Air Transportation.* New York: Columbia University Press, 1961.

Schlaifer, Robert, and S. D. Heron. *Development of Aircraft Engines;*

Development of Aviation Fuels, Two Studies of Relations Between Government and Business. Boston: Division of Research, Graduate School of Business Administration, Harvard University, 1950.

Schwartz, Bernard. *The Professor and the Commissions.* New York: Knopf, 1959.

Smith, Henry Ladd. *Airways: The History of Commercial Aviation in the United States.* New York: Knopf, 1942.

Sobotka, Stephen P., and others. *Prices of Used Commercial Aircraft, 1959–1965: A Research Report.* Evanston: The Transportation Center at Northwestern University, 1959.

Spencer, Francis A. *Air Mail Payment and the Government.* Washington: The Brookings Institution, 1941.

Taaffe, Edward J. *The Air Passenger Hinterland of Chicago.* Chicago: University of Chicago Press, 1942.

Taylor, Frank J. *High Horizons, Daredevil Flying to Modern Magic Carpet — the United Air Lines Story.* Rev. ed. New York: McGraw-Hill, 1958.

Thomas, Aaron Joshua, Jr. *Economic Regulation of Scheduled Air Transport, National and International.* Buffalo: Dennis & Co., 1951.

Thruelsen, Richard. *Transocean, The Story of an Unusual Airline.* New York: Henry Holt, 1953.

United Research, Inc. *Federal Regulation of the Domestic Air Transport Industry.* Cambridge, Mass.: 1959.

Veale, S. E. *Airliners and Airways of Today.* London: Pilot Press, 1947.

Wheatcroft, Stephen. *The Economics of European Air Transport.* Manchester: Manchester University Press, 1956.

Wilson, G. Lloyd, and Leslie A. Bryan. *Air Transportation.* New York: Prentice-Hall, 1949.

Wolfe, Thomas. *Air Transportation.* New York: McGraw-Hill, 1950.

Zacharoff, Lucien, ed. *Vital Problems of Air Commerce.* New York: Duell, Sloan, Pearce, 1946.

Zook, Paul D. "Local and Feeder Airlines and Public Policy." Unpublished dissertation, University of Illinois, 1954.

ARTICLES AND PERIODICALS

Adams, Joseph P. "Future Local Airline Service Depends on State Support," *Journal of Air Law and Commerce,* XX (Autumn 1953), 403–415.

———— "Future of the Local Service Carriers: Public Service vs. Federal Subsidy," *Journal of Air Law and Commerce,* XXIII (Spring 1956), 127–147.

———— "Low-Price Air Travel," *Congressional Record,* XCIX (May 20, 1953), A2911–A2912.

Adams, Russell B. "The Air Route Pattern Problem," *Journal of Air Law and Commerce,* XVII (Spring 1950), 127–140.

"Adequacy of Domestic Airline Service: The Community's Role in a

Changing Industry," *Yale Law Journal*, LXVIII (May 1959), 1199–1244.

Ades, A. E. "Airline Evaluation of Transport Aircraft," *Canadian Aeronautical Journal*, II (Oct. 1956), 277–283.

Adkins, L. D., and D. Billyou. "Developments in Commercial Aircraft Equipment Financing," *Business Lawyer*, XIII (Jan. 1958), 199–219.

"Air Cargo — A Symposium," *Law and Contemporary Problems*, XV (Winter 1950), 1–121.

Airlift, XXIII-XXIV (June 1959–May 1961).

"Airline Orders for Turbine-Powered Aircraft with Years of Delivery, 1958–1963," *Esso Air World*, XI (May-June 1959), 1–4.

Allen, Roy. "The Turbine Transport and the Commercial Scene," *Aeronautics*, XXXIX (Nov. 1958), 22–36.

American Aviation, IX-XXII (June 1945–May 1959).

Anderson, Dole A. "Airline Self-Sufficiency and the Local Air Service Problem," *Journal of Air Law and Commerce*, XXI (Winter 1954), 1–14.

"Approval of Purchase Price in Sale of Airline Properties under the Civil Aeronautics Act," *University of Chicago Law Review*, XV (Winter 1948), 343–351.

Arata, Winfield H., Jr. "Aircraft Growth, Local Transport Category," *Aero/Space Engineering*, XVIII (Nov. 1959), 42–47.

Aschenbeck, Lloyd B. "Passenger Air-Line Economics," *Aeronautical Engineering Review*, XV (Dec. 1956), 39–45.

"Ashbacker Rule and the CAB: Cumbersome Procedure v. Public Interest," *Virginia Law Review*, XLIV (Nov. 1958), 1147–1165.

Aviation, XXXIII-XLV (1934–1946).

Aviation Week, XLVI-LXXIII (1947–1960).

Baker, R. J. "Some Problems in Airline Turbine Transport Operation," *Canadian Aeronautical Journal*, IV (Oct. 1958), 289–295.

Balch, Bernard R. "Abandonment of Intrastate Segment of Interstate Air Route," *Journal of Air Law and Commerce*, XVII (Winter 1950), 107–112.

Ballard, F. A. "Federal Regulation of Aviation," *Harvard Law Review*, LX (Oct. 1947), 1235–1281.

Barnes, Leslie O. "Airline Subsidies — Purpose, Cause and Control," *Journal of Air Law and Commerce*, XXVI (Autumn 1959), 311–322.

——— "The Case for the Local Service Airlines," *Journal of Air Law and Commerce*, XX (Spring 1953), 197–202.

Bates, Gilbert L. "Current Changes in Trunkline Competition," *Journal of Air Law and Commerce*, XXII (Autumn 1955), 379–405.

Belmont, Daniel M. "A Pattern of Interstation Airline Travel," *Proceedings of the American Society of Civil Engineers, Journal of the Air Transport Division*, LXXXII, no. 987 (May 1956), 1–16.

——— "A Study of Airline Interstation Traffic," *Journal of Air Law and Commerce*, XXV (Summer 1958), 361–368.

Bendiner, Robert. "The Rise and Fall of the Nonskeds," *The Reporter*, XVI (May 30, 1957), 29–34.

Berge, Stanley. "Competition to the Extent Necessary: An Historical Introduction," *Journal of Air Law and Commerce*, XXII (Spring 1955), 127–130.

―――― "Regulation of Air Coach Service Standards," *Journal of Air Law and Commerce*, XX (Winter 1953), 25–33.

―――― "Subsidies and Competition as Factors in Air Transport Policy," *Journal of Air Law and Commerce*, XVIII (Winter 1951), 1–11.

Black, Louis E., Jr. "Realignment of the Domestic Airline Route Pattern," *Journal of Air Law and Commerce*, XV (Autumn 1948), 409–433; XVI (Winter 1949), 20–39.

Bluestone, David W. "The Problem of Competition Among Domestic Trunk Airlines," *Journal of Air Law and Commerce*, XX (Autumn 1953), 379–402; XXI (Winter 1954), 50–87.

Braden, Charles W. "The Story of the Historical Development of the Economic Regulation of Transportation," *I.C.C. Practitioner's Journal*, XVIII (April 1952), 659–690.

Brownell, George A. "The Air Coordinating Committee: A Problem in Federal Staff Work," *Journal of Air Law and Commerce*, XIV (Autumn 1947), 405–435.

Buckley, James C. "The Effect of Airport Distance on Traffic Generation," *Proceedings of the American Society of Civil Engineers, Journal of the Air Transport Division*, LXXXII, no. 978 (May 1956), 1–19.

Bunke, Harvey C. "Commercial Aviation and the Civil Aeronautics Act of 1938," *Southern Economic Journal*, XX (April 1954), 356–368.

―――― "The Fetish of Separating Subsidy from Air Mail Payments," *Journal of Air Law and Commerce*, XX (Summer 1953), 273–281.

Burt, W. C., and J. L. Highsaw, Jr. "Regulation of Rates in Air Transportation," *Louisiana Law Review*, VII (Nov. 1946), 1–22; VII (March 1947), 378–397.

"Carriers — Regulation. In General — CAB Conditions Approval of Route Transfer upon Provisions for Benefit of Adversely Affected Employees," *Harvard Law Review*, LXIV (Feb. 1951), 664–666.

Cherington, C. R. "The Essential Role of Large Irregular Air Carriers," *Journal of Air Law and Commerce*, XIX (Autumn 1952), 411–422.

Cherington, Paul W. "Objectives and Strategies for Airline Pricing," *Journal of Air Law and Commerce*, XVIII (Summer 1951), 253–265.

―――― Review of Gill and Bates's *Airline Competition. Journal of Air Law and Commerce*, XVII (Winter 1950), 116–118.

"Civil Aeronautics Board Policy: An Evaluation," *Yale Law Journal*, LVII (April 1948), 1053–1084.

Cohen, S. R. "Political and Economic Prospects of the Jet Age," *Journal of Air Law and Commerce*, XXIV (Autumn 1957), 398–409.

Cohu, LaMotte T. "The Paradox of the Airlines," *Journal of Air Law and Commerce*, XV (Summer 1948), 307–320.

Craig, Peter S. "A New Look at Section 416(b) of the Civil Aeronautics Act," *Journal of Air Law and Commerce*, XXI (Spring 1954), 127–158.

Crane, John B. "The Economics of Air Transportation," *Harvard Business Review*, XXII (Summer 1944), 495–509.

Davis, William J. "State Regulation of Aeronautics in the Southwest," *Southwestern Law Journal*, VII (Spring 1953), 293–299.

Desoutter, D. M. "Turboprop Efficiency for Short-Stage Airlines," *Aeronautics*, XXVI (April 1957), 26–39.

"Discretion of the CAB in Determining Rates Based on Carrier's 'Need,'" *Columbia Law Review*, LIV (April 1954), 626–628.

Douglas, Donald W., Jr. "Let's Look at Airlift," *National Defense Transport Journal*, XIV (May-June), 38ff.

Douglas of Kirtleside, Lord. "The Economics of Speed, An Examination of the Future Roles of Jet and Turbo-prop Transport Aircraft," *Journal of the Institute of Transport*, XXVII (May 1957), 115–131.

Duggan, Robert N. "An Administrative Agency, in Granting Authority as Provided by Statute, Must Make Its Findings in Such Detail That a Reviewing Court May Determine Whether the Court Is Within the Statutory Authority," *Georgetown Law Journal*, XLV (Winter 1956–57), 282–286.

Durham, J. A., and M. J. Feldstein. "Regulation as a Tool in the Development of the Air Freight Industry," *Virginia Law Review*, XXXIV (Oct. 1948), 769–809.

Dyment, J. T. "Selection of the Vickers Vanguard by Trans-Canada Air Lines," *Canadian Aeronautical Journal*, IV (May 1958), 149–155.

Ernst & Ernst. "Report Covering Preliminary Study of Methods of Compensation for Carriage of Domestic Air Mail and for the Operation of Air Transportation Service Essential to the Public Interest," *Journal of Air Law and Commerce*, XVII (Winter 1950), 86–93.

Fox, A. H. "Fare-Fixing in Air Transport," *Three Banks Review*, no. 35 (Sept. 1957), 23–35.

Gambrell, E. S., and G. A. Smith. "Separation of Subsidy from Air Mail Payments," *Journal of Public Law*, I (Spring 1952), 71–96.

Gardner, Sir George. "Some Aspects of Future Air Transport Possibilities," *Canadian Aeronautical Journal*, V (Oct. 1959), 324–339.

Gellman, A. J. "The Regulation of Competition in United States Domestic Air Transportation: A Judicial Survey and Analysis," *Journal of Air Law and Commerce*, XXIV (Autumn 1957), 410–434; XXV (Spring 1958), 148–181.

Gifford, Gilbert L. "The Evolution of Air Mail Rate Making," *Journal of Air Law and Commerce*, XXII (Summer 1955), 298–342.

Glenn, C. H. "Will We Be Able to Operate a Turbojet Transport Economically?" *Canadian Aeronautical Journal*, V (Jan. 1959), 24–30.

Godehn, Paul M., and Frank E. Quindry. "Air Mail Contract Cancellations of 1934 and Resulting Litigation," *Journal of Air Law and Commerce,* XXI (Summer 1954), 253–276.

Goodrick, M. George. "Air Mail Subsidy of Commercial Aviation," *Journal of Air Law and Commerce,* XVI (Summer 1949), 253–279.

―――― "The Air Route Problem in the United States," *Journal of Air Law and Commerce,* XVIII (Summer 1951), 281–298.

Gorrell, Edgar S. "Rationalization of Air Transport," *Journal of Air Law and Commerce,* IX (Jan. 1938), 41–47.

Gray, Horace M. "The Passing of the Public Utility Concept," *Journal of Land and Public Utility Economics,* XVI (Feb. 1940), 8–20.

Greenspun, Nathaniel. "Problems of Regulating and Subsidizing American-Flag International Air Transportation," *Public Policy,* IV (1953), 11–44.

Grossman, William L. "Reasonable Operating Ratio Versus Fair Rate of Return," *Journal of Air Law and Commerce,* XXI (Winter 1954), 15–19.

Hackford, R. R. "The Colonial Air Lines Challenge to U.S.–Canadian Transport Agreement," *Journal of Air Law and Commerce,* XIX (Winter 1952), 1–10.

Hale, G. E., and R. D. Hale. "Competition or Control, IV: Air Carriers," *University of Pennsylvania Law Review,* CIX (Jan. 1961), 311–360.

Hall, Sir Arnold. "The Influence on Civil Aviation of Some Current Researches," *Journal of the Institute of Transport,* XXVI (May 1955), 101–118.

Hamstra, J. Howard. "Two Decades — Federal Aero-Regulation in Perspective," *Journal of Air Law and Commerce,* XII (April 1941), 105–147.

Harbeck, William J. "Transfer and Revocation of Certificates of Convenience and Necessity under the C.A.A. of 1938," *Journal of Air Law and Commerce,* XVI (Autumn 1949), 471–482.

Harvey, d'Arcy. "Airline Passenger Traffic Pattern Within the United States," *Journal of Air Law and Commerce,* XVIII (Spring 1951), 157–165.

Healy, Kent T. "Workable Competition in Air Transportation," *American Economic Review,* XXXV (May 1945), 229–242.

Hector, Louis J. "Problems in Economic Regulation of Civil Aviation in the United States," *Journal of Air Law and Commerce,* XXVI (Winter 1959), 101–107.

―――― "Problems of the CAB and the Independent Regulatory Commissions," *Yale Law Journal,* LXIX (May 1960), 931–964.

Henzey, William V. "Labor Problems in the Airline Industry," *Law and Contemporary Problems,* XXV (Winter 1960), 43–56.

Hibbard, Hall L., and Clarence L. Johnson. "The Constellation Family — and How It Grew," *SAE Journal,* LXIII (Sept. 1955), 66–71.

Hickey, E. J., Jr. "Surface Carrier Participation in Air Transportation under the Civil Aeronautics Act," *Georgetown Law Journal,* XXXVI (June 1948), 125–153.

Hirshleifer, Jack. "Peak Loads and Efficient Pricing: Comment," *Quarterly Journal of Economics,* LXXI (Aug. 1958), 451–462.

Howell, Paul L. "The Rate of Return in Air Transport," *Law and Contemporary Problems,* XXIV (Autumn 1959), 677–701.

"ICAO Study on Jet Economics Causes World-Wide Comment," *ICAO Bulletin,* VII (Nov. 1958), 103–115.

Jaworski, Adam. "Inter-Industry Relationship of the Air Transport Industry," *Canadian Aeronautical Journal,* II (Nov. 1956), 329–336.

——— "Trans-Canada Airlines' Progress, 1946–1950 — A Comparison with U.S. Trunk Lines," *Journal of Air Law and Commerce,* XIX (Summer 1952), 305–316.

"Jet-Age Transport Conference, Aug. 15–17, 1957," *Journal of the Air Transport Division, American Society of Civil Engineers,* LXXXIII (Dec. 1957), 1–248.

Johnson, Edwin C. "Committee Report to the Senate on Separation of Air-Mail Pay from Subsidy," *Journal of Air Law and Commerce,* XVIII (Summer 1951), 320–350.

——— "Utilizing Trunk-Line Profits to Support Local Air Service," *Journal of Air Law and Commerce,* XX (Spring 1953), 203–205.

Jones, Harold A. "The Anomaly of the Civil Aeronautics Board in American Government," *Journal of Air Law and Commerce,* XX (Spring 1953), 140–157.

——— and Frederick Davis. "The 'Air Coach' Experiment and National Air Transport Policy," *Journal of Air Law and Commerce,* XVII (Winter 1950), 1–21; XVII (Autumn 1950), 418–435.

Kahn, Mark L. "The National Airlines Strike: A Case Study," *Journal of Air Law and Commerce,* XIX (Winter 1952), 11–24.

——— "Regulatory Agencies and Industrial Relations: The Airlines Case," *American Economic Review,* XLII (May 1952), 686–698.

——— "Wage Determination for Airline Pilots," *Industrial & Labor Relations Review,* VI (April 1953), 317–336.

Kaysen, Carl. "On Defining a Subsidy," *Public Policy,* IV (1953), 3–10.

Keefer, R. J. "Airline Interchange Agreements," *Journal of Air Law and Commerce,* XXV (Winter 1958), 55–67.

Keyes, Lucile S. "National Policy Towards Commercial Aviation — Some Basic Problems," *Journal of Air Law and Commerce,* XVI (Summer 1949), 280–297.

——— "Passenger Fare Policies of the Civil Aeronautics Board," *Journal of Air Law and Commerce,* XVIII (Winter 1951), 46–77.

——— "A Reconsideration of Federal Control of Entry into Air Transportation," *Journal of Air Law and Commerce,* XXII (Spring 1955), 192–202.

Kintner, E. W. "The Current Ordeal of the Administrative Process: In Reply to Mr. Hector," *Yale Law Journal,* LXIX (May 1960), 965–977.

Koontz, Harold D. "Airline Subsidies Can Be Eliminated," *Public Utilities Fortnightly,* XLVIII (Dec. 6, 1951), 805–816.

—— "Domestic Air Line Self-Sufficiency: A Problem of Route Structure," *American Economic Review*, XLII (March 1952), 103–125.

—— "Economic and Managerial Factors Underlying Subsidy Needs of Domestic Trunk Line Air Carriers," *Journal of Air Law and Commerce*, XVIII (Spring 1951), 127–156.

Landis, James M. "Air Routes under the Civil Aeronautics Act," *Journal of Air Law and Commerce*, XV (Summer 1948), 295–302.

Lansing, J. B., J.-C. Liu, and D. B. Suits. "An Analysis of Interurban Air Travel," *Quarterly Journal of Economics*, LXXV (Feb. 1961), 87–95.

Lewis, B. W. "State Regulation in Depression and War," *American Economic Review*, XXXVI (May 1946), 384–404.

Linnert, Theodore G. "Airline Appraisal of Crash-Fire Problem," *Airports & Air Transportation*, IX (July-Aug. 1955), 63–66.

Lipsey, R. G., and K. Lancaster. "The General Theory of the Second Best," *Review of Economic Studies*, XXIV (1956–57), 11–32.

Locklin, D. Phillip. "A Critique of Proposals to Separate Subsidy from Air Mail Pay," *Journal of Air Law and Commerce*, XVIII (Spring 1951), 166–186.

Loening, Grover. "Air Freight in Competition with Motor Transport," *Aeronautical Engineering Review*, XVI (June 1957), 70–73.

McDonald, John J. "Jet Airliners: Year of Decision," *Fortune*, XLVII (April 1953), 124–129, 242–248; XLVII (May 1953), 128–131, 216–218.

McGregor, G. R. "The Economics of Civil Turbine Operation," *Canadian Aeronautical Journal*, III (Dec. 1957), 332–335.

MacIntyre, Malcolm A. "The Railway Labor Act — A Misfit for the Airlines," *Journal of Air Law and Commerce*, XIX (Summer 1952), 274–288.

Maclay, H. K., and W. C. Burt. "Entry of New Carriers into Domestic Trunkline Air Transportation," *Journal of Air Law and Commerce*, XXII (Spring 1955), 131–156.

McWilliams, R. J. "Airline Planned Maintenance," *Canadian Aeronautical Journal*, IV (Sept. 1958), 217–223.

—— "Operations Research — Some Airline Applications," *Canadian Aeronautical Journal*, V (Nov. 1959), 369–374.

Magnusson, Jon. "Observations of the Economic Regulations of the Civil Aeronautics Board," *Journal of Air Law and Commerce*, XVIII (Spring 1951), 181–191.

Margoshes, S. L. "Price Earnings Ratio in Financial Analysis," *Financial Analysts Journal*, XVI (Nov.-Dec. 1960), 125–132.

Marvin, L. P., Jr. "Air Mail Subsidy Separation," *Georgetown Law Journal*, XL (Jan. 1952), 161–240.

Mayhill, G. Roger, "A Critique of the C.A.A. Studies on Air Traffic Generation in the United States," *Journal of Air Law and Commerce*, XX (Spring 1953), 158–177.

Montgomery, J. "Price as a Factor in the Determination of Air Carrier

Merger and Acquisition Cases," *George Washington Law Review*, XVI (June 1948), 509–523.

Moore, J. P., and K. R. Hahn. "Regulation of Irregular Air Carriers," *Cornell Law Quarterly*, XXXV (Fall 1949), 48–76.

Mott, Basil J. F., Jr. "The Effect of Political Interest Groups on C.A.B. Policies," *Journal of Air Law and Commerce*, XIX (Autumn 1952), 379–410.

Murphy, Charles J. V. "The Plane Makers under Stress," *Fortune*, LXI (June 1960), 134ff; LXII (July, 1960), 111ff.

—— and T. A. Wise. "The Problem of Howard Hughes," *Fortune*, LIX (Jan. 1959), 79–82, 160–171.

Murray, Roger F. "Regulation of Airline Securities," *Harvard Business Review*, XXVIII (May 1950), 71–76.

Neal, George C. "The Status of Non-Scheduled Operations under the Civil Aeronautics Act of 1938," *Law and Contemporary Problems*, XI (Winter-Spring 1946), 508–523.

Netterville, Victor S. "Local Service Airlines: Trunkline Suspensions in Aid of the Local Service Experiment," *Southern California Law Review*, XXV (April 1953), 229–264.

—— "The Regulation of Irregular Air Carriers: A History," *Journal of Air Law and Commerce*, XVI (Autumn 1949), 414–444.

"A New Approach to Airline Rates and Competition," *Journal of Air Law and Commerce*, XIX (Spring 1952), 231–237.

O'Connell, Joseph J., Jr. "Air Mail Pay under the Civil Aeronautics Act," *Indiana Law Journal*, XXV (Fall 1949), 27–41.

—— "Legal Problems in Revising the Air Route Pattern," *Journal of Air Law and Commerce*, XV (Autumn 1948), 397–408.

O'Mahoney, Joseph C. "Legislative History of the Right of Entry in Air Transportation under the Civil Aeronautics Act of 1938," *Journal of Air Law and Commerce*, XX (Summer 1953), 330–350.

Osborn, Richards C. "Recent Developments in Air Transportation," *Current Economic Comment*, XV (May 1953), 21–34.

Paradiso, Louis J., and Clement Winston. "Consumer Expenditure-Income Patterns," *Survey of Current Business*, XXXV (Sept. 1955), 23–32.

Pfeiffer, Paul N. "Shortening the Record in CAB Proceedings through Elimination of Unnecessary and Hazardous Cross-Examination," *Journal of Air Law and Commerce*, XXII (Summer 1955), 286–297.

Phillips, A. "Concentration, Scale, and Technological Change in Selected Manufacturing Industries, 1899–1939," *Journal of Industrial Economics*, IV (June 1956), 179–193.

Plaine, H. H. E. "The Pattern of State Aviation Legislation," *Insurance Counsel Journal*, XV (Jan. 1948), 58–69.

Polson, Robert K. "The Rise and Fall of Aircraft Values," *Skyways*, XVII (Oct. 1958), 57, 78.

Proctor, Jesse W., and Julian S. Duncan. "A Regression Analysis of Airline Costs," *Journal of Air Law and Commerce*, XXI (Summer 1954), 282–292.

"Public Regulation of Domestic Airlines: Proposal for Structural and Subsidy Reform," *Yale Law Journal,* LX (Nov. 1951), 1196–1217.

Putnam, Carleton. "The Illusion of Air Line Subsidy," *Journal of Air Law and Commerce,* XVII (Winter 1950), 32–42.

Rasenberger, Raymond J. "Legislative and Administrative Control of Air Carrier Subsidy," *George Washington Law Review,* XXV (March 1957), 397–427.

Ray, James G. "The Feeder Airline Story," *Journal of Air Law and Commerce,* XVI (Autumn 1949), 379–387.

Redford, Emmette S. "A Case Analysis of Congressional Activity: Civil Aviation, 1957–58," *Journal of Politics,* XXII (May 1960), 228–258.

"Regulation of the Purchase Price of Air Routes: The Public Burden Issuing from the 'Second Marquette' Doctrine," *Harvard Law Review,* LXI (Feb. 1948), 523–531.

"Reimbursing Airline Strike Losses with Federal Subsidy: The Railway Labor Act Aloft," *Yale Law Journal,* LXVIII (Nov. 1958), 77–97.

Reynolds, Lloyd. "Cutthroat Competition," *American Economic Review,* XXX (Dec. 1940), 736–747.

Richmond, Samuel B. "Creating Competition Among Airlines," *Journal of Air Law and Commerce,* XXIV (Autumn 1957), 435–464.

———— "Interspacial Relationships Affecting Air Travel," *Land Economics,* XXXIII (Feb. 1957), 65–73.

Rickenbacker, Eddie. "The Operating Ratio as a Yardstick for Measuring Airline Profits," *Journal of Air Law and Commerce,* XX (Summer 1953), 253–263.

Rieser, Carl. "George T. Baker's Feud with the World," *Fortune,* LXI (March 1960), 154ff.

Rizley, Ross. "Some Personal Reflections after Eight Months as Chairman of the Civil Aeronautics Board," *Journal of Air Law and Commerce,* XXII (Autumn 1955), 445–452.

Ryan, Oswald. "Economic Developments in Air Transportation and Their Implications," *Congressional Record,* XCVIII (March 10, 1952), A1541–A1543.

———— "Economic Regulation of Air Commerce by the States," *Virginia Law Review,* XXXI (March 1945), 479–513.

———— "Problems of Our Domestic Air Transportation," *Notre Dame Lawyer,* XIX (March 1943), 35–99.

"Sale of Airline Certificates of Convenience and Necessity," *Columbia Law Review,* XLVIII (Jan. 1948), 88–104.

Sammons, H. "Replacement of Piston Engines by Gas Turbines in Air Liners," *Journal of the Royal Aeronautical Society,* LXII (Feb. 1958), 94–104.

Saunders, Dero A. "The Airlines' Flight from Reality," *Fortune,* LIII (Feb. 1956), 91ff.

Schubert, Glendon A., Jr. " 'The Public Interest' in Administrative Decision-Making: Theorem, Theosophy, or Theory?," *American Political Science Review,* LI (June 1957), 346–368.

"Selected Topics in Aviation Law — A Symposium," *Southwestern Law Journal,* VII (Spring 1953), 135–277.

"Separation of Control between Surface and Air Carriers," *Journal of Air Law and Commerce,* XIX (Autumn 1952), 484–490.

Sharp, Walter M. "Some Considerations on the Financing of the Air Transport Industry in the Jet Era," *Robert Morris Associates Bulletin,* XXXIX (Oct. 1956), 25–34.

Sheehan, Robert. "What's Eating the Airline Pilots?" *Fortune,* LIX (April 1959), 122ff.

Slichter, Sumner H. "Notes on the Structure of Wages," *Review of Economics and Statistics,* XXX (Feb. 1950), 80–91.

Smith, C. R. "Government Policy Concerning Airline Subsidy," *Journal of Air Law and Commerce,* XXV (Winter 1958), 79–82.

———— "Government Policy for Air Transportation," *Journal of Air Law and Commerce,* XXI (Autumn 1954), 448–453.

———— "What the Airlines Expect from the 1961 Jet Fleet," *Fortune,* LIV (July 1956), 112ff.

Smith, Nelson Lee. "Regulation of Returns to Transportation Agencies," *Law and Contemporary Problems,* XXIV (Autumn 1959), 702–732.

Spurgeon, R. W. "Subsidy in Air Transport," *Journal of the Institute of Transport,* XXVII (Nov. 1956), 15–25.

Stentzel, L. L. "Developments in Irregular Air-Carrier Operations," *Public Utilities Fortnightly,* LVIII (Dec. 6, 1956), 899–906.

Stern, J. A. "Airline Planning for Jets," *Canadian Aeronautical Journal,* IV (April 1958), 117–120.

Stone, Franklin M. "Comments on the Hector Memorandum," *Federal Bar News,* VII (May 1960), 142–155.

Stryker, Perrin. "United *vs.* American: There's More than One Way to Run an Airline," *Fortune,* LXIII (Feb. 1961), 96ff.

"Supreme Court Construction of Mail Rate Subsidies to Airlines," *Journal of Air Law and Commerce,* XXI (Spring 1954), 239–244.

Sweeney, Edward C. "Policy Formation by the Civil Aeronautics Board," *Journal of Air Law and Commerce,* XVI (Spring 1949), 127–161.

Taaffe, Edward J. "Air Transportation and United States Urban Distribution," *Geographical Review,* XLVI (April 1956), 219–238.

———— "A Map Analysis of United States Airline Competition. Part I — The Development of Competition," *Journal of Air Law and Commerce,* XXV (Spring 1958), 121–147; "Part II — Competition and Growth," *Journal of Air Law and Commerce,* XXV (Autumn 1958), 402–427.

———— "Route Elasticity of Demand — Geographic Application of an Economic Concept," *Annals of American Association of Geographers,* XLVII (June 1957), 180–182.

Taylor, M. M. "Economic Regulation of Intrastate Air Carriers in California," *California Law Review,* XLI (Fall 1953), 454–482.

Thomas, A. J., Jr. "Federal Regulation of Air Transportation — Rates and Business Practices," *Southwestern Law Journal,* III (Winter 1949), 1–49.

Tipton, Stuart G., and Stanley Gewirtz. "The Effect of Regulated Competition on the Air Transport Industry," *Journal of Air Law and Commerce,* XXII (Spring 1955), 157–191.

Torgerson, H. W. "History of Air Freight Tariffs," *Journal of Air Law and Commerce,* XV (Winter 1948), 47–63.

Vatter, H. G. "Closure of Entry into the Automobile Industry," *Oxford Economic Papers,* n.s. IV (Oct. 1952), 213–234.

Westwood, Howard C. "Choice of Air Carrier for New Air Transport Routes," *George Washington Law Review,* XVI (Dec. 1947), 1–103; XVI (Feb. 1948), 159–237.

——— and E. W. Jennes. "Compulsory Interchange of Aircraft between Connecting Air Carriers," *Virginia Law Review,* XXXIV (Jan. 1948), 1–25.

"What's Wrong with the Airlines?" *Fortune,* XXXIV (Aug. 1946), 73ff.

Wheatcroft, Stephen. "Earning Power and the Jet v. Turboprop Controversy," *Shell Aviation News,* no. 235 (Jan. 1958), 6–7.

——— "European Air Transport Economics," *Journal of the Institute of Transport,* XXVII (Sept. 1957), 181–188.

Whitehead, Herbert H. "Effects of Competition and Changes in Route Structure on Growth of Domestic Air Travel," *Journal of Air Law and Commerce,* XVIII (Winter 1951), 78–90.

Wisehart, Arthur M. "The Airlines' Recent Experience under the Railway Labor Act," *Law and Contemporary Problems,* XXV (Winter 1960), 22–42.

Woods, J. G. "Factors Considered by the Civil Aeronautics Board in Merger, Consolidation, or Acquisition of Control of Airline Cases," *Georgetown Law Journal,* XXXVII (Nov. 1948), 66–73.

Wright, Theodore P. "Some Economic Factors in Air Transportation," *Aeronautical Engineering Review,* XVI (April 1957), 45–51.

Young, A. S., Jr. "Compulsory Inauguration and Extension of Air Carrier Routes," *Georgetown Law Journal,* XXXVIII (Nov. 1949), 81–93.

Zinbarg, Edward D. "Price-Earnings Ratios and Yields," *Analysts Journal,* XV (Aug. 1959), 35–42.

Zook, Paul D. "Recasting the Air Route Pattern by Airline Consolidations and Mergers," *Journal of Air Law and Commerce,* XXI (Summer 1954), 293–311.

GOVERNMENT DOCUMENTS

New York, State of. Department of Commerce. *Survey of Airport Landing Fees at Airports in the United States, September, 1952.* Albany: 1953.

Organization for European Economic Cooperation, Technical Assistance Mission No. 103. *Federal Regulation of Transport in the U.S.A.; How Transport Problems are Solved in a System of Federated States.* New York: Columbia University Press, 1953.

Port of New York Authority. Aviation Department, Forecast and Analysis Division. *Air Travel Forecasting, 1965–1975*. New York: 1957.

—— *Forecast of the United States Domestic Air Passenger Market, 1965–1975*. New York: 1957.

U.S. Air Coordinating Committee. *Civil Air Policy, A Report by the Air Coordinating Committee by Direction of the President*. Washington: 1954.

U.S. Board of Investigation and Research, *Public Aids to Domestic Transportation*. U.S. Congress, House of Representatives, H. Doc. 159, 79th Cong., 1st sess. Washington: 1945.

U.S. Civil Aeronautics Board. *Annual Report*. Washington: 1939–1958.

—— *Cost Standards — Domestic Scheduled Air Carriers*, by F. H. Crozier, Special Advisor to the Board. Washington: 1950.

—— *Materials Relative to Competition in the Regulated Civil Aviation Industry, 1956*. U.S. Congress, Senate, Select Committee on Small Business, Committee Print, 84th Cong., 2nd sess. Washington: 1956.

—— *The Role of Competition in Commercial Air Transportation*. U.S. Congress, Senate, Select Committee on Small Business, Subcommittee on Monopoly, Committee Print, 82nd Cong., 2nd sess. Washington: 1952.

—— Office of Carrier Accounts and Statistics. *Competition Among Domestic Air Carriers*. Washington: Air Transport Association of America, 1951–1958. (Published twice annually.)

—— —— *Monthly Report of Air Carrier Traffic Statistics*. Washington: 1940–1959. (Title varies.)

—— —— *Quarterly Report of Air Carrier Financial Statistics*. Washington: 1946–1959. (Title varies.)

—— —— *Forecast of Airline Passenger Traffic in the United States: 1959–1965*. ["Air Transport Economics in the Jet Age," Staff Research Report No. 1.] Washington: 1959.

—— —— *General Characteristics of Turbine-Powered Aircraft*. ["Air Transport Economics in the Jet Age," Staff Research Report No. 2.] Washington: 1960.

U.S. Congress, House of Representatives. *Airline Equipment Investment Program, Communication for President of United States Transmitting Report Concerning Status and Economic Significance of Airline Equipment Investment Program*. H. Doc. 430, 85th Cong., 2nd sess. Washington: 1958.

—— Committee on Appropriations. Subcommittee. *Department of Commerce and Related Agencies Appropriations for 1957*. Hearings, 84th Cong., 2nd sess. Washington: 1956.

—— —— *Department of Commerce and Related Agencies Appropriations for 1958*. Hearings, 85th Cong., 1st sess. Washington: 1957.

—— —— Subcommittee on Independent Offices. *Independent Offices Appropriations for 1960*. Hearings, 86th Cong., 1st sess. Washington: 1959.

—— Committee on Government Operations. *Study and Survey of Ad-*

ministrative Organization, Procedure and Practice in the Federal Agencies: Agency Response to Questionnaire, Part IIA, Independent Agencies. 85th Cong., 1st sess. Washington: 1957.

———— Committee on Interstate and Foreign Commerce. *Aircraft Equipment Loans and Capital Gains.* Hearings on H.R. 5822 and H.R. 7993, 85th Cong., 2nd sess. Washington: 1958.

———— ———— *Permanent Certificates for Local Service Air Carriers.* Hearings on H.R. 526 and H.R. 2225, 84th Cong., 1st sess. Washington: 1955.

———— ———— Subcommittee. *Investigation of Regulatory Commissions and Agencies.* Hearings, 85th Cong., 2nd sess. Washington: 1958.

———— ———— Subcommittee on Transportation and Communications. *Civil Air Policy.* Hearings on H.R. 4648, H.R. 4677, H.R. 8902, and H.R. 8903, 84th Cong., 1st and 2nd sess. Washington: 1956.

———— Committee on the Judiciary. Antitrust Subcommittee (Subcommittee No. 5). *The Airlines Industry.* Report pursuant to H. Res. 107, H. Rep. No. 1328, 85th Cong., 1st sess. Washington: 1957.

———— ———— *Monopoly Problems in Regulated Industries — Airlines.* Hearings, 84th Cong., 2nd sess. Washington: 1957. 4 vols.

U.S. Congress, Senate. Committee on Appropriations. Subcommittee. *Department of Commerce and Related Agencies Appropriations, 1957.* Hearings on H.R. 10899, 84th Cong., 2nd sess. Washington: 1957.

———— Committee on Interstate and Foreign Commerce. *Air-line Industry Investigation.* Hearings pursuant to S. Res. 50, 81st Cong., 1st sess. Washington: 1949. 3 vols.

———— ———— *Legislative Program and Statement of Policies of Civil Aeronautics Board.* Hearings, 82nd Cong., 1st sess. Washington: 1951.

———— ———— *Provide Permanent Certificates for Local Service Air Carriers.* Hearings on S. 3759, H.R. 8898, and Amendments "I" and "J" to S. 2647, 83rd Cong., 2nd sess. Washington: 1954.

———— ———— *Reinvestment of Capital Gains by Air Carriers.* Hearings on S. 1753 and H.R. 5822, 85th Cong., 1st sess. Washington: 1957.

———— ———— *Reinvestment of Capital Gains on Sale of Airlines Flight Equipment.* Hearings on S. 3449, 84th Cong., 2nd sess. Washington: 1956.

———— ———— *Revision of Civil Aeronautics Act.* Hearings on S. 2647, 83rd Cong., 2nd sess. Washington: 1954.

———— ———— *Separation of Air Mail Pay from Subsidy.* Hearings on S. 436, S. 535, S. 1137, S. 1756, S. 1757, and S. 1870, 82nd Cong., 1st sess. Washington: 1951.

———— ———— Subcommittee. *Permanent Certificates for Local Service Air Carriers.* Hearings on S. 651, 84th Cong., 1st sess. Washington: 1955.

———— ———— Subcommittee. *Regulation of Transportation of Passengers and Property by Aircraft.* Hearings on S. 3027, 74th Cong., 1st sess. Washington: 1935.

———— ———— Subcommittee. *Regulation of Transportation of Passengers and Property by Aircraft*. Hearings on S. 2 and S. 1760, 75th Cong., 1st sess. Washington: 1937.

———— ———— Subcommittee on Aviation. *Guaranteed Loans for Purchase of Aircraft and Equipment*. Hearings on S. 2229, 85th Cong., 1st sess. Washington: 1957.

———— ———— Subcommittee on Aviation. *Supplemental Air Service*. Hearings, 85th Cong., 1st sess. Washington: 1958.

———— Committee on the Judiciary. Subcommittee on Antitrust and Monopoly. *The Insurance Industry: Aviation, Ocean Marine, and State Regulation*. Report pursuant to S. Res. 238, Report No. 1834, 86th Cong., 2nd sess. Washington: 1960.

———— Select Committee on Small Business. *Annual Report*. Report No. 1068, 82nd Cong., 2nd sess. Washington: 1952.

———— ———— Subcommittee. *Future of Irregular Airlines in the United States Air Transportation Industry*. Hearings, 83rd Cong., 1st sess. Washington: 1953.

U.S. Department of Commerce, Civil Aeronautics Administration. *A Program of Charges for the Use of the Federal Airways System: A Report of the U.S. Department of Commerce*. Washington: 1953.

———— *Statistical Handbook of Aviation, 1956*. Washington: 1956.

U.S. Federal Aviation Agency. *Statistical Handbook of Aviation, 1960*. Washington: 1960.

U.S. Interstate Commerce Commission. *Regulation of Transportation Agencies*. U.S. Congress, Senate, S. Doc. 152, 73rd Cong., 2nd sess. Washington: 1934.

U.S. Library of Congress. Legislative Reference Service. *Subsidies to Transportation*, by B. N. Behling. Public Affairs Bulletin, No. 86. Washington: 1950.

U.S. President's Air Policy Commission. *Survival in the Air Age*. Washington: 1948.

Index